Introduction to the Talmud and Midrash

Introduction to the Talmud and Midrash

HERMANN L. STRACK

A TEMPLE BOOK
ATHENEUM, NEW YORK, 1974

Published by Atheneum
Reprinted by arrangement with
The Jewish Publication Society of America

Library of Congress catalog card number 59-7191
ISBN *0-689-70189-6*
Manufactured in the United States of America by
The Murray Printing Company,
Forge Village, Massachusetts
Published in Canada by McClelland and Sewart Ltd.
First Atheneum Printing September 1969
Second Printing December 1972
Third Printing February 1974

TABLE OF CONTENTS

PRELIMINARY REMARKS

PART I
INTRODUCTION TO THE TALMUD

PART II
INTRODUCTION TO THE MIDRASHIM

NOTES

INDEXES

APPENDICES

The Translator's Preface

This English translation of the late Professor H. L. Strack's work is to all intents and purposes a sixth edition of the original. It was prepared, according to instructions of the author as transmitted by his widow, from a copy of the fifth German edition revised by the author and marked: "Manuscript ready for the Printer. For the English translation." The corrections were either noted on the margins or on separate slips. It was also the author's wish that numerous corrections which he had received from Dr. Samuel Klein of Novo-Zamki in Czechoslovakia (now Professor in the Institute of Jewish Studies at the Hebrew University of Jerusalem) as well as those contained in Professor Alexander Marx's review in the *Jewish Quarterly Review*, New Series, XIII (1922–23), 352–365, should as far as feasible be incorporated in this translation. These conditions the translator has complied with. He has, moreover, without in any manner altering the words of the author, recast the work to this extent only that he has thrown into footnotes numerous parenthetical remarks and other by-work inserted by the author in the body of the text. Likewise, the matter appearing here as Appendices I–IV has been taken out of the body of the book and placed at the end. It is hoped that these innovations will serve to make the book more readable in its English garb, while in no wise impairing its eminent usefulness as a work of reference.

From the Author's Preface to the First Edition

The following Introduction to the Talmud is the first attempt to give objective and scientific information concerning the whole of the Talmud and to lead into the study of this literary monument equally remarkable for its origin, compass, contents, and the authority which has been accorded to it. I have striven honestly to let myself be influenced neither by polemical nor by apologetic interests, but to serve the truth alone. I shall consider myself amply rewarded for my laborious work if I shall succeed to remove many a prejudice, whether with those who are unconditionally hostile to the Talmud or with its over-zealous admirers, and to pave the way for a more just and calm appraisal.

May 6, 1887.

From the Foreword to the Fourth Edition

The third edition appeared some eight years ago and consisted of a reproduction by photographic process (except for a few addenda) of the second edition, which was published in 1894 and was for some time out of print. Because of other duties which claimed my entire time it was not possible for me to proceed to a new revision until now. This revision has turned out very thorough-going. The arrangement of the material has been made clearer. And the compass, in spite of the brevity of expression and the use of abbreviations, has been enlarged by three signatures; not only have I made additions and corrections in matters of detail but I have also inserted anew longer sections and augmented considerably bibliographical data in order to present to scholars, Christian as well as Jewish, a useful reference book. Any one who earnestly desires to obtain information concerning the Talmud or any part thereof will now be able, even without the knowledge of the languages of the original texts, to acquire generally adequate instruction.

Even at the present moment, certain ignorant agitators (most of them are at the same time malevolent) seek to make the Christian-German people believe that the Jews "are solicitous, with every possible means at their hands, to keep the Talmud a secret book," for fear lest its contents should become known, indeed, that they consider it a crime worthy of death for any Jew to make its contents known.* Over against this accusation it suffices to refer the reader to chapter XIV of this book (especially to § 2) and to single out of all Jewish scholars Professor Wilh. Bacher (who, unfortunately, died Dec. 25, 1913), who, by his publications on the Haggada, has done much to make known one main portion of the contents of the Talmud.

The Talmud (I repeat a statement which I have been solemnly making for many years) *contains no report or utterance which*, assuming, of course, that it is to be found there, *any Christian scholar, who is at home in the language and the subject matter, is not able to find.* As to the gaps, due to censorship in particular, there are scarcely ten rabbis in Germany who possess all the four publications named by me, see page 86 and n. 34, which I possess in my own library. Among the entire body of Jews there is not a single piece of literature or an oral tradition which is inaccessible to learned Christians. The Jews make no efforts whatsoever to conceal anything from the Christians, nor could they if they would. The Talmud, the Shulhan Aruk, and other Jewish literary works are secret books only for those—Jews no less than Christians—who have not acquired the necessary studies for a reading of the original texts nor know anything about the translations that are in existence. For such people, Caesar's *Bellum Gallicum* will be equally a secret book. May this Introduction to the Talmud, also in its fourth issue to the public, help to further a knowledge of truth and thereby also a just judgment.

June 2, 1908.

* Let me show by one example at least how utterly ridiculous this accusation is. When, in 1912, I proceeded to publish in photo-typic reproduction, the only complete Babylonian Talmud in existence, almost all the individual persons who made it possible by subscriptions in advance were Jews.

FOREWORD TO THE FIFTH EDITION

For a number of years it has been regretted in many quarters that my *Introduction to the Talmud* is wholly out of print. In these times, so hard for Germany, it has been my comfort and encouragement that so soon after the Great War, thanks to the aid of clear-sighted men in Frankfort on the Main and in Holland, England and America, I am in a position to let this book go forth again and that too in an entirely new shape. This fact is a proof that German science still lives and is recognized by former enemies. It has been my earnest desire to demonstrate that this recognition is deserved.

In obedience to a desire expressed by many, I have added, in addition to a short chapter on the Tosephta, an Introduction to the Midrashim. In what now forms the first part of the book, I have not only added references to the literature of the last twelve years but also much more besides, by utilizing both my own investigations and those of others. Entirely new is the third Appendix, an alphabetically arranged list of those chapters of the Babylonian Talmud which have Gemara. I am especially indebted for friendly help to Professor Ed. Baneth, Dr. S. Eppenstein, Dr. A. J. Epstein in Berlin, Dr. J. Theodor in Bojanowo; in regard to matters of detail to Professor Ismar Elbogen in Berlin, Dr. Saul Horovitz in Breslau, Professor S. Krauss in Vienna, Professor D. Heinr. Laible in Rothenburg on the Tauber, Professor Alexander Marx in New York and Dr. F. Perles in Königsberg.

Although, on the sixth of May, I reached the age of seventy-two years, I have not known for myself "an eight-hour day," and for this work in particular, by the side of other duties, I laboriously collected within the last year thousands of single data and strove to shape them into a single work. I am very well aware of the fact that even now, indeed just now, much in this work is in need of supplementation and correction; on the other hand, I am certain that there is not a scholar, even among Jews, who will not be able to learn from it or at least be stimulated in one respect or another. Anyone who will aid by appropriate communications to make this work come nearer and nearer to that degree of perfection which is attainable by man, may be sure of my warmest thanks.

The *Introduction to the Talmud and Midrash*, it may be permitted to be mentioned on this occasion, will be followed by a larger work which has been preparing for two decades: *A Commentary on the New Testament*, by Hermann L. Strack and Paul Billerbeck, which it is hoped will begin printing (by the same publishers) this winter.

Berlin-Lichterfelde West
October 18, 1920.

HERMANN L. STRACK

PRELIMINARY REMARKS

§1. ABBREVIATIONS

A. Names of Tractates in Mishna, Talmud, Tosephta

Bekor.: Bekoroth
Ber.: Berakoth
Bikk.: Bikkurim
B. B.: Baba Bathra
B. Ḳ.: Baba Ḳamma
B. M.: Baba Meṣi'a
Giṭ.: Giṭṭin
Hor.: Horayoth
Zeb.: Zebaḥim
Ḥag.: Ḥagiga
Ḥul.: Ḥullin
Ṭohar.: Ṭoharoth
Yad.: Yadaim
Yeb.: Yebamoth
Kil.: Kil'aim
Kerith.: Kerithoth
Keth.: Kethubboth
Meg.: Megilla
Mid.: Middoth
Mak.: Makkoth
Maksh.: Makshirin
Men.: Menaḥoth
Maas.: Ma'asroth
M. Ḳ.: 'Mo'ed Ḳaṭan
M. Sh.: Ma'aser Sheni
Me'il.: Me'ila
Miḳw.: Miḳwaoth
Neg.: Nega'im
Ned.: Nedarim
Soph.: Sopherim
Sanh.: Sanhedrin
A. Z.: 'Aboda Zara
Eduy.: 'Eduyyoth
Erub.: 'Erubin
Arak.: 'Arakin
Pes.: Pesaḥim
Ḳid.: Ḳiddushin
Ṙ. h. (or H.): Rosh Ha-shana
Shebu.: Shebu'oth
Shabb.: Shabbath
Sheḳ.: Sheḳalim
Taan.: Ta'anith
Tem.: Temura
Terum.: Terumoth
T. = Talmud
Bab. T. = Babylonian Talmud
Pal. T. = Palestinian Talmud
Tos. = Tosephta

B. Midrashim

R. = Rabba; Gen. R., Exod. R., Lev. (or Levit.) R.; Numb. R., Deut. R.—Midr. Cant. = Midrash Canticles; Midr. Lam. = Midrash Lamentations; Midr. Ḳoh(eleth); Pesiḳtha K. = P. deRab Kahana; Tanḥ(uma).

C. Titles of Books

Bacher (Wilh.), *Terminologie* I = *Terminologie der Tannaiten*, Leipzig, 1899; *Terminologie* II = *Terminologie der Amoräer*, Leipzig, 1905.

Tradition u. Tradenten = *Tradition u. Tradenten in den Schulen Palästinas u. Babyloniens*, Leipzig, 1914.

Brüll (Jakob), מבוא המשנה = *Einl. in die Mischnah*, 2 volumes, Frankf. o. M., 1885-1876 (volume I in chapter XIII usually without mention of the number of the volume). *Jbb.* (or *Jahrbücher*) = N. Brüll, *Jahrbücher für Jüd. Geschichte u. Litteratur*, 10 volumes, Frankf. o. M., 1874–1890.

Derenbourg (Joseph), *Essai sur l'histoire et la géographie de la Palestine, 1e partie, Paris*, 1867.

Frankel (Zechariah), מבוא המשנה, Leipzig, 1859 (cited simply by mentioning page). מבוא הירושלמי, *Einl. in den jerusalemischen T.*, Breslau, 1870 (cited as *Einleitung*).

Graetz (Heinrich), *Geschichte der Juden*, 4th edition, volumes I, II and III, Leipzig, 1908-1909.

Halevy (Isaak), דורות הראשונים, see chap XIII, § 1.

Hamburger II = *Real-Encyclopädie für Bibel u. Talmud, Abtheil. II; Die talmud. Artikel*, Strelitz, 1883.

Levy (J.), *Neuhebräisches u. Chaldäisches Wörterbuch*, 4 volumes, Leipzig, 1876-1889.

Rosenthal (Ludw. A.), *Entstehung* I, II, III = *Über den Zusammenhang, die Quellen u. die Entstehung der Mischna*, 3 volumes, Berlin, 1918. (Volumes I and II in second edition). *Mischna* = *Die M., Aufbau u. Quellenscheidung. Erster Theil: Die Ordnung Seraim*, Strassburg, 1903–1906 (Ber. to Shebi'ith, Maas.).

Schürer (Emil), *Geschichte des jüdischen Volkes im Zeitalter Jesu Christi*, 4th edition, 3 volumes, Leipzig, 1901-1909.

Weiss (Is. H.), דור דור ודורשיו (sometimes cited as *Dor*), 1st to 3rd volume, Vienna, 1871-1876.

Wolf, B. H. = J. Chr. Wolf, *Bibliotheca Hebraea*, 4 volumes, 4to, Hamburg, 1715-1733.

Zunz (L.), *GV.* = *Die gottesdienstlichen Vorträge der Juden*, 1832, 2nd edition, 1892.

'Festschriften' (mostly 'zum 70. Geburtstag'): A. Berliner, Frankf. o. M., 1903. | H. Cohen, 'Judaica,' Berlin, 1912. | H. Grätz, Breslau, 1887. Jak. Guttmann, Leipzig, 1915. | A. Harkavy, St. Petersburg, 1908. | Isr. Hildesheimer, Berlin, 1890. | Dav. Hoffmann, Berlin, 1914. | Kaufm. Kohler, *Studies in Jewish Literature*, Berlin, 1913. | Isr. Levy, Breslau, 1911. | Maybaum, Berlin, 1914. | M. Steinschneider [80th birthday], Leipzig, 1896. | L. Zunz [90th birthday], Berlin, 1884.

Cat. Bodl. = M. Steinschneider, *Catalogus librorum Hebraeorum in bibliotheca Bodleiana*, Berlin, 1860, 4to.

Cat. Brit. Mus. = (Zedner), *Catalogue of the Hebrew Books in the Library of the British Museum*, London, 1867.

Cat. Ros. = M. Roest, *Catalog der Hebraica u. Judaica aus der L. Rosenthal'schen Bibliothek*, 2 volumes, Amsterdam, 1875.

Diḳd. = Diḳduḳe Sopherim = Raph. Rabbinovicz, *Variae lectiones in Mischnam et in Talmud Babylonicum*, 16 volumes, Munich, 1868ff. (see p. 82γ).

JbJLG = *Jahrbuch der Jüdisch-Literarischen Gesellschaft.* Frankf. o. M., from 1903 on.

JbJGL = *Jahrbuch für jüdische Geschichte u. Literatur*, Berlin, from 1898 on.

JE or *Jew. Enc.* = *Jewish Encylcopedia*, 12 volumes, New York, 1901-1906.

JQR = *Jewish Quarterly Review*, London 1889–1908 (20 volumes).

N. S. = New Series, Philadelphia, from 1910-11 (thus far 21 volumes).

Magazin = *Magazin für die Wissenschaft des Judenthums*, Berlin, 1874 ff.

MGWJ, or *Monatsschrift* = *Monatsschrift für Geschichte u. Wiss. des Judts.*, Breslau, 1852ff.

HBG = *Hebr. Bibliographie*, הַמַּזְכִּיר, by M. Steinschneider, 21 volumes, Berlin, 1858-1882.

ZHBG = *Zeitschrift für hebr. Bibliographie*, volumes I, II, III, Berlin, 1896-1899; volume IV ff., Frankf. o. M., 1900 ff.

ZDMG = *Zeitschrift der Deutschen Morgenländischen Gesellschaft*, Leipzig, 1847 ff.

REJ = *Revue des études juives*, Paris, from 1880 (thus far 86 volumes).

PRE = *Realencyklopädie für protestantische Theologie und Kirche*, 3rd edition, Leipzig, 1896 ff.

D. PLACES OF PUBLICATION

Frank . o. M. = Frankfort on the Main

§2. TRANSLITERATION OF HEBREW CHARACTERS

א '; Not indicated as an inflectional ending, at the beginning of a word and after a vowel or vocal shewa, also at the beginning of syllables: יומא Yoma; אברהם Abraham; גאון Gaon; גאונים Geonim.

ו w; ז z; ח ḥ; ט ṭ; כ, כּ k; ס שׂ s; ע '; פ ph; פּ p; צ ṣ; ק ḳ; שׁ sh; ת th; תּ t.

The last syllable is usually the accented one and except in some inflectional endings, long; hence as a rule only the accentuation of the penultimate syllable is indicated by the use of an accent or a macron.

§3. MODE OF CITATION

a. Passages from the Mishna and from the Tosephta are cited by naming the tractate, the chapter and the section: Pe'a 8.2; in the case of the Tosephta it is customary also to add the page number of Zuckermandel's edition: Tos. Pe'a 1.4 (Zuck. 18).

b. The Babylonian Talmud is cited according to tractate, folio and page: Shabb. 31a or Babyl. Shabb. 31a, for the reason that the contents of the single pages are the same in almost all editions from the 3rd Bomberg edition, Venice, 1548, on.

In the Amsterdam edition after 'Arakin (34 leaves) pagination continues as follows: Me'ila 37 = M. 3 of most of the prints; M. 56 = M. 22; Ḳinnim 56a to 59a = Ḳ. 22a to 25a; Tamid 59b to 67b = T. 25b to 33b; Middoth 68a to 71b = Mid. 34a to 34b; Kerithoth 73 to 100 = K. 1 to 28; Temura 101 to 134 = T. 1 to 34.

The older editions are in part printed somewhat in a less crowded manner. Thus Ber. 22a of the first Venice edition corresponds almost exactly to fol. 21a of the more recent editions.

Of later editions, that of Cracow, 1616-1620 especially, has an entirely different content of the pages, see p. 86 ff.

c. Palestinian (Jerusalem) Talmud: tractate, chapter, folio and column (according to the Venice or Cracow edition in which each page has two columns): Pal. Mak. 2.31d. Frequently the line is also indicated. Some scholars cite the Palestinian Talmud as they do the Mishna, i. e. by mentioning the number of the paragraph (halakah). This method, however, is not to be recommended, since the editions do not agree in the numbering, also because some sections are much too long.

d. Midrashim. The simplest way as a rule is to indicate book, chapter and verse. Sometimes it will do to refer to the section or parasha; it is not advisable to cite by folio and page unless an edition is referred to which is easily accessible or is the only one in existence: Examples: Gen. R. 2.18 (par. 17) = Midrash, Genesis Rabba on Gen. 2.18. Mekiltha on Exod. 14.22 (Friedmann 31b). Siphre Numb. 5.15 (Friedm. §8). Siphre Deut. 6.5 (Friedm. §32). Siphra Emor, 21.6 (Weiss 94b) = Siphra on Levit. 21.6. Pesiktha K. 154b = Pesiktha de Rab Kahana, ed. Buber, fol. 154b. Yalḳuṭ I §261 = Yalḳuṭ Shim'oni on Exod 16.21ff. Midr. Cant. 3.11; it is awkward to cite by the initial words of the verse referred to (here צְאֶינָה וּרְאֶינָה).

e. In citations α and γ refer to the first and last thirds of the page respectively, δ to the notes.

PART I

INTRODUCTION TO THE TALMUD

CHAPTER I

Definition of Terms

§ 1. Mishna. The verb *shanah* means (a) 'to repeat,' (b) 'to study (something handed down orally,'[1] (c) 'to teach.'[2] Accordingly the noun *mishnah*[3] denotes (a) 'study,'[4] (b) 'oral lore'[5]—in contradistinction to *miḳra* 'reading, lection,' applied to the recitation of a scriptural text.[6] The oral lore or the body of ancient Jewish traditional learning is of a threefold variety: (a) Midrash, exposition of the Scriptures, particularly of the Pentateuch; (b) Halakoth, traditional statements of law, in categorical form, without regard to their derivation from the Scriptures;[7] (c) Haggadoth, scriptural expositions of a non-halakic character, proverbs, parables, narratives.

Mishna signifies specifically: (1) the entire content of the traditional law as far as it had been developed by the end of the second post-Christian century; (2) the sum of the teachings of any one of the teachers active up to that date (Tannaim); (3) a single statement of law,[8] in which sense the term *halakah* was also employed; (4) any collection of such statements, as when reference is made to '*Mishnayoth Gedoloth*, the great Mishna collections, e. g. the Mishna of Ḥiyya,[9] of Hoshaiah, of Bar Ḳappara';[10] (5) *par excellence* by Mishna is meant the collection made by Judah ha-Nasi ('Rabbi') which, however, in the form in which it has come down to us, contains many additions and modifications.

§ 2. Mathnitha. Of the same signification as the Hebrew *mishnah* is the Aramaic *mathnitha*, from *teni*, *tena* 'to hand down orally, study, teach.' Statements of the Mishna are cited in the Talmud by means of *tenan* and *tenayna*, 'we have studied, we hand down.' Recognized statements from the Baraitha (§ 3) are introduced with the formula *teno rabbanan*, 'our teachers have taught'; other citations from the Baraitha, by means of *tene* and femin. *tanya* (partic. pass.), 'it has been taught' (with particles: *we-hathanya, kidthanya*). Frequently also: *tane peloni*, 'So and So taught.' In the Babylon. Talmud we meet often with *tanni* 'to propound explanations to the Mishna' (partic. *methanne*, infin. *tannoye*).[11]

Tanna (plur. *Tannaim*) stands for (a) Tannaite, a teacher mentioned in the Mishna or belonging to mishnic times, (b) one who hands down tannaitic statements. The Amoraim, the teachers of the post-tannaitic period, had at their side in the schools men conversant with the oral law, who retained in their memory, and on occasion communicated, the statements of older authorities. At times these living libraries were spoken of as 'baskets full of books' (*Ṣanna dimle sifre*) in contradistinction to the 'eminent scholars' (*Ṣurba merabbanan*),[12] and it was said of them that they destroy the world, *ha-Tannaim meballe 'olam*,[13] insofar as they confined themselves to the subject-matter stripped of exposition and mode of application. Rab had a Tanna in the person of Isaac ben Abdimi.[14] Such Tannaim (in Hebrew *Shonim*) are referred to both in Palestine and in Babylonia to the end of the gaonic period. While written texts must have been available, recourse was had as a rule to these Tannaim for the reason that along with the text they carried on its traditional meaning in however limited a degree.[15] In consequence of lapses of memory on the part of these Tannaim, the Amoraim naturally experienced difficulties in interpreting the Mishna.[16] A knowledge of Rabbi's Mishna is presupposed with every Amora as a matter of course.[17]

§ 3. Baraitha, lit.: the extraneous one (supply *mathnitha*), is the generic name for all tannaitic teachings and dicta not included in the Mishna of Rabbi.[18] Hence *mathnithan* 'our Mishna,'[19] in contradistinction to *baraitha*.[20] It is often difficult to grasp the full sense of a Baraitha because we cannot form an opinion of the original context of which it formed a part.[21] Then again the discussion in the Talmud points at times to a formulation at variance with the extant text.[22] Baraithoth are adduced in the Palest. Talmud which are wanting in the Babyl., and vice versa;

nevertheless we must not conclude that they were unknown.[23] Statements which are cited in the Babyl. Talmud from a Baraitha appear frequently in the Palest. as dicta of an Amora.[24] It is greatly to be wished that the scattered remains of the Baraitha in the two Talmuds be collected and critically edited.[25]

§ 4. Gemara.[26] The verb *gemar*, 'to complete,' assumes in the Babyl. Talmud also the meaning 'to study (master the subject completely),' as in the often cited saying of Hillel, addressed to a heathen who wished to become a proselyte: *zil gemor*, 'Go, study.'[27] Hence the noun *gemâr* denotes 'that which has been learned, knowledge acquired by study.'[28] Gemara[29] has come to be the specific term for the so-called 'second constituent part of the Talmud,' i. e. the collection of the discussions relative to the Mishna at the hands of the Amoraim. This usage proceeds from *gemar* in the sense of 'to complete,' Gemara being interpreted as 'completion' or 'perfection.'[30] In this sense, however, the term, when it occurs in the current printed editions of the Talmud, comes from the hand of the censor who thus replaced the word 'Talmud' of the manuscripts and the older prints. Nevertheless, we abide by this modern usage, firstly, because of the circumscribed meaning which is free from ambiguity, and secondly, for the reason that at least one passage in the Talmud proves for it a more ancient lineage.[31]

§ 5. Talmud signifies: (a) as an infinitival noun from the simple stem *lamad* ('to study'), 'studying, study' (as theoretical activity, in contrast to *ma'ase* 'action,' i. e. practice, observance); (b) as a noun drawn to the Pi'el *limmad* ('to teach, instruct'),[32] 'instruction,' particularly that which has its starting point in Holy Writ;[33] (c) from *limmad* in the sense 'to derive a statement by exegetical means or otherwise,' the discussion of halakic statements with a view to elucidating the basis upon which they rest;[34] (d) the discussions concerning the Mishna of Rabbi on the part of the Amoraim.[35] We are wont to designate as Amoraim (*'Amora* lit.: 'speaker'; pl. in the Palest. Talmud *'Amorin*, in the Babyl. *'Amorae*) the Jewish doctors who were active from the time of the conclusion of the Mishna to about the end of the fifth post-Christian century; (e) Talmud is the comprehensive designation for the Mishna and the discussions (in the Aramaic tongue) which are joined thereto. This is the customary signification of the term in modern times, so also in the present volume. In its contents, the Talmud consists both of Halakah and of Haggada.

There are two Talmuds: the Babylonian, in which the individual Mishna sections are followed by the discussions of the scholars who resided in Babylonia, and the Palestinian (or Jerusalemitic), which is substantially concerned with the opinions of the Amoraim resident in Palestine.

§ 6. Midrash. The verb *darash* means, in post-biblical Hebrew,[36] 'to search out a scriptural passage, expound it,' then also 'to find something by exposition.'[37] Midrash denotes (a) in general, 'investigation,' both in the sense of 'study, theory,'[38] and with the meaning of 'exposition';[39] (b) specifically with reference to occupation with the Scriptures.[40] Hence *Beth ha-Midrash* 'house of study, where the scholars devoted themselves to the study of the Scriptures (the Law)';[41] (c) concretely, Midrash (pl. Midrashim) is the term for those literary works, some of them quite ancient, which contain scriptural interpretation of the haggadic, more rarely of the halakic, character; often then Midrash is outright the title by which such a literary work is known.[42]

The Aramaic equivalent *derash*, *derasha*[43] denotes both scriptural exposition and its concrete results. *Darshan*, Aram. *darosha*, means 'expounder (of the Scriptures), preacher.'[44]

§ 7. Halakah, from *halak* 'to go, follow,'[45] means literally 'going, walking,' then figuratively: the teaching which one follows, the rule or statute by which one is guided, the categorical religious law.[46] The expression *wa-halakah kidbaraw* occurs in the Mishna rarely,[47] but frequently in the Baraithoth. The plural *halakoth* is used to denote both individual statements of law and collections of such statements.[48]

How does anything become Halakah? In the first place, when it has been held in acceptance for a long period.[49] Secondly, when it is possible to have it vouched for by a recognized authority (*dibre Sofrim*). Thirdly, when it is supported by an accepted proof from Scripture, *din*. Fourthly and principally, by majority vote.[50]

§ 8. Haggada, in the Palest. Talmud with weakening of the laryngal, *'Aggadah*.[51] It is universally recognized that Haggada, a nomen actionis of *higgid*, denotes all scriptural interpretation which is non-halakic in character. W. Bacher was, however, the first to set forth the origin of this signification.[52] In the ancient Midrashim we find quite frequently *higgid* in the sense of *limmad*.[53] The students of Scripture search (*darash*) in Holy Writ, and the Scripture word tells, *maggid*, them then something which transcends the first impression conveyed by the scriptural expression. This term might be used also with reference to halakic exposition; but as a matter of fact it came soon to be employed preëminently with regard to non-halakic exposition, in which sense the connotation then persisted. With the nomen actionis *haggadah*, likewise, the scriptural word is to be mentally supplied as subject.[54]

CHAPTER II

Sketch of the History of the Talmud

§ 1. The Beginnings of Traditional Lore.

The Babylonian exile marks a turning point of the greatest significance in the history of the Jews. Not only was the native country lost together with political independence, but also, in consequence of the destruction of the Temple, the sole place of sacrificial worship, the center of the entire cult of Jahveh. Nevertheless the hope of the restoration was kept alive, resting as it did on God's word by the mouth of the prophet Jeremiah that the dominion of the Chaldees would last seventy years and that after the expiration of this period God would be found of His people and bring them back to their own land.[1] The sole condition named by God was: "when ye shall search for Me with all your heart."[2] How was the people to search for God? The pious were able to express their devotion to God neither by sacrifices nor by solemn worship in thronging assemblies. Naturally they would shun all manner of idolatry and the contact with idolaters; they would furthermore cultivate a scrupulous conduct which manifested itself likewise in works of love towards their neighbors. Then piety was exemplified on the one hand by keeping the Sabbath holy, and on the other by taking heed to the Word of God. The Word of God was at hand firstly in the prophetic message, whether in writing by the older prophets or in the spoken admonitions of the prophets of the exile;[3] secondly, and this is of utmost moment for our present purposes, in the will of God deposited in the pentateuchal Law. Two considerations led the people to pay particular attention specifically to the Law. In the first place, they pondered over the reasons which brought down all the evil upon the nation, God's own elect people; and then again, there was the hope for the restoration of the whole cult and of political independence. Thus in the Babylonian exile the learning which had the Scripture for its basis arose.[4] A contributory favorable cause in its development was the cessation of prophecy and the gradual suppression of the Hebrew speech, the language of the Law and the other monuments of God's revelation aforetimes. Already Ezra is expressly named *sofer mahir be-Torath Moshe*.[5] Not only had Ezra "set his heart to seek the law of the Lord, and to do it, and to teach in Israel statutes and ordinances,"[6] but he also took with him to Jerusalem teachers, *mebinim*.[7] On the occasion of the solemn reading of the Law by Ezra mention is made of Levites as teachers of the people, *mebinim 'eth ha-'am*, who were in need of a presentation of the sense.[8]

The written, i. e. the pentateuchal, law had been completed at the very least since the times of Ezra (earlier periods do not enter into consideration for our present purposes): nothing could be added and nothing could be taken away or in any other wise altered. Yet the constantly changing conditions of life required new regulations, and some sort of an organization must have been in operation from the times of Ezra on to make the Law effective in the life of the community, to preserve it, and to widen its scope.[9] We need not, of course, accept the Jewish traditional opinion that there existed in those early days a body of 120 men called the 'Great Synagogue,' since it is held by modern scholars quite plausibly that the notion is a pure invention resting on the account in Neh. 8–10.[10]

The orthodox Jewish conception of the manner in which the statutes were gradually enlarged and developed, may be studied in the works listed below.[11] We read in the Talmud, that *taḳḳanoth* were instituted by Moses, Joshua,[12] David, Solomon.[13] Ten[14] or eleven[15] Taḳḳanoth are attributed to Ezra, nine to Joḥanan ben Zaccai.[16]

Such statutes, if it was thought that they had been in immemorial usage, were termed *halakah le-moshe missinai* 'statutes given by God on Sinai.'[17] We meet with this expression three times in the Mishna,[18] but frequently in the Gemara.[19] Maimonides, in his introduction to the Mishna,[20] enumerates thirty-one statutes of this kind.[21]

In addition, in all probability as far back as the times of Ezra or the period immediately succeeding, the law was maintained or enlarged by the scholars in a manner suitable to the post-exilic conditions through the operation of scriptural exposition, *midrash.* It seems, however, that this procedure had in the course of time fallen into disuse until it once more gained ascendancy through Hillel and his successors.[22] The grounding of a statute in Scripture by means of subtle interpretation served, in the first place, to widen the written Law so as to meet new conditions. Secondly, it imparted to the oral law the requisite authority. We find Joḥanan ben Zaccai giving expression to the fear that the statute concerning impurity in the third degree will be abrogated by future generations for want of scriptural foundation; then came Akiba and supplied the proof.[23] As a simple statement of fact and with no thought whatsoever of calling into question the validity of the statutes referred to, it is observed: "The dissolution of vows hangs in the air and has no ground (in Scripture) to rest on. The Halakoth concerning the Sabbath (especially the kinds of labor forbidden thereon), the festal (private) offering (*ḥagigah*) and the mal-appropriation of sacred property (*me'ilah*) are as mountains suspended by a hair: little of Scripture and many Halakoth. Judicial cases and the Temple service, the statutes concerning purity and impurity as well as forbidden marriages have much to rest on."[24] However, since it was insisted on that all these statutes possessed equal validity, an impetus was given to the endeavor to secure for them all an equal or at least a similar foundation in Scripture.

In many cases it is quite certain that the Halakah antedates the scriptural proof by which it is propped up, for example the definition of 'the fruit of a goodly tree' (Lev. 23.40) or of 'eye for eye' (Exod. 21.24), *sheḥiṭa min ha-ṣawwar* (Hul. 1.4), *'isha niḳneth be-kesef* (Ḳid. 1.1), *basar be-ḥalab 'asur ba-'akilah u'ba-hana'ah.*[25] So also the regulation concerning the number of stripes (39 instead of 40).[26]

It is maintained by orthodox Jewish scholars that from the very beginning, i. e. from the time of the giving of the Law on mount Sinai, there had been in existence an oral law, carried on traditionally. According to D. Hoffmann,[27] "Mikra and Mishna, the Bible word read from the written book and the teachings heard at the mouth of the sages, are for the Israelite the two sources from which he draws the Torah received by Moses from God on Sinai (Ḳid. 40b). The Torah is one, although the source from which it issues is twofold; the teaching which comes to us from the Mishna of the sages is of the identical date and identical origin as that which is derived by interpretation from the scriptural word, 'all is given by the One God and communicated by one and the same prophet.' Hence when we speak of written lore *Torah shebikthab* and oral lore *Torah shebe-'al pe*, we have in mind one and the same law of God, derived in part from the divine Word committed to writing and in part from the authoritative statements of the teachers of tradition." This view, however, is untenable. In the first place, it is contradicted by the quite certain conclusions of sound pentateuchal criticism;[28] then nothing in the Old Testament points in that direction with compelling force; the Talmud[29] entertains wholly erroneous notions concerning chronology, thus reducing the 185 years from the restoration of the Temple to the fall of the Persian empire (516–331 B.C.E.) to thirty-four, hence with a loss of 151 years consigned to oblivion; lastly, the traditional chain of the carriers of tradition in the first chapter of Aboth is incomplete. One example will suffice to show how desultory often the attempted argumentation from the Old Testament is. All that at least Judah ha-Nasi[30] can find in Scripture upon which to rest the rules concerning the ritual mode of killing animals for food is contained in the two words *ka'asher ṣiwithika* ('as I have commanded thee') Deut. 12.21, although the reference is clearly and simply to v. 15 above. The orthodox opinion is discarded by L. Löw.[31]

The whole of the matter which had grown up and was constantly growing up in addition to the pentateuchal Torah was handed down by word of mouth during a long period. Philo[32] speaks of 'myriads of unwritten customs and usages' (*μυρία ἄγραφα ἔθη καὶ νόμιμα*).[33] Of special importance is the observation of Josephus:[34] "The Pharisees have made many ordinances among the people, according to the tradition of their fathers, whereof there is nothing written in the laws of Moses; for which cause they are rejected by the sect of the Sadducees, who affirm that they ought to keep the written ordinances, and not to observe those that are grounded upon the tradition of the fathers" (νόμιμά τινα παρέδοσαν τῷ δήμῳ οἱ φαρισαῖοι ἐκ πατέρων διαδοχῆς, ἅπερ οὐκ ἀναγέγραπται ἐν τοῖς Μωυσέως νόμοις, καὶ διὰ τοῦτο ταῦτα τὸ Σαδδουκαίιον γένος ἐκβάλλει, λέγον ἐκεῖνα δεῖν ἡγεῖσθαι νόμιμα τὰ γεγραμμένα, τὰ δ'ἐκ παραδόσεως τῶν πατέρων μὴ τηρεῖν). Likewise in other passages in which mention is made, whether in Josephus or in the New Testament, of the 'tradition of the elders' (παράδοσις τῶν πρεσβυτέρων)[35] or the 'ancestral tradition' (πατρῷα παράδοσις),[36] there is nothing that in any manner points to the traditional law in a written form. The first attempts to write down the traditional matter, there is reason to believe, date from the first half of the second post-Christian century, at which time the arrangement subsequently kept up is already in evidence, whether according to subject-matter or in exegetical form according to the sequence of the biblical passages. The conjecture may be advanced that the Jews were led to codify in a definitive form and thus also to commit to writing their oral traditions with a view, in part at least, to the New Testament canon then in process of formation.

§ 2. The 'Interdict on Writing down'.

According to an opinion widely held, it was categorically forbidden to commit to writing the traditional (lit. oral) law, *Torah shebe-'al pe*. It is even maintained by a number of scholars that the interdict was in force not only as regards Halakah, but also with reference to Haggada. So specifically by J. S. Bloch:[1] "The Jewish people, despite its marvelous many-sidedness, its high endowment and its mental versatility, forbore to enrich its literature by so much as a single leaf during the centuries from the close of the biblical canon to the writing of the Mishna, from the constitution of the Maccabean priestly monarchy to the conclusion of the amoraic period"; he speaks[2] of an interdict "directed against the committing to writing of anything, whether Halakah or Haggada."[3]

When did this interdict originate? Obviously it was unknown to the translator of Ecclesiasticus into Greek (132 B.C.E.).[4] M. Joel asserts[5] that the disallowance 'to write down Halakoth' ascends to the reign of Salome Alexandra (76–67 B.C.E.), but he offers no proof whatsoever.[6] Joel contends further[7] that "in the first Christian century, on the top of the injunction against the writing down of Halakoth, it was forbidden to publish Aramaic translations of scriptural books," but the statement cannot be regarded as substantiated by citing the example of Gamaliel I who ordered a Targum of the book of Job to be immured.[8] Bloch[9] would make us believe that "the interdict on any further literary activity may be found in the closing verses of Ecclesiastes, which constitute the postscript to the canon from the hands of the Great Synagogue"! However, Eccles. 12.12 cannot be interpreted in this manner, nor can the haggadic interpretation of the verse in the Midrash[10] be seriously accepted.

If we turn to the principal passage in the Talmud[11] bearing on this question, we obtain the following facts. It is quite true that the Palestinian Amora Joḥanan bar Nappaḥa (who lived in the third post-Christian century) delivered himself of the opinion that "he who writes down Halakoth is as one who commits the Torah to flames."[12] It is furthermore true that Judah bar Naḥmani, the interpreter of Joḥanan's brother-in-law Simeon ben Laḳish found in Exod. 34.27 support for his deduction that "what is said orally may not be said in writing, and vice versa"[13] and that this interpretation of the biblical passage had been current in the school of Ishmael.[14] But we must bear in mind, in the first place, that both Joḥanan and Judah bar Naḥmani lived as late as the third century; then, Joḥanan speaks only of committing to writing Halakoth, and his language which is grossly Oriental does not sound as if he were enacting a law; as for Judah, as his position indicates, he is no authoritative personality; lastly, whether we take the first or the second saying, we are in a position to adduce positive evidence that neither in point of time nor of place was the proscription regarded as in the nature of a law.

I. Testimonies for the writing down of haggadic material. A. In Palestine: 1. Ḥiyya (an uncle of Rab's) reads in the bathhouse a haggadic work on the Psalms.[15] 2. Jacob bar Aḥa, a contemporary of Rab, found written 'in the Haggada book of the academy.'[16] 3. It is told of Joḥanan and Simeon ben Laḳish that they 'were studying a Haggada book.'[17] 4. Rabba bar bar Ḥana states: When we studied with Joḥanan, he was wont, whenever he repaired to a privy, to hand us a Haggada book, if he happened to have one with him.[18] 5. Joḥanan said: This is certain, He who studies Haggada from a book, will not so soon forget it.[19] 6. The harsh language which Joshua ben Levi, a contemporary of Joḥanan, and his pupil Ḥiyya bar Ba use concerning committing to writing Haggada and studying from Haggada books[20] proves at any rate that such writings were then in existence. 7. Ze'ira (about 300 C.E.) vexed the masters of Haggada and called their writings books of witchcraft, *sifre ḳisme.*[21] Abba bar Kahana, however, said to him: Why do you vex them? Ask them, and they will answer you.[22] 8. Casual references in patristic literature.[23]

What is said about variants found in the Bible codex written by the hand of R. Meir[24] is to be taken quite literally and need not refer at all to masoretic notes or haggadic expositions jotted down in the margin (see Ad. Blumenthal, *Rabbi Meir*, 1888, 24, 134f.). Comp. Epstein, 'Biblische Textkritik bei den Rabbinen,' in the *Chwolson-Festschrift*; also *OLZ*, II, 200.

Midrash Tanḥuma belongs to a period entirely too late to affect our question. "The Israelites in Egypt had scrolls, *megilloth*, with which they delighted themselves, *mishta'ash'in*, on Sabbaths."[25]

Nor is the passage Ber. 10a to the point. "Simeon bar Pazzi ordered the Haggada of Joshua ben Levi." The meaning is that he recited it in proper sequence (see ch. XV, § 2). Nothing is said of writing; comp. Taan. 8a: Resh Laḳish ordered (reviewed) the Halakoth forty times before he stepped up to Joḥanan.

B. Babylonia. 1. Rab Ḥisda (died about 309 C.E.) says to Taḥlipha bar Abina with reference to certain foreign (Greek) words: "Write it in your Haggada book and explain it."[26] 2. Rab Papa (died 375 C.E.) and Rab Huna bar Joshua found in a Haggada book[27] that Rab Ḥisda and Rabba bar Huna interpreted the name Sinai in the identical manner.[28] 3. Rab Naḥman bar Jacob (died 320 C.E.) was wont, when he repaired to a privy, to hand to one of his pupils a Haggada book, if he happened to have one with him.[29] 4. It is said of Raba (*Raba* died about

352 C.E.) that he ordered certain orphans to restore a wool-shear[30] and a Haggada book which were claimed as the property of some one else.[31]

C. Writings mentioned by title. 1. Megillath Taanith,[32] the 'Scroll of Fasts,' a record of those days which it is not lawful to keep as fast days, for the reason that in times past some joyous event had occurred thereon. The Aramaic text was probably composed in part before the destruction of Jerusalem; its present form dates from the reign of Hadrian.[33]

Text: G. Dalman, *Aramäische Dialektproben*, Leipzig, 1896, 1–3, 32–34; Ad. Neubauer, *Mediaeval Jewish Chronicles*, II (Oxford, 1895), 3–25; M. Grosberg, *Masseketh M. T.*, Lemberg, 1905 (40 + 84 pp.; 28–32 deal with the later additions); A. E. Bornstein, *M. T.* (with commentary), Jerusalem, 1908 (272 pp.); S. Zeitlin, 'M. T. as a Source for Jewish Chronology and History in the Hellenistic and Roman Periods,' *JQR.*, N. S., IX, 71–102; X, 49–80 (deals specifically with the chronology of the Books of the Maccabees).

2. *Megillath Yuḥasin*, a scroll with genealogies and divers records, no literary work, is no longer extant. It is cited by Ben Azzai (about 100 C.E.).[34] The books reported to have been found in the Temple, *shel me'onim*, *hi'*, and *za'aṭuṭim*,[35] it is contended by J. Z. Lauterbach,[36] were writings of the same character.

3. *Sefer Yuḥasin* contained expositions and amplifications of the genealogies in the Book of Chronicles. "Rab said: From the time that the Book of Genealogies was hidden, the strength of the wise has failed and the light of their eyes has grown dim."[37] The contents of this book were taught as oral tradition by the Palestinian Amora Jonathan ben Eleazar.[38] Mar Zuṭra, a contemporary of Ashi, states that it took 400 camels to carry the load of the haggadic interpretations of the genealogies running in the First Book of Chronicles (8.37f. to 9.43f.) from Azel to Azel. Obviously an exaggeration, but it shows that there existed then many books of haggadic matter.

4. *Megillath Ḥasidim*,[39] or *Megillath Setharim*.[40] David Hoffmann,[41] who prefers the reading *Megillath Ḥarisim*,[42] believes that it was an Essene writing.[43]

5. *Sefer Beth Ḥashmonai*,[44] i. e. the First Book of the Maccabees which, according to Eusebius,[45] bore the title Σαρ βηθ σαρβαναιελ. The corrupt words should read: Σφαρ (= *sefer*) βηθ Ασμωναιειν.[46]

6. In numerous places mention is made of written Targums.[47] There was no ban on the writing of Aramaic translations of the Bible; it was merely forbidden to read publicly from a written Targum.[48]

II. Testimonies for the writing down of Halakoth. 1. In the 'Scroll of Fasts' it is said under the rubric of the fourteenth day of the month Tammuz: The Book of Decrees, *Sefar Gezeratha*, was done away with. Apparently it was a penal code disapproved of by the Pharisees. The event occurred at the accession of Alexandra, 76 B.C.E., or at the outbreak of the Great Revolt, 66 C.E.

2. Joḥanan ben Nuri, a contemporary of Aḳiba, receives from an old man *Megillath Sammanin*, a catalogue of the spices used in preparing the incense, which had been an heirloom of the family of Abṭinas.[49] However, we are dealing here with a writing which was composed for private use.

3. Rab found with Ḥiyya a *Megillath Setharim* (according to Rashi, a scroll which was kept secret because of the interdict), in which were found halakic statements by Isi ben Judah.[50]

4. Mention is made of a halakic Midrash on Leviticus in the times of Eleazar ben Pedath.[51]

5. Samuel, head of the school of Nehardea (died about 254 C.E.), sent to Johanan thirty-nine camel loads[52] of questions which had reference to the laws concerning Ṭerepha.[53]

6. Joḥanan's contemporary Ḥilpha[54] had in his possession a book of notes[55] of halakic matter.[56] Such books were also in the possession of Joshua ben Levi, Levi (230 C.E.) and Ze'iri.[57]

No inference as to the existence of written halakic records can be made from the use of the verb *'ashkaḥ*, 'to find.' Joshua ben Levi said: In twenty-four passages it is said that the court may anathematize a person guilty of affront to a scholar. Eleazar asked: Where? Joshua answered: *leki tashkaḥ*, when you will find it, i. e. search and you will find. *Nefaḳ daḳ we'ashkaḥ telath*, he went out, reflected and found three passages (of the Mishna).[58]

A similar reply was made by Joḥanan to Eleazar.[59] The expression *'atha we 'aithi mathnitha bideh*[60] signifies the introduction of a statement of law, hitherto unknown in the school, on the part of one who retained it mentally. What is reported of Ḥiyya[61] shows merely that he took pains to have copies made of the five books of Moses (nothing is said of copying the Mishna). The debates between Rab and Mar Samuel on certain readings in the Mishna concern divergences caused by mishearing rather than by misreading.[62] When Abaye and Raba are divided on the text of B. M. 6.5, whether we should read *kemas'oi* or *lemas'oi*,[63] it would seem as if neither had before him a written Mishna.

On the basis of the data which have been presented it must be concluded that there is nothing to point to an interdict on the writing down of Halakoth, and still less so on the writing of haggadic matter, formally promulgated and universally recognized. It should be conceded, however, that again and again voices were raised in powerful opposition against writing, specifically against writing down Halakoth. It is not that writing per se was frowned upon, rather writing for the purpose of public use. If every teacher had been free to compose his own code of laws and to transmit it to his disciples, the unity of Judaism would have been endangered. Then writing as a means of giving permanence to the traditional law would have precluded the process of modifying this law in accordance with the peculiar time conditions in each period. At all events, in the schools of the Amoraim the discussions went on with no written copy in evidence to serve as a basis.[64] Rather, the Amoraim availed themselves of the services of scholars whose business was to carry mentally the tannaitic teachings (often they were likewise called Tannaim).[65] Because it was disallowed to write down for public use the recitations of the teachers, it became a duty to name the communicant with every statement heard.[66] Frequently we meet with the inculcation: *ḥayyab 'adam lomar bilshon rabbo.*[67] Whenever possible, the names of older authorities for a given statement should be specified: if you are able to lead back the chain of tradition up to Moses, do so.[68]

The circumstance that the oral law remained unwritten was a trait which distinguished Israel from the other nations. Judah

b. Shalom[69] said: "Moses was desirous that the Mishna should be written down likewise. God, however, foresaw that the nations would in time translate the Torah into Greek and read it in Greek and then say: 'We are Israel.' Therefore God said to him (Hosea 8.12): 'Were I to write for them (the Israelites) the whole abundance of My law, they would be accounted as the strangers.' Now, however, the Mishna is the secret of God, and the Lord makes His secret known only to them that fear Him (Ps. 25.14)."[70] Or: "God gave them the oral law, that by this they might be distinguished (*meṣuyyanin*) from the other nations. Hence it was not given in writing, or else the other nations would falsify it, as they have dealt with the written Torah, and then say that they were Israel."[71] On the other hand, the formation of the New Testament and its growing recognition acted as a spur for the Jews by codifying the oral law to create an authoritative supplementary continuation of the Old Testament.

It is quite true that written Haggadoth and especially written Halakoth are in earlier times far less frequently alluded to than we are disposed to expect. But it must be remembered that in antiquity people did not take to writing as readily as we do now, and because of the high cost of parchment much writing was indeed out of the question. On traveling in *'asia* (*'asia*), Meir found not so much as one copy of the Scroll of Esther and was compelled to write one from memory.[72] Even Rabbi found himself in the delicate situation that, when after an illness he had forgotten thirteen classes of Halakoth[73] which he had previously taught himself, he had to learn them afresh partly from Ḥiyya and partly from a certain fuller.[74] Of course, this does not mean that it was not customary then to write anything at all nor, specifically, that Rabbi wrote nothing.

As opinions diverge among students on the question of an enforced interdict on the writing of Halakoth, so also concerning the time when our Mishna and subsequently both Talmuds were committed to writing.

1. According to one opinion, the Mishna was committed to writing by Rabbi himself, the Palestinian Gemara by Joḥanan, the Babylonian Gemara by Rab Ashi and Rabina. So (a) Rabbenu Nissim[75] in the introduction to the *Sefer ha-Mafteaḥ*;[76]

(b) Samuel ha-Nagid (1027–1055, secretary and adviser to king Habus of Granada and to his son Badis) in his *Introduction to the Talmud*; (c) the well-known poet and philosopher Judah Ha-levi in his *Kuzari*;[77] (d) Abraham ben David in his *Sepher ha-ḳabbala* (written in 1160); (e) Moses Maimonides, in his introduction to the Mishna[78] and still more unreservedly in his preface to *Mishne Torah*; (f) Menaḥem b. Solomon Meiri of Perpignan, in his work *Beth ha-beḥira*;[79] (g) Ḥisdai Ḳresḳas; (h) Prophiat Duran (about 1391); (i) Isaac Abrabanel (1437–1508); (j) Abraham Zakuth, *Sepher Yuḥasin* (written in 1504),[80] and in general the Talmudists of Spain, Italy and Germany. Of modern scholars we may single out: (k) Z. Frankel;[81] (l) I. H. Weiss;[82] (m) Hamburger;[83] (n) J. Brüll;[84] (o) Wolf Jawitz.[85]

2. The contrary opinion is to the effect that the Mishna was not committed to writing by Rabbi, nay, that the Amoraim had no written Mishna before them; both Mishna and Gemara were committed to writing for the first time by the Saboraim (as the successors to the Amoraim are named). So in particular the French scholars: (a) Rashi (R. Solomon Yiṣḥaḳi, 1040–1105);[86] then (b) several Tosaphists;[87] (c) Zerahiah Ha-levi (in Lunel, died 1186), in his *Sepher ha-maor*; (d) Moses of Coucy (near Soissons, about 1240), in his *Sepher miṣwoth gadol*; furthermore (e) Simeon ben Ṣemaḥ Duran (died in 1444), in his *Responsa*;[88] (f) Jacob Ḥagiz (*Ḥagiz*, died in 1674), in the introduction to his Commentary on the Mishna.[89] Among moderns may be named: (g) Hirsch Chajes, in *Torath Nebiim*;[90] (h) Samuel David Luzzatto, in the introduction to *'Oheb Ger* (Philoxenus);[91] (i) Grätz;[92] (j) L. Löw;[93] most circumstantially (k) J. S. Bloch.[94] Among Christian scholars: (l) Johannes Morinus.[95]

The Epistle of the Gaon Sherira deals with this question in a significant manner. It was written in the year 1298 of the Seleucid era (987 C.E.) and was addressed to Jacob b. Nissim and the men of Kairwan. Unfortunately it is extant in two recensions, a 'Spanish'[96] and a 'French'[97] which give a contradictory answer to the present question.

The editions of Sherira's Epistle by B. Goldberg,[98] J. Wallerstein,[99] Ad. Neubauer,[100] A. Hyman[101] are unsatisfactory. The French translation, with introduction and notes, by L.

Landau[102] is devoid of scientific importance. All these editions have been superseded by the critical edition of B. Lewin,[103] in which the text is printed according to both recensions (pp. 1–122), preceded by a minute introduction (pp. i–lxxii) in which we may single out the part dealing with the two recensions (p. xlvii ff.) with an adequate treatment of the question concerning the writing of the Mishna.

It is certain that the Mishna existed in writing in the times of the emperor Justinian (527–565).[104]

§ 3. The traditional law up to the codification of the Mishna by Rabbi.

According to a trustworthy (ancient and unanimous) tradition, Rabbi, i. e. Judah Ha-nasi (born 135 C.E.), the great-grandson of Gamaliel I, is held to have been the editor of the code of traditional law which has come down to us and is known as the 'Mishna' *par excellence.* Just how much of it was written by Rabbi himself is a subject of debate. Certainly in its present compass the Mishna cannot go back to Rabbi. It is quite evident that the work was in the course of time enlarged by numerous additions.[1] Such are obviously in particular all those sections in which Rabbi's own opinions are adduced with the explicit mention of his name,[2] or divergent views of his contemporaries, then opinions which do not square with those taught by Rabbi elsewhere. Though rarely, authorities are cited from times subsequent to Rabbi's.[3] But also otherwise there is reason to believe that the text underwent alteration.[4] Thus elements from the Tosephta were inserted at an early date.[5] The first business of the textual criticism of the Mishna is to collect the variants of all important manuscripts of the Mishna.[6] The next step is to collate the Mishna texts in the two Talmuds. The Mishna which is printed in front of the Palestinian Gemara is by no means the Palestinian recension.[7] A third piece of work is to ascertain the text presupposed in the discussions of the Babylonian and Palestinian Amoraim. Lastly, a study must be made of ancient citations (in the works of the Geonim, Isaac Alfasi, Rashi, etc.).[8]

The purport of Rabbi's Mishna was not to serve as a storehouse of halakic material, but solely, as Maiminides has recognized, to teach the authoritative norm (Halakah). It is held that when an opinion is delivered anonymously, that is the recognized norm.[9] Then again the rule is that "we follow the first authority,"[10] but this rule has usually force only when the first opinion is cited anonymously. When it is added: "But the sages say,"[11] their authority prevails as a rule.[12] When opinions which are disapproved of are suffered to remain, it is accounted for in part by considerations of deference; at the same time it becomes possible to attach further discussion.[13]

Halakic codifications antedate the effort of Rabbi. Jose ben Ḥalaphta, a contemporary of Meir, apostrophizes the tractate Kelim: "Hail to thee, Kelim,[14] that beginning with uncleanness thou endest with cleanness."[15] Meir and Nathan conspire to expose Rabban Simeon b. Gamaliel II by bidding him recite the tractate Uḳṣin of which he was ignorant; whereupon Jacob b. Ḳorshai seats himself near by Simeon's chamber and proceeds to rehearse the tractate *peshat, geras u'thena*; Simeon listens and memorizes it, and on the following day he is able to recite the whole of it.[16] Accordingly the tractate Uḳṣin had then assumed complete shape with which Meir, Nathan and Jacob b. Ḳ. were familiar and which Simeon b. G. might likewise be expected to command. Is it not reasonable to suppose that the matter had at least in part been committed to writing? In all probability, by this time most of the Tannaim of standing had composed written collections of Halakoth for the purpose of refreshing their memory while preparing their lectures in private, though not for use in the school house; possibly also those who were preachers owned similar collections of Haggadoth in writing. Of course, we do not know just how much had then been written down and how much was memorized by constant rehearsing. The codifiers of comprehensive Mishna works availed themselves of collections of this sort, in particular when they dealt with specific parts of the entire field of traditional lore. It is in this sense that certain tractates (i. e. in the oldest elements which go by no name, *setham*) are attributed to certain Tannaim, as e. g. Middoth to Eliezer ben Jacob, who lived when the Temple was still standing,[17] Tamid and Yoma to Simeon of Mizpah (a contemporary of

Gamaliel I[18])[19], Ḳinnim to Joshua ben Hananiah,[20] Kelim to Jose ben Ḥalaphta.[21] (According to Hoffmann,[22] in general, Yebamoth and Yoma go back to Aḳiba, Neziḳin to Ishmael, Sanhedrin to Meir, Taanith to Rabban Simeon ben Gamaliel II).

Rabbi made of Meir's Mishna the groundwork of his own code, which he called by the same name and which was more comprehensive, taking note of the later development. According to Johanan bar Nappaḥa, "our Mishna, whenever an opinion is reported anonymously, rests on Meir, the Tosephta on Nehemiah, Siphra on Judah ben El'ai, Siphre on Simeon ben Joḥai, but all of them ultimately on R. Aḳiba."[23] From this passage as well as from the circumstance that the same Jose ben Ḥalaphta speaks repeatedly of "Aḳiba's Mishna,"[24] it follows that a similar codification had been undertaken by Aḳiba.[25] This Mishna of Aḳiba was probably at no time committed to writing as a whole, though parts may have been written down. The same holds good of Meir's codification. Great stress was laid on memorizing and retaining in memory the enormous material; witness the remark of Dosthai ben Jannai in the name of Meir: "When a scholar forgets a single word of his Mishna, they account it to him as if he forfeited his life."[26]

Nor was Aḳiba's Mishna the first attempt at codification. This we may gather, in addition to the evidence adduced above,[27] from the remark of Jose ben Ḥalaphta: "This is Aḳiba's Mishna, but the earlier Mishna[28] taught differently."[29] D. Hoffmann[30] endeavors to prove that long before Aḳiba there had been in existence a codified Mishna composed before the destruction of the Temple by the schools of Shammai and Hillel. M. Lerner[31] goes farther in maintaining that Hillel and Shammai themselves codified the six orders of the Mishna, while Isaac Halevy[32] would fain persuade us that the beginnings of the Mishna ascend to the times of the Men of the Great Synagogue. This much is certain that many of the differences between the Shammaiites and Hillelites point to the existence of a Mishna text.

L. Rosenthal[33] believes that identical or similar phraseology in mishnic statements justifies the inference that they were composed at one and the same time.[34] He then seeks to show[35] that in the older parts a polemical attitude to Sadducee teaching is recognizable, and he goes so far as to maintain that we are in a position to distinguish two strata: of these the one, which he calls the primitive anti-Sadducaean Mishna, deals with general manifestations, while the other goes more into detail. So soon as this polemic recedes, order according to subject-matter becomes gradually the rule in the scholastic lectures. This process may be seen in the source S, which contains the pronouncements of the Shammaiites and Hillelites.[36] A further source is JE, consisting of teachings which with certainty or at least probability go back to the Shammaiite, Eliezer ben Hyrcanus, and the Hillelite, Joshua ben Hananiah.[37] Akiba[38] frequently broke up the sequence of the old order of instruction and established new concatenations;[39] his innovations became particularly marked in Neziḳin. Of Akiba's pupils, Meir[40] and Judah ben El'ai[41] range themselves often on opposite sides. Meir arranges Akiba's Mishna, while Judah harks back to the Mishna of the older Tannaim. Jose and Simeon illuminate and vitalize the material with their elucidations.[42] The greater number of the statements by Simeon ben Gamaliel II[43] occur in Nashim and Neziḳin;[44] there are in many respects points of contact with the traditions of his house and with Jose.[45] Rabbi[46] based himself upon the scholastic course of Meir and Judah,[47] but at the same time the course pursued by Jose exercised a potent influence;[48] another feature was that he appended the names of the Tannaim from the disciples of Akiba to his own day,[49] and then again excluded this and the other item.[50] Of the additions introduced may be singled out the pieces opening with *zeh ha-kelal*[51] or with *ma'aseh*.[52]

When the occasion presented itself, legal statutes, it goes without saying, were enacted, quite independently of the text of the Bible; so at least at first.[53] But when it came to teaching the Halakah, the form of Midrash was resorted to at an early date, in all probability long before the form of Mishna was at all thought of.[54] The presentation of the body of traditional lore took on the form of scriptural exposition, the written Torah served as the thread for stringing together the traditional matter. Josephus speaks of *ἐξηγηταὶ* (*τῶν νόμων*), Philo of *νόμων ἑρμηνεῖς*. The Talmud[55] designates Shemaiah and Abtalion as great sages and great expounders, *darshanin*, who might be expected to be able to tell Israel (i. e. by deduction from Scripture) that the festival offering sets aside the Sabbath. There existed no Mishna, i. e. a course of instruction in the law in comprehensive form and in proper sequence according to subject-matter, in the times of the Sopherim preceding the "five Pairs."[56] According to Lauterbach,[57] Jose ben Joezer was still teaching in the form of Midrash, though his statement as reported in our Mishna[58] lacks the exegetical foundation. The activity of the Sopherim, so Lauterbach argues, was disrupted by the transition from the Persian dominion to the Greek, and he makes a point of the gap in Aboth 1 (between Simon the Just and Antigonus of Socoh). After this transition, the teachers set about on the one hand to expound the Law by means of novel principles of exposition, and on the other to teach as independent Halakoth whatever had been accepted as authoritative.[59] The Pharisees made themselves indispensable to the people by teaching in the Mishna form, a novel method of their own invention, though the Midrash form continued by the side of the other.[60] Subsequently the division in method created a distinction in the schools, some cultivating the Midrash form and others the Mishna form.[61] The older Halakah, since it disapproved of the expositional methods of the more recent one, largely adhered to the Mishna form. One example: Akiba endeavors to prove that with a thanksgiving-offering there should go half a log of oil. Whereupon Eleazar ben Azariah retorts: If you go on arguing the whole day about inclusion and exclusion, it is no concern of mine: half a log is the established tradition going back to Moses on Sinai.[62]

It is certain that the form of the Mishna as it has come down to us has been influenced in numerous places by the halakic Midrash.[63] In several instances statements of our Mishna are presented in the extant Tosephta in the form of Midrash.[64]

It is worthy of note that the basic passages of the Pentateuch to which the Mishna offers expositions, expansions, etc. are for the most part not cited at all, but are taken for granted. Thus in the tractate Kil'aim neither Levit. 19.19 nor Deut. 22.9–11 are cited; without any introduction whatsoever the opening reads: "Wheat and rye-grass (*zunin*) are no mixed seed."[65]

When in numerous places the order according to subject-matter to be expected from the name of the tractate is departed from, the supposition is justified that the intention was to facilitate the retention in memory by collocating as many statutes as are similar in one respect but quite dissimilar otherwise.[66] Then again matters or cases are brought together with analogous distinctions,[67] or because they refer to the same person,[68] or because they go by the same number,[69] or because the sentences rhyme or follow alphabetic order.[70] In general, we meet with association of ideas of diverse kind,[71] and sometimes the connection is quite of a loose order.[72]

Here and there unevenness in the treatment of the material resulted from the process of compilation, inasmuch as the succeeding codifiers took over a number of tractates, barring additions, in the form in which each had been cast by its first editor.[73]

Thus it is that within the tractates, especially if we apply a modern standard, there is manifested a woeful lack of systematic arrangement. It appears that from an early date the principle had been to order the tractates substantially according to their size (number of chapters). As Hoffmann tells us:[74] "Herein the pedagogical interest clearly manifests itself. The teacher who would teach an entire order of the Mishna preferred to open his course with the largest tractate, at a time when the pupil applied himself to the new subject with zeal and concentrated attention. The smaller tractates were taught last when the student's mind had become sluggish. One must remember that what mattered most at first was the memorizing of the Mishna rather than a penetrating understanding of its contents."

Rabbi's Mishna very soon put all the other codifications of the Mishna in the background; with the Amoraim it enjoyed canonical authority. A concurrent factor lay in the circumstance that Rabbi had taken counsel with his Beth-din.

CHAPTER III

The Division of the Mishna (the Talmuds, the Tosephta) and the Arrangement of its Parts

§1. Orders, Tractates, Chapters.

The extant Mishna (likewise the Babylonian Talmud and, as far as it is preserved, the Palestinian) consists of six main divisions (*sedarim*, Orders).[1] Hence it is that the Jews are wont to call the Talmud by the name of 'Shas' (Sh. S. = *Shishshah sedarim*).[2] Each Seder has a number (7–12) of Tractates (sing. *masseketh*,[3] Aramaic in the traditional pronunciation *massekta*,[4] plur. usually *massektoth*).[5] The Tractates are divided into chapters (sing. *pereḳ*), the chapters into sections or legal paragraphs (sing. *mishnah* or, as in the Palestinian Talmud, *halakah*).

The Babylonian Talmud is frequently published or, as the case may be, bound in twelve folio volumes;[6] the Palestinian in one or (according to the number of the extant Orders) in four volumes.

The names of the six Orders are: 1. Zera'im 'Seeds.' Chief contents: Agriculture and fruits of the field. 2. Mo'ed 'Festivals.' 3. Nashim 'Women.' 4. Neziḳin[7] 'Damages'; euphemistically also Yeshu'oth 'Deeds of help.'[8] Main contents: Civil and criminal law. 5. Ḳodashim "Holy things." Main contents: Sacrifices and devoted things. 6. Ṭoharoth 'Purities,' euphemistically for tum'oth 'that which is ritually impure.'[9] The names of several Orders are repeatedly mentioned in the Gemara.[10]

The sequence as given above is attested at an early date, so by Simeon ben Laḳish in the third Christian century.[11] According to Abraham Geiger,[12] "it would seem as if the Orders were arranged to follow according as the matters they treat of were of more frequent or of rarer occurrence." Frankel[13] attempts to justify the sequence on logical grounds.

The names of the Tractates are of ancient date. Certainly the Amoraim were familiar with them.[14] They are derived for the most part from the subject-matter, but sometimes the opening word furnished the name.[15]

The number of the Tractates is now sixty-three (eleven in the first Order, twelve in the second, seven in the third, ten in the fourth, eleven in the fifth, and twelve in the sixth). Originally, however, the three 'Gates' (Baboth) at the head of the fourth Order constituted a single Tractate, named likewise *neziḳin*.[16] Because of its inordinate size, it was subsequently divided into three.[17] Then Makkoth formed in earlier times the concluding part of Sanhedrin.[18] Maimonides[19] is constrained to admit, unwillingly enough, that in the codices Makkoth is joined to Sanhedrin and counted with it as one Tractate. Thus there results a total number of sixty, which is expressly attested by Isaac Nappaḥa:[20] " 'There are threescore queens' (Cant. 6.8), these are the threescore Tractates of Halakoth."[21]

The sequence of the Tractates. It is quite manifest that several tractates, from the nature of their subject-matter, do not fit in with the Seder in which they are placed. Thus Berakoth is alien to Zera'im, Aboth (a collection of sententious sayings) to Neziḳin. Nedarim and Nazir are only partially akin to Nashim.[22] What is then the principle according to which the tractates were arranged within the single Orders? It is impossible to give a decisive answer to this question, for the reason that the sequence[23] varied at different times and we know too little about the oldest arrangement(s). Certain sequences are expressly attested in the Talmud.[24] Maimonides, who ignores these talmudic references (possibly they represent later interpolations), exerts himself quite considerably in the introduction to his Commentary on the Mishna to explain rationally that sequence which he considers to be the original: related subjects are brought together, then priority is given to the things that are indispensable, or the sequence is determined by that in the written Torah. Abraham Geiger,[25] on the other hand, has advanced the theory that the tractates are arranged within the Sedarim according to size (number of chapters).[26] This theory is borne out in five of the Sedarim,[27] and in the first Seder at least as regards the latter part.[28] Nevertheless, we should seek perhaps for a more rational explanation. One might conjecture that the primitive arrangement was dictated by the location of the laws in question in the Pentateuch. In support of this proposition it will do well to remember that, within the several tractates, quite a number of regulations appear in a certain sequence which can be explained only by the collocation of the corresponding laws in the Pentateuch.[29]

The chapters. The division into chapters is likewise exceedingly ancient. In the Gemara, a number of chapters are cited by their names which are in vogue to this day and which are formed of the opening words.[30] All told there are 523 chapters: 74 in Zera'im,[31] 88 in Mo'ed, 71 in Nashim, 73 in Neziḳin,[32] 91 in Ḳodashim,[33] 126 in Ṭoharoth. Others count 524 or 525 chapters by adding a fourth chapter to Bikkurim or (and) a sixth to Aboth. With regard to the sequence of the chapters, only a few instances of variation occur.[34]

§ 2. Tabular Survey of the Tractates in Mishna, Talmuds and Tosephta; see Appendix I at the end of the volume.

§ 3. Alphabetical List of Tractates in the Mishna; see Appendix II.

§ 4. The Opening Words of those Chapters in the Babylonian Talmud which have Gemara, in alphabetical order; see Appendix III.

CHAPTER IV

Contents of the 63 Tractates of the Mishna according to the Order of Moses Maimonides

§ 1. First Order: Zera'im, eleven Tractates.

1. Berakoth, 'Benedictions'; treats of benedictions and prayers, especially the daily prayers. Nine chapters. 1. The time for the Shema' in the evening and in the morning, posture of the body in reciting, the benedictions in front and after. 2. Stops in the Shema', permission to interrupt this prayer in order to greet a person; praying with silent voice, laborers on the top of a tree or a wall, a person newly wedded.[1] 3. Dispensations from the Shema'. 4. The times for the morning, afternoon, evening prayer and for the Additionals; whether one may pray the Eighteen Benedictions (Shemone 'esre) also in the form of an abstract; of him whose prayer is opus operatum; praying in a dangerous place, while on horseback or driving; of the Additional Prayer. 5. Position and inward preparation for prayer; prayer for rain; Habdala (benediction at the exit of the Sabbath); leading in prayer; losing oneself in prayer. 6. Benedictions when partaking of fruits of the tree, fruits of the soil, bread, wine and other means of sustenance, while drinking water, over incense after the meal. 7. Common benediction after meals. 8. Differences between the schools of Hillel and Shammai touching the washing of hands and the benedictions, especialy those at meals. 9. Benedictions on diverse occasions (in commemoration of miracles or of idolatry rooted out, with natural phenomena, at receiving news, when one builds a new house or purchases new furniture, when entering and leaving a city, at fortunate and unfortunate events); respect for the Temple mount: "Blessed be the God of Israel from everlasting to everlasting"; uttering the name of God at salutations.

2. Pe'a 'Corner,' Levit. 19.9f.; 23.22; Deut. 24.19ff.; of the corner of the field and in general of the dues to the poor. Eight

chapters. 1. Which things are similar to Pe'a in having no limit set to them in the Law; the limit and place of Pe'a as determined by the rabbis; of which plants and within what time Pe'a is given, and how long it is free from tithing. 2. Whereby fields or plantations of trees are divided from one another; exceptions and specific regulations (e. g. carob trees, two threshing-floors, two sorts of produce). 3. Special cases: small plots, harvesting at different times, community property; validity of transfers depending on the reservation of a small part of the soil. 4. How Pe'a is to be given; gleanings, *leḳet*; produce in ant holes. 5. More about gleanings; the forgotten sheaf, *shikḥa*. 6. The same subject continued. 7. The dues of the poor from oliveyards and vineyards. 8. What time one may glean; trustworthiness of the poor with regard to their dues; the poor tithe; the wayfaring poor; who is entitled to receive the dues of the poor.

3. Demai[2], 'The Dubious,' i. e. fruits concerning which it is not certain whether the tithe for the Levites, the heave-offering for the priests and, in those years in which it is due, the second tithe have been given. Seven chapters. 1. Which fruits are exempt from the right of Demai; how the Demai tithe is distinguished from the ordinary second tithe; in which cases fruits are exempt from the right of Demai; for what purpose Demai fruits may be applied. 2. Of which fruits of the land of Israel the Demai offerings must be made everywhere; who is trustworthy with regard to the observance of the Demai regulations; purchase and sale. 3. To whom it is permissible to give Demai for food; in which cases Demai fruits which one lets go out of his hands must be tithed. 4. Who deserves credence with reference to Demai; the things to be observed on the Sabbath in relation to the tithe. Those that cannot be trusted in regard to tithing. 5. How the offerings are segregated. 6. The right procedure when one has leased a field or with community property; fruits raised in Syria. 7. When one is invited over the Sabbath by one who is not trustworthy; the deliverance of the Demai offerings in certain cases; what should be observed when something of which it is certain that no tithe has been given (*ṭebel*) has been mixed with Demai.

4. Kil'aim, 'Diverse Seeds,' Levit. 19.19; Deut. 22.9ff., un-

lawful mingling of things (plants, animals, clothing) belonging to one genus but of different species. Nine chapters. 1. Which species of plants, and which of animals, constitute Kil'aim towards one another. 2. What is to be done when two distinct seeds have been mingled or when one wishes to sow a field previously sown with other seeds or to sow in one and the same field different seeds. 3. Beds of cabbage, onions, gourds and other kinds of beds. 4, 5. Vineyards. 6. Arbors of grape vines, *'aris*. 7. More about vines (shoots, etc.). 8. The various kinds of Kil'aim. Kil'aim of cattle (yoking together), bastards and a number of other (mostly wild) animals. 9. Kil'aim of clothing.

5. Shebi'ith, 'Seventh year,' Exod. 23.11; Levit. 25.1ff.; according to Deut. 15.1ff. the year in which debts are released[3], *shemiṭṭah*. Thus e. g. the years 164–63 and 38–37 B.C.E. were sabbatic years. Ten chapters: nine treat of the rest of the land, the tenth of the release of debts. 1. Fields in which there are trees (orchards) and to what time they may be tilled. 2. Fields free from trees. 3. Manuring; fencing in; opening up of quarries; tearing down a wall; removal of stones. 4. Gathering of wood, stones, weeds; trimming and pruning; when one may commence to eat that which grows in the field in the sabbath year and when it may be taken home. 5. What is to be observed with white figs, arum (*luf*), summer onions, madder (*pu'ah*); what may not be sold or lent. 6. Difference in the provinces with regard to the seventh year. The things that may not be exported from the land of Israel and that the priests' heave-offering may not be taken into the land. 7. What is subject to the law of the seventh year. 8. How that which grows in the seventh year may be used. 9. Which vegetables one may buy. The use to which that which grows in the seventh year may be put and the removal thereof. 10. The releasing of debts. § 4 deals with the *Prosbul*, *προσβολή*.[4]

6. Terumoth, 'Heave-offerings'—the so-called great priests' heave-offering, Numb. 18.8ff., comp. Deut. 18.4, and the heave-offering from the tithe *terumath ma'aser*, or the tithe which is set aside for the priests from the levites' tithe, Numb. 18.25f. Eleven chapters, which treat mainly of the great heave-offering. 1. Persons whose act of setting aside is ineffective; that the setting aside must not be done according to measure, weight and number.

2. One may not set aside the heave from the clean for the unclean, nor from the unclean for the clean, nor from one species for another species. Difference between that which is done in error and that which is done with design, both in regard to the heave-offering and in other cases. 3. In which cases the heave-offering must be given twice. How the heave is determined and in what order. When one blunders in speech. Offerings by non-Jews. 4. The setting aside and measure of the great heave. Concerning mixing up the heave with other fruits, *medumma'*.[5] 6. Restitution of heave eaten or stolen. 7. Further regulations concerning restitution and mixture. 8. Further norms concerning substitution. Heave wine which has been suffered to stay uncovered. Remarks concerning the danger of poisoning. Defilement of the heave. Women in danger of being defiled by heathens. 9. What is to be done when heave has been sown. 10. In which instances even the taste which is taken on by certain things from the heave renders them prohibited. 11. To what use the heave may be put.

7. Maasroth or Maaser Rishon, 'Tithes' or 'First Tithe,' Numb. 18.21ff., the tithe which appertains to the Levites. Five chapters. 1. Of which fruits the tithe is to be given and at what time it becomes due. 2–4. In which cases such fruits may be eaten (enjoyed) without giving the tithe.[6] 5. Application of the tithing due in the case of transplanting, selling, or with after-wine (lora) or with produce found in ants' holes. Some further plants and species of seed which are free from tithing.

8. Maaser Sheni, 'the Second Tithe', Deut. 14.22ff., comp. 26.12ff.,[7] which or the equivalent of which in money was to be consumed in joyous celebration in Jerusalem. Five chapters. 1. The second tithe may not be alienated. What may be bought with the money for which it is exchanged. 2. More about the use to which the second tithe is put. The procedure when money realized from the second tithe has been mixed up with other money or when it is desired to exchange that money for other money (so as to facilitate the transportation to Jerusalem). 3. Of the fruits of the tithe taken to Jerusalem it is not permitted to spend for porters' hire;[8] no heave may be bought with the

money of the second tithe; this money may be exchanged in Jerusalem for ordinary fruits and these for ordinary money. What is to be done with a tree the boughs of which overtop the wall of Jerusalem. Defilement of the second tithe. 4. For what price the second tithe may be redeemed. He that redeems his own fruits is bound to add a fifth of the estimated value (according to our mode of expression: one-fourth).[9] To what extent something found is to be regarded as consecrated. 5. A vineyard in its fourth year and the redemption of its fruits (comp. Levit. 19.24). The removal (*bi'ur*) of the tithe. Abrogation of the confession customary on that occasion (Deut. 26.13–15) on the part of the high priest Johanan (John Hyrcanus) and other repeals instituted by him.

9. Ḥalla, 'Heave from the Dough,' comp. Numb. 15.18ff. Four chapters. 1. Whereof Ḥalla must be given. Wherein Ḥalla and the Heave-offering coincide. 2. A woman, even when naked, may set aside Ḥalla of the dough, if she is seated, for in this posture it is possible for her to cover her secret parts. Of 5/4 of a ḳab of flour Ḥalla must be given. The size of Ḥalla is 1/24, for those who bake to sell 1/48. 3. How one deals with Ḥalla according to the condition of the dough and its owner. 4. Which species of produce may be computed together to bring up the quantity requisite for the giving of Ḥalla to its full measure. How different countries are distinguished with regard to Ḥalla.

10. Orla, 'Uncircumcision' (of trees), comp. Levit. 19.23. Three chapters. 1. Under what circumstances trees and vineyards are subject to the law of Orla. 2. In which instances ordinary things which are permissible for use stay permitted when Orla and (or) Kil'aim is mixed up with them. In connection therewith discussions concerning that which is lawful when heave or Kil'aim is intermixed with other things, as well as concerning other prohibited mixtures. 3. On dyes and fire made with Orla. Varying application of the laws concerning Orla and Kil'aim in the land of Israel, in Syria and elsewhere.

11. Bikkurim, 'First Fruits,' comp. Deut. 26.1ff.; Exod. 23.19. Three chapters. 1. Who may not offer the First Fruits at all and who may offer them but without reciting the formula

prescribed in Deut. 26. Whereof and from what time on they may be offered and how under given conditions they may be replaced by others. 2. Wherein First Fruits, the Heave-offering and the Second Tithe coincide. It is then discussed how the fruit Ethrog used with the festive wreath on the Feast of Booths, the animal Kewi (*Kewi*, antelope?) and human blood may be distinguished from similar things. 3. How the First Fruits are taken to Jerusalem.[10]

§ 2. Second Order: Mo'ed, Twelve Tractates.

1. Shabbath, 'Sabbath,' comp. Exod. 20.10, 23.12; Deut. 5.14; furthermore Exod. 34.21, 35.2f., 16.22ff.; as well as Jerem. 17.21ff.; Amos 8.5; Nehem. 10.32, 13.15ff. The pentateuchal regulations may be summed up in a few sentences. The exceedingly circumstantial rulings of the Mishna have been spun out from the fact that in Exod. 35 the command of sabbath rest and the ordinances referring to the structure of the Tabernacle are placed in juxtaposition. In order to understand the rules governing the carrying (movement) from one place to another which play so great a part we must take note of the diversity in the four kinds of localities:[11] (a) *reshuth ha-rabbim*, public domain, squares or streets of at least sixteen cubits in width outside a town or in unwalled cities; (b) *reshuth ha-yaḥid*, private territory, localities enclosed on all sides by walls which are at least ten handbreadths high, also walled cities when the gates are not shut at night; (c) *karmelith*[12], neutral ground, localities which show characteristics both of public and of private territory, for which reason intercourse between them and those territories is forbidden; hence on the one hand private property which as with fields, meadows, projecting roofs is not fenced in, and on the other hand blind alleys and other localities avoided by general traffic (such as canals, depressions or embankments of a certain minimal depth or height, on streets and squares, also the sea);[13] (d) *maḳom paṭur*, free domain, open, unforbidden territory[14] from which it is lawful to maintain intercourse both with private and with public property. But this freedom must not be abused so as to make for transit from public to private property and vice versa. Such free domains are, for example, embankments (depressions) of at

least three handbreadths in height (depth) and of less than four handbreadths in width, then the air space ten handbreadths above public territory or Karmelith.[15]

The matter of the twenty-four chapters is disposed with not much of system. 1. In what diverse manners it is unlawful to take something from one domain, *reshuth*, to another. What may still be done on Friday before the Sabbath sets in, and on the other hand what one must forbear to do at that time. Concerning eighteen regulations on which it was voted in the assembly which met in the upper chamber of Hananiah ben Hezekiah ben Garon in favor of the Shammaiites against the Hillelites. 2. Illumination on the Sabbath. 3, 4. Keeping warm or warming up cooked food on the Sabbath. 5. Wherewith an animal may be led or covered on the Sabbath (halter, cover, etc.). 6. Wherewith women or men may or may not go out on the Sabbath (ornaments, amulets, false teeth, wooden legs, etc.). 7. How many sin-offerings one is liable to according to circumstances because of inadvertent violation of sabbath rest. § 2 the thirty-nine main classes of forbidden labor,[16] *'aboth melakoth*. 7, § 3f. and ch. 8. Concerning the quantities by the carrying of which on the Sabbath one incurs guilt. 9, §§ 1–4. Scriptural passages as proofs or catchwords for defilements, things lawful and unlawful, which have nothing to do with the Sabbath but are inserted here because 8.7, where the question turns upon carrying a potsherd on the Sabbath, Isai. 30.14 had been cited as catchword. Then additional regulations concerning what or how much it is unlawful to carry on the Sabbath. 10. Carrying on the Sabbath: to the threshold and from there inside or outside; carrying in an unwonted manner; two men carrying a loaf of bread; the carrying of a corpse, the carrying of a living human being. 11. Concerning throwing: into the street, into the sea, on land, etc. 12. Building, hammering, sawing, boring, plowing, weeding, trimming of trees, gathering of wood or grass; writing two letters. 13. Weaving, spinning, sewing, tearing, washing, dyeing; hunting. 14. Catching and wounding, hunting, preparing salt water, forbidden medicaments. 15. Tying knots, folding garments, making beds. 16. Behavior during a conflagration.[17] 17. Which utensils may be taken into one's hand on the Sabbath. That it is permissible to close a shutter. 18. What may be removed on the Sabbath. One may pull calves and foals of asses, so may a mother walk her child (but she must not carry it). An animal may be assisted at bringing forth on festival days; for the sake of a woman giving birth the Sabbath may be broken. 19. Circumcision on the Sabbath, day of circumcision; defective consummation of circumcision. 20. Straining wine and feeding cattle. 21. How vessels are handled in which objects repose which one may not take into one's hand on the Sabbath. Clearing the table. 22. Sundry regulations concerning the preparation of food and drink, also on bathing on the Sabbath. 23. Borrowing; casting lots; renting; walking a distance within the Sabbath day's limit (2000 cubits) with the intention of continuing when Sabbath is out from the point reached; what may be done to a dead body. 24. Feeding cattle on the Sabbath.

2. Erubin, 'Blendings,' three expedients for circumventing certain specially irksome regulations contained in the laws about the Sabbath: (a) '*Erub Teḥumin*, a blending in thought of boundaries. In order that one may walk on the Sabbath beyond 2000 cubits, one deposits on the preceding day at the place where the Sabbath limit terminates food sufficient for two meals, thus as it were establishing residence there, by means of which fact leave is given him to proceed from there 2000 cubits farther. (b) '*Erub ḥaṣeroth*, a blending in thought of courts. It is not permissible on the Sabbath to carry anything from one private domain (see above, p. 34) to another. Hence those who have their dwellings around one and the same court combine their several domains by depositing in one of the dwellings food prepared on Friday from joint contributions. A cognate mode is the '*erub maboi*, blending of a blind alley (literally of the entrance) or *shittuf maboi* (*shittuf* = jointure) by means of food; but the act must be preceded by blocking the blind alley or a space enclosed by walls on three sides by means of a beam and lath. (c) '*Erub tabshilin*. When a festival occurs on Friday, it is properly unlawful to cook for the Sabbath. It was therefore customary to prepare something for the Sabbath as early as the eve of the festival, thus effecting a blending between festival and Sabbath which made it lawful to prepare all the remaining food on the

festival for the Sabbath. This third species of Erub is dealt with in Beṣa 2.

Ten chapters. 1. Erub Maboi. How an encamping caravan may transform, by fencing in, a public domain into a private. 2. How one may make use on the Sabbath of a well in a public domain and under what conditions one may carry in a garden. 3. Wherewith and where the Erub of boundaries may be made; whereby an Erub becomes void; Erub of boundaries with a condition; when a festival is followed by the Sabbath; the new year. 4. Transgression of the Sabbath-day's journey. 5. The territory surrounding a city and how the limit for the Sabbath journey is measured. 6. Erub of the courts. 7. More about Erub of the courts; Shittuph Maboi. 8. Erub of the boundaries for pious purposes (house of mourning, wedding); how much of food is to be deposited for this kind of Erub. More about Erub of the courts. 9. Roofs. 10. Numerous laws of a diverse character relating to the Sabbath, which properly belong into the preceding tractate: when one has found tephillin (phylacteries); how one may carry home a child born in the field; whether it is permissible to roll together a biblical volume which on reading has become unwound; passing water; expectorating; drinking; catching up water; what is lawful in the sanctuary, but forbidden abroad, *ba-medinah*, for example § 14: "When a priest has a wound on his finger, he may bind it up with bast in the sanctuary, but not elsewhere."[18]

3. Pesaḥim, 'Paschal Lambs, Passover-offerings': Exod. 12; 23.15; 34.15ff.; Levit. 23.5ff.; Numb. 28.16ff.; Deut. 16.1ff. Ten chapters. 1–3. Searching for and removing leaven; whereof the unleavened cakes (*maṣṣoth*) may be prepared; the bitter herbs. 4. What labors are permitted on the eve of the festival and how long. Six things done by the men of Jericho (of which only one appertains to Passover).[19] 5. The killing of the Passover lamb. 6. How far the Passover lamb sets aside the Sabbath; at what time and whereof a festival sacrifice is offered in addition to it; what obtains when on the Sabbath one sacrifice has been interchanged with another. 7. The roasting of the Passover lamb; what happens when it has become unclean, and in which case it may be offered in a condition of uncleanness; what is eaten

thereof. 8. The persons that may eat of the Passover lamb; the place for eating it; associations (community eating). 9. The Passover festival of the second month (see Numb. 9.10ff.); the Passover festival at the time of the exodus; instances in which Passover lambs had been interchanged. 10. The order of the Passover meal as it proceeds with the four cups of wine which it is obligatory to partake of on this occasion (in § 3 it is mentioned that after the destruction of the Temple the Passover lamb is no longer eaten since it cannot be offered).

4. Sheḳalim, 'Shekels.' Eight chapters, treating of the half a shekel tax which, having originated in the times of Nehemiah in the amount of a third of a shekel (Nehem. 10.33), had been raised, probably not much later, to the amount first mentioned (comp. Exod. 30.12ff.) and served to defray the costs of the maintenance of the worship in the second Temple. 1. How on the first of Adar[20] the summons goes out for the payment of the tax; how the money changers[21] on the fifteenth in the provinces and on the twenty-fifth in the sanctuary, set up their counters, for the reason that the tax must be paid in ancient (holy) coin. The persons obligated to pay the tax. 2. The exchanging; shekels lost or purloined; diverse sorts of coin. The various uses to which moneys may be put which have been collected for definite purposes. 3. The manner in which the money paid in is taken out of the treasury. 4. What was purchased therewith. When a person has consecrated his fortune, to what use it may be put. 5. The fifteen offices in the sanctuary and their chiefs. The four seals, *ḥothamoth* (marks), for marking the measures of diverse meal-and wine-offerings. 6. The thirteen sacrificial boxes, thirteen tables and thirteen gates in the sacntuary. Where the ark of the covenant was hidden. 7. Money, meat or cattle which one has picked up in Jerusalem and in the sanctuary. Seven ordinances of the court of justice. 8. Saliva, utensils, butchers' knives when run across in Jerusalem. Purification of the temple veil. The costliness of the veil in front of the sanctuary. Shekels and firstlings discontinued after the destruction of the Temple.

5. Yoma, literally 'The Day' (in Aramaic), i. e. the Day of Atonement, also Kippurim[22] or Yom ha-kippurim,[23] comp. Levit. 16. Eight chapters. 1. Preparing the high priest. 2. How four

times a day lots are drawn for service. How the sacrificial victims were put upon the altar.[24] 3. Further preparations for the high priest (bathing, ablutions, putting on the garments). Bringing near his bullock, his first confession of sins. The golden lots of Joshua ben Gamla for the two goats. Improvements in the sanctuary on the part of Ben Ḳaṭṭin, king Monobazus and queen Helena. Blame for those who refused to instruct others. 4. Casting lots upon the two goats. Second confession of sins by the high priest. Peculiarities of the Day of Atonement with regard to offering incense, ascending the altar and the ablution of hands and feet. 5. How the high priest enters the holy of holies thrice (*'eben shethiah*, 'stone of foundation,' in that place): with the incense, with the blood of the bullock, with the blood of the goat. Purification of the altar of gold. 6. Third confession of sins by the high priest. Sending away the other goat for Azazel. 7. Scriptural portions read or recited by the high priest and the benedictions pronounced by him. The remaining part of his service. 8. Prohibitions concerning eating, drinking, working on the Day of Atonement; the fasting of children; procedure in the case of danger to life. The means of atonement (sin-offering, guilt-offering, death, Day of Atonement, repentance). When no atonement is effected.

6. Sukka, 'Booth', or Sukkoth treats of the 'Festival of Booths,' Levit. 23.34ff.; Numb. 29.12ff.; Deut. 16.13ff. Five chapters. 1. Concerning the setting up of the festival booth. 2. More about the character of the same; concerning eating and sleeping therein; persons exempt from this obligation. 3. The festive wreath *Lulab* (comp. Levit. 23.40; Nehem. 8.15), consisting of a branch of the palm, a branch of myrtle, a branch of willows of the brook and Ethrog. 4. How many days each ceremony of the festival lasts. The libation of water. 5. Manifestations of joy at the drawing and pouring out of the water (comp. Isai. 12.3). Concerning the participation of the twenty-four priestly divisions in the festival sacrifices. Stray remarks concerning the distribution of the sacrificial portions and of the showbread among the priestly divisions.

7. Beṣa, 'Egg' (from the initial word) or Yom Tob, 'Festival.' Of that which must be observed on festivals, among other matters

also of the difference between Sabbath and festivals with Exod. 12. 16 as a point to fall back upon.—For an understanding of the tractate the following terms are important: *mukan*, what was prepared or set aside for Sabbath or festival on an ordinary day; *mukṣeh* (literally: something separated, remote from thought), that which lacks the preparation or designation just spoken of (for the reason that the object in question has not been thought of at all or at least not in the requisite manner);[25] *nolad*, that which has just come into existence, which accordingly lacks the antecedent designation referred to, e. g. animals just born, new-drawn milk, utensils or garments just finished.—Five chapters. 1. Opens up with the mention of the much-cited dispute in the schools concerning the Egg. According to the school of Shammai it is permissible to partake of an egg derived from a hen which had been intended for eating purposes (not for laying eggs), when that egg was carried on a festival and laid on the Sabbath immediately following, or was carried on a Sabbath and laid on the festival immediately following; according to the school of Hillel, it is not. Then follows a series of differences between these two schools. What of edibles or of garments one may send to another as a gift on festival days. 2. Erub Tabshilin (see above, p. 36(c). Further differences between the schools just named. Three points on which Rabban Gamaliel was strict, three on which he was lenient. Three things which R. Eleazar ben Azariah permitted. How a handmill in which pepper is ground and a child's carriage become unclean. 3. Catching and killing birds on festival days. How one buys on festival days meat, beverages and the like without negotiating as to quantity and price. 4. Transporting food; which kind of wood may be used for cooking and how it is to be split.[25] Prohibited formation of vessels; the prohibition of generating fire. 5. The relation of Sabbath and festival with regard to things permitted and things forbidden. Cattle and other posessions with reference to the Sabbath day's journey.

8. Rosh Ha-shana, 'New Year's Festival.' According to Numb. 28.11ff., comp. 10.10, each new moon was solemnly observed; but with peculiar solemnity was observed the new moon of the seventh month (in the ecclesiastical year, amounting

to the first of the civil year, i. e. Tishri), see Levit. 23.24f.; Numb. 29.1ff. Four chapters. 1. Divers new years (Nisan, Elul, Tishri, Shebat). Four times in the year God sits in judgment. Six times messengers are sent from Jerusalem on account of the new moon. Testimony in regard to the appearance of the new moon. 2. More about this testimony; sanctification of the new moon. Rabban Gamaliel as Nasi (patriarch) and R. Joshua. 3. Blowing the shophar. The requisite devotion (Exod. 17.11; Numb. 21.8). 4. Blowing the shophar before and after the destruction of Jerusalem. The festival wreath on the Festival of Booths before and after the destruction of Jerusalem. How long one may go on to receive the testimony concerning the new moon. Order of the benedictions on new year's day: Malkiyyoth[26] (recitation of ten biblical verses in which the Kingdom of God is mentioned), Zikronoth (ten verses referring to God's compassionate remembrance), Shopharoth (ten verses with the word Shophar occurring therein).

9. Taanith or in the plural Taaniyyoth 'Fasting.' Four chapters. 1. From what time on rain is made mention of (in the second of the eighteen Benedictions), when one commences, in the absence of rain, to pray for it (in the ninth Benediction) and when to fast (at the first three days, then again three days and lastly seven days) and in what manner public mourning is ultimately manifested. 2. Order of the seven days' fasts and the prayers appertaining thereto. On which of these days even the officiating priests do fast. On which days it is not permissible to appoint fasts. 3. The events for which otherwise fasting and (or) blowing an alarm is prescribed. Honi, who drew circles *ha-me'agel* and was answered as often as he prayed for rain. At what time, when rain is forthcoming, the fasting is cut short. 4. The institution of the body of delegates present at the Temple sacrifices and consisting of priests, Levites and Israelites, *ma'amadoth*; how they fasted and read portions of the Scriptures. The seventeenth day of Tammuz, the ninth of Ab. How the fifteenth of Ab was kept.[26a]

10. Megilla 'The Scroll of Esther,' means any scroll, specifically the scroll of Esther which is read in the synagogue on the day of Purim (comp. Esth. 9.28).[27] Four chapters. 1. On what

day the Megilla is read in the month of Adar. How in this connection there is a difference between walled cities on the one hand and unwalled cities and villages on the other hand. Then follows an enumeration of other instances of a difference obtaining between similar things or cases, e. g. between Sabbath and festivals; the books of Holy Scripture may be written in all languages *bekol lashon* (according to Rabban Gamaliel only in the Greek language), Tephillin and Mezuza only in square script *'ashurith*; great and small high places; Jerusalem and Shiloh. 2. How the Megilla should be read appropriately. In this connection it is stated which commandments may be kept during the whole day and which during the whole night. 3. The subject matter of this chapter is really foreign to this tractate. Selling holy objects, including a synagogue; concerning synagogues in ruins; the scriptural portions read on the Sabbaths of Adar; those read on festivals and on fast days.[28] 4. § 1 Of the reading of the Esther Scroll; then of other liturgical lections from Torah and Prophets. § 3 for which actions ten persons are required; § 4 interpreting (translating); § 8 improper behavior with reference to Tephillin; § 9 who is to be silenced when leading in common prayer and when acting as interpreter of the Scriptures;[29] which parts of Scripture may be read but not translated; what may not be read as Haphṭara.

11. Moed Ḳaṭan[30] or, after the opening words, Mashkin 'One may irrigate.'[31] Three chapters. Regulations concerning the intervening festival days, i. e. the days which intervene between the first and seventh day of Passover or between the first and eighth day of Tabernacles.[32] On these days it was permitted to perform certain kinds of work, albeit partly in a manner somewhat differing from the normal (the restrictions are of rabbinic origin). 1. Agricultural labors, graves, coffin, marrying, sewing;[33] making a parapet, repairs. 2. Pressing olives or wine; buying; arranging layers. 3. Shaving, washing, writing. Mourning on Sabbaths, solemn festivals and the lesser festival days.

12. Ḥagiga 'Festival Offering.' Three chapters, treating of what is to observed on the three pilgrimage festivals (Passover, Festival of Weeks, F. of Booths, comp. Deut. 16.16f.). 1. The persons upon whom it is obligatory to appear on these festivals

in the sanctuary; how much is to be spent; whereof the festival offerings may be taken and wherein they must consist.[34] 2. This chapter, together with the end of the first chapter, has extremely little to do with the exact subject. § 1 the things in which not every one may be instructed and those concerning which one should not inquire at all; § 2 the difference of opinion between Jose ben Joezer and Jose ben Johanan[35] and in general between the five 'Pairs' concerning *semikah*; § 6 the necessity of definite intent in connection with ritual ablution of hands; § 7 degrees of (Levitical) purity. 3. How far holy meat requires stricter handling than the heave and so on. With §§ 7, 8 the subject matter of the tractate is resumed: how during the festival wine and bread belonging to an observant Jew are not defiled by contact with an ordinary person; of the cleansing of the vessels in the sanctuary after the festival.

§ 3. Third Order: Nashim, Seven Tractates.

1. Yebamoth[36] 'Sisters-in-law' or Nashim 'Women'[37] treats for the most part of the levirate Deut. 25.5ff.; comp. Ruth 4.5; Matth. 22.24; in part also of prohibited marriages, Levit. 18, etc. *Yabam* means the husband's brother, i. e. the brother of a deceased husband who left no issue; *yebamah* the widow whom the husband's brother must marry; *yibbem* to marry the deceased brother's wife; *yibbum* and *yebamuth* (52b) consummation of this marriage; *ḥaliṣah* the act of loosing the shoe; *ḥalaṣ* denotes in post-biblical Hebrew: (a) to perform the act of ḥaliṣa (on the part of the woman); (b) to grant ḥaliṣa (on the part of the husband's brother, who thereby sets the widow free to marry someone else); *ḥaluṣah* a widow to whom ḥaliṣa was granted. Sixteen chapters. 1. Which degrees of kinship between the woman and the husband's brother release her as well as her co-wives from ḥaliṣa and from marrying the husband's brother. § 4 how the adherents of the school of Shammai and their opponents of the school of Hillel came to terms in a spirit of toleration in matters involving intercourse with one another.[38] 2. When a third brother is born after one of the two has passed away. Marriages prohibited by the *Sopherim* (comp. 9.3) or for reasons of sanctity. Betrothal with one of two sisters who cannot be

told apart. Other marriages which a man may not contract (such as may give rise to evil report). 3. When two of four brothers have married two sisters. 4. When the deceased brother's wife is found to be with child. When during her waiting period she falls heir to property. The duty to marry the deceased brother's wife falls to the eldest brother. The duration of the waiting period for women who become widowed or divorced after contraction or consummation of marriage; the same for those repudiated and those betrothed. Mamzer (bastard). 5. The relation of ḥaliṣa and bill of divorcement. 6. Those a high priest or an ordinary priest may not marry. The duty to raise children. 7. Usufruct *millug* and iron fund *ṣon barzel* slaves, and how far they may partake of the heave. Whereby wives or daughters of priests are excluded from partaking of the heave. 8. Those crushed or maimed in their privy parts with reference to the heave and the levirate marriage. In this connection also (comp. Deut. 23.2ff.) concerning non-admission or admission to the congregation of Ammonites, Moabites, Egyptians and Edomites. 9. Which women belong lawfully to their husbands but are forbidden to their deceased husband's brothers, and vice versa. When a woman may or may not partake of the heave or tithe. 10. When husband or wife upon insufficient evidence of death of the other conjugal party remarries. Cohabitation on the part of a boy nine years and one day old. 11. Concerning deflowered virgins, proselytes and changelings. 12. The ceremonies of ḥaliṣa. 13, 14. Refusal *me'un* on the part of a minor to remain with her husband to whom she had been given in marriage by her mother or her brothers. Deafmute (*ḥeresh*) women and men with reference to the levirate. 15, 16. specifically of the trustworthiness of testimony concerning the husband's death, whereupon the widow left behind may marry another man.

2. Kethubboth 'Marriage Settlements,' comp. Exod. 22.16. Kethubbah denotes both the document[39] and the sum settled therein by the husband upon his wife in case of divorce or death. Thirteen chapters.[40] 1. Wedding day for virgins Wednesday, for widows Thursday. Amount of the Kethubba. Trustworthiness concerning lost virginity. 2. More about declarations made by women, including such as had been captives, concerning their

status. The credibility of witnesses who testify to their own advantage or to the advantage of one another; the trustworthiness of adults with reference to observations made during their minority. 3. The fine for seducing a young woman (*na'arah* Deut. 22.25ff.). 4. To whom the fine money goes. A father's rights, a husband's rights and duties. The sons inherit after their mother's death her Kethubba; what the daughters or the widow is entitled to after the death of father or husband. 5. Augmenting the Kethubba. Duties of husband and wife towards each other (in marital and material respect). 6. What a wife has acquired through her own labor or through inheritance. The calculation of that which a wife brings with her. A daughter's dower. 7. The right to divorce with certain vows and when a wife commits offenses against the law of Moses or that of Judaism (*dath Moshe wihudith*); also when the husband is afflicted with an offensive ailment or is engaged in a labor with an offensive smell. 8, 9. Property which falls to a woman during marriage; a wife's claim upon property left by her husband. 10. Adjudication of claims when a man leaves behind more than one wife. 11. The rights of widows, specifically concerning sale of the Kethubba. 12. The rights of a stepchild; the right of the widow to remain in her husband's house. 13. Decisions by the judges Hanan and Admon. The superior merit of dwelling in the land of Israel and in Jerusalem.

3. Nedarim 'Vows (and their disannulment)', comp. Numb. 30. Eleven chapters, treating (not of that which one dedicates, but) of vows (also oaths *shebu'ah* and bans *ḥerem*) by which something is abjured. 1. Which expressions and deformations (e. g. Ḳonam, Ḳonaḥ, Ḳonas for Ḳorban)[41] stand for vows. 2. Which expressions do not stand for vows. Wherein an oath differs from Ḳorban and other vows. Vows with reservation. Evasions. 3. Four classes of vows which are not valid at the outset.[42] Venial falsehoods. How certain expressions in the vow are to be interpreted. 4, 5. When, by means of a vow, it is denied to a person to have enjoyment from his fellow. (5. 4: *hareni 'aleka* and *hare 'at 'alai*). 6, 7. When by a vow a person renounces food, clothing, bed, house, city. 8. (including 7. 8, 9) of the vow of renunciation for a limited period. Interpretation

of certain vows. 9. From which vows of renunciation one may be absolved by a scholar. 10. Who may disanull the vows of wife or daughter. 11. Which vows of wife or daughter may be disanulled.

4. Nazir 'Nazirite'; *Neziruth* 'Nazirate', comp. Numb. 6. Nine chapters. 1. Which expressions make the Nazirate binding. The period of duration of the Nazirate (ordinarily and at the same time minimally thirty days). The Samson Nazirate. 2. Which Nazirate vows stand. Junction of two Nazirates. 3. Time of shaving the hair. 4. Remission and disanulment of Nazirate vows. 5. When something has been consecrated in error and the application to the Nazirate. When the victim intended for the Nazirate offering is stolen. Nazirate vows on condition (a sort of wager). 6. The things forbidden to the Nazirite. The sacrifices when a Nazirite has been defiled and upon completion of his term. 7, 8. Concerning a Nazirite's defilement, specifically the kind proceeding from a dead body. 9. Nazirate vows of women and slaves. *Tum'ah Yeduah* and *tum'ath ha-tehom*. What constitutes a place of sepulture. Whether Samuel was a Nazirite.

5. Giṭṭin 'Bills of Divorcement',[43] comp. Deut. 24.1. Nine chapters. 1. Transmission of a bill of divorcement from abroad. Authentication or withdrawal of bills of divorcement and bills of manumission. 2. Authentication of a bill of divorcement from abroad. Subsequent signatures. Writing material. The persons who may write a bill of divorcement and those who may transmit it. 3. The bill of divorcement must be written expressly for the woman in question. Having on hand formularies for bills of divorcement, deeds of sale etc. A lost bill of divorcement; supposition that the giver is alive (or, as the case may be, dead); substitute messengers. 4. Withdrawal of a bill of divorcement. Ordinance by Gamaliel I on this subject, similarly concerning the case when husband or wife or both have more than one name. In this connection several other ordinances by Gamaliel I and in general by the Hillelites with a view to good order, *mippene tikkun ha-'olam*. Re-marrying a divorced wife. 5. Ordinances touching compensation for damage and the validity of certain actions, partly with a view to the same motive (*mippene tikkun*

ha-'olam). Ordinances dictated by the desire for peaceful relations, *mippene darke shalom.* 6. Transmission of the bill of divorcement by messenger. How far an oral order with reference to a bill of divorcement is valid.[44] 7. Divorce in cases of sickness. A bill of divorcement on condition. 8. Throwing the bill of divorcement at the woman; making use of an old bill; misleading data in a bill of divorcement. A bald bill of divorcement, *geṭ kereaḥ.*[45] 9. The wording of the bill of divorcement; which bills are valid and which not valid. Causes for divorce.[46]

6. Soṭa 'The Woman Suspected of Adultery', comp. Numb. 5, 11ff. Nine chapters. 1. How the husband manifests his jealousy. How the suspected woman is exhorted in the great court of justice. How she is presented. § 7 'With whatsoever measure a man meteth, they mete to him. She adorned herself for sin, and so God makes her ugly', etc. Other examples of divine retribution. 2. Writing of the billet and adjuration of the suspected woman. 3. The offering of jealousy and the fate of her that is found to have been defiled.[47] Differences between Israelites and priests, between males and females with regard to rights and penalties. 4. In which cases a woman is not given the water of the curse to drink. 5. That the water of the curse operates likewise on the adulterer. Other interpretations of the Scriptures propounded *bo ba-yom*[48] by Akiba and Joshua ben Hyrcanus. 6. Testimony concerning the woman's infidelity. 7. Formulae, etc. which may be recited in all languages and those which may be recited in Hebrew only. 8. The allocution of the priest anointed for warfare and, in general, exposition of Deut. 20.2–9. 9. Breaking the neck of a heifer in the case of an untraced murder, Deut. 21.1–9. At what time this ceremony as well as the application of the water of jealousy fell into disuse. Concerning the cessation of other customs, things and virtues. (Baraitha: Indications of the advent of the Messiah.)

7. Ḳiddushin 'Marrying', the actions by which a man acquires a woman to be his spouse (*'erusin* or *liḳḳuhin*; distinct from *nissu'in*, the induction into the husband's home which marks marriage proper and takes place, in the case of a virgin, ordinarily twelve months later, and in the case of a widow as a rule thirty days later). Four chapters. 1. How a wife is acquired

by a man (by the gift of an amount of money no matter how small, by a document in which the man manifests his intention, by cohabitation). The manners in which the acquisition of slaves, cattle, chattels and real estate is consummated. Which commandments are obligatory upon men only and which also upon women. § 9: which commandments are to be observed only in the land of Israel. § 10: Retribution for deeds. 2. Betrothal through a proxy. Whereby betrothals become invalid. 3. Betrothals on conditions. When the one party denies the fact of betrothal. In all cases of valid betrothals the child follows the father. 4. Which marriages are on a footing of parity; probing descent. Authentication of marriages contracted abroad. Maxims of morality.

§ 4. Fourth Order: Neziḳin. Ten Tractates.

1. Baba Ḳamma, 'First Gate,' that is of the tractate *neziḳin*.[49] In the first Gate the discussion concerns damages in the narrower sense (including theft, robbery and mayhem), in the other two Gates principally legal points with reference to chattels (II. 1–9) and real estate (II. 10, III).

Ten chapters. 1. The four principal species of damages according to Exod. 21.33, 22.5f.: (a) *ha-shor* the ox, according to the Palestinian Talmud in short *ḳeren* (horn), i. e. damage specifically by goring; according to the Babylonian Talmud in short *regel* (foot), i. e. damage which an animal perpetrates in walking. (b) *ha-bor* a pit left uncovered; also damages caused by objects thrown into the street. (c) *ha-mab'eh* he who grazes, according to the Palestinian Talmud *shen* (tooth) and *regel* (treading under foot), according to an opinion in the Babylonian Talmud a damage caused by a human being. (d) *ha-hab'er* setting fire, damaging through incendiarism, *'esh*. The distinctions obtaining between these species. What time, for which goods, with reference to which place and persons damages are to be paid, and that from the best of one's field. Computing damages. Difference between *mu'ad* (proved as noxious) and *tam* (innocuous, tame, from which injury proceeds either sporadically or only accidentally). 2. How far an animal does injury by stamping, eating, goring, etc. and concerning the compensation. A human being must always pay full compensation for damages done by him (is accounted as *mu'ad*). 3. Damages perpetrated by human beings through letting things stand in public places, through colliding. The goring ox. 4. More about the goring ox. 5. The same. The pit uncovered. What is said of the ox, pertains likewise to other cattle. 6. Damages by grazing cattle and by fire. 7. Compensation for stolen property (double; four-or fivefold). Cattle which may not be kept in the land of Israel.[50] 8. Mayhem and outrage. The offender is in duty bound to apologize, the offended person to forgive. 9. Compensation, when the thing stolen has changed in value or when anything has been vitiated by an artisan. Species of compensation, when the thief has perjured himself. 10. Several other cases of compensation (e. g. when a stolen thing has passed to other hands). That, because of the suspicion of theft, one may not buy from a shepherd wool, milk or a kid, from fruit watchers fruit or wood. Which waste products belong to the manufacturer or artisan.

2. Baba Meṣi'a, 'Middle Gate', a tractate particularly much in use. Ten chapters. 1. Of things, especially those found, claimed by two persons. That minor children, women and Canaanitic slaves have no claim to finds. Which documents, when found, must be restored. 2. Publication of found articles. Conducting back stray cattle. Assistance at loading and unloading. The precedence of the teacher as compared with one's father. 3. Concerning things left in storage. 4. Concerning buying, the term for reconsidering, unlawful profit (a sixth and over; Ona'a defrauding, comp. *hona* Levit. 25.14, 17), debased coin. In which cases even what is worth one peruṭa (small copper coin = 1/8 of an issar or 1/192 of a denarius) is of moment. Five cases, in which the compensation must be augmented by a fifth. With reference to which objects the law of Ona'a has no validity. One must not exercise Ona'a even with words. Fraudulent mixing of wares and other manipulations by sellers. 5. *neshek* (interest) and *tarbith* (speculating on the rise of prices). Cession of objects, on the condition of half of the profit, for selling or using. It is lawful to pay interest to non-Jews or to take interest from them. Lending and accommodation. 6. The hiring of laborers[51] and of cattle. Responsibility for that which

is committed to one's care (an accomplished piece of work, a pledge). 7. Feeding laborers. Force majeure, *'ones*, absolves a caretaker or lessee from the obligation of compensation. Which conditions are not valid. 8. When something hired, borrowed, bartered, or olive-trees sold for cutting down have changed in value. When the object of a sale is doubtful. Renting a house. 9. Leasing a field. At what time the laborer may demand his hire. Taking in pledge. 10.[52] Claims arising from the collapse of structures. What may be done in or on public places. Using the space between two superimposed gardens.

3. Baba Bathra 'Last Gate.' Ten chapters. 1. Dividing property held in partnership. How far a division may be demanded. 2. Restrictions upon the use to which private or public property may be put (from considerations of the neighbor, of public welfare, etc.). 3. Usucaption *ḥazaḳah* (the presumption of legal title to property held in uninterrupted and undisputed possession). How one may not build towards a common court or a public square. 4. What goes with the sale of immovable property. 5. What goes along with the sale of movable property (e. g. ships, cattle) and trees. Reconsideration on the part of the buyer on account of false statements by the seller. How things bought are taken possession of. Procedure in measuring and weighing.[53] 6. To what extent the seller must vouch for his wares. When one has a cistern in some one else's house or a garden in some one else's garden. Dimensions for dwellings, streets, sepulchers. 7. The measuring of fields for sale.[53] 8. Law of inheritance. 9. Division of property. Concerning gifts and the bridegroom's friends *shoshebenim*, *παρανύμφιοι*, also concerning betrothal gifts. 10. The drawing up of documents (bill of divorcement, Kethubba, etc.). Bail.

4. Sanhedrin, *συνέδριον* 'Court of Justice', treats in eleven chapters of the courts of justice and of judicial procedure, in particular of criminal law. 1. For the disposition of which questions or actions three men are requisite; the small sanhedrins with a membership in each of twenty-three, the great sanhedrin in Jerusalem with seventy-one members. 2. Privileges of the high priest and of the king. 3. Election of arbitral judges. Which persons may be neither judges nor witnesses. Examination

of witnesses. Announcement of the sentence. 4. Differences between civil and criminal cases. How the judges sat. Cautioning the witnesses in criminal cases. 5. As to what and how the witnesses are questioned. How the judges meet in conference. 6. Punishment by stoning. Burying the executed criminals. 7. The four species of capital punishment: stoning, burning, decapitation, strangulation. Which crimes are punished with stoning. 8. Of the wilful and stubborn son (Deut. 21.18ff.). The burglar. Whom it is lawful to kill in order to prevent him from committing a gross crime. 9. Which criminals are burnt and which decapitated. Which cases of homicide are not to be reckoned as murder. When criminals sentenced to death are mixed up so that it is not known which crime was committed by the individual persons. When a man is guilty of two crimes for which two distinct modes of punishment by death are prescribed. One who relapses (and is placed in the *kippah*[54]). Who may be put to death without court sentence. 10.[55] Who has and who has not a part in the world to come. The banned city, Deut. 13.13ff. 11. Which criminals are strangled. The rebellious (dissenting) teacher *zaḳen mamre*.[56] The false prophet.

5. Makkoth 'Stripes,' treats of the lashings to which a person is condemned by a court (Deut. 25.1ff.). Three chapters. Originally Sanh. and Mak. formed one tractate (see p. 27), in which first capital and then corporal punishments were discussed. 1. In which cases false witnesses are subjected to stripes instead of retaliation (Deut. 19.19). Then more elaborately on false witnesses. 2. The one who commits unpremeditated homicide and the cities of refuge (Deut. 19.19ff.; Numb. 35.19 ff.). 3. Which sins are punishable by stripes. Number of stripes.[57] Execution of the punishment. The punishment of scourging exempts one from the punishment of extermination. Reward for fulfilling even one commandment. Why God gave numerous commandments.[58]

6. Shebuoth 'Oaths', comp. Levit. 5.4ff. Eight chapters. 1. Two main species of oaths which divide into four.[59] Other acts similarly circumstanced. Statements concerning the cognisance of being unclean (Levit. 5.2) which is one of these acts. How atonement is effected for doing something in an unclean state

and for other transgressions of law by various kinds of offerings. 2. Further particulars about becoming aware of being unclean, *yedi'oth ha-tum'ah*. 3. The (2 or 4) species of oaths. A wanton oath (*shebu'ath bittui*) and an oath in vain (*shebu'ath shaw*). 4. The oath of testimony. 5. Denial by oath of that which one has appropriated or retained wrongly or by force, *shebu'ath ha-pikkadon*, Levit. 5.21ff. 6. The oath imposed by judges. In which case one may not swear. 7. Oaths in matters of hire, business and the like (mostly cases in which the plaintiff swears). 8. Four species of keepers (for pay, for no pay, one who borrows, one who hires).

7. Eduyyoth[60] 'Testimonies' (on the part of later teachers concerning the statements of older authorities), according to tradition[61] taught in the selfsame day *bo ba-yom* in which Eleazar ben Azariah was elected head of the academy, Nasi, after the deposition of Gamaliel II. The epithet *behiretha*, 'The Chosen One', is met with in the Talmud.[62] Altogether a hundred statements; in addition forty cases in which the Shammaiites were lenient and the Hillelites more rigorous (4.1–5. 5). These numbers seem to be intended. For the most part the statements recur in the Mishna in other places (according to the subject matter). Eight chapters. 1. Three statements of law in which the scholars (*hakamim*) go neither with Hillel nor with Shammai. Why the opinions of these or of other individual scholars have been handed down, although they have not become law. Three cases in which the school of Shammai disagreed with Shammai. Ordinances in which the school of Hillel prevailed and questions concerning which it yielded to the school of Shammai. 2. Four statements by Hananiah, the prefect of the priesthood. Three by Ishmael. Three questions discussed by others but settled for the first time by Joshua ben Mathiah. Three points of difference between Ishmael and Akiba. Three statements enunciated before Akiba. Statements of law and sayings by Akiba. 3. Dosa ben Archinus, Joshua ben Hananiah, Zadok, Rabban Gamaliel, Eleazar ben Azariah. 4. Points on which the school of Hillel was more rigorous than that of Shammai. 5. Further ordinances of the same kind. The things Akabiah ben Mahalalel would not retract. 6. Five statements attested by Judah ben Baba. Dispute

concerning defilement by parts severed from a dead (live) animal (human being). 7. Joshua, Zadok, Jakim, Papias, Menahem of Signa,[63] Nehuniah of Gudgeda.[64] 8. Joshua ben Bethera, Simeon ben Bethera, Judah ben Baba, Judah the Priest, Jose the Priest, Zechariah son of the Butcher, Jose ben Joezer,[65] Akiba, Eliezer and Joshua ben Hananiah. Diverse opinions concerning the activity of Elijah at his advent (Mal. 3.23f.).

8. Aboda Zara 'Idolatry.'[66] Five chapters. 1. Concerning the festivals of the idolaters. What may not be sold nor rented to idolaters. 2. Regulations to prevent closer intercourse with idolaters (being alone with an idolater; inns; acting as midwife; victuals, etc.). 3. Images (Rabban Gamaliel II in the Aphrodite baths at Acco) and other objects of idolatrous worship: mountains, hills, temples, trees. 4. What belongs to an idol. How an idol is destroyed (§ 7 Why God does not destroy the idols). Wine of idolaters. 5. More about this wine. How vessels bought from idolaters are cleansed.

9. Aboth '(Sayings of the) Fathers', also *pirḳe 'aboth.*[67] The primary purpose of this collection of maxims is to demonstrate the continuity and hence the weight of tradition (chapters 1, 2); then in the second instance to impart practical rules of wisdom. Five chapters. 1.1–15 sayings of the oldest teachers down to Hillel and Shammai. 1.16–2.4a sayings by men from the house of Hillel down to Gamaliel III, son of the compiler of the Mishna. 2.4b–2.7 further sayings by Hillel (in order to revert to the chain of tradition). 2.8–16 Joḥanan ben Zaccai and his five disciples. Tarphon. 3, 4. Maxims by more than forty authorities, only in part ordered chronologically.[68] 5. § 1–15 Anonymous maxims by number (with the numbers 10, 7, 4). § 16–19 Other anonymous moral reflexions. § 20 Judah ben Tema. § 21 The stages of life. § 22 Ben Bag-Bag. § 23 Ben He-He. 6. The Praise of the Law (Ḳinyan ha-tora, 'Acquisition of the Law', also called after the opening Pereḳ R. Meir) does not belong to the Mishna, but was added at a later period in order to provide reading matter for the sixth of the Sabbath afternoons between Passover and the Festival of Weeks on which it was customary to read Aboth. The essential part of the collection covers 1.1–15; 2.8–14; 5.1–5,

7–10,13–18. So far does the parallelism with Aboth de-Rabbi Nathan extend.

10. Horayoth 'Teachings, Decisions'. The tractate treats only of those decisions in matters of religious law which have been made by error. Three chapters. 1. Of the sin-offering which is then due Levit. 4.13f. 2. Differences, when erroneous decisions are complied with, between a court, the high priest, the prince and a private person. 3. The retiring high priest or prince (king) with reference to the sin-offering. Other differences between the anointed high priest and the invested one, between the high priest in office and when he has stepped out of office, between the high priest and a common priest. Precedence of the more frequent and the holier, of man over woman, of priests over Levites.[69]

§ 5. Fifth Order: Kodashim, 11 Tractates.

1. Zebahim 'Animal-Offerings',[70] comp. Levit. 1ff. Thirteen chapters. Of the requisite intention. Nor is it permissible to kill the paschal lamb ahead of time. 2. Whereby an animal-offering becomes unfit *pasul*, and whereby it is rendered an abhorred thing *piggul*.[71] 2. Despite which errors an animal-offering remains fit. 4. Of the sprinkling of the blood. Offerings of heathens. Whereat the intention must be aimed at in sacrificing. 5. The place where the victims are killed in accordance with the degree of their sanctity, the manner in which their blood is sprinkled, and the persons that may eat them. 6. More about the same subject, also concerning the offerings of birds. 7. Blunders in connection with the offerings of birds. 8. When victims, pieces of sacrifices or blood are mingled with other sorts. 9. To what extent that which is brought up on the altar may not be taken down again. What is hallowed by altar, stair or vessels. 10. Which offerings, because of greater frequency or holiness, take precedence of others in point of time. Partaking of sacrifices by the priests. 11. When the blood of a sin-offering lights upon a garment (or vessel). Of the cleansing of vessels, each in accordance with the sacrificial pieces prepared therein for eating. 12. Which priests receive no portion of sacrificial meat. The hides. Where the bullocks and goats are burned; concerning the

defilement of garments which is occasioned thereby. 13. Wrong actions in connection with sacrifice. 14. Sacrifices offered without. History of the places at which sacrifices might be offered.

2. Menaḥoth 'Meal-offerings,' comp. Levit. 2; 5.11ff.; 6.7ff.; 7.9f.; 14.10, 20; 23.13, 16; Numb. 5.11ff.; 6.13ff.; 15.24; 28; 29. Thirteen chapters. 1. The requisite intention; Pasul and Piggul. Taking one's handful. 2. More about Pasul and Piggul according to the various species of offerings. 3. Errors which still leave a meal-offering fit, kasher. How a meal-offering becomes unfit. This leads both here and in chapter 4 to the enumeration of things which render unfit one the other or which do or do not have an effect upon one another. The high priest's meal-offering. 5. Preparation of the meal-offering, especially the ingredients. The waving, *tenufah*, of the meal-offering. 6. Of which meal-offerings only a handful is taken to the altar and which go there entire. More about the preparation of meal-offerings. 7. The loaves of the thanksgiving-offering *todah*, of the consecration-offering *millu'im* and of the Nazirite-offering. 8. Whence the materials for the meal-offering are taken. The high priest's meal-offering. 9. The measures employed in measuring out the meal-offering. Drink-offerings. Vowing of meal-offerings and drink-offerings. 10. The sheaf of the waving, *'omer*.[72] 11. The loaves on the Festival of Weeks. The showbread. 12. Redemption of meal-offerings and of drink-offerings. Vowing of meal-offerings and of drink-offerings. 13. Regulations concerning sacrificial vows not accurately defined. The temple of Onias. 13.11: 'It amounts to the same, whether one offers much or little—provided one directs his intention to God.'

3. Ḥullin[73] 'Things profane, unhallowed,' also *sheḥitath ḥullin*[74], treats specifically of the killing of animals not intended for sacrifice,[75] and of other regulations which go with the eating of animal food. Twelve chapters. Who may kill an animal (ritually); wherewith one kills. Differences between pinching off *malaḳ* (the head of offerings of fowls) and (ritual) killing; in this connection differences of that which is allowable with turtledoves and with young pigeons, with the red heifer and with a young heifer, with priests and with Levites, with earthen vessels and with other vessels, etc. 2. Rules for ritual killing of animals.

When at killing an animal no blood flows. A diseased animal. Killing for idolatrous worship and for sacrifices. 3. Ṭerepha and Kasher. The marks of clean animals (birds, locusts, fish). 4. Animal embryos. Broken limbs. Afterbirth. 5. One may not kill the dam on the same day with the young (Levit. 22.28).[76] 6. Covering up the blood (Levit. 17.13). 7. The sinew of the thigh-vein (Gen. 32.32). 8. One may not seethe meat in milk (comp. Exod. 23.19; 34.26; Deut. 14.21).[77] 9. Defilement by Nebela, hides, bones, members, portions of meat. 10. The priests' dues from an animal that is killed. 11. The first of the shearings of sheep. 12. The law concerning the bird-nest (Deut. 22.6f.).

4. Bekoroth 'The Firstborn,' comp. Exod. 13.2, 12; Levit. 27.26f., 32; Numb. 8.16ff.; 18.15ff.; Deut. 15.19ff. Nine chapters. 1. The firstborn of an ass. 2. The firstborn of a clean animal. When more than one young animal is born. 3. Estimating whether an animal had brought forth young. Hair and fleece of the firstborn animal. 4. How long one may keep a firstborn animal before it is delivered to the priest. Authority of the recognized scholar *mumḥe* and the examination of the firstborn.[78] Incidentally the priest who is suspected with regard to the firstborn of cattle. Items concerning persons who are held in suspicion because of one or another transgression of law. 5. Concerning the firstborn of cattle with a blemish. 6. By which blemishes the firstborn are rendered unfit for sacrifice. 7. Which blemishes render a man unfit for priestly service. 8. The privileges of the firstborn with regard to inheritance. The privileges of the priest with regard to redemption money. 9. The tithe of cattle (Levit. 27.32).[79]

5. Arakin 'Estimations,' i. e. the amounts which are to be paid on the ground of a vow in each case according to age and sex (Levit. 27.2ff.) or when one has vowed to God the equivalent of a person. Nine chapters. 1. Who may fix these estimates and with reference to whom they are in place. 2. The statement that the minimum estimate may amount to one shekel and the maximum to fifty affords an opportunity for treating of other minima and maxima. 3. How with estimates the law is, at times in one and the same case, lenient towards one and

rigorous towards another person, so also on divers other occasions. 4. Calculating the equivalent according to the wealth of the vowing person and the age of the person to whom the vow refers. 5. Estimates when the vow is made according to weight or when the value of a limb or half of the equivalent of a person is the subject of a vow. Obligations of heirs. Seizure in the case of non-payment. 6. More about seizure. The procedure when obligations rest on that which is vowed. 7. Redemption of a field whether inherited or bought. 8. More about consecrated fields. That which is devoted (Levit. 27.28f.). 9. Redemption of a field that has been sold (Levit. 25.15ff.); walled cities (Levit. 25.29ff.).

6. Temura, 'Changing' a sacrificial beast, comp. Levit. 27.10, 33. Seven chapters. 1. With which objects a change may be effected. 2. How the sacrifices of individuals differ from those of the community. 3. The young of a sacrificial victim after a change has been made. 4. Change with a sin-offering and other regulations concerning sin-offerings (when a sin-offering had been lost and then found again). 5. How when a beast is big with young the dam and the young may be consecrated at once or singly. More about changing (5.5 formula of change). 6. What may not be brought upon the altar. 7. How the law differs with regard to that which has been consecrated for the altar and that which is destined for the maintenance of the Temple. What may be burnt or buried of consecrated things.

7. Kerithoth[80] 'Cuttings off.' The punishment of being cut off, frequently mentioned in the Tora (*karath* in varying forms Gen. 17.14; Exod. 12.15, etc.), is interpreted by the Jews to mean natural death when it occurs in the age of from twenty to fifty years (usually without leaving offspring).[81] Six chapters. 1. For thirty-six sins one is liable to the penalty of being cut off when they have been committed intentionally but without previous warning; when inadvertently done a sin-offering is requisite; in case of doubt an Asham talui. Concerning the sacrifices of women in childbirth. 2. Diverse instances of obligation to offer a sacrifice (a woman after repeated abortion, a woman-slave who was slept with, etc.). 3. Sin-offerings for eating tallow (*ḥeleb* in rabbinic usage: the fat which may not be eaten, different from *shomen*).

How one may become liable through one sin to four and even six sin-offerings. Several questions by R. Akiba. 4. Guilt-offerings in doubtful cases. 5. Eating of blood. Diverse cases, in which, according to circumstances, an Asham talui, an ordinary guilt-offering (Asham waddai) or a sin-offering is due. 6. When only after a beast had been designated for a guilt-offering certainty has arisen concerning the actuality or, as the case might be, the erroneous supposition of a sin. Power of the Day of Atonement. How, when one has laid aside money for the purchase of sacrificial victims or the victims themselves, one may employ that which has been laid aside.

8. Me'ila 'Trespassing' (upon consecrated things, from *ma'al* 'trespass'), comp. Numb. 5.6–8; Levit. 5.15f. Six chapters. 1. With which offerings trespassing takes place. 2. From what time on trespassing takes place with the different offerings, the loaves on the Festival of Weeks, the showbread. 3. Things which, though one may not make use of them, cannot be trespassed upon. 4. Of counting in with trespasses and with other things, specifically articles of food or clothing (with reference to incurring a penalty, Erub, impurity). 5. Use and usufruct of consecrated things. Whether more than one person may trespass upon the same object. 6. At what time the person commissioned and at what time the commissioning person becomes a trespasser.

9. Tamid, a contracted expression for *'olath tamid*, 'the daily (morning and evening) offering,' comp. Exod. 29.38ff.; Numb. 28.3ff. Seven chapters. 1. The night watch of the priests in the sanctuary. The prefect over the lots (*ha-memunneh*). The clearing away of the altar. 2. More about the clearing of the altar. Fetching the wood. 3. Casting lots with regard to the various ministrations. Fetching the sacrificial lamb. Opening the great gate of the Temple. Cleansing the inner altar and the candlestick. 4. The lamb is killed and dismembered. The component parts of the victim are brought upon the altar. 5. The morning prayer. Preparation for offering incense. 6. Offering the incense. 7. When the high priest himself performed the sacrificial service. The priestly benediction. The songs of the Levites on the different days of the week.[82]

10. Middoth, Measures and appointments of Temple and

sanctuary. Five chapters. 1. The night watches in the sanctuary. Gates of Temple and court. The fire-place *beth ha-moḳed* at the north side of the court. 2. The Temple mount, walls and courts. 3. The altar of burnt-offering. The place of killing the victims at its north side. Laver, portico. 4. The Temple. 5. The court and its chambers. The chamber of hewn stones, *lishkath ha-gazith.*[83]

11. Ḳinnim, 'Bird nests.' Three chapters. The offering of doves (two turtledoves or two pigeons; the one for a sin-offering, the other for a burnt-offering), which was required from poor women in childbirth (Levit. 12.8) or from the poor who committed an offence with regard to Levit. 5.1ff. and which might be presented also as a voluntary burnt-offering (Levit. 1.14ff.). The principal contents are made up of a discussion of instances, in part of an extremely subtle invention, of birds which belong to different persons or (and) diverse species of offerings, being thrown together by accident.[84] Two illustrations: 1.2: 'When a sin-offering is thrown together with a burnt-offering or vice versa, even if the proportion were as of 1 to 10,000, all must die.' 2.3: 'When one woman is required to offer one pair of birds, the second two, the third three, the fourth four, the fifth five, the sixth six, the seventh seven pairs, and when then one bird flies from the first pair to the second, then one from the second to the third, then one from the third to the fourth and so on to the fifth, to the sixth, to the seventh, and then similarly back, by this flying to and fro each time one bird becomes unfit to serve as a counterpart (unfit to constitute one half in the pair which is required in each case); hence the first and the second woman possess no longer a pair for the offering, the third one pair, the fourth two, the fifth three, the sixth four, the seventh six. When this sort of flying away and returning occurs a second time, the third and fourth woman are without a pair for the offering, the fifth has one pair, the sixth two, the seventh five. When repeated a third time, only the seventh woman retains pairs, namely four.'

§ 6. Sixth Order: Ṭoharoth, 12 Tractates.

1. Kelim 'Vessels,' sometimes also *Toharoth,*[85] (inclusive of garments, covers, etc.). Thirty chapters indicate which species of

impurity are taken on by vessels.[86] Starting points in the Bible: Levit. 6.20f.; 11.32ff.; Numb. 19.14ff.; 31.20ff.—1. The chief impurities,[87] the degrees of impurity and of holiness. 2–4. Earthen vessels. 5–9. Ovens and hearths (comp. Levit. 11.35). 10. Vessels with close-bound covering (Numb. 19.15). 11–14. Vessels of metal. 15, 16. Vessels of wood, leather, bone, glass. 17. Damages which take away from an object of use its character as a vessel (incidentally points on measures). 18–20. Couches and other things which may be defiled through *midras* (lying, sitting, stepping on something). 21. Composite vessels: loom, plough, saw, bow. 22. Tables, benches, bridal chair, privy-stool. 23. Riding-equipage, pillows, nets. 24. Things which according to their condition are affected by defilement, each in a threefold manner. 25. Externals and internals, stands, rims, handles, etc. of vessels. 26. Sandals and pouches provided with thongs; hides, cases. How far a thing becomes capable of defilement by its designation. 27, 28. How large garments, sacks, hides, etc. must be so that they may be able to become defiled in one way or another. Several other points concerning the defilement of these and similar objects. 29. How much of cords, handles, hilts becomes unclean together with the object thereto belonging. 30. Vessels of glass and their damages.

2. Ohaloth 'Tents'[88] discusses impurity spread by a corpse. A corpse defiles not only (like other unclean things) by contact, but by the mere fact that one or a thing happens to be in the same Ohel (tent, house) with it, comp. Numb. 19.14: 'When a man dieth in a tent,[89] every one that cometh into the tent, and every thing that is in the tent, shall be unclean seven days.' Eighteen chapters. 1. Defilement by a dead body and its transfer. The 248 members of the human body. 2. How much of a dead body defiles in the tent, how much by contact and by carrying. 3. Adding up of that which defiles. Blood. Which apertures (e. g. doors, windows) and which spaces prevent and which further the spread of impurity. 4. Cabinets *migdalim* in the open and in a room with regard to impurity. 5. A covered pit (e. g. a cistern) in the unclean house. 6. How persons and vessels may become tents. Partition. 7. The slanting roof (the slanting sides) of anything that is roofed over. The doors of a house with

a corpse in it. Birth of a dead embryo. 8. Things which do or do not transmit impurity and (or) those which do or do not protect against it. 9. A species of basket, *kawwereth*. A tomb hewn in the rock. Barrel. 10. Apertures in the house. 11. The house with the roof cracked. When one leans out of a window over a corpse. When one is lying on the threshold of a house and the carriers of a corpse pass over him. More about the pit in the chamber. 12. Expansion or non-expansion of impurity upward and downward. 13. Measure of windows and other holes requisite for the progress of impurity. 14. Cornices, jetties and other projections. 15. Boards lying on the top or by the side of each other, similarly clay barrels, wainscotings. 16. The finding of one or more corpses. 17, 18. A place containing bones of dead bodies *beth ha-peras*. Houses and dwellings of heathens.

3. Nega'im 'Leprosy' (lit.: Plagues), comp. Levit. 13,14. Fourteen chapters. 1, 2. Species and appearances of leprosy. Inspection by the priest. 3. Time and criteria for pronouncing unclean. 4. Differences in the criteria of leprosy. How certain criteria recede and others emerge. 5. Doubtful cases in which the pronouncement is for unclean. 6. Size of the spot of leprosy. Which parts of the human body do not enter into count with regard to leprosy. 7. Changes in the spot of leprosy. When the criteria of leprosy or the spots of leprosy have been removed. 8. Breaking out of the leprosy. When one has grown wholly white through leprosy. 9. The boil of leprosy *sheḥin* and burning *mikwah*. 10. Scurf (of the head or beard, Netheḳ). 11. Leprosy of garments. 12, 13. Leprosy of houses. 14. Cleansing the leper.

4. Para 'Red Heifer,' comp. Numb. 19. Twelve chapters. 1. Age of the red heifer, the heifer of Deut. 21. 3 and of sacrificial victims in general. 2. Required properties of the red heifer. 3, 4. Preparations for killing the red heifer; killing; preparing the ashes. 5. Vessels for the ashes and for the water of sprinkling. 6. How the ashes and the water may become unfit. 7. That no other operation is permissible between the drawing of the water and the pouring in of the ashes or during these very actions. 8. Storing the water of sprinkling. Mediated transfer of impurity where the immediate kind is precluded ('What made thee unclean did not defile me; but thou madest me unclean'). Differ-

ent species of water. 9. How the water of sprinkling becomes unfit. 10–12. How a person clean with reference to the water of sprinkling becomes unclean. Defilement of the water of sprinkling. The hyssop. 12. Effective and uneffective sprinkling. Effect of the sprinkling on objects tied up.

5. Ṭoharoth 'Purities', euphemistically for: Impurities; treats of the less weighty defilements the effect of which lasts only until the setting of the sun. Ten chapters. 1. Nebela (cattle killed unritually). Computing unclean articles of food up to the size of an egg. When pieces of dough or loaves stick together or touch each other and one becomes unclean. 2. Different grades of uncleanness which are effected through contact with the unclean. 3. Mashḳin (see Tractate 8 of this Order) which have become solid and then again turn liquid. Modification in the egg-sized quantity of an impure object. With regard to impurity things are judged according to the status in which they are found. 4–6. Regulations concerning cases of doubtful impurity. Chap. 6 deals specifically with the condition of the place. 7, 8. How one who is faithfully observant *ḥaber* must be on his guard lest something of his be defiled particularly through one that is ignorant of the law.[90] Rule concerning the defilement of that which is partaken of by men (8. 6). More about Mashḳin. 9. Defilements of oil and wine in pressing and treading. 10. Treading.

6. Miḳwaoth[91] 'Baths of immersion';[92] comp. Levit. 15.12 and Numb. 31.23 (vessels); Levit. 14.8 (lepers). Comp. also Mark 7.4: 'And many other things there be, which they have received to hold, washings of cups and pots and brazen vessels and couches.' A bath of immersion must contain at least forty se'a (428 quarts) of (undrawn) water from springs, rivers, or rain. Ten chapters. 1. Six gradations of gatherings of water with reference to being clean and to cleansing. 2, 3. The minimum contents of forty se'a. When three logs (about three pints) of drawn water come into a tub which is not full it is not permitted to fill it up to forty se'a by rain water, but the whole of the water must be drawn out. 4. How rain water may be directed into a bath of immersion. 5. Springs, spring water, the sea, running water, dripping water, sea waves. 6. What goes together with a

bath of immersion (holes, crevices). Immersing several vessels at one and the same time. Basins which are situated by the side of each other. 7. Which things (e. g. also snow, ice, hail) complete the measure of forty se'a. Colored water. 8. Baths of immersion in the Land of Israel and in other countries. Bathing of persons having had sexual emissions. 9. Which things when adhering to immersed persons or objects render the immersion ineffective. 10. How divers vessels are to be immersed.

7. Nidda '(A Woman's) Impurity,' comp. Levit. 15.19ff. (menstruation) and Levit. 12 (in childbirth). Ten chapters. 1, 2. The Nidda (Nidda signifies in post-biblical Hebrew not only the menstruum, but also the menstruating woman). 3. The woman in childbirth, according to the character of the issue. 4. The daughters of Cuthaeans, of Sadducees (this is the correct reading) and the non-Israelitish woman (Nokrith). More about women in childbirth. 5. Concerning varying ages. 6. A statement concerning the puberty of females leads to a compilation of statements which are not reversible. 7–10. Observed spots of blood, etc.

8. Makshirin 'What Predisposes (to Impurity)', called also Mashḳin 'Liquids,' because solid or dry articles of nourishment become unclean through contact with the unclean only when they themselves have previously been moistened by one of the seven liquids (see 6.4). Comp. Levit. 11.34, 37f. Six chapters. 1–5. Of the requisite intent (demonstrated from *yuttan* verse 38). In chapter 2 it is shown incidentally how different regulations obtain in the cities according as the inhabitants are Jews, non-Jews, or mixed. 6. Of which things it may be assumed that they are mukshar (fit to become unclean). The seven Mashḳin: Wine, honey, oil, milk, dew, blood, water,[93] their sub-species and other liquids.

9. Zabim 'Those Affected with Unclean Issue,' comp. Levit. 15. Five chapters. 1. At what time one becomes completely *zab*; of the counting of the seven clean days. 2. The seven questions at the examination of the issue. 3–5. Defilement through one affected with an issue (contact, movement, etc.). Chapter 5 concludes with a comparison of diverse species of impurity and

with an enumeration of the things which render the heave unfit (pasul).

10. Ṭebul yom 'One who took on the same day a bath of immersion' and remains unclean after that until sundown (Levit. 15.5; 22.6f., etc.). Such a person may touch Ḥullin without scruple; on the other hand, though he does not defile the heave, ḥalla or consecrated things (meat or meal-offering) he does render them unfit, pasul. In four chapters the question is specifically treated how contact has an effect on the whole when it strikes only a part.

11. Yadaim 'Hands,' i. e. the ritual impurity and purification of the hands, comp. Matth. 15.2, 20; 23.25; Mark 7.2ff.; Luke 11.38f. It is not quite adequate to render *neṭilath yadayim*[94] as 'washing of hands,' since the ceremony consists in pouring water over the hands, not in washing nor in immersing them. Four chapters. 1. Quantity of water; vessels; unfit water; who may pour the water over. 2. First and second pouring; how the pouring over is done. 3. Whereby hands may become unclean. The Holy Scriptures, likewise, defile the hands.[95] Debate on Canticles and Koheleth. 4. Further decisions carried on the day on which Eleazar ben Azariah was made head of the academy (comp. Tractate Eduyyoth). Concerning the Aramaic portions of Daniel and Ezra. Differences between the Sadducees and Pharisees.[96]

12. Ukṣin 'Handles.' Three chapters: How handles, shells and also kernels participate in defilement when the fruit becomes unclean or defile the fruit along with themselves when they come in contact with anything unclean. 1. The handles and how far they are a Shomer. 2. Kernels, shells and encasing leaves. 3. A grouping of diverse matters according to presuppositions under which they are rendered mukshar (capable of becoming unclean).

CHAPTER V

THE PALESTINIAN TALMUD

§ 1. A Sketch of the History of the Palestinian Talmud.

The name *Talmud 'Ereṣ Yisra'el* 'Talmud of the Land of Israel' is met with as early as in Saadia Gaon,[1] then in the gaonic Responsa edited by A. Harkavy,[2] in Amram Gaon, Hananeel, Nissim ben Jacob,[3] Abulwalid.[4] Correspondingly, in Aramaic, Amram Gaon speaks of *Gemara de-'Ereṣ Yisra'el*; both recensions of the Halakoth Gedoloth of *Talmud de-Ma'arba*; Nissim ben Jacob, Isaac Alphasi and Shaare Teshuba No. 61[5] of *Gemara dibne Ma'arba.* The Tosaphoth[6] refer to the Hilkoth Ereṣ Israel. On the other hand, the appellation *Yerushalmi* which is equally old and now almost universally in use, is not at all appropriate;[7] Samuel ha-nagid (died 1055) and Samuel ibn Jami call it *'al-Shami, al-Talmud.*[8]

As Abraham ibn Daud[9] and Maimonides[10] would have it, the Palestinian Talmud was composed by Joḥanan. This opinion, however, is untenable; for Joḥanan died in 279 C.E.,[11] nevertheless, throughout the whole of the work we meet with sayings and discussions by Jonah and Jose II who lived at a much later date, likewise in Tiberias. Of a still later date are two other scholars frequently named: Mani II bar Jonah, master of a school in Sepphoris, through whose agency, it would seem, many utterances of the scholars of Caesarea[12] were merged into the scholastic tradition, and the eminent halakist Jose bar Abin. It is safe to assume that the Palestinian Talmud took on its present shape in all essentials some time during the succeeding generation at the beginning of the fifth century: the activities of the school of Tiberias ceased with the extinction of the patriarchate about 425 C.E. The work represents a collection of the matter then taught in the schools (beside Tiberias we may mention also Caesarea and Sepphoris[13]), it is not a literary product with anything like unity of conception. This conclusion is forced upon us in the first place by the glaring inequality of workmanship: in the first two Orders a very great number of tannaitic statements are introduced as handed down by Samuel (of Nehardea[14]), but in the third and fourth none; on the other hand, we meet in these Orders with numerous controversies between Mani and Abin II, while such are extremely rare in the Orders Zera'im and Mo'ed. The Tractate Neziḳin differs by its brevity and by deviations from the parallel passages in other tractates.[15] Much that is exceedingly in need of exposition is frequently left undiscussed or disposed of by an obscure suggestion which is in need of explanation itself. In the second place, unity of conception is precluded by the great frequency of repetitions.[16]

§ 2. The Absence of Many Tractates.

In Palestine, many laws which were applicable solely to the Holy Land were observed for centuries after the destruction of the Temple, whereas in Babylonia they had at no time been observed: hence the Palestinian Talmud has Gemara for all the tractates of Zera'im, but the Babylonian only to the tractate Berakot which deals with matters of universal application. In the sight of the holy places, the hope in the restoration of the ancient cult and of the religious life was more vivid in Palestine than in Babylonia; hence the Palestinian Talmud has Gemara in Sheḳalim. It stands to reason that the two last Orders were likewise studied and taught in Palestine. Several of the subjects treated of in the Tractate Hullin were, according to the testimony of the Babylonian Gemara,[1] taught more adequately and were better known in Palestine than in Babylonia.

Nevertheless, the editions of the Palestinian Talmud[2] contain just the first four Sedarim and the beginning of Nidda. In the second Seder the Gemara is wanting for Shab. 21–24, in the fourth for Mak. 3. Aboth and Eduyyoth are without Gemara in both Talmuds.

It is highly probable that the Orders Ḳodashim and Ṭoharoth, barring Nidda, were compiled only by word of mouth, and were at no time committed to writing. In the Geniza (lumber-room of the synagogue) at Old-Cairo numerous fragments have been found from the first four Sedarim and two from Nidda, chapters 1 and 3, but nothing else from the two last Orders.[3] In order to explain this absence, one might point to the disturbed political conditions which stood in the way of completing in literary form the parts wanting.[4]

Other scholars[5] have favored the view that at one time there existed a Palestinian Gemara of all the six Orders (for all or at least the greater part of the tractates). They explain the loss of Ḳodashim and Ṭoharoth (1) by the unpropitious times, the long and absolute absence of recognized seats of learning in Palestine, whereas in Babylonia the schools flourished with only slight interruptions; (2) by the circumstance that the Palestinian Talmud was held in lesser esteem and was less known. One might also invoke the testimony of Maimonides who[6] knows of five Orders of the Palestinian Talmud; likewise citations now and again from the Palestinian Talmud which are wanting in the extant text.[7] A. Epstein[8] distinguishes four categories of such citations: (a) such as were actually read in the text; (b) such as refer to Palestinian Midrashim;[9] (c) falsifications in kabbalistic or other interest; (d) inventions by preachers. Aptowitzer who has also written on the subject[10] points out that the German and French scholars cite the Palestinian Talmud frequently from a collectaneum which was much abbreviated, and then again amplified (principally from the Babylonian Talmud and the gaonic literature); the Spanish scholars from secondary sources (in particular from the commentary by R. Hananeel), so that frequently one is at a loss to say where the Palestinian Talmud stops and the citing source begins. As in the codex of the Palestinian Talmud there were incorporated in addition other works and dissertations, this led to further confusion by which authors were misled. Certain authors adduce kabbalistic works as Palestinian Talmud, and lastly here and there a supposed passage from the Palestinian Talmud rests on downright fabrication. Hence, according to Epstein as well as Aptowitzer, no conclusion can be drawn from citations that the compass of the Palestinian Talmud was once essentially larger.

The Tosaphists, it is true, had the Palestinian Gemara for the complete tractate Nidda.[11] Similarly Maimonides.[12] In a

Berlin Ms.[13] mention is made of the Palestinian Gemara for Uḳṣin (a tractate of the sixth Order).

Parts of the Palestinian Talmud continued to disappear in extremely late times. Thus Simeon ben Zemah Duran (fourteenth century) on Aboth (Leipzig 1855, 31a) and Issachar Berman Cohen (sixteenth century) in Mattenoth Kehunna on Gen. R. section 68 cite the Palestinian Gemara for Mak. 3.19, whereas we have this Gemara only for the two first chapters.

The contention of W. H. Lowe that the Cambridge Ms. Add. 470.1 embodies the Palestinian recension of the Mishna has in no wise been demonstrated by him.[14]

S. Friedländer (in reality Solomon Leb Friedland) of Szatmárhegy in Hungary claimed to have discovered in European Turkey a Spanish manuscript of the year 4972 era of creation = 1212 C.E. with a substantial part of the fifth Order (Zeb., Men., Ḥul., Bekoroth and beginning of Arakin), and the text of four tractates has actually been published by him under the title *Talmud Yerushalmi Seder Ḳodashim.*[15] If the romantic account of the find gave cause for doubts, they were allayed when two so eminent students of the Talmud as Solomon Buber (who furnished in the first of the two publications by Friedländer an exposition of the foreign words) and S. Schechter (who negotiated with Friedländer with a view to buying the manuscript) accepted the authenticity. Nevertheless, the manner in which Friedländer prevented others and myself from a personal inspection of the manuscript as well as of the transcripts (one supposedly ancient and another made by himself) was bound to arouse grave suspicion. At this writing there is no longer any doubt that the published text does not contain a hitherto unknown portion of the Palestinian Talmud, but for the most part excerpts from the portions known for long. It is quite a matter of indifference for us whence the remnant proceeds and whether Friedländer made up the material in its entirety out of whole cloth (possibly by making use of Maimonides' Code) or whether somehow there came to his hands collectanea prepared by others. The forgery has been demonstrated by a number of scholars.[16]

As far as extant, the Palestinian Talmud has Gemara for thirty-nine tractates, while the Babylonian has such only for thirty-six and one-half; nevertheless, in compass the latter is three times as large as the former, for the reason that the discussions in the Palestinian Gemara are much briefer.

§ 3. The Authority of the Palestinian Talmud.

Decisions in matters of religious law are rendered by the Jews on the basis of the Babylonian Talmud,[1] for the reason that it was first in getting to the West and because the teachers named therein, in part at any rate, lived later than those mentioned in the Palestinian. Only when the Babylonian does not oppose the Palestinian Talmud may the latter be followed.[2] The Haggada of the Palestinian Talmud contains in matters of historical fact more ancient and hence more trustworthy data for a knowledge of the Judaism of Palestine.

CHAPTER VI

The Babylonian Talmud

Name *Talmuda de-Babel*;[1] in Hebrew texts 'Talmud Babli' in contrast to *Talmud 'Ereṣ Yisra'el*. The Geonim, R. Nissim, Isaac Alphasi and others say *Talmud dilan* 'our Talmud.'

Only a small portion of the Jews returned to Palestine with Zerubbabel and Joshua (Jeshua), later with Ezra; the large mass remained in Mesopotamia.[2] Of old times the Torah was studied in Babylonia;[3] here it is necessary only to recall that Hillel was Babylonian by birth; mention may likewise be made here of Nahum the Mede. As early as the beginning of the second century of the Christian era Nehardea had been a seat of Jewish learning. The academy there rose to eminence under Mar Samuel (died 254); at the same time the academy in Sura flourished under Rab (died 247). After the destruction of Nehardea (259), Judah bar Ezekiel (died 299), the pupil of Rab and Samuel, founded the academy at Pum Beditha. Here were active, besides, Rabbah bar Naḥmani (died 330, frequently simply *Rabbah*), Joseph bar Ḥiyya (died 333) and Abaye, the pupil of both. Raba bar Joseph bar Hama (died 352) taught at Maḥuza on the Tigris. After Raba, Naḥman bar Isaac (died 356) was head of the academy which once more was transferred to Pum Beditha. Papa (died 375) founded the school at Naresh near Sura. After the death of Papa, Sura came once more to the front through Ashi (died 427). The sayings and controversies of Joseph and Rabbah together with those of Abaye and Raba occupy a considerable part of the Babylonian Talmud. Further material for study and discussion came to Babylonia through Palestinian Amoraim and such Babylonians as returned from Palestine. The most frequented gatherings for the purpose of study, called Kalla,[4] took place twice annually in the months of Adar (before Nisan) and Elul (before Tishri), though the date of the institution is not known; and on each occasion it was the wont to take up a single tractate (not necessarily in its entirety) for minute discussion. It is recorded that Raba participated in the direction of such gatherings,[5] and it is said of Ashi[6] that presumably just in these assemblies he went over at least certain tractates twice; it must be remembered that he was master at Sura for quite a long stretch of time, 375–424. Just as there were several codifications of the Mishna which at length were set aside by that of Rabbi, so there existed more than one Talmud resulting from the discussions centering on Rabbi's Mishna in the different schools. Thus we meet not at all infrequently with the expression: So and So taught *mishshemeh digmara*.[7] The Talmud which proceeded from the school of Ashi in Sura represents as it were selections from previous compilations;[8] that of Nedarim and Nazir alone seems to emanate from the school of Pum Beditha.[9] One further reason for assembling and ordering the material consisted in the persecutions directed against the Jewish religion by the Sassanian king Jezdegerd II (438–457) and his second successor Peroz (459–484). Peroz forbade the convocations of students and sought to force the Jewish youth into accepting the Persian religion. It was therefore imperative to counteract by a definitive compilation any fading of the material from memory.

Rabina II bar Huna (died 811 Seleuc. = 499 C.E.) was the last of the Amoraim, i. e. the last to deliver sayings and to teach them on the basis of oral tradition.[10]

After him followed those scholars who are named the Reflecting Ones, Examiners, because they reflected on the matter taught by the Amoraim, pondered over it, and made supplements thereto; they flourished from the end of the fifth to the middle of the sixth century and may be regarded as those who put the finishing touches to the Babylonian Talmud.[11]

At an early period[12] it was sought, rather skilfully, to aid the memory by means of all kinds of devices.[13] When halakic regulations or discussions came to be committed to writing, mnemonic signs *simanim* (a sort of tachygraphy: names of authorities and characteristic words for complete sentences; letters standing for words or sentences; catchwords, especially for the purpose of keeping distinct the names of authorities) were likewise employed, in the first instance, in order to economize time and writing material and to facilitate a clearer survey of the matter; then again it must be remembered that it was permissible to write down Halakoth only for personal use in private, but never for public use in lectures or in rendering decisions on religious questions. It is quite likely that as far back as the times of the Tannaim many a teacher or student had in his possession such notes, while books of halakic contents with sentences fully written out must have been rare. So also did the collectors and systematizers of the Babylonian Talmud frequently employ these mnemonic signs or take them over from their predecessors, thus placing them in front of the transcribed expositions to serve in a manner as titles or indexes of contents. As time went on it became customary more and more to discard these Simanim in the manuscripts and particularly in the printed editions, partly because they were superfluous and partly because they were no longer understood.[14]

Of the sixty-three tractates of the Mishna, twenty-six and one-half are without Babylonian Gemara.[15] These tractates were likewise discussed in the Babylonian schools during the fourth century,[16] but at no time was a formal compilation of a Babylonian Gemara on these tractates undertaken.[17] It must be remembered that a large part of the contents of these tractates had no relevancy outside Palestine; other portions had been dealt with in the Gemara on preceding tractates; the subject-matter of Aboth and Eduyyoth precluded a Gemara altogether (hence there is no Gemara on them even in the Palestinian Talmud).

The question whether the Babylonian Amoraim were acquainted with the Palestinian Talmud is answered negatively by Hirschensohn[18] and affirmatively by Yerushalimski[19] and Halevy.[20]

CHAPTER VII

The Extra-canonical Tractates

§ 1. The Tractates which are joined to the Babylonian Talmud.

At the end of the fourth Seder we find in the editions of the Babylonian Talmud (hence in the ninth volume) beside several other Additamenta the following tractates. Since they are of lesser standing and essentially date from later times than the tractates of the Mishna, we confine ourselves in each case to a few remarks.

(a) Aboth deRabbi Nathan, forty chapters, may be best described as a Tosephta to the tractate Aboth. The appellation after the Tannaite Nathan has no foundation in fact.[1] Joshua Falk wrote a commentary in Hebrew;[2] a Latin translation was made by Francis Tayler.[3] A recension differing from the current one has been published by Solomon Taussig,[4] and both recensions by S. Schechter.[5] Kaim Pollak has published a German translation of the current text with notes.[6]

(b) Sopherim from the times of the Geonim.[7] The contents are indicated in the title of Joel Müller's edition.[8] A text worthy of note is found in Mahzor Vitry.[9] We have numerous commentaries in Hebrew,[10] and the first five chapters have been rendered into Latin.[11]

(c) Ebel Rabbathi (Mourning),[12] frequently under the euphemistic title Semaḥoth (Joys). This tractate is known to have existed in Southern France at the end of the twelfth century, but it contains much older elements.[13]

(d) Kalla (Bride, a woman newly wedded) treats of marital relations.[14] There are two tractates of this name. The shorter (one chapter) in the ordinary editions of the Talmud and, as *hilkoth Kalla*, in Mahzor Vitry is properly a portion of the Halakoth Gedoloth. The longer (ten chapters) was published by Coronel and is now also printed in the Romm edition of the Babylonian Talmud.[15]

(e) Derek Ereṣ Rabba 'Moral Conduct,' eleven chapters. The principal part contains mostly maxims of conduct and it is possible that it dates from the time of the Mishna. One of the sayings occurring therein is cited in the Palest. Talmud[16] as found *bederek ha-'areṣ*.[17]

(f) Derek Ereṣ Zuṭa.[18] Nine chapters.[19] Another title for the first four chapters is *Yir'ath ḥet* 'Fear of Sin.'[20]

(g) Pereḳ ha-shalom, 'The Chapter concerning Peace.'[21] See in addition chapter XXIII, § 2b on Tanna debe Eliyyahu.

§ 2. The other 'small Tractates.'

Seven other 'small tractates' have been edited according to a Ms. of Carmoly by Raph. Kirchheim:[1]

(a) Sepher Tora concerning the writing of Scrolls of the Law (see § 1b).

(b) Mezuza, a diminutive parchment scroll with the words of Deut. 6.4–9; 11.13–21, in a longish holder which is affixed to the right doorpost. At the extreme end of the blank side is written *Kwzw bmwksz kwzw=yhwh 'Elohenu yhwh* (according to the alphabet ab. gd.).[2]

(c) Tephillin 'Phylacteries,' Matth. 23.5 φυλακτήρια.[3]

(d) Ṣiṣith 'Fringes,' Num. 15.37ff.; Deut. 22.22. Fringes of hyacinth blue (white) wool on the four corners of the upper garment, in later times on the small and large *tallith* ('prayer shawl'). Matth. 23.5 κράσπεδα.[4]

(e) Abadim 'Slaves.'[5]

(f) Kuthim 'Samaritans.'[6]

(g) Gerim 'Proselytes.'[7]

CHAPTER VIII

The Tosephta

Tosephta[1] literally: Addition, Supplement. The work so named is a collection of tannaitic statements and traditions, closely allied to the Mishna. It has like the Mishna six Orders, which are likewise divided into Tractates and Chapters.[2]

According to Joḥanan,[3] the Tosephta is based on the lectures of Nehemiah, a contemporary of Meir. With the Gaon Sherira[4] we may take the author to have been Ḥiyya bar Aba, the disciple and friend of Rabbi; for in the Tosephta we find exactly that which is attested in the Palest. Talmud as the opinion of Ḥiyya over against that of Hoshaia. The Tosephta is an independent work, as is also evidenced by the partially different arrangement of the Halakoth; the name Tosephta is misleading. The few passages in which Ḥiyya[5] and Rab are named are later accretions, as are the passages of the Mishna in which Rabbi is named.

The relation of our Mishna to the Tosephta has been obscured by later alterations in the texts. On the one hand, here and there an element from the Tosephta had crept into the text of the Mishna in Amoraic times;[6] on the other hand, we find in the Tosephta one or the other interpolation,[7] likewise sentences which originally had a place in the Mishna.[8] These mutual encroachments require accurate investigations extending not only to single items but to the whole Tosephta and the whole Mishna. However, the absence of critical editions (also of the Talmuds) makes such investigations rather difficult.

Z. Frankel[9] undertook to prove that the Tosephta was put together after the close of the Talmud out of two collections of Baraithas, one by Ḥiyya and the other by Hoshaia.

Adolf Schwarz has dealt with the problem of the Tosephta in a number of monographs.[10] In the (German) introduction to his last published work he has this to say on 'the relation of the Tosephta to the Mishna': The Tosephta represents the matter excluded (?!) from Akiba's Mishna and edited first by Nehemiah and then by Hiyya. Almost at every step it becomes apparent that the abrupt and unconnected sections of the Tosephta presuppose the Mishna, inasmuch as these, in themselves quite unintelligible, serve to explain and at other times to supplement the several points of the Mishna. Schwarz arranges the text of the Tosephta in accordance with that of the Mishna. By this arrangement an understanding of the contents is facilitated, but in no wise is the original text restored.

M. S. Zuckermandel,[11] seeks to demonstrate that in the Tosephta we possess the Palestinian Mishna (more accurately: the remainder of the Palestinian Mishna), whereas our Mishna was compiled anew in Babylonia. Schwarz,[12] however, rightly takes exception: 'If our Mishna was made up by the Amoraim of Babylonia, how does it happen that we possess even for those tractates of which no Babylonian Talmud is available, a brand-new Mishna? To say nothing about Tamid, Middoth and Ḳinnim, did Aboth also, this jewel of the whole Mishna, originate in Babylonia? . . . If the Amoraim had not treated the text of the Mishna exactly in the same manner as the Tannaites had dealt with the scriptural text, straining it until it said what they were bound to legalize in order to meet the exigencies of their own times, their dialectics would never have grown to be so formidably hair-splitting. And in spite of this all the Amoraim of Babylonia carry on . . . criticism with regard to the Mishna, emend . . . its text without any scruple, give preference to the Baraithoth over the Mishna. It is a psychological puzzle how Zuckermandel can insist that this Mishna in which the name of Rabbi occurs scarcely thirty times is a creation of the Babylonian Amoraim, while the Tosephta in which Rabbi is named more than 200 times is to be regarded as his proper Mishna.'[13]

CHAPTER IX

History of the Talmud Text

§ 1. General Remarks[1].

The text of the Babylonian Talmud received many additions after the compilation was completed by the Saboraim. Frequently it is quite easy to recognize these additions by the evidence from subject-matter, as when they interrupt the context of a discussion.[2] In other instances additions betray themselves by the change of idiom, in still other cases by the fact that they are wanting in all or certain ancient witnesses. An important handle is offered by the expression *lishna 'aḥrina* 'another version.' Of the ten examples adduced by Bacher,[3] five must certainly be struck off or at least are doubtful,[4] while others are omitted.[5] Of particularly frequent occurrence are decisions, i. e. statements as to what has become or has not become the norm (Halaka) on the basis of the preceding discussion.[6] M. Friedmann[7] shows by specimens how it is possible to indicate in print the diverse strata of the Talmud.

A multitude of tasks awaits here the student. Probably there never existed a uniform and universally recognized text; rather from the very beginning there must have been differences between what was taught at Sura and what at Pum Beditha.[8] These differences persisted and, moreover, were multiplied through the circumstance that to the end of the gaonic period the Talmud text was only on rare occasions read in the academies from a book, but for the most part it was recited from memory by those expert in traditional lore.[9] As early an authority as Saadia[10] occasionally expresses doubt concerning the correct reading. At the time of the Gaon Hai (died 1038) students in Babylonia itself were uncertain as to the authentic version in many a passage.[11] As a matter of fact the Geonim frequently say in their answers that the questions rest upon a text which diverges from the one in vogue in Babylonia. However, the latter was looked upon as authoritative.[12]

As to the text current in Spain, valuable material is afforded by Isaac Alphasi (1013–1103), Isaac ibn Gayyath, Moses b. Naḥman (in his comment. on the Talmud), Solomon ibn Adreth (died 1310) and his pupil Yom Tob ben Abraham, Nissim ben Reuben, Yalḳut ha-Makiri and Jacob ben Habib in the work En Ya'aḳob. This text is offered likewise in the Ms. Hamburg 169 (Ḥullin) and the printed editions of Fez[13] 1516–1521, for Erubin in a Ms. in Frankf. o. M., for Ḳiddushin in a codex of the British Museum[14] and in the edition of Faro in Portugal about 1494.[15] The Spanish texts are also cited with deference by Provençal and Northern French authors, so by Abraham b. David of Posquières, Zerahiah ha-Levi, Rabbenu Tam.—The ancient codex of the three Baboth, Hamburg 165, was written at Gerona. For the Franco-German text we may refer to the Munich codex 95, principally because it contains practically the whole Talmud.—Another type of text has emerged from the Yemenite manuscripts (Midrash ha-gadol) and the numerous fragments which were recovered from the Geniza in Old Cairo.

Here and there a reading may be obtained by looking up the parallel passages in old Midrashim.[16] It is to be regretted that of these literary works only the fewest are accessible in critical editions.

Has the text been altered designedly? Here and there it would appear that the original wording has been modified or shortened with an eye to the Christian Church, in particular by command of the censor[17] or because of an anticipation of the censor's displeasure.[18] Likewise it may have seemed desirable to accentuate the differences between the Jewish religion and the Christian. Thus we find wholly absent the expression so frequent in the Targums *memra de-yhwh ὁ λόγος τοῦ κυρίου* (the Targums were less rigidly censored); only once[19] is the passage in Isaiah 53 interpreted as referring to the suffering Messiah.[20]

First references to copies containing the whole of the Babylonian Talmud. It is reported that the exilarch Natronai ben Ḥabibai (banished in 773 from Babylonia) wrote out for the Jews of Spain a copy from memory.[21] According to a letter addressed in the year 953 from Babylonia to Spain, the Gaon Paltoi (842–858) had a copy of the Talmud written and annotated for Spain.[22] Maimonides[23] (1135 to 1204) relates that he had before him a fragment from a Gemara almost 500 years old. Moses b. Naḥman (died after 1267)[24] makes mention of correct Talmud copies proceeding from the Talmud academy of Hushiel (end of the tenth century).[25]

§ 2. Manuscripts (and Ancient Citations in lieu of them).

A. It goes without saying that such errors as are known by experience to be incidental to copying (omissions, misreading, lapses in writing) are met with in the manuscripts of the Talmud. These errors are the more disconcerting since in consequence of the repeated confiscations[1] and foolish destructions of Jewish manuscripts by fire[2] only a very small number of ancient Talmud copies are extant.

A list of extant manuscripts was published by F. Lebrecht.[3] It must be remembered that Lebrecht saw only a few manuscripts with his own eyes and that especially in the last decades we have come to know more about many of them, while some have come to light for the first time; it is therefore desirable in the highest degree that a new and thorough description of the entire manuscript material should be attempted. For supplementation and rectification the reader must be referred to the prefatory notices by R. Rabbinovicz.[4]

a. Mishna. 1. Parma, *Mss. codices hebraei biblioth. J. B. de-Rossi*, I (Parma 1803), No. 138, according to de-R. from the thirteenth century, up to one-half vocalized. 2. Berlin, Ms. Orient. Fol. 567, Orders 2 (beginning with Pesaḥim) to 4 with the commentary of Maimonides (in Hebrew); Ms. Or. Qu. 566–574 with Arabic comment. of Maimon.; No. 568 (three Baboth and Sanh., written in the year 1222, hence less than eighteen years after the death of Maimon.). 3. Hamburg No. 18, Orders 1–3 with comm. of Maimon. (Hebr.), of the year 1416, in Steinschneider's Catalogue No. 156. 4. Oxford, Bodleian Library, acc. to the new Catalogue by Neubauer and Cowley No. 393–407, Mishna with Arab. comm. of Maimon., No. 408, 409, 2662 (this number about 5/8 Of Mo'ed) with Hebrew translation of the same comm.; Nos. 2661, 2662–2669 contain fragments partially of high antiquity. 5. London, Brit. Museum. Mishna with Arab. comm. of Maim.: Cod. Or. 2217–2226, 2391–2394; Add. 27588. 6. Cambridge. University Library Add. 470, 1, accurately reproduced in print by W. H. Lowe under the misleading title 'The Mishnah on which the Palestinian Talmud rests', Cambridge 1883 (250 leaves).[5] 7. Petrograd. Fragments of the Mishna with the so-called Babyl. (superlinear) vocalization: M. Sh. 4.5–Ḥalla 4.2 (four pages in autotype reproduction)[6] and Bikk. 3.11 (also chapter 4)–Shab. 2.1; 23.3–Er. 1.3. Eduy. end and Zeb. 1–3 (five pages in autotype).[7] 8. New York. Prof. Alex. Marx possesses sixteen leaves of a vocalized Mishna Ms. (small folio, presumably tenth to eleventh century). 9. Budapest, an old codex of great value from the library of Dav. Kaufmann,[8] now in the Library of the Hungarian Academy of Sciences. 10. The text-critical work of Solomon Adeni, up to 1854 in the hands of N. Coronel,[9] has been printed in the large edition of the Mishna Wilna 1887, 1908f.

b. Palestinian Talmud. 1. The only manuscript of considerable compass is Scaliger 3 in Leiden.[10] This Ms. was one of the four which were made use of for the first print of the Palest. Talm. (Venice, 1523f.); as a comparison with the edition shows, it was taken for the best; the other three seem no longer to be extant. It contains just the parts printed, it must be regretted, inaccurately in the Venice edition.

2. Oxford, Bodleian Library, acc. to the new Catalogue by Neubauer a. Cowley: No. 365 Ber. with comm. by *'Eli'ezer 'Azkari* (?)[11]; No. 2671 M. Ḳ. one leaf; No. 2672 B. Ḳ. two leaves; No. 2674 Ber. two leaves.[12]

3. London, Brit. Museum, Cod. Orient. 2822–2824: Zera'im and Sheḳalim.[13]

4. Paris, Bibliothèque Nationale, Supplément Hébreu 1389. Zera'im incomplete, written in Safed 'avec le commentaire de R. Moise Syrileio . . . paraît être l'autographe de l'auteur.'[14]

5. Rome, Vatican Library, Cod. Hebr. 133. Zera'im.[15]

6. Lewis-Gibson, Hebrew Mss.: one leaf Giṭṭin 44b-d.[16]

7. L. Ginzberg,[17] all the fragments found in the Geniza;[18] extracts from the first edition of the Yalḳuṭ, Saloniki 1526/21;[19] variants from cod. Vatic. 133.[20]

c. Babylonian Talmud. 1. Munich, Cod. Hebr. 95, written in the year 1343, basis of the *Dikduke Sopherim*; edited by Herm. L. Strack.[21] Cod. Hebr. 6: Pes., Yoma, Ḥag.[22] Cod. Hebr. 140/41: M. Ḳ. beginning with fol. 19, R. H., Sukka, Taan., Meg. to fol. 28 and Yeb. beginning with 48a.[23]

2. Hamburg, No. 165 (previously No. 19) the three Baboth, written at Gerona in 1184.[24] No. 169 Ḥullin, Spanish text.[25]

3. Göttingen, Cod. Hebr. 3 (previously Orient. 13) Taan. in part, Meg., Ḥag., Yom Ṭob, M. Ḳ. in part (110 leaves, beg. of thirteenth century).[26]

4. Carlsruhe, Sanh., once in the possession of Reuchlin.[27]

5. Oxford, Bodleian Library, acc. to the Catalogue by Neubauer a. Cowley: No. 366 Zera'im and Mo'ed;[28] No. 367 Yeb., Kid.;[29] No. 368 Giṭṭin;[30] No. 369 B. B.;[31] No. 370 Tamid, Middoth, Me'il., Arak.; No. 373 Ḥul.; No. 375 Nidda; in addition (all incomplete) No. 2661, 2666, 2671, 2673, 2675–2678. No. 2673 contains the whole of the tractate Sukka, barring the opening words; No. 2673 half of Kerith., the oldest dated Talmud Ms. (4883 of creation = 1123 C.E.).[32]

6. London, Brit. Museum, Harley 5508 R. H., Yoma, Ḥag., Beṣa, Meg., Sukka, M. Ḳ., Taan. (236 leaves, prob. twelfth century). Add. 25717 Bek. (incomplete), Arak., Kerith. (102 leaves, fourteenth century). Or. 5531, six leaves from Shab., B. Ḳ., B. M.[33]

7. Cambridge. 'The Fragment of the Talmud Babli Pesachim of the ninth or tenth century, in the University Library, Cambridge'[34] may be mentioned here on account of the high antiquity assigned to the four leaves by the editor.

8. Florence, the National Library possesses the second oldest of the known Talmud Mss.: Bekor., Temura, Kerith., Tamid, Mid., Me'ila, Ḳinnim, completed in Elul 936 (or 937), i. e. 1176 (or 1177) C.E. The tractate Ber. constituting the beginning is from another hand. From the same hand or at any rate from the same period as the main part of the codex are prob. two other volumes: B. Ḳ., B. M. a. B. B., Sanh., Shebuoth.[35]

9. Parma (Foa 23, Perreau 60). The whole of the Talmud in four volumes, very small script of recent times. Fra Luigi subscribes himself as censor in the y. 1601.[36]

10. Rome. An exact description and evaluation of the Talmud Mss. which formerly belonged to the Palatina in Heidelberg is very much to be desired. According to the Catalogue of the Brothers Assemani[37] fifty-seven tractates of the Talmud and several of the so-called small tractates are contained in thirty-one codices.[38]

11. Paris, Bibliothèque Nationale No. 671,3 Ber.;[39] No. 1337 B. B., A. Z., Hor.; No. 1313 (or Supplément 183) several fragments of B. B.

12. New York. A Ms. brought by Ephr. Deinard from Yemen to New York and written 1546–1548 contains in two volumes Beṣa, Pes., Meg., M. Ḳ., Zeb.[40]

13. Numerous fragments from the Geniza preserved in Oxford, Petrograd and elsewhere still await a scientific evaluation. Six facsimiles of passages in the tractate Ber. (2b. 3a. 13a. 44b. 45b. 48a), have been published by N. Pereferkowitsch.[41]

B. The scarcity of old manuscripts is to a certain extent compensated by numerous citations in ancient authorities.

For the Palest. Talm. are of moment specifically: Eliezer ben Joel ha-Levi (first half of the thirteenth century);[42] Isaac ben Moses (thirteenth century) of Vienna.[43] B. Ratner (died 1917)[44] published a collection of variants from ancient sources and manuscript fragments; it is to be regretted that he worked rather carelessly and thus included much that is of no value whatever.[45]

For the Babylonian Talmud: The compendium of the Talmud by Isaac ben Jacob Alphasi, the Dictionary of Nathan b. Jehiel, the commentaries of Rashi and the Tosaphists.[46] In addition: Maimonides; Yalḳuṭ Shim'oni, Saloniki, 1526, 1521; *'aggadoth ha-Talmud*, Constantinople, 1511;[47] En Ya'aḳob by Jacob ibn Habib; Bezalel Ashkenazi, author of *shiṭṭah meḳubbeṣeth* (sixteenth century; of great importance for textual criticism, because Mss. were resorted to).

Raphael Rabbinovicz[48] began to collect with great industry the material obtainable for textual criticism from the sources just mentioned and elsewhere, specifically from the oldest editions of the Mishna and the Talmuds, with the edition Frankf. o. M. 1721 f. as a basis. Unfortunately the fifteen volumes published

1868–1886 contain only Orders 1, 2, 4 (without Aboth) as well as the tractates Zeb. and Men. A sixteenth volume, containing the tractate Ḥullin, was published by Ehrentreu.[49] Nor has sufficient account been taken of the linguistic variants found in the ancient witnesses.

§ 3. Editions.[1]

What has been said about the manuscripts does not exhaust the history of the text. Considering the great rarity of ancient manuscripts and because of the textual curtailments in the later prints of which we shall speak soon, great value attaches also to the old editions. For an accurate evaluation of the printed editions of the Babyl. Talm. we are indebted to Raph. Rabbinovicz.[2]

a. Mishna. First edition Naples, 1492 fol., with the commentary of Maimonides (in Hebrew). || Venice, Justiniani 1546–50 fol. || Venice, 1548 f., 4to with the commentary of Obadiah di Bertinoro. || Riva di Trento, 1559 fol.; Sabbioneta a. Mantua, 1559–63, 4to; Venice, 1606 fol., all with Maimon. (Hebr.) and Obadiah. || Prague, 1614–17 a. (enlarged) Cracow, 1642–44 with (Obadiah a.) the *Tosephoth Yom Tob* by Yom Ṭob Lipman Heller. || Cambridge, 1883.[3]

b. Palest. Talmud. First edition: Venice, D. Bomberg, ca. 1523/24 fol.[4] Following it: Cracow, 1609 fol.;[5] on the margin a brief commentary. From the Cracow edition: Krotoschin, 1886 fol. and Zhitomir, 1860–67 fol.;[6] Petrokow, 1900–1902. || Editions of single Orders (all in folio). Zera'im: Amsterdam, 1710; Capust, 1812; Mo'ed: Dessau, 1743, Sklow, 1812, Vienna, 1820f. Nashim: Amsterdam, 1754; Berlin, 1757. Neziḳin: Leghorn, 1770; Berlin, 1862. || Three editions with commentaries were left uncompleted: Z. Frankel, *Talmud Yerushalmi 'im . . . 'Ahabath Ṣion*, I (Ber., Pe'a), Vienna, 1874; II (Demai), Breslau, 1875. 4to. M. Lehman, *Talmud Yerushalmi* I, (Ber. with commentary by Shelomo Bekor Joseph Syrileio), Frankf. o. M., 1875. 50 leaves fol.[7]. A. M. Luncz, *Talmud Yerushalmi*, Talmud Hierosolymitanum . . . additis lectionibus codicum manuscriptorum[8] cum commentario, five parts,[9] Jerusalem, 1907–1917 fol.

c. Babylonian Talmud. Fragments of an edition Faro

(Portugal) 1494, Ber., Giṭ., Shebu., which with cod. 169 Hamburg Ḥul. form the remnants of a Spanish recension.[10]

Of the tractates printed at Fez 1516–1521 Erub. (1521) alone is extant complete. Of Ber., Yoma, Beṣa, M. Ḳ., Ḥag., Keth. and Ḳid. we possess only fragments.[11]

Joshua Solomon and his nephew Gershom of Soncino printed from 1488 to 1519 at Soncino (10), Barco (only Sanh. 1497) and Pesaro (21) at least twenty-five tractates.[12]

Daniel Bomberg in Venice (a Christian) has the merit of having printed the first complete editions of the Babyl. Talm., the first 1520 to 1523 fol.; the second was completed in 1531, fol. According to Rabbinovicz,[13] however, they are full of errors, and Gershom[14] complained: *ma'atiḳe Winiṣi'ah he'etiḳu mehadefus sheli*. Some of these errors were corrected in the edition of M. A. Justiniani (Venice, fol., 1546–51); Rabb.,[15] however, finds fault with the corrector's arbitrary procedure. F. Lebrecht[16] asserts that Just. nevertheless made use also of manuscripts and that the editor Joshua Boaz was an eminent scholar. | The third Bomberg edition, 1548 fol.; Ber. was reprinted from Justiniani.

Lublin I, fol. Rabbin. enumerates eleven tractates which were printed between 1559 and 1576 after Justiniani or in part after Bomberg. As twelfth may be named the tractate Giṭṭin printed in 1560 at Konsko Wola near Lublin.[17] || Joseph Jabez printed in 1563 ff. at Saloniki and 1583 ff. at Constantinople, fol., a great number of Talmud tractates.[18] The number of printed tractates is not accurately known; however, the two editions together are supposed to have made up a complete Talmud. Essentially after Bomberg. || The edition Basel, 1578–81 fol.[19] was mutilated in the most stupid manner by the censor[20] (Marcus Marinus Brixianus). The tractate A. Z. is wholly missing; the word Talmud has been replaced by Gemara[21] or something similar; Min (Judeo-Christian heretic) by Sadducee or Epicurean; Goi (non-Jew) by Kuthi (Samaritan) or Kushi (Ethiopian) and so on! Otherwise the text follows essentially Bomberg, the appendages (commentaries, etc.) were taken from Justiniani. This edition was held by the Jews in bad repute, so much so that all printers (with exception of Frankf. o. Oder 1697) who reproduced it placed on the title page the notice: 'after Justiniani.'

Cracow I, 1602–1605, fol., follows the Basel edition, but supplies most (by no means all) of the textual mutilations from Justiniani or Lublin, A. Z. from the edition of Cracow 1579. Cracow II, 1616–20, large 4to, after Cracow I, but in the matter of distributing the contents on the pages it goes its own way.[22] Lublin II, 1617–1639 fol., according to the Basel edition; a part (much less than in the Cracow edition) of the textual mutilations was supplied from Venice or Cracow. Ḥullin, Nidda and Seder Ṭoharoth were printed in Hanau, Ḥul. entirely after the Basel edition!

Amsterdam; 644–48 Immanuel Benveniste, large 4to, is regarded by many with especial esteem; but the title pages read exactly as in Cracow I and the text is that of Lublin II.

Frankf. o. Oder 1697–99, fol., follows according to the title page the Basel edition in all respects; as a matter of fact, however, many of the passages deleted there were restored after Amsterdam 1644 ff. and the tractate A. Z. was also incorporated.[23] After this edition: Amsterdam II, 1714–17, fol. (a few further gaps due to censorship were supplied)—Zera'im, Mo'ed, Yeb., Keth.; on account of a law-suit the printing was completed 1720–21 at Frankf. o. M.; Berlin and Frankf. o. Oder I, 1715–22 fol., and Frankf. o. M., 1720–22.[24] According to Rabb.,[25] the last named edition, prized because of its appendages, served as a basis for almost all of the subsequent editions, whether directly or indirectly. Sulzbach II, or 'Sulzbach Red,' because in this edition for the first time the names of the tractates on the title pages were printed in red ink, 1755–1763. Warsaw, 1875–79 with numerous commentaries. Twenty-five volumes, 4to.

N. Pereferkowitsch, *Talmud Babylonicum ad codices manuscriptos editionesque veterrimas correctum et completum.* I, Berachot, Petersburg, 1909 (136 pp.). The text is eclectic; P. should rather have followed a single definite recension.[26]

Edition with vocalized text: *Masseketh Giṭṭin*, Wilna, 1906 fol. (110 leaves).

The attacks and persecutions to which the Talmud was subjected at the hands of Christians had, in addition to what has been set forth above, still another consequence which has hitherto received but scant attention: in order to escape further attacks, the Jews themselves exercised censorship to a large extent not only in the manuscripts but also in the printed editions.[27]

So far as we know, Gershom of Soncino[28] was the first Jewish printer who exercised censorship on his own account. The few blank passages in the copies of the tractates printed at Soncino are to be explained in all probability as due to the gaps (occasioned by the censor or by dread of him) in the (Spanish) manuscript which was made use of;[29] on the other hand, the quite frequent omissions in the tractates printed at Pesaro appear to proceed from Gershom himself who was bound to bear in mind the duke's dependence upon the Pope.[30] Blank passages are found e. g. in A. Z. Pesaro, in the first Sulzbach print of tractate Sanh.,[31] frequently in Frankf. o. Oder 1697–99 and thereafter in many of the later editions, so as late as the Talmud edition printed by Jul. Sittenfeld at Berlin 1862 ff.[32] In 1835 (in the first instance for the Wilna print) Russian censorship made it unlawful to call attention to deletions by means of blanks.[33]

A part of the passages deleted by censorship in the Babyl. Talm. and its commentaries have been gathered in a few small publications, for the most part anonymous.[34] In addition to these there existed also this and the other printed compilation which did not appear in book form.[35]

CHAPTER X

A CHARACTERIZATION OF THE TALMUD

§ 1. How opinions clash.

1. There are few literary productions on which as contradictory judgments have been passed as on the Talmud. Among orthodox Jews the 'holy Talmud' is spoken of in terms of the highest reverence;[1] in the mind of many Christians it stands for a medley of absurd and coarse statements, as well as of hostile utterances against Christianity.

2. For the Talmud have stood up especially S. Klein,[2] Adolf Jellinek,[3] T. Cohn,[4] Emanuel Deutsch,[5] Ludw. Stern,[6] M. Joel,[7] Lewinsohn,[8] Samson Raph. Hirsch,[9] L. Munk,[10] M. Ehrentheil,[11] J. P. Ssuwalski,[12] M. Horovitz,[13] J. Eschelbacher,[14] Albert Katz.[15] Among Christians: Karl Fischer,[16] Aug. Wünsche.[17] Opinions of Christian scholars concerning the Talmud and in particular on the usefulness of its study have been brought together by K. Fischer,[18] Löwit,[19] Joseph Perles.[20]

3. Against the Talmud. Among Jews: Jacob Kittseer, Jr.,[21] E. Schreiber.[22]

The standard work of the literature hostile to the Talmud is that by Eisenmenger.[23] The original edition which was confiscated in consequence of agitation by the Jews of Frankfort was released only after an interval of forty years; for this reason Frederick I caused an exact reproduction to be printed with the number of the year 1711 and the place indicated as 'Königsberg in Prussia.'[24] Eisenmenger's polemic answered to the uncouth manner of an earlier period; we are apt to designate it as spiteful; we must also concede that repeatedly his translations are erroneous. On the other hand, the charge, often expressed among Jews, that he was a falsifier, cannot be substantiated; for he not only translates, but he gives in addition the place where his citation occurs and, moreover, reproduces the original wording.

On a much lower plane than the well-read and honest, even

though frequently bigoted Eisenmenger stand Aug. Rohling,[25] Jos. Rebbert[26] and J. B. Pranaitis.[27]

As to utterances made by converted Jews against the Talmud or against Judaism, caution is in place, since frequently they are occasioned by spite and (or) the desire to demonstrate the complete severance from their former religion, and often also disclose gross ignorance. The titles of the books themselves repeatedly give evidence of the malicious disposition of their authors.[28] Christ. Gerson's work[29] enjoyed among Christians for a long time too great a popularity. From our own times one example will suffice.[30]

4. Franz Delitzsch[31] and the Roman Catholic Jos. Kopp[32] furnish material to make possible a judicious opinion.

5. In order to account for the difference of opinions we must remember in the first place how their proponents go apart in their religious conceptions and in their bringing up (parentage, habits), and secondly how extraordinarily heterogeneous are the contents of the work on which judgment is passed, since this heterogeneity affords to every one who would form an opinion the opportunity for adducing utterances found in the Talmud which favor or at least seem to favor his particular view. Paul de Lagarde has referred to the Talmud as 'a veritable Pompeii of philology.'

§2. How a correct point of view may be obtained.

For a just estimate of the Talmud two requirements may be mentioned:

a. We must know not only the conditions (political and otherwise) and the notions (religious and otherwise) under which the Jews lived in Palestine and in Babylonia during the first five Christian centuries, but also how these conditions and notions came to be. If we thus e. g. observe in the Talmud 'the idea of God Judaized' (and accordingly the life and doings of God determined by the Torah), much of the offensiveness is lost and we can understand how the notion arose if we consider how with the Jews in the times after the Babylonian exile the 'Law' was so highly valued as to relegate to the background everything else.

b. One must bear in mind that *the Talmud is not a law-book,* not a code, in which every sentence is unconditionally valid. In the Mishna itself diverging opinions are placed in juxtaposition very frequently.[1] And the Gemara almost throughout takes on the nature of a lecture hall or of a collection of minutes of the discussions in which the Amoraim cleared up that which had been said by the Tannaim.[2] Direct statements as to what is Halakah, valid law, are rare in the Mishna;[3] frequent in the Baraithoth. Repeatedly the Saboraim added at the conclusion of a debate: 'The Halakah is as . . .'[4] What is religiously valid to-day the rabbi must ascertain by investigation. He is aided therein by such rules as are put together in Seder Tannaim we'amoraim, so § 16. 'Akiba's opinion is always authoritative in conflict with a single scholar, but not when he is opposed by more than one scholar.' The main business, however, is to consult the Codes which regulate practice and from them backward to go back to the older authorities (e. g. the responsa of the Geonim) and to the sources (the discussions in the Talmud). The Codes[5] which orthodox Jews consider as authoritative are specifically the Mishne Torah by Moses Maimonides, the Sepher Ha-miṣwoth ha-gadol by Moses of Coucy (about 1250), the Arba'a Ṭurim by Jacob ben Asher (died about 1340) and the Shulḥan Aruk by Joseph Ḳaro (1488–1575); but these Codes, especially the Shulḥan Aruk, *only in connection with the Commentaries thereon.*[6] 'Sources' are: Mishna, Tosephta, both Talmuds and the halakic Midrashim. When the sources contradict one another, then the Babylonian Talmud is given the preference.—Accordingly it is highly preposterous to cause all the utterances of a single rabbi found in the Talmud to stand without further ado as 'teaching of the Talmud' or to hold Judaism responsible for such utterances. As a rule one should cite, 'R. So and So says,' and in this connection not only indicate the period in which this teacher lived, but also note whether he met with opposition, whether the Halakah is after him and so on.

§ 3. Obligatory Character and Significance of the Talmud for Judaism.

a. The Haggadah is not binding.

Thus Samuel ha-nagid (in Granada, died 1055) says in his Introduction to the Talmud: Of the Haggada one need accept only what is plausible to the understanding. One hears frequently the statement adduced: 'The words of the Haggada are not to be refuted' in the sense that 'there is no call for refuting the words of the Haggada.' To my knowledge the statement is nowhere to be met with in the older period.[1] In older times the Haggada was certainly held in high repute: If thou wouldst know thy Maker, study the Haggada; for thereby thou wilt learn to know Him and to cleave to His ways;[2] or: By 'stay of water' (Isaiah 3.1) are meant those versed in Haggada who by means of the Haggada attract the hearts of men.[3] According to L. Baeck[4] objections began to be raised against the Haggada in the first decades of the second century when Christianity called for a definite stand, and these objections increased as the Church began its career as a power in the state. When we stop to think of the high importance which Judaism attaches to the right *doing* and of its contrast to Christianity which indulges in a scriptural exposition strongly reminiscent of the haggadic, we shall understand the disparaging remarks concerning the Haggada, as when e. g.[5] the Haggadist is spoken of as a man who is unable to enjoy his possessions: he cannot forbid and he cannot grant permission, nor pronounce aught unclean or clean.

b. Voices on the binding character of the Talmud or to the contrary.

α. S. R. Hirsch.[6] 'Beside the traditions reaching up to Moses,' the explications, handed down orally, of the written Mosaic Law, 'the Talmud contains also discriminating and didactic sayings; decisions and statements by later searchers and sages which flow from those traditions as deductions, applications or explications . . . and like them are invested with binding force, the so-called halakic part; or again we meet with individual opinions, proverbs, parables etc. which *lay no claim* to such *binding authority*, the so-called *haggadic* part . . . The Gemara . . . contains the debates as they were carried on in the schools, . . . hence also *contradictory opinions*, and practical validity attaches only to the definitive conclusions resulting therefrom, of the character of those[7] which are systematically compiled in the Codes.'

β. Ludw. Stern in Würzburg, likewise strictly orthodox, sets forth[8] 'that the Israelite is not bound to give credence to haggadic passages, which are not immediately open to understanding, according to their literal wording, but rather is warranted in taking them in that sense which comes to him after honest scrutiny, especially since for the immediately intelligible part of the *Haggada it is not belief* in the dogmatic sense, but only that *respect is demanded* which is due to the words of authors so highly learned.—However, unconditional validity belongs to the *Halakah,* and in accordance therewith Jewish life is regulated to the utmost detail; but in the form in which the Halakah presents itself in the Talmud it is *not* adapted to direct application as a *norm* for religious life . . . Probably the most difficult task of rabbinic learning is to establish a decision on the basis of talmudic discussion.' He continues to say 'that in the halakic discussions of the Talmud there occur thousands of propositions which, because they are not valid as decisions, are only of theoretical significance.'

γ. Leopold Stein (point of view of extreme reform, was rabbi at Frankfort o. M., died 1882):[9] 'The Talmud appears only as an aggregate of opinions taught, but nowhere as a closed Code.' It 'is for us in no wise a confessional work or a source of divine communication.' It 'must be completely divested of any title to higher validity as if it contained even a jot of Mosaic revelation and Sinaitic communication not found explicitly in Scripture.' We must 'state regretfully that infinitely much of that which the Talmud passes off for such necessary explanations of the written, pentateuchal Law turns out to be harmful commandments of men, which circumstance has dimmed the splendor of our religion only too well.'

δ. Isaac M. Wise (of the same leanings):[10] The Talmud is not quoted or even mentioned in this book, although almost every paragraph thereof can be supported by Talmudical passages, and consequently it must contain many good and even excellent passages, also in the estimation of the author. American rabbis, the author included, having declared in various conferences the authority of the Talmud abrogated, it could only be consulted as a historical record, to show how the ancient expounders of the Law understood this or that passage of the Bible.

ε. Ludw. Philippson[11] represents the point of view of moderate reform.

c. The significance of the Talmud for Judaism.

One voice in the stead of many may be adduced. F. Perles:[12] 'The Halakah was an unexampled disciplining of the will of downright heroic proportions. For it imparted to the Jews of a whole millennium the moral strength to achieve the most difficult tasks and to suffer for their religion. To it in the first instance we are most peculiarly indebted for that which to this day we have regarded as our highest good, the flower and fruition of our religion, I mean the Jewish family virtues. Nevertheless . . . we must on the other side own that in this straining of the legal requirements there lurked a danger by no means small . . . Inasmuch as the Halakah took too little account of the personal bent of mind and the moral judgment of the individual, it is just the more forceful personalities that were hampered in their unfoldment so that one may, at least in this respect, not go wrong in speaking of the "yoke of the Law".' 'The Talmud accomplished the historic miracle of injecting into Jewry, dispersed amidst a hostile world, again and again an indestructible vitality and at the same time of stamping it with that uniform character which it has preserved to this day despite all dissolving influences . . .' The Talmud 'was made by Jews for Jews without . . . sidelong glances at the world without. Long before the Jews had renounced all hope of propaganda . . . Thus it stood not in need of any accommodations to the rest of the world and was left free to mould Judaism in all purity.'

CHAPTER XI

Hermeneutics of the Talmud and Midrashim

§ 1. Introductory Remarks.

An effort was made to prove by far the greatest number of the regulations of the 'Oral Law,' in part from the outset and in part at least subsequently,[1] from the written Torah, the Pentateuch, occasionally also from other biblical books. Of these hermeneutics it is to be noted that they very frequently not only appear to be, but really are wide of the mark. Nevertheless they are not, as it is often believed, entirely arbitrary, but bound to certain rules *middoth* which one must know in order to form a correct opinion of the talmudic exposition of the Scriptures. In the Haggada the same rules are employed, but in a still freer manner, and a part of the rules mentioned in § 4 (the thirty-two Middoth) apply even exclusively to it; so it comes about that in haggadic discussions joined to a Bible word it is quite often a case not of bringing out the sense, but of bringing it in or thoughts loosely connected by means of playing on words or by anything else that will support the memory. According to orthodox Jewish opinion[2] it was the merit of M. L. Malbim[3] to 'demonstrate brilliantly and irrefutably how all *derashoth* of our great teachers, all their deductions of the oral law from the written rest upon the rules of logic and of the Hebrew language . . . In the introduction *Ayeleth ha-Shaḥar* . . . he gives a summary presentation of the rules and principles discovered by him in the course of his investigations.'[4]

§ 2. The oldest norms of interpretation.

a. The Seven Middoth of Hillel were not invented by Hillel; they represent merely a compilation of the main kinds of the method of evidence customary from that time on. It is certain that Hillel stressed the need of scriptural interpretation in contrast to the statements of abstract Halakah.[1]

1. *Kal Wa-ḥomer.*[2] Inference a minori ad maius, from the light (less important) to the heavy (more important) and vice versa.[3]

2. *Gezerah Shawah,*[4] literally: similar injunction or regulation. 'Inference by Analogy,' by virtue of which, because in two pentateuchal passages words occur which are similar or have the identical connotation, both laws, however different they may be in themselves, are subject to the same regulations and applications.[5]

3. *Binyan 'ab mikkathub 'eḥad,* literally: constructing a family.[6] 'In consequence of the exegetical rule designated by this expression there is applied to a number of biblical passages which go together as to the contents any specific regulation which is found only in one of them. Thus the principal passage imparts to all the remaining passages a common character which unites them in one family.'[7]

4. *Binyan ab mishshene Kethubim.* So the rule is called when the deduction just mentioned rests on two biblical passages.[8]

5. *Kelal u-ferat u-ferat u-Kelal.* 'The General and Particular, the Particular and General,' i. e. detailed determination of the General by means of the Particular, of the Particular by means of the General. This rule, which with Schwarz we should rather count as two, is divided in the thirteen Middoth of Ishmael into eight (Nos. 4–11). In advance of Ishmael, Neḥuniah ben Ha-ḳana had shown a preference for this method of interpretation.[9]

6. *Keyoṣe bo bemaḳom 'aḥer.* 'To which something Similar in another Passage,' i. e. exposition by means of another similar passage.[10] If with Schwarz we count No. 5 as two Middoth, this No. 6 is to be deleted.

7. *Dabar ha-lamed me'inyano.* Something that is deduced from the Context.[11]

b. These seven Middoth are by no means the only exegetical rules in vogue during the old Tannaitic times. Hillel himself made use in addition of the form of inference *heḳḳesh* in order to demonstrate that the Passover offering may be offered on the Sabbath.[12] *Hiḳḳish* to conform two subjects to one another by juxtaposition or by the use of analogous phraseology.[13] Several of the rules enumerated in 3–5 are very old.

§ 3. The thirteen Middoth of R. Ishmael.

Ishmael[1] rejected the straining interpretation put upon single words, aye, letters, and formulated the principle: *dibberah Torah kilshon bene 'Adam* 'the Torah speaks the language of the children of men.'[2] He reasoned, in a manner similar to that of Hillel, by means of distinct modes of inference. Ishmael's thirteen Middoth are held by the Jews in high repute (they form an element in the daily morning prayers, so as early as the Siddur of Rab Amram); but in essence they are merely an expanded edition of the seven Middoth of Hillel.[3] S. R. Hirsch[4] has compiled numerous sayings of ancient authorities (Rishonim and Aḥaronim) to the effect that these Middoth were handed down from Sinai. Similarly Is. Unna:[5] 'The rules according to which the oral law is derived from the written law were handed down from Sinai, and it is not without cause that the Baraitha de Rabbi Ishmael has been received into our order of prayers. The unity of written and oral law is the pillar upon which rabbinic Judaism rests, with that it stands and falls.'[6]

New is Ishmael 13: *shene Kethubim ha-makḥishin zeh 'eth zeh 'ad sheyabo ha-Kathub ha-shelishi weyakri'a benehem.* When two verses contradict one another, the contradiction is removed by a third verse.[7]

The Karaite Judah Hadassi (1149 C.E.) incorporated these Middoth into his religious system: Eshkol ha-kopher, Eupatoria, 1836, No. 162. The text is found in the introduction to Siphra.[8]

§ 4. The two and thirty Middoth.

Abulwalid ibn Ganaḥ is the first to cite the thirty-two Middoth which are ascribed to Eliezer ben Jose Ha-gelili. The text has been repeatedly copied and reprinted from the third part of the *Sepher Kerithuth* by Samson of Chinon. Still earlier is the textual form in Judah Hadassi (No. 155ff.). In manuscript form this Baraitha is found e. g. in the introduction to *midrash ha-gadol*[1] and in *midrash ha-ḥefeṣ.*[2] The number 33 in the two Yemenite Midrashim has arisen through bisection of the 29th Middah.[3]

In the Talmud itself the thirty-two Middoth are not mentioned; nevertheless we read:[4] 'Wherever thou hearest the words of Eliezer ben Jose Ha-gelili in the Haggada, incline thine ear like unto a funnel.' At least a part of these Middoth is older than this Eliezer.

The first four rules treat of Inclusion and Exclusion. Already Nahum of Gimzo applied *ribbuyın u-mi'utin*, and Akiba learned it from him.[5] Eliezer ben Hyrcanus likewise made use of this method.[6]

1. *Ribbui.* The particles *'af, gam, 'eth* indicate an inclusion or amplification.[7]

2. *Mi'ut.* The three particles *'ak, raḳ, min* point to a limitation, exclusion or diminution.[8]

3. *Ribbui 'aḥar ribbui.* When two of the particles named are joined.[9]

4. *Mi'ut aḥar mi'ut.* When two limiting or excluding particles are joined.[10]

5. *Ḳal wa-ḥomer meforash.* Explicit inference a minori ad maius and vice versa.[11]

6. *Ḳal wa-ḥomer sathum.* When such an inference is merely suggested.

7. *Gezerah shawah* a. 8. *Binyan 'ab.*[12]

9. *Derek Ḳeṣarah.* Abbreviated or elliptical phraseology.[13]

10. *Dabar shehu' shanui.* Repetition is made use of to bring out a point.[14]

11. *Siddur shenneḥelaḳ.* A context which is disrupted, namely by Soph pasuḳ (or any other disjunctive accent).[15]

12. *Dabar sheba lelammed wenimṣa lamed.* Something is adduced for comparison, but in this process fresh light is shed upon that itself.[16]

13. *Kelal she'aḥaraw ma'aseh we'eno 'ella perato shel ri'shon.* When a General is followed by an action, then that is the Particular of the former.[17]

14. *Dabar gadol shenithlah beḳaton mimmennu lehashmi'a ha'ozen bederek shehi' shoma'ath.* Something important is compared with something trivial that a clearer understanding may be facilitated.[18]

15. *Shene kethubim ha-makḥishim* . . .[19]

16. *Dabar ha-meyuḥad bimḳomo.* Significant use of an expression.[20]

17. *Dabar she'eno mithparesh bimkomo umithparesh bemakom 'aḥer.* A circumstance not clearly enunciated in the principal passage is referred to in another passage, especially with a view to supplementing a pentateuchal passage from a non-pentateuchal.[21]

18. *Dabar shenne'emar bemikṣatho we-hu' noheg ba-kol.* A specific case of a type of occurrences is mentioned, although the whole type is meant.[22]

19. *Dabar shenne'emar ba-zeh wehu' ha-din laḥabero.* A statement is made with reference to one subject, but it is true just as well with reference to another.[23]

20. *Dabar shenne'emar ba-zeh we'eno 'inyan lo 'abal hu' 'inyan laḥabero.* A statement does not go well with the passage in which it occurs, but is in keeping with another passage and may then be applied to that passage.[24]

21. *Dabar shehukkash bishte middoth we'atah nothen lo koaḥ ha-yafeh shebbishtehen.* Something is compared with two things and so only the good properties of both are attributed to it.[25]

22. *Dabar sheḥabero mokiaḥ 'alaw.* A proposition which requires to be supplemented from a parallel proposition.[26]

23. *Dabar shehu' mokiaḥ 'al ḥabero.* A proposition serves to supplement a parallel proposition.[27]

24. *Dabar shehayah bikelal weyaṣa min ha-kelal lelammed 'al 'aṣmo yaṣa.* Is in force with haggadic interpretation.[28]

25. *Dabar shehayah bikelal weyaṣa min ha-kelal lelammed 'al ḥabero.* Modification of Ishmael 8.[29]

26. *Mashal.* Parable.[30]

27. *Neged.* Corresponding significant number.[31]

28. *Ma'al.* Paronomasia.[32]

29. *Gematria.*[33] (a) Computation of the numeric value of letters:[34] (b) Secret alphabets or substitution of letters for other letters.[35]

30. *Notrikon.*[36] Breaking up a word into two or more, exposition of the single letters to stand for just as many words which commence with them.[37]

31. *Mukdam shehu' me'uḥar ba-'inyan.* Something that precedes which is placed second.[38]

32. *Muḳdam u-me'uḥar shehu' beparashioth.* Many a biblical section refers to a later period than the one which precedes, and vice versa.[39]

§ 5. Concluding Remarks.

Still other rules were in use both for Halakah and for Haggada. Specifically, Eleazar ben Azariah and Aḳiba,[1] but also Eliezer ben Hyrcanus,[2] in their interpretation of Scripture, followed the rule 'Every biblical section which is found close by another is to be interpreted with an eye to that one', *Kol parashah shehi' semukah la-ḥabertah lemedah hemenah.*[3]

In conclusion a few additional specimens from mishnic exegesis which at the same time may serve as further proof that the Halakah availed itself not only of the thirteen Middoth of Ishmael. Thus Aḳiba sets up Ribbui as an hermeneutic principle;[4] the same teacher forces an absolute infinitive.[5] In the same manner a plural is made to yield an implication,[6] or a superfluous Waw (Aḳiba),[7] or the duplication of a word (Rabbi).[8] A renewed scientific examination of the hermeneutics of the Tannaim has not been rendered superfluous by G. Aicher's publication.[9]

CHAPTER XII

TEXTUAL SPECIMENS IN TRANSLATION

§ 1. Ḥullin 8. 1 with Gemara 103b-104b.

Mishna. No meat may be boiled with milk, save meat of fish and locusts. It is also forbidden to bring it to table together with cheese, save meat of fish and locusts. He who vows to abstain from meat, is still free to partake of fish and locusts.

Gemara. Meat of fowl, cooked with milk, is thus forbidden biblically.[1] Not so according to R. Akiba. For he says [§ 4]: 'It is not forbidden in the Bible to cook game and fowl with milk.'[2]—Let me, however, cite the final clause of the Mishna [here § 1]:[3] 'He who vows to abstain from meat, is still free to partake of fish and locusts.' Accordingly fowl is forbidden to him. This would go with Akiba who said: 'All things, in regard to which a messenger asks for instructions, belong to the same category,'[4] as is taught Ned. 7.1: When a person vows not to eat vegetables, *yereḳ*, he is permitted to eat gourds; Aḳiba forbids it. They said to Aḳiba: 'One may say to an agent, may he not? "Fetch me vegetables," and the agent will answer: "I found only gourds." He replied: 'Quite so. Would the agent say that he found only peas? Hence gourds come within the category of vegetables, but not peas.'

Hence the first clause of the Mishna [according to which it is forbidden in the Bible to cook food in milk] corresponds to the opinion of the sages, while the conclusion [according to which fowl is held to be meat] would answer to that of Akiba. Rab Joseph said: 'Rabbi taught in accordance with different Tannaim; as regards vows he concurred with Akiba, but as regards meat and milk with the sages.'—Rab Ashi said: 'The whole goes with Akiba, and this is what he meant: It is unlawful to cook any kind of meat with milk, some meats on biblical grounds (meat of cattle), other meats in accordance with the scholars, Sopherim (meat of game and fowl); save the meat of fish and locusts which is forbidden neither on biblical grounds nor according to the Sopherim.'

Mishna. And it is forbidden to bring it[5] to table together with cheese . . .

Gemara. Rab Joseph said: Inferentially it follows that fowl with milk is forbidden biblically; for if you were minded to say that it is forbidden only rabbinically, then eating itself would constitute a rabbinical prohibition—how then could it be forbidden by the rabbis to bring to table for fear it would lead to eating?—[Query:] Whence can you prove that the rabbis have no power to enact a preventive measure for the sake of something which is merely forbidden by the rabbis?[6]—[Answer:] From the Mishna Ḥalla 4.8: 'Ḥalla from outside Palestine[7] may be eaten by a priest in the presence of a non-priest at the same table and may be given to any priest.'

Abaye rejoined: Granted. If it were a case of Ḥalla brought to Palestine from outside Palestine, then a preventive measure by the rabbis with a view to Palestinian Halla which is forbidden in the Bible would be in place and therefore from the fact that such a measure is absent this conclusion[8] might be justified. The Mishna, however, speaks only of Ḥalla outside Palestine where there is no occasion whatsoever for a rabbinical preventive measure.[9] But in the present instance, if you permit one to serve fowl and cheese, the next thing will be that he will serve meat and cheese and then eat 'meat with milk' which is forbidden in the Bible.[10]—Rab Shesheth[11] raised an objection: After all, either[12] is cold.[13]—Abaye replied: There is an apprehension that it will be served in a hot dish.[14]—[Objection:] After all, this dish is but a second vessel,[15] and a second vessel would not any more effect boiling. [Answer:] But it is to be apprehended that it will be served in the first pan.

§ 2. Baba Meṣi'a 1.8 with Gemara 20a–21a.

B. M. chap. 1 deals with finds. The main subject in the discussion which follows here is the Symphon. *Symphon*, from the Greek τὸ σύμφωνον, properly denotes: an agreement; then specifically: a clause whereby a contract is voided when certain conditions supervene, as e. g. when subsequently a defect is discovered in the thing purchased.[1]—In the present section, *S.* refers to the cancellation of a promissory note so that *S.* is 1. a receipt written in advance; 2. one written after payment, but not delivered; 3. a private memorandum of payment in the creditor's papers; 4. a receipt on the face of the promissory note.

Mishna. When one finds documents relating to legal assessment[2] or to alimony,[3] documents relating to ḥaliṣa[4] or letters of protest[5] or documents relating to Berurin or any (other) judicial documents, he must return (his find). When one finds in a bag or case[6] a roll of bills or a bundle of bills, he must return (his find). How much is a bundle of bills? Three tied together. Rabban Simeon, son of Gamaliel, said: (The three bills) belonging to one who borrowed from three persons (the finder) returns to the debtor; but (the three) belonging to three persons who borrowed from one (and the same) person (the finder) returns to the creditor.—When one finds a bill (belonging to some one else) among his own and does not know what the nature of it is,[7] let (this bill) lie untouched until Elijah comes.[8]—When a Symphon is found therewith, (the finder) shall be guided by the contents of the Symphon.

Gemara. What are documents relating to Berurin, *shiṭre berurin*? According to the interpretation here (in Babylonia) they mean briefs concerning the pleas of litigants.[9] Jeremiah says: The one (litigant) chooses one and the other another[10] (to constitute a court of arbitration).

M. He must return any judicial document.—*G.* In the court of Rab Huna there was found once a bill of divorcement[11] in which was written: 'In the town Shewiri, situate on the river Rakis.' Then spoke Rab Huna: 'We must take into consideration that there may be two towns by that name.'[12] Then Ḥisda spoke to Rabbah: 'Go (and) ponder for in the evening Rab Huna will question thee concerning it.' So he went, pondered and found[13] that the Mishna (here B. M. 1.8) says:[14] 'Any judicial document must be returned.' Whereupon Rab Amram said to Rabbah: 'How canst thou draw an inference from a civil case to a matter touching a religious prohibition?' The reply was: 'O thou devoid of sense (*tarda*)! We find in the Mishna (also): Documents relating to ḥaliṣa and letters of protest.[15] Then did a cedar column of the school house collapse. The one gentleman said: 'It collapsed on account of what happened to me,' and the other: 'It collapsed on account of what happened to me.'

M. When one finds (documents) in a *ḥaphisa* or *deloskama*.—What is *ḥaphisa?* Rabbah bar bar Hanah says: 'A small bottle of skin.' What is *deloskama?* Raba, son of Samuel, says: 'A knapsack (*θύλακος*) of an old man.'

M. A roll of bills or a bundle of bills etc.—*G*. The Rabbanan have handed down: 'What is a roll of bills? Three wrapped together, *kerukin*. And what is a bundle of bills? Three tied together, *ḳeshurin*.'—From which one might infer that a knot is a mark of identification? (Not at all,) Ḥiyya taught (that a bundle means) three (bills,) rolled into one another.—If this be the case, then (this) would amount to the same as a 'roll'?—(By no means,) (it is) a roll when each (bill) touches (with its end) the beginning of the other;[16] (on the other hand) a bundle, when they lie on the top of one another and are (then) rolled together.—

What does (the finder) cry out? The number.[17] Why are three mentioned? It should hold good even in the case of two. But as Rabina says:[18] 'He cries out: Coins!'—so here likewise he cries out: 'Bills!'[19]

M. Rabban Simeon, son of Gamaliel, said: (Three bills) belonging to one who borrowed from three persons (the finder) returns to the debtor etc.—*G*. For if you should think that they (were lost) by the (3) creditors—how could they (the bills) come together?[20]—[Reply:] Perhaps (the three creditors) came (simultaneously) in order to have them certified [i. e. each creditor's bill by the court scribe]! [Rejoinder: But the case stands so] that they had been certified! [Reply:] Suppose they were dropped by the court scribe?—[Rejoinder:] No man will leave his certified bills with the court scribe!

M. (three bills) belonging to three persons who borrowed from one person, (the finder) returns to the creditor etc.—*G*. For if you should think that they (the bills were lost) by the debtors (then I ask:) how did they (the bills) come to be together?[21] [Reply:] Perhaps they (the three debtors) had gone to have them written.[22]—[Rejoinder: But the case stands so] that they (the bills) are written by three different clerks! [Reply:] Perhaps (the three debtors) came (simultaneously) to have them certified [i. e. each one's bill by the clerk of the court]?—[Rejoinder:] The creditor will (it is true,) have his bill certified, (but) not the debtor.

M. When a Symphon is found therewith, (the finder) shall be guided by the contents of the Symphon.—Jeremiah, son of Abba, says in the name of Rab: A Symphon which goes out of the hands of the creditor,[23] even though it be written by his own hand, is to be taken as a jest and is (therefore) disqualified. It is needless to say that when it (the S.) proceeds from the hands of a professional scribe it is disqualified; for it might be said that this scribe chanced upon him (the creditor) and wrote it (the S.). But even if it be written by his own hand, the S. is disqualified, (for) he (the creditor presumably) thought: He (the debtor) will come perchance at twilight and pay me; if then I give him not it (the S.), he will not give me my money; hence I will have (the S.) written (in advance) and give it to him when he pays me my money.

We find it said in the Mishna:[24] 'When a Symphon is found therewith, (the finder) shall be guided by the contents of the Symphon.'—[Answer:] As Saphera said (further below): 'When it is found among his (the creditor's) torn bills'[25]—so here likewise (the meaning is) that it (the S.) was found among his torn bills.

Come and listen: [It is said:[26]] 'When one finds among his bills (the memorandum:) "The note of Joseph, son of Simeon, has been paid," then both bills[27] are (considered as) paid.'—[Answer:] As Saphera said (there): 'When it (the bill) is found among his torn bills,' so here likewise (the meaning is) that it (the Symphon) was found among his torn bills.

Come and listen: [It is said:][28] 'We[29] swear that our father gave us no instructions concerning it (in his last will), that our father spoke nothing to us concerning it (otherwise) and that we have found[30] among our father's papers nothing (to indicate) that this bill has been paid.'—Saphera said: When it (the promissory note) was found among his (the father's) torn bills.

Come and listen: [It is said:[31]] 'A Symphon, on which there are witnesses, is authenticated by those subscribed to it *beḥothe-*

maw.'[32] Say (rather): It is authenticated on the part of those subscribed to it *meḥothemaw*;[33] for the witnesses are questioned whether payment has been made or not!

Come and listen:[34] 'A Symphon, on which there are witnesses, is valid.' What sort of witnesses?—Witnesses of authentication.[35] This follows also conclusively from the final clause: 'But if there be no witnesses therewith,[36] it (the Symphon) is disqualified.' What is the meaning of 'No witnesses therewith'? If the meaning were that no witnesses at all are subscribed thereto, would it be necessary to say that it is disqualified? (No,) but the question turns upon the witnesses of authentication (just referred to).

The identical text: 'A Symphon, on which there are witnesses, is authenticated by those subscribed to it. But if there be no (such) witnesses therewith and it come from the hand of a third person (*shalish* depositary) or it come immediately under the subscription of the promissory note, then it is valid.' (For) when it comes from the hand of a third person, it is valid for the reason that (apparently) the creditor had deposited it with the third person. And if it come right under the signature of the promissory note, (it is) likewise (valid): for if no payment had been made, the creditor would not have invalidated his bill (by the Symphon).

CHAPTER XIII

The More Important Teachers

§ 1. Bibliography.

I. Jewish authors. (a) Works in the Hebrew language: Abraham ben Samuel Zakuto (died 1515), Sefer Yoḥasin, ed. Filipowski, London, 1857, 10–80, 97–203. || Simeon Peiser, Sefer naḥlath Shim'oni, Wandsbeck, 1728 fol. (68 and 69 leaves)—a list of those passages in which persons of the Old Testament and Tannaim are mentioned in the Babyl. Talmud and in the Midrashim called Rabboth. || Jehiel Heilprin (d. 1728), Seder ha-Doroth, Carlsruhe, 1769 and frequently; more orderly arrangement by Naphtali Maskileison, Warsaw 1882 (see J. Rachlin in *Ha-kerem*, 1887, 193–222 and S. Buber in *Oṣar ha-siphruth*, IV, 163–180). || Jacob Brüll, Mebo ha-Mishna, I, Frankf. o. M., 1876. || Z. Frankel (d. 1875), Darke ha-Mishna, *Hodegetica in Mischnam librosque cum ea conjunctos.* I (no further volume has appeared): *Introductio in Mischnam*, Leipzig, 1859; Mebo ha-Yerushalmi, *Einleitung in den Jerusalemischen Talmud*, Breslau, 1870. Since Frankel takes up fol. 53b to 131b the Palestinian Amoraim in alphabetical order, we cite his work in §8ff. only exceptionally. This list is supplemented by Bacher, *Agada der paläst. Amoräer*, I, 567–570. || J. H. Weiss, Dor Dor we-Dorshaw, *Zur Geschichte der jüdischen Tradition*, vol. I–III, Vienna, 1871, 76, 83. Against him Judah Ha-levi Lipschitz, S. Dor Yesharim, Petrokow, 1907, 1910 (104, 124). || Wolf Jawitz, Sefer Toldoth Yisrael, vol. VI (fall of the Jewish state to the death of Rabbi), Cracow, 1907; VII (Amoraim), Berlin, 1909; VIII (Amoraim to the close of the Talmud), Berlin, 1912. || A. Hyman, Toldoth Tanna'im we-'Amoraim, London, 1910 (1246), lives of the persons mentioned in Talmud and Midrash, in alphabetical order. || J. D. Eisenstein, Osar Yisra'el, II, New York, 1908, enumerates 1812 Amoraim of whom he claims that 245 had not been listed in previous works, see p. 85–95. || Isaac Halevy (d. 1914), Doroth ha-Rishonim. Frankf. o. M. (vol. III: Pressburg). There have appeared: vol. I c (end of the Hasmoneans to the end of the Roman procurators), 1906 (736); I e (destruction of the Temple to the close of the Mishna), 1918 (890); II (to the close of the Talmud) 1901 (619); III (Saboraim and Geonim), 1897 (315). In his all too sharp polemics against H. Grätz, Frankel and Weiss, Halevy is often materially in the right, but on the positive side he advances much that is untenable. He has adherents and opponents equally passionate. To the former belong especially H. Kottek, *Fortschritt oder Rückschritt in der jüd. Wissenschaft*, Frankf. o. M., 1902 (80) and W. Jawitz, 'Neue jüd. Geschichtsforschung u. einige ihrer wichtigsten Resultate,' *Jahrb. d. Jüd.-Liter. Gesellschaft*, IV (1906), 283–292. Opponents: J. Elbogen, *Monatsschrift*, 1902, 1–48; N. Kronberg, ibid., 439–448; Isr. Lévi, *Revue des Etudes Juives*, XLIII (1901), 279; A. Epstein, ibid., XXXVI, 222–236; XLIV, 45–61; XLVI, 197–211 (ordination et autorisation); R. Leszynsky, *Monatsschrift*, 1912, 567–580, 690–699. W. Bacher, *Revue des Etudes Juives*, XLIV, 132–151, while dismissing again and again his opinions, accepts several; against Bacher: Kottek, *Jahrb. d. Jüd.-Liter. Gesellsch.*, II (1904), 85–184. A mediating position is maintained by D. Hoffmann in *Zeitschr. f. hebr. Bibliogr.*, V (1901), 100–107 and by E. Atlas, *Or we-ṣel b'Toldoth Yisra'el* in the annual *ha-Shanah* I (Warsaw, 1901), 102–124.

(b) J. Derenbourg, *Essai sur l'histoire et la géographie de la Palestine d'après les Talmuds et les autres sources rabbiniques*. I (the only one published): *Histoire . . . depuis Cyrus jusqu'à Adrien*, Paris, 1867 (486). || Jul. Fürst, *Kultur-u. Literaturgeschichte der Juden in Asien*. I (sole) part, Leipzig, 1849 (318), treats only of Babylonia. M. Braunschweiger, *Die Lehrer der Mischnah. Ihr Leben u. Wirken*, Frankf. o. M., 2d ed., 1903 (319). || Albert Katz, *Biographische Charakterbildungen aus der jüdischen Geschichte u. Sage*, Berlin, 1905 (215 p.; 12 biographical sketches: Hillel . . . Simeon ben Johai). || Wilh. Bacher, *Die Agada der Tannaiten*, 2 volumes, Strassburg 1884, 1890 (457 a. 578); vol. I, in 2d ed., 1903 (496). I quote after the first edition, the page numbers of which are indicated in the second ed. on the inner margin. Idem, *Die Agada der babylonischen Amoräer*, ibid., 1878 (151); *Die Agada der palästinensischen Amoräer*, 3 vol., ibid., 1892, 1896, 1899 (587, 545 a. 803).

H. Kottek, '*Die Hochschulen in Palästina u. Babylonien*,' in *Jahrbuch der Jüd.-Liter. Gesellschaft*, III (1905), 131 to 190. || S. Funk, *Die Juden in Babylonien*, Berlin, 1902, 1908 (170 a. 160).

II. Christian authors: O. J. Ottho, *Historia doctorum Misnicorum*, Oxford, 1672; with notes by Hadr. Reland (not named), Amsterdam (about 1698); repeated in J. Chr. Wolf, *Bibl. Hebr.*, IV, 336–447. An alphabetical list of the teachers of the Mishna with notes in Wolf, *B. H.*, II, 805–865; additional names, IV, 330–336; a partial list of the Amoraim after Bartolocci's *Bibliotheca Rabbinica* III, with some explanations, in Wolf II, 865–882. || E. Schürer, *Geschichte des jüd. Volkes* § 25, IV (down to Akiba). *Verzeichnis der Personennamen in der Mischna*, Leipzig, 1913 (23). || H. Tj. de Graaf, *De Joodsche Wetgeleerden in Tiberias van 70–400 n. C.*, Groningen, 1902 (175).

§ 2. The oldest period and the five 'Pairs.'

Concerning Ezra and the Men of the 'Great Synagogue' see above p. 9. The oldest bearers of Tradition, whose names we know, are those named Aboth 1.2 f.; Simeon the Just, apparently the high priest Simeon I, ca. 300 B.C.E.,[1] and Antigonus of Socoh, who is mentioned just once more in Aboth deRabbi Nathan 5, where it is said that the Sadducees and Boethusians derived from Zadok and Boethus, reputed disciples of Antigonus.

Right after Antigonus, but in a manner that the phrase suggests a gap[2] in the chain of tradition (*Ḳibbelu mehem* instead of *Ḳibbelu mimmennu*), five pairs (*zug*, plural *zugoth*) of teachers are named Aboth 1.4–15; of these teachers accordingly two in each case must be regarded as contemporaries. It is, however, an error when the tradition Ḥag. 2.2 (where the same ten names recur) claims that of each pair the first was the president (*nasi*) and the second the vice-president (*ab beth din*) of the great Sanhedrin. In reality the high priest presided over this body.[3]

Jose ben Joezer of Zereda and Jose ben Johanan.[4] The first is designated Ḥag. 2.7 as a saint among the priesthood.[5]

Joshua ben Perahiah and Mattai[6] of Arbel (Irbid, north-west of Tiberias). Anachronistically the first is said Sanh. 107b, Soṭa 47a to have been a teacher of Jesus.[7]

Judah ben Ṭabai[8] and Simeon ben Shaṭaḥ. The statement of Mishna Sanh. 4.6 that the latter caused eighty women to be hanged in Ashkelon is erroneous, since the city had been an independent municipality from 104 B.C.E. on. During the reign of Alexander Jannaeus (103–76 B.C.E.) and particularly of Salome Alexandra (76–67) it was through him that the Pharisaic party carried off the victory.[9]

Shemaiah and Abtalion.[10] Josephus names *Σαμαίας* in the year 47 B.C.E.[11] But in the other two passages[12] in which Josephus couples *Σαμαίας* with *Πωλλίων* in the year 37 it is safe to assume that he referred to Abṭalion and Shammai, and the identification of the *Σαμαίας* in 15.1 with the one in 14.9 seems to be an error perpetrated by Josephus.[13]

The Bene Bathyra[14] or *zikne Bathyra*[15] had risen to prominence when Hillel arrived from Babylonia.[16] Their name seems to be derived from the colony which Herod permitted to be established in Batanea by Jews who had come from Babylonia.[17]

Hillel, *ha-zaken*, the Elder, also named 'the Babylonian', because he was descended from a family of Babylonian exiles, a teacher of great prominence, at the same time celebrated for his patience and humanity. His chief activity, it seems, is to be placed in the times of Herod I, and immediately after. E. Renan was the first to suggest that Hillel taught Jesus, but though the opinion has been often repeated by Jews it has no foundation to rest on and is extremely improbable. Neither was Hillel a reformer.[18]

Shammai,[19] sometimes with the epithet *ha-Zaḳen* the Elder.[20] Jerome:[21] Sammai igitur et Hellel non multum priusquam dominus nasceretur orti sunt in Judaea, quorum prior dissipator interpretatur, sequens profanus [!]; eo quod per traditiones et *δευτερώσεις* suas legis praecepta dissipaveri<n>t atque maculaveri<n>t. In all likelihood Jerome misunderstood the saying of Hillel concerning the scattering (*pizzar*, Aram. *baddar*), i. e. spreading of the Torah.[22]

§ 3. First Generation[1] of Tannaim.

A short (historically inaccurate) list of the older teachers is given by Jerome[2]: Sammai et Hellel ex quibus orti sunt Scribae et Pharisaei, quorum suscepit scholam Acibas, quem magistrum Aquilae proselyti autumnant, et post eum Meir, cui successit (?) Joannan filius Zachai, et post eum Eliezier (!) et per ordinem Telphon (*Tarfon*) et rursum Joseph Galilaeus et usque ad captivitatem Jerusalem Josue.

School of Shammai *beth Shammai* and School of Hillel *beth Hillel.* They differ from one another specifically with reference to religious dues, the observance of Sabbath and festivals, laws of marriage and purity, but these differences concern throughout externalities which (for the non-Jew) are trivial. So at the very opening of Ber. 1.3: 'The School of Shammai said: One should recite the Shema' in the evening while lying down and in the morning while standing, for it is written, Deut. 6.7: when thou liest down, and when thou risest up; but the School of Hillel said: One may recite it according to one's convenience (in any condition or posture).' For the most part the Shammaiites incline to rigorous decisions; exceptions Eduy. 4, 5. Repeatedly the Hillelites yielded to the Shammaiites.[3] Very rarely disciples of Shammai are mentioned as such by name: Dosthai of Kephar Jathma[4] and Joezer *'ish ha-birah.*[5] Hananiah ben Hezekiah ben Garon was likewise a Shammaiite;[6] in his chamber the teachers met and decided eighteen questions to suit the Shammaiites.[7]

Akabiah ben Mahalalel.[8]

Rabban[9] Gamaliel I, usually *ha-zaken*, teacher of the apostle Paul.[10] 'When R. G. died, fear of the law ceased and purity and continence died.'[11] G. was probably a son of Hillel.[12]

The Court of the Priests.[13]

The three judges in matters of police and traffic:[14] Admon ben Gaddai, Ḥanan ben Abishalom ('the Egyptian'),[15] Nahum the Mede who witnessed the destruction of the Temple.[16]

Hananiah,[17] the prefect of the priesthood *segan ha-Kohanim*, hence at the time of the second Temple and, since he is given this title regularly, probably the last to hold this office.[18]

Neḥoniah ben Ha-ḳana,[19] teacher of Ishmael, who learned from him his predilection for employing the rule of the Universal and Particular.[20]

Rabban Simeon ben Gamaliel I, at the time of the war with Rome, according to Josephus[21] *ἀνὴρ πλήρης συνέσεώς τε καὶ λογισμοῦ δυνάμενός τε πράγματα κακῶς κείμενα φρονήσει τῇ ἑαυτοῦ διορθώσασθαι.*

R. Zadok[22] had been prominent during the war with Rome, but is also mentioned as associating in Jabneh with Gamaliel II, Eliezer and Joshua.[23] Since he had a grandson of the same name, it is frequently doubtful which of the two Zadoks is meant.[24]

Rabban Joḥanan ben Zaccai,[25] a pupil of Hillel, was active after the destruction of Jerusalem in Jabneh, later also in Berur Ḥail,[26] and like Moses, Hillel and Akiba was 120 years old when he died.[27] Through founding the academy at Jabneh he became of utmost importance for the preservation of Judaism. Aboth 2. 8 f. names as his five disciples: Eliezer ben Hyrcanus, Joshua ben Hananiah, Jose the Priest, Simeon ben Nathanel, Eleazar ben Arak. Many timely regulations are ascribed to him (so e. g. abolition of the water of cursing Num. 5).[28]

R. Eliezer ben Jacob the Elder, from whom we have many statements which deal specifically with the Temple and its equipment.[29] The traditional matter taught by him is pronounced[30] *ḳab wenaḳi*, i. e. small in compass but trustworthy.[31]

R. Ḥanina ben Dosa, a contemporary of Johanan ben Zaccai.[32] A legendary performer of miracles.[33]

Ḥananiah ben Hezekiah ben Garon;[34] Simeon of Mizpah;[35] Measha;[36] Zechariah ben Ḳebuṭal.[37] Hanina[38] ben Antigonus.[39]

Nahum of Gimzo (in south-western Judea), Akiba's teacher. With the epithet *'Ish gam zo*, because in all untoward circumstances he was wont to say, "This also is for the good."[40] He applied the rule of Inclusion and Exclusion, *ribbui* and *mi'ut*.[41]

§4. Second Generation of Tannaim (about 90–130 C.E.).

A. Older Group.

Rabban Gamaliel II, son of Simeon ben G. I, frequently, in contradistinction to his grandfather of the same name, designated as G. of Jabneh, *G. de-Yabneh*; successor to Johanan ben Zaccai; was considered by the Jews ca. 90–110 as highest authority, so much so that when at a certain time he was deposed on account of his overbearing demeanor from his dignity as head of the academy, *yeshibah*, and Eleazar ben Azariah was put into his place, the dignity of Nasi was restored to him so soon as a reconciliation had been effected with the offedded R. Joshua;[1] nevertheless it was arranged that G. delivered discourses on three Sabbaths and Eleazar on one.[2] A voyage by sea to Rome is said to have been undertaken by him in company with Eleazar ben Azariah, Joshua ben Ḥananiah and Akiba in the year 95 C.E.[3] During his time Samuel the Little[4] composed the execration of the *minim* in the Shemone Esre prayer.[5] The report of the church fathers Justin, Epiphanius and Jerome that the Jews pronounced in their daily prayers curses against the Christians, previously disputed, has received manuscript substantiation through a find by S. Schechter in the Geniza of Old Cairo.[6]

R. Papias.[7] Frequently confounded with Pappus ben Judah.[8]

R. Dosa ben Archinus.[9]

R. Eliezer ben Hyrcanus,[10] in the Mishna just R. Eliezer,[11] brother-in-law of Rabban Gamaliel II, frequently in dispute with Joshua ben Hananiah and (or) Akiba. He had his school at Lydda,[12] which then already is mentioned by the Aramaic name *motheba rabba*.[13] He took the lex talionis literally (eye for eye, Ex. 21.24; Lev. 24.19), while Ishmael required compensation.[14]

There is no foundation in the thesis of C. A. Tötterman[15] that Eliezer was drawn to Christianity. Because he would not renounce his opinion, he was put under the ban by the Synedrium of Jabneh.[16]

Joshua ben Hananiah,[17] in the Mishna just R. Joshua,[18] very often in controversy with Eliezer ben Hyrcanus, was active at Peḳiin (Beḳiin).[19]

Jose the Priest, Simeon ben Nathanel and Eleazar ben Arak were, like Eliezer ben H. and Joshua, disciples of Johanan ben Zaccai.[20]

R. Eleazar[21] ben Azariah at Jabneh, a priest of distinction and exceedingly wealthy; for a brief period head of the school in the place of Gamaliel II, then alternately with him.[22]

R. Eleazar[23] ben Zadok,[24] son of the elder Zadok,[25] had a grandson of the same name.[26]

Abba Saul ben Baṭnith (son of the Batanean woman), business associate of Eleazar ben Zadok.[27]

Samuel the Little.[28]

Simeon ha-paḳoli, the dealer in cotton, ordered the Eighteen Benedictions at the time of Gamaliel II.[29]

Ben Paṭuri.[30]

R. Eleazar of Modi'im, at the time of the Hadrianic war.[31]

R. Levitas of Jabneh, probably in pre-Hadrianic times.[32]

B. Younger Group of the Second Generation.

a. R. Ishmael ben Elisha, ordinarily just R. Ishmael, of priestly descent, was as a boy released from captivity in Rome by Joshua ben Hananiah. Pupil of Neḥoniah ben Haḳana. He lived for the most part at Kephar Aziz on the frontiers of Edom.[33] Two of his exegetical teachings were: 'The Torah speaks the language of men'[34] and 'The Torah speaks after the manner of human speech.'[35]

b. R. Akiba ben Joseph, ordinarily just R. Akiba. Up to the age of forty he was ignorant of the Law, *'am ha-'areṣ*,[36] and hostile to scholars; nevertheless he won for himself a name which was illustrious above all others. His school was situated at Bene Beraḳ (Ibn Ibraḳ east of Jaffa); but we find him also at Lydda and at Jabneh. He flourished ca. 110–135. It is well known how he acclaimed Bar Kokeba as the Messiah. It is reported of him by way of praise that he knew how to evolve from each tittle (*ḳoṣ*, *κεραία*) of the written Law mountains of Halakoth.[37] It must be owned, however, that this report, according to which Moses, seated behind the eighth row of Akiba's pupils and listening, was not able to comprehend their discussions, is not without a satirical implication. Akiba's compilation of the Mishna has been spoken of above.[38] He is mentioned in the Mishna, over and above the passage Aboth 3.13–16, more than 270 times. Siphra on Lev. and Siphre on Deut. 12–26, as well as extracts especially communicated in Midrash hagadol and Yalḳuṭ Shim'oni[39], are midrashic works which follow Akiba's system.[40] In addition to the passage on Isai. 8.11[41] Akiba is mentioned by Jerome once more in the Epistle to Algasia c. 10.[42]

c. R. Tarphon, to whom Jerome[43] refers as Telphon,[44] attended in his boyhood the Temple service, but is most frequently named in connection with Akiba. His permanent residence was at Lydda, where there was a large school and where scholars were domiciled as far back as three decades before the destruction of the Temple.[45] T. was hostile to Judeo-Christians.[46]

R. El'ai, pupil of Eliezer ben Hyrcanus, father of Judah (ben E.).[47]

Aquila *'Aḳilas ha-ger*, according to Epiphanius, of Sinope in Pontus, pupil of R. Eliezer and of R. Joshua ben Hananiah, translated under the influence of Akiba the Old Testament into Greek.[48]

R. Johanan ben Tortha, combated Akiba's support of Bar Kokeba.[49]

Pappus ben Judah, also simply Pappus (without the title Rabbi), haggadist.[50]

R. Johanan ben Nuri at Beth She'arim near Sepphoris, in debate specifically with Akiba.[51]

R. Jose Ha-gelili, the Galilean, in debates specifically with Akiba, Tarphon and Eleazar ben Azariah; statements concerning sacrifices and the Temple service.[52]

R. Eleazar *ḥisma*, pupil of Joshua ben Hananiah, together with Johanan ben Nuri supervisor in the school of Rabban Gamaliel II.[53]

R. Johanan ben Beroḳa, pupil of Joshua ben Hananiah.[54]

R. Simeon ben Nannus (*νάννος* dwarf), also simply: Ben Nannus.[55]

R. Jose, son of the woman from Damascus, pupil of Eliezer, haggadist.[56]

R. Hananiah[57] ben Teradion, at Siknin in Galilee, by his daughter Beruriah father-in-law of R. Meir, suffered martyrdom by death through fire soon after Akiba.[58]

R. Jose ben Ḳisma (Ḳosma?).[59]

R. Eleazar ben Peraṭa.[60] To be distinguished from his grandson of the same name.[61]

R. Judah ben Baba, with the cognomen *ḥasid*, well-known as having ordained seven pupils of Akiba soon after his death; he fled and was slain by Roman soldiers.[62]

Simeon ben Azzai, ordinarily simply Ben Azzai.[63] Ben Azzai, Ben Zoma, Elisha ben Abuiah and Akiba went into 'paradise' *pardes*, i. e. immersed themselves into theosophic speculation; but only Akiba emerged without detriment to faith and intellectual faculty.[64]

Simeon ben Zoma, ordinarily simply Ben Zoma.[65]

Elisha ben Abuiah, called by Letteris the 'Faust' of Judaism; repeatedly spoken of as *'aḥer* (he who should not be named); was teacher of R. Meir.[66]

R. Hananiah[67] ben Gamaliel II.[68]

R. Hananiah ben Judah.[69]

R. Simeon ben Tarphon.[70]

R. Eleazar ben Judah of Bartotha,[71] also without naming the father *'El'azar 'ish B.*[72]

R. Simeon of Teman (*ha-Temani*).[73]

d. To this generation are likewise reckoned the older pupils of Akiba, namely:

Hananiah ben Hakinai.[74]

R. Simeon of Shiḳmona.[75]

R. Ḥidḳa.[76]

Outside Palestine taught: Mathiah ben Heresh[77] immediately before the Hadrianic war, in Rome.[78]

R. Judah ben Bathyra,[79] in Palestine with Eliezer ben Hyrcanus; subsequently presided over a school at Nisibis *Neṣibin*, where Johanan the maker of sandals and Eleazar ben Shammua studied Torah under him.[80]

Hananiah, nephew (brother's son) of Joshua ben Hananiah, resided in Babylonia *Nehar Pakud*.[81]

§ 5. Third Generation of Tannaim. (Ca. 130–160 C.E.).

a. School of R. Ishmael.[1] The most prominent pupils of Ishmael were R. Josiah and R. Jonathan.[2] They are very frequently mentioned in Mek. and in Siphre,[3] but not in the Mishna. The reason why these were passed over is to be found in the circumstance that Meir and Rabbi followed the opinions of Akiba in opposition to Ishmael.

Abba Ḥanin (Ḥanan), who is frequently mentioned as deliverer of utterances by Eliezer ben Hyrcanus, seems likewise to have belonged to this circle.[4]

b. The later pupils of Akiba.[5] We may list here eight pupils of whom the first four are those most frequently named:

R. Meir,[6] pupil first of Ishmael, then of Akiba. Elisha ben Abuiah was likewise his teacher. M. resided for the most part in Tiberias or in the neighboring Ḥammetha; husband of Beruriah. The keenest mind of his period,[7] noted also as an haggadist. 'One third of his discourse was Halakah *shema'ta*, another third Haggada *'aggadta*, and a third part parables *mathle*.'[8] His compilation of the Mishna rested on that of Akiba and served as a foundation for that of Judah Ha-nasi.[9] Outside Aboth 3.8; 4.10; 6.1 he is mentioned in the Mishna 330 times,[10] in the Tosephta 452 times.[11]

R. Simeon ben Johai,[12] in the Mishna always simply R. Simeon: Aboth 3.3; 4.13b and approximately 325 times.[13]

R. Jose ben Halaphta, in the Mishna always simply R. Jose: Aboth 4.6 and approximately 330 times, in Sepphoris, a worker in leather; chief authority for the accepted Jewish chronology as fixed in Seder Olam Rabba.[14]

R. Judah ben El'ai (Il'ai).[15] In the Mishna always simply R. Judah (Aboth 4.13a and more than 600 times), on account of his eloquence called *rosh ha-medabberim*.[16]

R. Nehemiah, often in controversy with Judah ben El'ai.[17]

R. Eleazar ben Shammua, in Mishna and Baraitha always simply R. Eleazar, born in Alexandria; he even visited his teacher Akiba in prison in order to be instructed by him.[18]

R. Eliezer[19] ben Jacob (the younger scholar of this name),[20] second half of the second cent.[21]

R. Johanan the maker of sandals *ha-sandlar*, from Alexandria.[22]

c. To the same generation, in post-Hadrianic times, belong:

Eliezer[23] ben R. Jose Ha-gelili, eminent haggadist.[24]

R. Joshua ben Ḳarḥa ('Baldhead,' *ḳarḥa* or *ḳaraḥa*?).[25] [26]

R. Eleazar ben Zadok II, grandson of E. ben Zadok I.[27]

R. Jose ben Yasian, contemporary of Rabban Simeon ben G. II, also simply Ben Yasian;[28] probably the same as *R. Yosi b'Rabbi 'Asi.*[29]

Rabban Simeon II ben Gamaliel II, father of Judah Ha-nasi, transferred at the request of Akiba's pupils the seat of the Synedrium from Jabneh to Usha. His son praises his humility.[30]

R. Ishmael, son of Johanan ben Beroḳa, belonging to the circle of Rabban Simeon ben Gamaliel II.[31]

Abba Saul. His time is determined by the fact that he had a controversy with Judah ben El'ai.[32]

R. Ḥananiah ben Akabiah,[33] probably son of Akabiah ben Mahalalel,[34] highly esteemed by Rab on account of his keen intellect.[35]

R. Hananiah ben Akashiah.[36]

Isi[37] ben Akabiah.[38]

Isi[39] ben Judah, perhaps identical with Isi (Jose) the Babylonian (a pupil of Eleazar ben Shammua)[40] and also with Jose ben Judah of Kephar Ha-babli.[41]

R. Nehorai, contemporary of Jose ben Halaphta, probably a resident of Sepphoris.[42] According to N. Brüll[43] identical with R. Nehemiah; but Bacher[44] is opposed to this identification.

Reuben ben *'Iṣterobeli* or *'Esterobeli.*[45]

Abba Jose ben Dosethai (Dositheus).[46]

§ 6. Fourth Generation of Tannaim.

a. The Contemporaries of Rabbi.

R. Dosethai ben Jannai, handed down utterances by Meir, Jose and Eleazar.[1]

R. Simeon ben Judah of *kefar 'akus.*[2]

Ahai ben Josiah (J. probably a pupil of Ishmael).[3]

R. Jacob, son of a daughter of Elisha ben Abuiah.[4]

Symmachus ben Joseph, Σύμμαχος, halakist, pupil of R. Meir.[5]

R. Isaac, mentioned frequently in Mek. and Siphre.[6]

R. Jose ben Kipper, pupil of Eleazar ben Shammua, repeatedly in the Tosephta.[7]

R. Dosa, who handed down utterances of R. Judah (not identical with Dosa ben Archinus).[8]

R. Dosethai ben Judah, who handed down utterances of Simeon ben Johai.[9]

R. Eleazar b. Simeon (ben Johai).[10]

R. Phineas ben Jair, the ascetic, son-in-law of Simeon ben Johai; he seems to have resided at Lydda.[11]

R. Ishmael ben Jose (ben Halaphta).[12]

R. Eleazar ben Jose (ben Halaphta).[13]

R. Menahem ben Jose (ben Halaphta), also simply: R. Menahem.[14]

Eurydemus ben Jose (ben Halaphta).[14a]

R. Jose ben Judah (ben El'ai), often in controversy with Rabbi.[15]

R. Judah ben Laḳish hands down statements in the name of Simeon ben Gamaliel II, in halakic controversy with Jose ben Judah (ben El'ai).[16]

R. Eleazar ben Judah.[17]

R. Simeon ben Eleazar (ben Shammua?), pupil of Meir, often in debate with Rabbi, frequently in the Tosephta.[18]

R. Jose ben Meshullam, in debate with Simeon ben Eleazar.[19]

R. Nathan, with the epithet Ha-babli, because he had migrated from Babylonia to Palestine in the time of Rabban Simeon ben Gamaliel II. He had held in the latter's academy the respected office of Ab beth din (deputy), Meir serving as Hakam (speaker). At a later period we find him frequently debating with Rabbi. It is possible that the recension of the Mishna tractate Aboth which lies at the base of Aboth deRabbi Nathan proceeded from him.[20]

R. Eleazar[21] ha-ḳappar ('dealer in asphalt'),[22] father of Bar Ḳappara.[23]

Abba Eleazar ben Gamla.[24]

R. Simeon ben Jose ben Laḳonia, brother-in-law of Eleazar ben Simeon, uncle of Jonathan ben Eleazar (ben Simeon) whom he brought up.[25]

R. Simeon ben Menasia, was together with Jose ben Meshullam at the head of an association *'edah ḳedoshah*, whose members spent all their time in the study of the Torah (prayer) and labor.[26]

R. Mana[27] in Acco,[28] not to be confounded with the two Palestinian Amoraim Mani or Mana.[29]

R. Judah ben Tema (time?).[30]

b. R. Judah Hanasi 'the Prince' or 'the Patriarch,' frequently just Rabbi, occasionally Rabbenu[31] or *Rabbenu ha-ḳadosh*;[32] a saint not in the sense of the Catholic church, but on the ground of his strictly moral mode of life;[33] son of Rabban Simeon ben Gamaliel, born, according to Abba bar Kahana, on the day when Akiba died, hence in the year 135 C. E. He spent his boyhood in Usha, where he was instructed by Judah ben El'ai. He studied also Greek and had a liking for this language.[34] Later on he was a pupil of Simeon ben Johai, of Eleazar ben Shammua, of Nathan (whose opinions, however, he subsequently opposed quite frequently), of Jacob ben Ḳorshai;[35] he was also taught by his father. After his father's death he moved his residence and the school to Beth Shearim, likewise in Galilee; during the last seventeen years of his life he resided at Sepphoris. He had great wealth and a very high reputation. He also owned estates east of the Jordan.[36] It is not possible to ascertain just how much historical truth there is in the narratives concerning his friendship with the emperor Antoninus; the emperors that might be thought of are Marcus Aurelius Antoninus (161–180) and Septimius Severus (193–211) who for a time resided in Palestine.—The time of his death is unfortunately uncertain. Rapoport, D. Hoffmann,[37] Is. Halevy[38] and H. Kottek have pronounced in favor of the year 193; the majority of scholars settle upon a date later by almost a quarter of a century, so now D. Hoffmann.[39] In addition to Aboth 2.1 f.; 4.20c; 6.9a, Rabbi is mentioned in the Mishna about thirty times.[40]

§ 7. Fifth Generation of Tannaim.

Semi-Tannaim; younger contemporaries of Rabbi, in part his disciples. They constitute the transition to the period of the Amoraim when Rabbi's Mishna is recognized as the authoritative compilation of traditional law.

Gamaliel III, son of Rabbi, designated by him as his successor in the dignity of Nasi.[1]

R. Ḥiyya, Ḥiyya the Elder (*Rabba*).[2] Ḥ. bar Abba, was born at Kaphri near Sura in Babylonia, came to Palestine at a somewhat advanced age, there he resided at Tiberias and supported himself by trading in silk wares; disciple and friend of Rabbi, uncle of Rab;[3] his part in the Tosephta was discussed above;[4] he also participated in the compilation of the Midrash Siphra on Levit. 'Any Baraitha not edited by R. Hiyya or R. Oshaia is erroneous (untrustworthy).'[5]

Bar Ḳappara,[6] properly R. Eleazar ben R. Eleazar ha-Kappar,[7] also *R. 'E. ha-Ḳappar b'Rabbi*;[8] teacher of Hoshaia and of Joshua ben Levi, had his school at Caesarea.[9]

R. Simeon ben Ḥalaphta, friend of Ḥiyya, resided at *'Eṣ Te'enah* near Sepphoris, repeatedly glorified in legends.[10]

Levi bar Sisi (Sosius?), in the Babyl. Talmud as a rule simply Levi,[11] disciple of Rabbi.[12]

R. Simai, father of Nahum ben Simai.[13]

R. Banna'a[14] or Bannaia ('Builder').[15] His deliverances handed down chiefly by Joḥanan bar Nappaḥa.[16]

R. Jonathan ben Amram, pupil of Rabbi.[17]

R. Jose ben Saul, pupil of Rabbi whose utterances he handed down.[18]

R. Judah ben Naḳosa hands down opinions in the name of R. Jacob.[19]

Rab Huna, the scholarly exilarch, contemporary of Rabbi. His corpse was brought to Palestine.[20]

§ 8. First Generation of Amoraim.

A. Palestine.

R. Hama bar Bisa, father of Hoshaia Rabba.[1]

R. Ephes,[2] of Southern Judea, subsequently the successor of Rabbi as head of the academy in Sepphoris.[3]

R. Ḥanina,[4] came in mature age from Babylonia to Palestine, pupil of Rabbi, successor to R. Ephes in Sepphoris.[5]

R. Jannai, was exceedingly rich, dwelt in Sepphoris, in contradistinction to his grandson of the same name (*R. Yanai Ze'era*) also with the epithet *Saba*, 'the Elder,' pupil of Ḥiyya, teacher of Joḥanan.[6]

Judah a. Hezekiah, the sons of Ḥiyya, came together with their father from Babylonia to Palestine.[7] Judah was a son-in-law of Jannai; Hezekiah was the editor of Mek. deR. Simeon.

R. Jonathan ben Eleazar, usually simply R. Jonathan, belonged to the circle of R. Ḥanina and dwelt likewise in Sepphoris; pupil of Simeon ben Jose ben Laḳonia, teacher of Samuel bar Naḥman.[8]

Bar Pedaiah, or with full name: Judah bar Pedaiah, nephew of Bar Ḳappara, teacher of R. Joshua ben Levi.[9]

R. Hoshaiah;[10] son of Ḥama ben Bisa, in contradistinction to the Amora of the third generation also with the epithet Rabba (*Rabbah* 'the Great or Elder'); pupil of Bar Ḳappara and of R. Ḥiyya, teacher of Joḥanan; resided in Sepphoris, later in Caesarea. Like Ḥiyya a. Bar Ḳappara he compiled Mishnayoth.[11]

Judah II, son of Gamaliel III,[12] the Patriarch, grandson of Rabbi, in friendly relations with Hoshaiah in particular, but also with the school head Joḥanan (bar Nappaḥa).[13]

R. Jose ben Zimra. His daughter was married to a son of Rabbi. Eleazar ben Pedath handed down his haggadic sayings.[14]

R. Simeon ben Jehozadak. His sayings were handed down by Joḥanan.[15]

R. Joshua ben Levi, at Lydda, one of the most eminent Amoraim of Palestine in the first half of the third century, especially noted for his occupation with Haggada; pupil of Bar Ḳappara, of Judah bar Pedaiah and of Phinehas ben Jair; teacher of Simeon ben Pazzi and of Tanhum ben Ḥanilai.[16]

R. Zabdai ben Levi belonged to the circle of Hoshaiah, was on friendly terms with Joshua ben Levi whom he survived and with Rab.[17]

R. Ḥiyya ben Gamda, resided in Palestine and Babylonia, handed down utterances by the last Tannaim Simai and Jose ben Saul.[18]

B. Babylonia.

Rab Shela, had been head of the school at Nehardea when Rab returned from Palestine.[19]

Abba bar Abba, usually named after his famous son, 'Samuel's father,' was also in Palestine where he was on terms of friendship with Levi bar Sisi.[20]

Ze'iri or Ze'ira, the Elder, a Babylonian belonging to the circle of Joḥanan, pupil of R. Ḥanina (bar Ḥama)[21] in whose name he often hands down decisions.[22]

Ḳarna, one of the *dayyane golah*, 'judges of the captivity;'[23] occupied himself in particular with the laws of damages, *Nezikin*.[24]

Mar Uḳba(n) I, probably exilarch about 210–240 C.E. It is recorded that he presided over the court at Kaphri.[25]

Abba Arika (died 247 C.E.) 'the Tall,' on account of his extraordinary stature, properly Abba, ordinarily simply Abba; nephew (son of the sister) of Ḥiyya, followed his uncle to Palestine[26] in order to study with Rabbi. Founder and first principal of the college at Sura on the Euphrates 219 C.E. His high reputation is shown e. g. in the statement[27] *hilketha k'Rab be'isure ben leḳula ben leḥumra*, 'The religious decision in (ritual) prohibitions is according to the opinion of Rab whether on the side of leniency or on that of rigorism.'[28] Of him it is said in several passages *Tanna hu' u-faleg*, 'he is accounted a Tanna and may run counter to an opinion accepted in the Mishna.'[29]

Rabbah bar Ḥana, son of R. Ḥiyya's brother, colleague of his cousin Rab and like the latter a pupil of Rabbi, from whom he received authorization to render religious decisions.[30]

Assi (Issi, Assa), held in high esteem by Rab a. Samuel.[31]

Mar Samuel (died 254), called also *Shemu'el Yarḥena'ah* 'the Astronomer' and 'Arioch the Great'),[32] son of Abba bar Abba; director of the college at Nehardea. His is the often cited statement *dina demalkutha dina*, 'the law of the government (even of the non-Jewish) is in full force.'[33] Rab Huna succeeded him in Nehardea after an intermission of five years due to political disturbances.[34]

§ 9. Second generation of Amoraim.

A. Palestine.

R. Joḥanan bar Nappaḥa (*nappaḥa* the Smith), usually simply R. Joḥanan. His teachers were in particular Jannai, Hoshaiah a. Ḥanina ben Ḥama; among his colleagues Simeon ben Laḳish is most eminent. A contemporary of his was also Rab Judah bar Ezekiel.[1] Joḥ. taught at first in Sepphoris, where he was also born, subsequently in Tiberias. According to a report communicated by Sherira (*'omrin* they say) he presided over the college for eighty years. On account of *melek*, this number cannot refer to the duration of his life; his activity in Tiberias cannot have been that long but will have covered fifty to sixty years. Is this number faulty or are we to count in the time when he taught at Sepphoris? According to Sherira (who, however, was less well informed about Palestine than he was about Babylonia) Joḥ. died in the year 590 Sel. = 279 C.E. Halevy has endeavored to show that Joḥ. who certainly must have reached a high old age was born between 175 and 180 C.E. and died about 290.[2]

R. Simeon ben Laḳish, usually called Resh Laḳish, was married to Joḥanan's sister and like him resided in Tiberias; but he predeceased him.[3]

R. Ḥilpha,[4] youthful colleague of Joḥanan.[5]

R. Isaac ben Eleazar, usually *I. ben Ḥaḳula*, contemporary of R. Joshua ben Levi and of R. Joḥanan.[6] He delivered a eulogy at Johanan's funeral.[7]

R. Alexander[8] handed down sayings by Joshua ben Levi and should accordingly not be reckoned to the first generation of Amoraim.[9]

Rab Kahana, in the Palest. Talmud invariably minus the title, was a pupil of Rab, moved from Babylonia to Palestine where he belonged to the circle of Johanan and Simeon ben Laḳish. The collection of homilies which usually goes by the name of Pesiḳtha deRab Kahana[10] dates from a later period; it was ascribed to Rab Kahana solely for the reason that the first of its Haphṭarah pericopes (Jer. 1.1) begins with a saying by R. Abba bar Kahana (faultily contracted to Rab K.).[11] Not fewer than six Babylonian Amoraim were named Rab Kahana and three of them came to Palestine.[12]

R. Ḥiyya bar Joseph likewise wandered from Babylonia to Palestine and became there a pupil of Joḥanan; he is frequently mentioned in debate with him.[13]

R. Jose ben Ḥanina,[14] older pupil of Joḥanan's; controversies between the two are extant. His most prominent pupil was Abbahu.[15]

R. Ḥama bar Ḥanina, son of Ḥanina bar Ḥama at Sepphoris.[16]

R. Measha, grandson of Joshua b. Levi.[17]

R. Simlai (Samlai), son of Abba, hailed from Nehardea, then resided at Lydda,[18] later on in Galilee in attendance upon Jannai at Sepphoris; his sayings were handed down by R. Tanḥum bar Ḥiyya.[19]

R. Ḥanina, father of Aḥa b. Ḥanina.[20]

R. Jonathan of Beth Gubrin (Eleutheropolis), hands down a saying by Joshua ben Levi.[21]

Mani I, also *Mana* bar Tanḥum, Joḥanan's contemporary.[22]

Reuben, eminent haggadist, contemporary of Mani I, delivers sayings by Ḥanina bar Ḥama.[23] His traditionaries were Bebai[24] and Phinehas.[25]

R. Abba (or *Ba*) bar Zabdai (or *Zabda*), for a short time also in Babylonia, survived Rab Huna of Sura, and was still among the circle of Ammi and Asi in Tiberias.[26]

R. Tanhum ben Ḥanilai,[27] traditionary of Joshua ben Levi, belongs in part to the third generation.[28]

B. Babylonia.

Rab Huna (died 297 C.E.), Rab's successor in the principalship of the college at Sura; in point of fact also Samuel's successor, since after the death of the latter, on account of political disturbances, no college principal was appointed at Nehardea for some time.[29]

Rab Judah bar Ezekiel (died 299), usually simply Rab Judah, pupil of Rab, founder of the college at Pum Beditha, after Rab Huna's death for two years the most eminent college head in Babylonia. He is reckoned among those who guarded the study of the Torah from oblivion.[30] It is unknown why the epithet *shinena*[31] was applied to him. According to Hai the meaning is: 'large-toothed;' Bacher would have it refer to his iron perseverance; others to his keen intellect. He taught the tractate Neziḳin with especial thoroughness. His large stature is also spoken of.[32]

Epha a. Abimi, the 'keen intellects' *ḥarifin* of Pum Beditha.[33]

Mar Uḳba(n) II, exilarch like his grandfather Mar U. I, through his mother grandson of Rab, handed down sayings by Samuel.[34]

Giddel, younger pupil of Rab, in whose name he handed down many sayings.[35]

Rab Ḳaṭṭina (Ḳeṭina?) a. Geniba, both in Sura, likewise pupils of Rab.[36]

Rab Adda (Ada) bar Ahaba, at Sura, was supposedly born on the day when Rabbi died and died on the day that Abin the Elder was born;[37] pupil of Rab, famous for his long life and piety.[38]

Rabbah bar Abuha, at Maḥuza, father-in-law of Rab Naḥman.[39]

Rab Matthena, pupil of Samuel, then probably of Rab Judah.[40]

Rab Jeremiah bar Abba,[41] older pupil of Rab, for a time in Palestine.[42]

§ 10. Third Generation of Amoraim.

A. Palestine.

R. Samuel bar Naḥman,[1] pupil of Jonathan ben Eleazar; eminent haggadist; was active in Tiberias. He was born in Palestine, but was twice in Babylonia: once for a longer period in his youth, later on on an official mission for the purpose of enacting intercalation in Babylonia. His principal pupil and traditionary was Ḥelbo.[2]

R. Isaac II, in the Babyl. Talmud frequently with the epithet *nappaḥa* 'the Smith,' pupil of Joḥanan, was active partly at Tiberias, partly (probably at a subsequent time) in Caesarea; for some time also in Babylonia where he consorted in particular with Naḥman bar Jacob. One of the most prolific haggadists (frequently in debate with Levi), but prominent also as an halakist.[3]

R. Levi, pupil of Johanan, friend of Abba bar Kahana, father-in-law of Zechariah; his principal traditionary is Joshua of Siknin; frequently named as haggadist.[4]

R. Eleazar ben Pedath, usually without naming the father;[5] by birth a Babylonian, was instructed in his native country by Rab and Samuel and in Palestine by Joḥanan; for three years and a half he acted as the substitute of the latter in the principalship of the school at Tiberias, but the two died in the same year. His principal traditionaries are Abbahu and Benjamin ben Japheth.[6]

R. Abbahu,[7] one of the later pupils of Joḥanan, a pupil also of Jose ben Ḥanina, principal of the school in Caesarea. He was a student of the Greek language and culture; engaged in disputations with Christians.[8]

R. Ammi (ben Nathan),[9] pupil of Joḥanan a. Hoshaiah. Highly reputed teacher at Tiberias. Very frequently mentioned with Asi and Ḥiyya II; they were contemporaries of the emperor Diocletian.[10]

R. Asi,[11] emigrated from Babylonia; there he was taught by Samuel; subsequently in Palestine by Joḥanan.[12]

R. Judah III, the Patriarch,[13] son of the inconsequential Gamaliel IV, pupil of Joḥanan. He commissioned Ammi and Asi to erect schools for children. In his time the emperor Diocletian visited Palestine.[14]

R. Ḥiyya II, bar Abba, probably a brother of Simeon bar Abba, emigrated in his youth from Babylonia to Palestine where he was taught by Joḥanan.[15]

Simeon bar Abba,[16] emigrated from Babylonia to Palestine, probably a brother of Ḥiyya II, son-in-law of Samuel at Nehardea, was taught by Ḥanina and especially by Joḥanan.[17]

R. Simeon,[18] or, as he was called in Babylonia, R. Simeon ben Pazzi, pupil and traditionary of Joshua ben Levi, resided in southern Palestine, frequently in debate with Ḥanina ben Papa, teacher of Tanḥum ben Ḥiyya a. Hilkiah who frequently handed down sayings in his name.[19]

R. Ze'ira (Ze'era) I, a Babylonian, pupil of Rab Judah bar Ezekiel, against whose wishes he betook himself to Palestine. There he entered into close relations with Ammi, Asi a. Abahu. As Ze'ira's pupils are considered especially Jeremiah, Abba b. Zebina a. Haggai.[20] He had no predilection for the Haggada:

'The Haggada may be turned hither and thither, and we learn nothing (for practice) therefrom.'[21]

R. Abba II, a Babylonian, pupil of Rab Huna and of Rab Judah, was repeatedly in Palestine and at last settled permanently, at first in Caesarea (consorting with Abbahu) and then in Tiberias (consorted with Ammi a. Asi).[22]

R. Samuel bar R. Isaac, pupil of Ḥiyya II bar Abba, father-in-law of Hoshaiah II, was for a time also in Babylonia among the circle of Rab Huna; his most prominent pupil and traditionary is Jeremiah.[23]

R. Hela,[24] by the side of Ze'ira I the most prominent scholar at the beginning of the fourth Christian century at Tiberias; the former called him *banyah de'oraitha* 'builder of the Torah,' i. e. a great scholar.[25] He was a teacher of Abin I, Jonah a. Jose.[26]

R. Zeriḳa,[27] pupil of Eleazar ben Pedath and of Ammi; consorted with Jeremiah a. Judah bar Simon.[28]

Hoshaiah (II) a. Hananiah, brothers, who hailed from Babylonia, and, because they were not ordained, designated as *ḥabrehon derabbanan* 'companion to scholars;' pupils of Joḥanan at Tiberias, where they sustained themselves meagerly as shoemakers, both glorified by posterity in legends. Hoshaiah married a daughter of Samuel bar Isaac.[29]

R. Jannai, son of Ishmael.[30]

R. Judan bar Ishmael, perhaps a brother of Jannai.[31]

R. Josiah, pupil of Joḥanan a. of Rab Kahana; in order to distinguish him from the Amora of the same name at Huṣal who belonged to the second generation, he is frequently designated as 'the contemporary of Eleazar (ben Pedath).'[32]

R. Abba bar Mèmel,[33] distinguished halakist; consorted with Ze'ira I, Samuel b. Isaac a. Jeremiah; Jose bar Abin hands down sayings in his name.[34]

R. Jacob bar Idi, pupil of Joḥanan.[35]

R. Isaac bar Naḥman, pupil of Joshua ben Levi.[36]

R. Bebai,[37] pupil of Abbahu, to be distinguished from the nearly contemporaneous Babylonian Amora.[38]

R. Abba bar Kahana, pupil of Joḥanan, eminent haggadist; his principal traditionary is Berechiah.[39]

R. Ḥanina b. Pappai,[40] pupil of Samuel b. Naḥman, debates frequently with Simon b. Pazzi, was active by the side of Abbahu at Caesarea, temporarily also in Babylonia, largely glorified in legends.[41]

R. Benjamin ben Levi, essentially haggadist. Traditionaries: Judan[42] a. Huna.[43]

R. Aḥa b. Ḥanina had controversies with Ḥanina b. Pappai, handed down sayings e. g. of Joḥanan a. Joshua ben Levi, resided for some time also in Babylonia.[44]

Tanḥum bar Ḥiyya of Kephar Acco, resided at Tiberias, pupil of Simon ben Pazzi,[45] consorted with Assi a. Ḥanina b. Pappai.[46]

R. Abba of Acco became noted for his modesty.[47]

B. Babylonia.

Rab Huna b. Ḥiyya, successor to R. Judah b. Ezekiel at Pum Beditha, 299–309.[48]

Rab Ḥisda (died 309 C.E.), pupil a. friend of Rab Huna, after the death of Rab Judah for ten years head of the school at Sura, preeminently an haggadist, noted for his keen discussions *pilpule d'Rab Ḥisda*.[49]

Rab Hamnuna.[50]

Rabbah bar Rab Huna (died 322), after the death of Ḥisda for thirteen years head of the school at Sura.[51]

Rab Isaac bar Abdimi.[52]

Rab Nahman bar Ḥisda.[53]

Rab Shesheth, pupil of Samuel, hence at first in Nehardea, then in Maḥuza, founded a school at Shilhi. By memory he commanded a comprehensive knowledge of the traditional material.[54]

Rami (R. Ammi) bar Abba, by the side of R. Eleazar ben Pedath a. R. Ḥiyya II.[55] A number of haggadic sayings by him are cited.[56]

Rab Naḥman bar Jacob (died 329), usually simply Rab Naḥman, pupil of Samuel, with whom his father had the position of a court scribe.[57] N. married a daughter of Rabba b. Abuha at Maḥuza and was a celebrated guest with the Palestinian Isaac II.[58] In Naḥman's house Masoretic studies were largely cultivated.[59]

Rabbah[60] bar bar Ḥana,[61] was for some time in Palestine, subsequently at Pum Beditha a. at Sura. R. has become particularly known by his fantastic accounts of his sea voyages etc., which partake of the nature of Münchhausenian adventures.[62]

Ulla bar Ishmael,[63] emigrated from Palestine to Babylonia, but repeatedly returned to visit his native country.[64]

Rabba(h) bar Naḥmani, also simply Rabba(h), died 339, successor to Rab Huna bar Ḥiyya as director of the school at Pum Beditha, was probably at no time in Palestine. Because of his keen dialectics he was spoken of as '*oḳer harim* 'uprooter of mountains!' In a question relating to leprosy he decides between God a. the *Yeshiba shel ma'alah*, the upper (celestial) college.[65]

R. Raḥba of Pum Beditha, traditionary of his teacher Judah bar Ezekiel.[66]

Rab Joseph (bar Ḥiyya), died 333, honored for the reason of his comprehensive knowledge of traditional lore with the epithet Sinai; after the death of Rabba(h) for two years and a half head of the school at Pum Beditha. The edition of the Targum on the Prophets is attributed to him.[67]

§ 11. Fourth Generation of Amoraim.

A. Palestine.

R. Jeremiah, a Babylonian by nativity, pupil of Ze'ira I, after whose death he became the recognized authority of the school at Tiberias, handed down sayings by Ḥiyya II bar Abba; teacher of Hezekiah, Jonah, Jose a. Ze'ira II.[1]

R. Haggai, likewise pupil of Ze'ira, prominent member of the school at Tiberias, father of Jonathan, traditionary of Isaac II.[2]

R. Ḥelbo, pupil of Samuel bar Naḥman, closely associated with Ammi, temporarily in Babylonia in the school of Rab Huna; Berechiah was his pupil.[3]

R. Aḥa of Lydda, later at Tiberias, pupil of Jose b. Ḥanina a. of Tanḥum b. Ḥiyya, teacher of Huna b. Abin. He was a recognized authority in the field of Halakah, much more so as haggadist.[4]

R. Abin I[5] or, by abbreviation, Rabin,[6] hailed from Babylonia, where he also resided subsequently for some time. Friend of Abaye (died 338). His teachers: Asi a. Hela. Traditionaries: Judan, Huna, Phinehas (b. Ḥama) a. Berechiah. In many passages it is impossible to hold him apart from his son who bore the same name and who was born on the day he died.[7]

R. Samuel b. Ammi. Haggadic sayings of his are extant.[8]

R. Ḥanina b. Isaac, haggadist. Traditionaries: Joshua b. Nehemiah a. Huna.[9]

R. Ḥanina b. Aḥa, prob. son of Aḥa b. Ḥanina.[10]

R. Ḥanin (Ḥanan) of Sepphoris, traditionary of Samuel b. Naḥman. His traditionary is Phinehas.[11]

R. Judan, frequently traditionary to former authorities, pupil of Abba II (R. Ba) a. teacher of Mana II.[12]

R. Huna,[13] with full name R. Huna b. Abin, pupil a. traditionary of Jeremiah a. of Aḥa, by the side of Jose an authority of the school at Tiberias, resided for a time in Babylonia, frequently in haggadic debates with Judan. His principal pupil was Tanḥuma bar Abba.[14]

R. Ḥasdai.[15]

R. Judah bar Simon, also: son of S. b. Pazzi,[16] of Lydda; pupil of his father Simon b. Pazzi a. of Ze'ira, debates esp. with Aibo.[17]

R. Aibo, in debate with Judah bar Simon.[18]

R. Joshua b. Nehemiah, exclusively haggadist, occurs almost only in midrashic literature.[19]

R. Ḥanina b. Abbahu, son of the head of the school at Tiberias.[20]

R. Ahaba (Aḥawa) ben Ze'ira, son of Ze'ira I at Caesarea, where Mani II attended his lectures; specifically an haggadist.[21]

R. Dimo or Abudimi,[22] the 'voyager to Babylonia' who delivered at Pum Beditha, esp. in the presence of Abaye, Palestinian statements of law and traditions.[23]

Hillel II, patriarch 330–365, son of the patriarch Judah III, is named just twice in connection with Halakoth.[24] He is credited with having reduced the Jewish calendar to system.[25]

B. Babylonia.

Abaye, lived approximately 280–338/39 C.E., son of Kailil who was a brother of Rabba(h) bar Naḥmani. He was taught by this Rabba(h) and in particular by Joseph; then he succeeded the latter and served for five years as head of the school at Pum Beditha.[26]

Raba, 299–352, with full name Raba bar Joseph bar Ḥama, pupil of Rab Naḥman (bar Jacob) a. of Rab Joseph; head of a school at Maḥuza on the Tigris. With Abaye a. Raba talmudic dialectics reached its highest point; much space is given in the Talmud to their debates (*hawayoth de Abaye we-Raba*, keen discussions which penetrate into the smallest detail).[27] Except in six instances, the Halakah has decided in favor of Raba against Abaye.[28]

In order to guard against confusion, the name of the son of Naḥmani is written Rabbah with h and sounded Rabba or Rabbah (with dagesh), while that of bar Joseph is written Rabba (with Alef at the end) and sounded Raba (Beth without dagesh).

R. Adda II bar Ahaba, contemporary a. pupil of Abaye a. Raba.[29]

Rab Naḥman bar Isaac, died 356, was together with Raba pupil of Naḥman bar Jacob. After the death of Raba he was head of the school at Pum Beditha, whither the school of Maḥuza had been removed. Since Rab Naḥman bar Isaac is also spoken of as Rab Naḥman for short, it is at times difficult to keep him apart from his teacher N. bar Jacob.[30]

R. Rami bar Ḥama, son-in-law a. pupil of Ḥisda, died about 350.[31]

R. Idi bar Abin I, pupil of Ḥisda, about 350, at Naresh, subsequently at *Shekanṣib*.[32]

R. Joseph bar Ḥama at Maḥuza, pupil of R. Shesheth.[33]

Rabbah bar Mari, a Babylonian who intermittently resided in Palestine.[34]

R. Aḥa bar Jacob in Paphunia.[35]

R. Abba bar Ulla, often for short *Rabba 'Ulla*.[36]

Rabba bar Shela.[37]

§ 12. Fifth Generation of Amoraim.

A. Palestine.

R. Jonah, pupil of Jeremiah a. Hela. Jonah a. Jose II were ca. 350 C.E. heads of the college at Tiberias. In the times of

Ursicinus (U. since 351 general of Gallus who was general of Constantius and his co-emperor in the Orient).[1]

R. Jose II bar Zabda, similarly pupil of Hela.[2]

Judah IV, the Patriarch, approximately 385–400, son of Gamaliel V, grandson of Hillel II. With his son Gamaliel VI the patriarchate in Palestine ceased to exist.

R. Phinehas (with full name: Phinehas b. Ḥama), pupil of Jeremiah, belonged to the circle of Jose and was a contemporary of the patriarch Judah IV.[3]

R. Hezekiah, pupil of Jeremiah, head of the school at Caesarea.[4]

R. Berechiah (in the Midrashim frequently: B. Ha-kohen), pupil of Ḥelbo, frequently mentioned as traditionary.[5]

R. Jose bar Abin (Abun), also Jose be R. Bun, the last of prominent halakists in Palestine, teacher of Abin II.[6]

Samuel b. R. Jose be R. Bun (or: b. Jose b. Abin).[7]

R. Abin II, born on the day his father Abin I[8] died, in the 3d and 4th Order of the Palest. Talm. very frequently by the side of Mani II, frequently in the Tanḥuma Midrashim.[9]

R. Mani II, *Mana*, also *Muna*,[10] son of Jonah, pupil of Jose II, Hezekiah a. Judan; resided and taught mainly at Sepphoris. His pupil was the haggadist Azariah, his chief traditionary Naḥman. Very frequently in the Palest. Talm.[11]

R. Hananiah[12] II, of Sepphoris, frequently in conjunction with Mani, in whose favor he declined the dignity of head of the school.[13]

R. Judah ben Shalom, in the Palest. Talm. uniformly Judan.[14]

R. Jonah of Bozrah, *R. Yonah Boṣraya.*[15]

R. Tanhuma (Tanhum) bar Abba, more exactly Berabbi Abba, pupil of Huna, made a beginning with a systematic compilation of the Haggada and its fixation in literary form; it seems plausible that his collections of Midrashim, which are not extant, have served as the basic element in the Pesiḳtha deRab Kahana, the Pesiḳtha Rabbathi a. the Tanḥuma (Yelammedenu) Midrashim. He concludes the series of the more prominent Palestinian haggadists. A noteworthy saying of his: 'When a non-Jew, goi, salutes thee, answer: Amen.'[16]

R. Naḥman, pupil a. traditionary of Mani II.[17]

R. Azariah, pupil of Mani II, hands down sayings of Judah bar Simon.[18]

Ulla II, several times in the Palest. Talm. (does not occur in the Babyl. Talm.), a younger contemporary of Raba. Subsequently he removed from Palestine to Babylonia.[19]

Ze'ira II, pupil of Jeremiah, belonged to the circle of Mani.[20]

B. Babylonia.

Rab Papa bar Ḥanan, died 375 C.E., pupil of Abaye a. Raba, founder of the school at Naresh near Sura. Is fond of citing proverbs in the mouth of the common people (*'Amri 'inshe*).[21]

Rab Huna, son of Rab Joshua *Rab Huna breh d'Rab Yehoshu'a*, like Papa a pupil of Raba, erudite and wealthy.[22]

R. Bebai bar Abaye.[23]

R. Ḥama at Nehardea,[24] after Rab Naḥman bar Isaac head of the school at Pum Beditha for twenty-one years (356–377).[25]

R. Papi, pupil of Raba, teacher of Ashi, at Maḥuza.[26]

Dimi of Nehardea, head of the school at Pum Beditha (385–388 C.E.).[27]

Raphram I ben Papa at Pum Beditha, pupil of Rab Ḥisda,[28] successor to Dimi.[29]

Rab Zebid, also named Z. of Nehardea, master in Pum Beditha 377–385.[30]

§ 13. Sixth Generation of Amoraim: Babylonia.

Amemar, teacher of Ashi, restores the school at Nehardea and is its head for a considerable time.[1]

Rab Kahana at Pum Nahara (close by Nehardea), pupil of Papa a. of Huna b. Joshua, teacher of Ashi.[2]

Rabina I, died ca. 420, pupil of Raba, in friendly relations with Rab Naḥman bar Isaac; colleague of Rab Aḥa bar Raba, later of Rab Ashi.[3]

Huna bar Nathan, pupil of Papa, mentioned several times by Ashi, was, as Sherira reports, exilarch.[4]

Rab Ashi, died 427, also with the honorific title *Rabbana Ashi*;[5] for fifty-two years head of the school at Sura, where in the Kalla months Adar a. Elul (in each month a tractate) he went through the whole of the Talmud and a great part of it twice.[6]

Rab Kahana, head of the school at Pum Beditha, died 414.

Rab Aḥa bar Raba, *Rab 'Aḥa breh d'Raba*, son of Raba bar Joseph,[7] died 419, as the last head of the school at Pum Beditha, debates frequently with Rabina I.[8]

Mar Zuṭra, friend of Ashi, died 417.[9]

Mar bar Rabina.[10]

§ 14. Seventh Generation of Amoraim: Babylonia.

The following were heads of the school at Sura:

Meremar or Rab Yemar, Ashi's successor 417–432.[1]

R. Idi bar Abin II, pupil of Papa 432–452.[2]

Rab Naḥman bar Rab Huna 452–455.

Mar bar Rab Ashi (Ṭabyomi) 455–468.[3]

Rabba Tosphaa 468–470.[4]

Rabina (Rab Abina) II bar Huna, 470–499, nephew of Rabina I.[5]

The following at Pum Beditha:

Rab Gebiha of Kathil 419–433.[6]

Rab Raphram II 433–443.[7]

Rab Riḥumai (Niḥumai) 433–449.[8]

Rab Sama son of Raba, *Sama breh d'Raba* 449–476.

Rab Jose.[9] Jose a. Rabina II are designated by Sherira as *Sof Hora'ah*, the last Amoraim.

§ 15. The Saboraim.[1]

Sabora'e, those judging on the ground of reflection, plural of *Sabora*. *Sebar* to reflect; noun *sebâr*, *sebârâ* result of reflection.[2]

Sherira[3] names the following Saboraim, who belong in part to the second half of the fifth century, but otherwise to the first half of the sixth:

A. Older circle of Saboraim:

Sama bar Judah, died 594.

Rab Aḥai bar Rab Huna, died 506. In another version[4] with the addition *mibbe Ḥathim* of Be Ḥathim.[5]

Rab Riḥumai (var.: Niḥumai), died 506.

Rab Samuel bar R. Abbahu of Pum Beditha, died 506.[6]

Rabina of Amuṣia,[7] died 510.

Rab Aḥa, son of (Rabba bar) Abuha, died 510.

Rab Taḥna[8] a. Mar Zuṭra, sons of Rab Ḥinena, died 515.

Rabba Joseph (var.: Rab Jose), head of the school at Pum Beditha, died 520.[9]

B. Younger circle of Saboraim:

Rab Ena at Sura (var.: Giza).[10]

Rab Simona at Pum Beditha.

Rabbai of Rob, *Rabbai me-Rob*, at Pum Beditha. Some would count him as Gaon.[11] In that case the period of the Saboraim would close with Rab Simona in 540.

Simona a. Rabbai might be counted as the first of the Geonim.[12] According to the ordinary conception, the first Gaons were, in Sura: Mar bar Rab Ḥanan of Isḳiya, since 589; in Pum Beditha: Rab Mar ben Rab Huna, since 609. End of the Gaonate: Samuel Ha-kohen b. Ḥophni in Sura, died 1034, Rab Hai in Pum Beditha, died 1038. The title Gaon was applied in still later times to the heads of the schools in Palestine and then in Egypt.[13]

CHAPTER XIV

Literature

§ 1. Introductions.

1. A survey of the "Introductions to the Talmud" was given by J. H. Weiss in *Beth Talmud*, I (Vienna, 1881), 26–31, 53–60, 85–89, 115–112, 153–159, 181–184; II (1882), 1–8.

J. Hamburger, *Real-Encyclopädie für Bibel u. Talmud*, II: the Talmudic articles A-Z. Strelitz 1883 (1331 pp.); Supplementary volume I, Leipzig 1886 (158). [Very many misprints. The author had practically no knowledge of the works of Christian scholars].

The booklet Seder Tannaim Va'amoraim, composed during the Gaonic period, may be considered as the oldest attempt at an introduction to the study of the Talmud. The first or chronological part deals with the succession of the teachers of the Law; the second or Halakic part shows how the Halaka may be derived from the Mishna and Gemara (see above page 89) and how certain terms are to be explained.—It was published by S. D. Luzzatto in Kerem Ḥemed IV, 184–200; Salomon Taussig, *Neweh Shalom*, I (Munich, 1872); H. Grätz (see immediately under Joseph Ibn Aḳnin). M. Grosberg, *Seder 'Olam Zutta 'im Seder T. we 'A. ha-shalem*, London 1910 (16 and 112). Al. Marx, 'Neue Texte des S. T. V.' in *Lewy-Festschr.* 392–399 and Hebrew, 155–172. The Halakic part was published by H. J. D. Azulai, Shem ha-gedolim, and by Filipowski in '*Sepher Yuḥasin*,' London, 1857, 251–253; in German translation by D. O. Straschun, *Der Tractat Taanit . . . ins Deutsche übertragen* (Halle, 1883), Introduction, pp. 11–19. Compare in addition J. Brüll in *Jahrbücher*, IV, 43–45: M. Steinschneider, *Geschichtsliteratur der Juden*, I (1905), § 11.

Concerning Samuel ben Ḥophni's Arabic introduction which was made use of by Samuel Ha-nagid compare A. E. Cowley in *Harkavy-Festschrift*, Hebrew, 161–163; A. Marx, *JQR*, N. S., I, 435 f.

Samuel Ha-nagid (Ibn Nagdila; not Ibn Nagrela, comp. *HBg* III, 89; XIII, 123), in Granada, died 1055. The *Mebo ha-Talmud*, incorporated in *Halikoth Olam* of Jeshua Ha-levi and in the more recent Talmud editions (in Pinner, *Berachoth*, Introduction, fol. 12a–17a), is only a part (consisting mostly of explanations of various terms) of a larger work. Regarding two fuller manuscripts (New York and Rome) see *ZHBg* IX, 140.

Moses ben Maimon (1135–1204) placed at the head of his Commentary on the Mishna an Introduction to the Talmud, specifically to the Mishna, which is usually referred to as a Preface to the Order Zera'im. The Arabic original was published by Edw. Pococke, *Porta Mosis*, Oxford, 1655. B. Hamburger, *Maimonides, Einl. in die Mišna, Arabischer Text mit umgearbeiteter hebr. Übersetzung des (Jehuda) Charizi und Anmm.*, F. o. M, 1902 (17 and 73). Comp. also Pinner, *Berachoth*, Introduction, fol. 1b and 12a.

Joseph (ben Judah) ibn Aḳnin, subsequently favorite pupil of Maimonides, wrote in the Arabic language an introduction to the Talmud, which, together with the *Seder Tann. Va'am.*, was published (by H. Grätz) in the *Jubelschrift für Z. Frankel*, Breslau 1871 (18 and 37), Comp. *HBg*, XIII, 38–43; M. Steinschneider, *Die Hebr. Übersetzungen des Mittelalters*, Berlin 1893, 920. The surname Ibn Aḳnin is questionable; comp. S. Eppenstein in the collective work *Moses ben Maimon*, II (Leipzig, 1914), 58–60.

Samson (ben Isaac) of Chinon in France, beginning of the fourteenth century: *Sepher Kerithuth* (Book of the Making of the Covenant, comp. *ZDMG*, 1909, 208), Constantinople, 1515; Cremona, 1558; Verona, 1647; Warsaw, 1884. On the 32 Middoth see above chapter XI, § 4.

Isaac (ben Jacob) Ḳanpanṭon died 1643, *Darke ha-talmud* (published for the first time Constantinople about 1520); Venice 1565 etc.; lastly edited by J. H. Weiss, Vienna, 1891 (20).

Jeshua Ha-Levi, of Tlemcen, wrote about 1467 in Toledo his *Halikoth 'Olam*. First editions: Lisbon (?) about 1490 and Constantinople 1510. With an unsatisfactory Latin translation by Constantin L'Empereur, under the title *Clavis Talmudica*, Leiden, 1634 (printed again by Bashuysen 1714).—Commentaries: by Joseph Ḳaro (died 1575): *Kelale ha-talmud* in the editions Saloniki 1598, Venice 1639, Leghorn, 1792, and by Solomon Algazi (seventeenth century): *Yabin Shemuah* in the Venice and Leghorn editions.

Beṣalel Askenazi, sixteenth century, in Egypt. His *Kelale ha-talmud* contain methodological notes by the most eminent commentators on the Talmud. Published from an incomplete Ms. in the Library of the Jewish Theological Seminary of America in the Hoffmann-Festschrift, 369–382 and Hebrew part 179–217 and reprinted Berlin 1914.

Solomon (ben Eliakim) Finzi (not: Panzi, see Cat. Bodl. No. 6914), of Rovigo (sixteenth century): *Maphteaḥ ha-gemara*, first published in the collective work *Tummath Yesharim*, Venice 1622; with a Latin translation by Ch. H. Ritmeier; *Clavis Gemarae*, Helmst. 1697, 4to, afterwards by Bashuysen 1714.

Moses Ben Daniel of Rohatin in Galicia: *Sugiyyoth ha-talmud*, Zolkiew 1693; in Bashuysen's *Clavis Talmudica Maxima* (containing: Jeshua's *Halikoth Olam*, *Mebo ha-gemara* by Samuel Ha-nagid, *Maphteaḥ ha-gemara* by S. Finzi and the *Sugiyyoth ha-talmud*, all with a Latin translation; in addition several treatises by B.), Hanau 1714, 4to (140 and 552).

Jacob ben Samuel Ḥagiz (died 1674) in the introduction to his Mishna commentary, Eṣ Ḥayyim (Leghorn 1653 f., Berlin 1716 f.). Comp. also Teḥillath Ḥokmah, Verona 1647, Amsterdam 1709.

Malachi Cohen (second half of the eighteenth century) *Yad Mal'aki*, Leghorn 1767, 4to; Berlin 1852; Przemysl, 1888.

Hezekiah Abulafia, *Sepher Ben Zeḳunim*. Leghorn 1793. The first part, *Yesod Olam*, is methodological.

Ṣebi (Hirsch ben Meir) Ḥayyoth (Cat. Brit. Mus. and Cat. Ros.: Ḥayas; the successors write their name Chajes), *Mebo ha-talmud* Zolkiew 1845, 4to (28 leaves).

Ḥayyim Bloch, Mebo ha-talmud, Berlin 1853 (76),

J. S. Zuri-Schesak, *Toldoth ha-deromim beyaḥasehem 'el ha-gelilim*, I, Paris 1914 (150); *Geschichte der Methodologie in den Hochschulen Judäas, Galiläas, Suras, und Nehardäas*, I, Jerusalem 1914 (160). These publications (the second likewise is written in Hebrew) is known to me only from *JQR*, N. S. VII, 422–424.

The publications named thus far, insofar as they do not contain a chronological part corresponding to that of Seder Tannaim, are mostly of a methodological character (in Maimonides and Joseph ibn Aḳnin also other matters).

2. Introductory literature in the narrower sense of the word:

a. To the Mishna: Z. Frankel, *Darke ha-mishnah, Hodegetica in Mischnam librosque cum ea conjunctos.* Pars prima [more did not appear]: Introductio in Mischnam. Leipzig 1859 (342).

With it goes: *Hosaphoth u-maphteaḥ lesefer Darke ha-mishna, Additamenta et Index ad librum H. in M.*, Leipzig 1867 (68). In support of the traditional point of view and against this important work wrote: S. R. Hirsch in: Jeschurun 1859 [and several articles in his *Gesammelte Schriften*, 1912, 322–434]; B. Auerbach, *ha-Ṣophe 'al Darke ha-Mishna* (54) and S. Klein, *Meppine Ḳoshet* (32) and (against Rapoport) *ha-'emeth we-ha-shalom 'ehabu* (32), all three F. o. M. 1861. For Frankel: S. J. Rapoport, *Dibre shalom we'emeth*, and S. J. Kämpf, *Mamteḳ sod*, both Prague 1861. Comp. J. Dobschütz in *MGWJ*, 1901, 262–278. On this controversy see also *Me'iruth 'enayim, Beleuchtung des Frankel'schen Streites*, Vienna 1861 (38) against the defenders of Frankel in the *Allgemeine Zeitung des Judentums*, and Zweifel, *Shalom 'al yisrael* IV (Zhitomir 1873), 13–64.

Jacob Brüll, *Mebo ha-mishna, Einl. in die Mischnah*, F. o. M., I: *Leben u. Lehrmethode der gesetzeslehrer von Esra bis zum Abschlusse der M.*, 1876 (293). II: *Plan u. System der M.*, 1885 (167).

The works of Frankel and Brüll are written in Hebrew, similarly that of Weiss, *Dor Dor We-Doreshaw*, and that of Is. Halevy, *Doroth ha-rishonim*, see above p. 105–106.

N. Krochmal (1785–1840) *More Nebuke ha-zeman*, Lemberg, 1851, chapter 13.

Z. M. Pineles, *Darkah shel Torah*, Vienna, 1861 (280). Against him Waldberg, *Kak hi Darkah shel Torah*, Jassy 1864. 68. Comp. *JE*, X, 45.

Abraham Geiger, 'Einiges über Plan u. Anordnung der M.', in: *Wissenschaftl. Zeitschrift für jüdische Theologie*, II (1836), 474–492. || Tob. Cohn, 'Aufeinanderfolge der M.-ordnungen,' in: Geiger's *Jüd. Zeitschrift für Wissenschaft und Leben*, IV (1886), 126–140. || W. Landsberg, 'Plan und System in der

Aufeinanderfolge der einzelnen Mišnas:' *MGWJ*, 1873, 208–215. || J. Derenbourg, 'Les sections et les traités de la Mischnah': *REJ*, III (1881), 205–210.

J. H. Dünner, 'Veranlassung, Zweck und Entwickelung der halakhischen und halakhisch-exegetischen Sammlungen während der Tannaim-Periode:' *MGWJ*, 1871, 137 ff., 313 ff., 363 ff., 416 ff., 449 ff. | By the same author: 'R. Jehuda Ha-nasis Anteil an unsrer M.,' *MGWJ*, 1872, 161 ff., 218 ff. || Joach. Oppenheim, *Toldoth ha-mishna, Zur Geschichte der M.*, Pressburg 1882 (52) [from *beth Talmud* II]. || M. Lerner, 'Die Ältesten Mišna-Kompositionen,' in: *Mag.*, 1886, 1–20; '*Die Grundlagen der M.*' in: *Hoffmann-Festschrift*, 346–361 (against Is. Halevy, see above page 22); also (on the oldest M.) *Torath ha-mishna*, I, Berlin 1914 (28).

D. Hoffmann, *Die Erste Mischna und die Controversen der Tannaim*, Berlin 1882 (54) [a Hebrew translation by S. Grünberg appeared Berlin 1913 (64)]; 'Zur Kritik der M.' in *Mag.*, VIII (1881), 121–130, 169 to 177; IX, 96–105, 152–163; XI, 17–30, 88–92, 126–127.

J. Bassfreund, 'Zur Redaktion der M.:' *MGWJ*, 1907, 291–322, 429 to 444, 590–608, 678–706; printed separately Berlin 1913 (60).

Ludwig A. Rosenthal, *Über den Zusammenhang, die Quellen und die Entstehung der Mischna*, Berlin 1918. I: Die Sadduzäerkämpfe u. die Mischnasammlungen vor dem Aüftreten Hillel's, 2d edition (164); II: Hillel bis Akiba, 2d edition (151); III: Von Akiba's Tod bis zum Abschluss der Mischna (132). | *Die Mischna, Aufbau und Quellenscheidung.* I, 1 [Ber. to Shebiith], Strassburg 1903 (29 and 156); Maas. 1906 (64); M. Sh. 1909 (52) [ingenious and stimulating, but much that is not proved].

L. Ginzberg, '*Zur Entstehungsgeschichte der M.*' ('*ein-bein* clauses, see above p. 252 n. 67), in: *Hoffmann-Festschr.*, 311–345.

S. M. Schiller-Szinessy, in *Encyclopedia Britannica*, ninth ed., XVI, 502–508; J. Z. Lauterbach in *JE*, VIII, 609–619; Hamburger II, 789–798.

b. To the Palestinian Talmud: Z. Frankel, *Mebo ha-Yerushalmi, Einl. in den jerusalemischen T.*, Breslau 1870 (158 double pages). || S. J. L. Rapoport, in: *Kerem Ḥemed* I (1833), 83–87. || Abr. Geiger, 'Die jerusalemische Gemara im Gesamtorganismus der talmud. Literatur': *Jüd. Zeitschr. f. Wissensch. und Leben*, 1870, 278–306. || 'Der jerusalemische T. im Lichte Geigerscher Hypothesen,' in *MGWJ*, 1871, 120–137. || J. Wiesner, *Gib'ath Yerushalayim*, in: *ha-Shaḥar* II, Vienna 1872. || M. Schwab, *Le T. de Jerusalem traduit*, 2d ed., Paris 1890, I, p. l-lxxxiii.

c. To the Babylonian Talmud: N. Brüll, 'Die Entstehungsgeschichte des bT.s als Schriftwerkes,' in: *Jahrbücher*, II (1876), 1–123.

d. To the Talmud in general. M. Steinschneider, *Cat. Bodl.* columns 209–290. || The famous letter of Sherira Gaon, see above p. 19. || E. M. Pinner, *Tractat Berachoth*, Berlin 1842, fol. The introduction to the Talmud in front consists of 24 pages in Hebrew and German. The introduction by Maimonides and the introduction to the Talmud by Samuel Ha-nagid, the 13 and the 32 Middoth (see above chapter XI, § 3, 4), a list of the biblical verses quoted in the Mishna with a few notes regarding the manner in which they are introduced, a list of the Simanim (see above p. 71), remarks on the *Bath Ḳol.* || Weiss, *Dor Dor we-Dorshaw*, III and Halevy, *Doroth ha-rishonim* I[e], 2.3 (see above chapter XIII, § 1).

H. Graetz, *Geschichte der Juden*, 4th ed.: vom Untergang des jüd. Staates bis zum Abschluss des T., Leipzig 1908 (483); V: bis zum Aufblühen der jüdisch-spanischen Kultur, 1909 (572).

Z. Frankel, 'Beiträge zur Einl. in den T.:' *MGWJ*, 1861, 186–194, 205–212, 258–272. Wertheimer, *Le T.* Première leçon. Histoire de la formation du T., Geneva, 1880 (32). || J. Lewy in the *Jahresbericht des jüd.-theolog. Seminars*, Breslau 1895, p. 1–23. || The article "T." by J. Derenbourg in Lichtenberg's *Encyclopèdie des sciences religieuses*, XII (Paris 1882), 1007–1036; Hamburger II, 1155–1167; S. M. Schiller-Szinessy in *Encyclop. Britannica*, 9th ed., XXIII, 35–39; A. Darmesteter, *REJ*, XVIII (1889), Actes et conférences, p. ccclxxxi to dcxlii (English translation by H. Szold, Philadelphia 1896 (97)); S. Schechter in Hastings' *Dictionary of the Bible*, V (1904), 57–66 and W. Bacher (M. Richtmann, J. Z. Lauterbach, Ludw. Blau), *JE*, XII, 1–37.

M. Mielziner, *Introduction to the T.*, 2d ed., New York 1903 (297). [The first part is practically an excerpt of my Introduction; praiseworthy are the sections on Hermeneutics, Terminology and Methodology, p. 117–264]. || M. L. Rodkinson, *The History of the Talmud from the Time of its Formation about 200 B.C. up to the Present Time*, New York 1903 (229); London, 1908 (450).

W. Bacher, *Tradition und Tradenten in den Schulen Palästinas und Babyloniens*, Leipzig 1914 (704). [pp. 1–72 very important and full essays introductory to the Talmud. The author died before he was able to present in a finished form the remainder of the enormous material. See on the whole work Horovitz, *MGWJ*, 1916, 66–73; 153–159].

Popular writings: S. Bernfeld, *Der Talmud*, Berlin, 1900 (120). S. Funk, *Die Entstehung des T.s* 2d ed., Leipzig 1919 (127); *Talmudproben*, Leipzig 1912 (135).

Christian authors: J. Chr. Wolf, *Bibl. Hebr.*, II, 657–993; IV, 320 to 456. || A. G. Wähner, *Antiquitates Ebraeorum*, I (Gött. 1743), 231 to 584. || B. Pick, *The Talmud what it is*, New York 1887 (147).

e. Reference works: M. Steinschneider, 'Über talmudische Realindices, Onomastica und dgl.,' in: *Serapeum*, 1845, 289–301. || Ad. Jellinek, *Ḳontres ha-kelalim*, Vienna 1878 (32). [Bibliography of writings on methodology of the talmud and Seder Tann. Va'am.]; *Kontres ha-maphteaḥ*, *Bibliographie der Nominal-, Verbal-und Real-Indices zum babyl. und jerusal. T.*, *zur Midrasch-und Sohar-Literatur und den alphabetisch geordneten Hagadasammlungen*, Vienna 1881 (36).

Isaac ben Samuel Lampronti (1679–1756, physician and rabbi in Ferrara), *Paḥad Yiṣhaḳ*. The letters A-M of this encyclopedia to the Talmud and Decisors (*poseḳim*) appeared Venice, Reggio, Leghorn, 1750–1840 in 5 folio volumes, N till the beginning of Ḳ, Lyck, 1864–1874 in 5 volumes; the last 4 parts Berlin, 1885–1888.

S. J. L. Rapoport, *Sepher Erech Millin* [encyclopedia of Talmud, Targum, Midrash]. Part 1: Prague 1852 (282). 4to || M. Katzenellenbogen, *Sepher Alpha betha* [encyclopaedic dictionary of the Talmud]. Part 1: ד–א. Frankfort o. M., 1855 (254).

M. D. Cahen, *Sepher Sekiyyoth ha-ḥemdah. Repertorium talmudicum* sive memorabilia omnia de personis et rebus, quae in utroque Talmude et Midraschim occurrunt . . . Item series integra commentatorum Talmudicorum medii aevi. Lyon, 1877 (228).

M. Guttmann, *Maphteaḥ ha-talmud*, Budapest. I (A to *Abraham*) 1908 (320); II (to *'elle*) 1917 (480). Comp. V. Aptowitzer, *MGWJ*, 1910, 419 ff., 553 ff.

Ḥayyim Shalom Slivkin, S. *Ispaḳlaria ha-me'irah*, Warsaw, 1902. 1904 (137 and 120). [A list of the halakic and haggadic utterances in the Babylonian Talmud, arranged according to the names of the Tannaim].

§ 2. Translations.

Erich Bischoff, *Kritische Geschichte der Talmud-Übersetzungen aller Zeiten u. Zungen*, F. o. M. 1899 (110).

1. Mishna. *Mischna . . cum Maimonidis et Bartenorae commentariis integris.* Accedunt variorum auctorum notae ac versiones. Latinitate donavit ac notis illustravit Guilielmus Surenhusius. Amst. 1698–1703. 6 volumes folio [Hebrew text above the Latin. (At least 26 tractates are translated by others); Maimonides and ʻObadia of Bertinoro in latin; besides these the notes by Arnoldi (Tamid), Coccejus (Sanh. and Mak without the excerpts of the Gemara), L'Empereur (B.Ḳ, Mid.), Guisius (Zeraʻim to the end of Maʻas. 1), Houting (R.H.), Leusden (Aboth), Lund (Taʻan.), Peringer (ʻA.Z.), Seb. Schmidt (Shab., ʻEr.), Sheringham (Yoma), Wagenseil (Sota, without the excerpts of the Gemara). Compare Bischoff, p. 20–23, 104 f.].

Mishnayoth Berlin 1832–34. 6 parts 4to. [Text vocalized, Commentary *melo kaph naḥath*; translated into German, brief introductions and notes in Hebrew characters published by the "Gesellschaft von Freunden des Gesetzes und der Erkenntnis," usually named after J. M. Jost].

Johann Jacob Rabe, *Mischnah oder der Text des Talmud . . . übersetzt und erläutert.* Onolzbach 1760–63. 6 parts 4to. [The translation of the M. edition, Vienna 1817–1835, is based upon this excellent work]. *Mischnajoth* . . . Hebr. text mit Punktation, deutscher Übs. und Erklärung, Berlin; I, Seraim, von A. Sammter, 1887 (196). IV, Nesikin, von D. Hoffmann, 1898 (384). II, Moʻed, von Ed. Baneth, 1920. Volumes III

(Petuchowski), V (J. Cohn), VI (D. Hoffmann) have not yet been completed.

Die Mischna, Text, Übersetzung und ausführliche Erklärung herausgegeben von G. Beer u. O. Holtzmann, Giessen 1912 ff. There have appeared so far: Holtzmann, Ber. and Middoth; Beer, Pes.; Albrecht, Kil. and Ḥalla; Windfuhr, B.K. and Hor.; Fiebig, R.H.; Meinhold, Yoma; W. Bauer, Pe'a. The parts are of unequal merit. The work on Ber. is poor. (Comp. V. Aptowitzer in *MGWJ*, 1913, 1914).

H. L. Strack, *Ausgewählte Mišnatraktate*, nach Handschriften und alteṇ Drucken herausgegeben (Text vocalized), übersetzt und mit Berücksichtigung des Neuen Test. erläutert, Leipzig. (There have appeared thus far: Aboth, Ber., Yoma, Sanḥ-Mak., A.Z., Pes., Shab., see below § 3D.).

Eighteen Treatises from the Mishna. Translated by D. A. de Sola and M. J. Raphall, London 1843 (368). [Ber., Kil.; Shab., 'Erub., Pes., Yoma (only chapter 8), Sukka, Beṣa, R.H., Taan., Meg., M.Ḳ.; Yeb. (chapters 6,8 and several smaller parts omitted), Keth., Giṭ., Ḳid.; Ḥul; Yad.].

Joseph Barclay, *The Talmud.* A translation of eighteen Treatises from the Mishna, with Notes and Appendix. London 1878 (380). [Ber., Shebiith; Shab., Pes., Yoma, Sukka, R. H., Taan., Ḥag.; Sanh., A. Z., Aboth; Tamid, Mid.; Neg., Para, Yad.—Baraitha concerning the Tabernacle].

2. Palestinian Talmud. Biagio Ugolini edited and translated into Latin 20 tractates in his *Thesaurus antiquitatum sacrarum*, volumes XVII–XXX (Venice 1755–65 fol.), Volume XVII: Pes.; XVIII Sheḳ, Yoma, Sukka, R.H., Taan., Meg., Ḥag., Beṣa, M. K.; XX: Maas., M. Sh., Ḥalla, Orla, Bik.; XXV: Sanh., Mak.; XXX: Ḳid., Soṭa, Keth.

Moise Schwab, *Le Talmud de Jerusalem traduit pour* la première fois, Paris, 11 volumes, II–XI: 1878–1889; I in 2d edition 1890 (172 pages. Introduction et tables générales, 176 pages, Ber.). The first edition of the first volume bears the title: *Traité des Berakhoth du T. de Jérusalem et du T. de Babylone traduit pour la permière fois en français* (1–217 Pal. T.; 219 ff. Bab. T.).

Aug. Wünsche, *Der Jerusalemische Talmud in seinen haggadischen Bestandtheilen übertragen.* Zurich 1880 (297. Comp. *Theol. Litztg*, 1880, No. 16).

3. Babylon. Talmud. Laz. Goldschmidt, *Der Babylonische Talmud herausgegeben nach der ersten*, zensurfreien Bombergschen Ausgabe . . ., nebst Varianten . . . der Münchener Talmud handschrift [except for volume XV only after *Diḳd.*] möglichst sinn-und wortgetreu übersetzt vol. I, II, III, VII Berlin, vol. VI, VIII Leipzig, large 4to. I: Zera'im, Shab. 1897 (61 and 730) [2d edition Leipzig 1906 with corrections in the plates]; II: Erub., Pes., Yoma 1901 (31 and 1044); III: Sukka, Yom Ṭob, R. H., Taan., Meg., M. Ḳ., Ḥag., Sheḳ. 1899 (22 and 902); V: Nazir, Soṭa, Giṭ., Ḳid., 1912 (38 and 1009); VI: B. Ḳ., B. M., B. B. 1906 (44 and 1420); VII: Sanh., Mak., Shebu., A. Z., Hor., Eduy., Aboth 1903 (31 and 1194); VIII: Zeb., Men., Ḥul. 1909 (36 and 1286).

Mich. L. Rodkinson, *New edition of the Babylonian* Talmud Original text, edited, corrected, formulated (!) and translated into English. New York 1896 ff. Vols. I–VIII: Mo'ed [and Ebel Rabbathi]. Volume IX ff.: Neziḳin [vol. IX contains besides Aboth also Aboth de R. Nathan, Derek Ereṣ Rabba and D. E. Zuṭṭa.] Volumes X–XII: B. Ḳ. and B. M. [A free and largely abbreviated translation. As far as I have seen, the original text is appended only in the 4th volume for Sheḳ. and R. H.] According to *REJ*, IX, 266 there appeared in London (Boston) a new edition ['punctuated'] in 10 volumes.

Occupying a middle position between a translation and a summary of the contents are the two works by Isr. M. Rabbinowicz: *Législation criminelle du Thalmud.* Organisation de la magistrature rabbinique . . . (Synhedrin et Makhoth et deux passages du traité Edjoth) Paris 1876 (40 and 232) and: *Législation civile du Thalmud.* Nouveau commentaire et traduction critique. 5 Volumes, Paris, I: Les femmes, les païens selon le Thalmud 1880 (91 and 466); II: B. Ḳ. 1877 (84 and 509); III: B. M. 1878 (54 and 486); IV: B. B., 1879 (51 and 420); V: La médecine, les païens, 1879 (70 and 431).

Aug. Wünsche, *Der Babylonische Talmud in seinen haggadischen Bestandtheilen.* Wortgetreu übs. und durch Noten erlaütert.

Leipzig Ia: [Zera'im, Mo'ed] 1886 (16 and 552). Ib: [Nashim] 1887 (378); II: [Baboth] 1888 (224); III: [end of Nezikin] 1889 (470); IV: [Ḳodashim, Ṭoharoth] 1889 (201) [not carefully done].

4. Translations of single tractates see § 3D.—Professor Heinr. Laible informs me by letter that Ms. translations of parts of the Talmud by J. J. Raba are found in the State Library at Berlin: Codices mspti Germanici 4to, No. 377–393. Unfortunately I have been prevented by illness from examining the manuscripts named.

§ 3. Commentaries.

A. Commentaries on the Mishna.

a. J. N. Epstein, *Der Gaonäische Kommentar zur Ordnung* Tohoroth, eine kritische Einl., Berlin 1915 (160). [The commentary dating from the time immediately after Saadia is to be published anew by Epstein, since Rosenberg's (*Ḳobeṣ ma'ase yede Geonim Ḳadmonim*, Berlin 1856) is very unsatisfactory].

b. Moses Maimonides (1135 to the end of 1204) wrote between the age of 23 and 30 a commentary on the Mishna in the Arabic language. (*Kitab al-Siraj*, The Book of Luminary, is a title by which it came to be known later, probably due to the fact that Maimonides himself was called by the honorific title *ha-maor*, comp. M. Steinschneider, *Die heb. Übersetzungen des Mittelalters*, Berlin 1893, 922). 'Of the various men [as to the names see *Cat. Bodl.* column 1883] who undertook to make the commentary accessible [in translation] particularly to those of northern Europe, some understood Arabic or Hebrew but moderately, some were moreover also untutored Talmudists. One can hardly conceive with what carelessness these men unprepared for their task went about their work . . . The translation of Seder Ṭoharoth is the poorest of all' (Derenbourg). The Hebrew translation is found in many editions of the Mishna (Naples 1492, Riva di Trento 1559, fol. etc.) and in most of the editions of the Talmud.

Parts of the Arabic original were first published by: Edw. Pococke, *Porta Mosis*, Oxford 1655: the introductions to Orders

Ḳodashim and Ṭoharoth and to Men.; interpretation of Sanh. 10 a. the "Eight Chapters" (as for these see below p. 147).

J. Derenbourg, *Seder Taharoth 'im Perush ha-rab R. Moshe ben Maimon, Commentaire de Maimonide sur la Mischnah Seder Tohorot* publié en arabe et accompagné d'une traduction hébraique, Berlin 1887–1889 (236, 244 a. 276; the introduction of Maimonides to Ṭoharoth is important); comp. in addition Derenb. in: *Zunz-Festschr.* part I, 152–157.

More recent publications (mostly doctoral theses of individual parts of the original with corrected Hebrew translations and notes.—° indicates that the translation is wanting). B. Hamburger, Introduction, Frkf. o. M. 1902. || Ber.: Ernst Weill, Strassburg 1891; Pe'a: D. Herzog, Berlin 1894; Demai: J. Zivi, Berlin 1891; Kil.: Sal. Bamberger, Frkf. o. M. 1891; Ḥalla: Sel. Bamberger, Frkf. o. M. 1895. || Shab. 8–12: M. Katz° 1903, Shab. 13–18: Urbach° 1904, Shab. 19–24: L. Kohn° 1903, all three parts Budapest; Erub. 2.5, 6.2, 8.2: D. Grünewald, *MGWJ*, 1900, 452–454 (corrections of the Hebrew translation); Pes.: H. Kroner, Berlin 1901; J. M. Toledano (*Yede Moshe*) Safed 1915, from a Ms. Sassoon which the editor took for an autograph (in an Appendix the vocalized words of this Ms. of Mo'ed and Nashim); Sheḳ. 1–4: Borsodi,° Budapest 1904; Yoma 1–4: Em. Hirschfeld,° ibid. 1902; Yoma 5–8: Vidor,° ibid. 1904; Sukka 1–3: Lövinger,° ibid. 1904; Beṣa: H. Kroner, Munich 1898; M. Friedländer, R. H. 1.3–3.1, in: *Hildesheimer-Festschr.*, Hebr. part 95–103; Sal. Bamberger, R. H. 1. 1f. 3. 2–end, in: *Hoffmann-Festschr.*, Hebr. part 248 to 260; Taan.: B. Sik, Budapest (Berlin) 1902; Taan. 1, 2: A. Kallner, Leipzig 1902; Meg.: S. Behrens, Frkf. o. M. (Diss. Breslau) 1901; M. Ḳ. and Shab. 5–7: J. Simon, Berlin 1902. Keth, 1, 2: S. Frankfurter, Berlin 1903; Keth. 3–5: M. Frankfurter, Berlin 1904; Keth 6–8: G. Freudmann, Berlin 1904; Keth. 9 to 11: L. Nebenzahl, Frkf. o. M. 1907; Nazir 1–4: F. Weiss, Berlin 1906; Giṭ.: H. Goldberg, Berlin (Diss. Strassburg) 1902; Ḳid.: A. B. Nurock, Berlin 1902. || B. B. 1–4: J. Sänger, Berlin 1912; B. B. 5–10: Imm. Lewy, Berlin (Diss. Tübingen) 1907; Sanh. 1–3: M. Weiss, Berlin 1893; Sanh. 4, 5: J. Bleichrode 1904; Sanh.: M. Gottlieb, Hannover 1906; Mak.: J. Barth, Leipzig 1881 (comp. J. Derenbourg, *REJ*, II 335–338);

Mak., Shebuoth: M. Gottlieb, Hannover 1911; Eduy. 1. 1–1. 12: M. Beermann, Berlin 1897; Eduy 5, 6: A. Garbatti, Berlin 1906; A. Z.: J. Wiener, Berlin 1895; Aboth: Ed. Baneth,° Berlin 1905, comp. *MGWJ*, 1905, 616–619. From Ed. Baneth we have further in the *Hildesheimer-Festschr.*, Hebr. part 57–76 Aboth 1 in Arabic with a new Hebrew translation and in the *Lewy-Festschr.*, Hebr. part 76–103, corrections of the translation by Samuel ibn Tibbon. Ḥullin 3, 4: M. Wohl, Frkf. o. M. (Berlin) 1894; Bekor.: J. Löwenstein, Berlin (Diss. Erlangen) 1897; Arakin: Isr. Schapiro, Jerusalem 1910. || Tamid: M. Fried, Frkf. o. M. 1903; Middoth: J. Fromer, Frkf. o. M. (Diss. Breslau) 1898. Many of these publications have been reviewed by S. Bamberger *JbJLG.* I, II.

M. Wolff, *Musa Maimuni's Acht Capitel*, arab. u. deutsch mit Anmm., 2d edition, Leiden 1903 (96 a. 40). | J. Wolff, *Maimounide, les 8 chapitres ou Introduction à la Mischna D'Aboth*, traduit de l'Arabe, Lausanne 1912 (79). | Jos. Gorfinkle, *The Eight Chapters of Maimonides on Ethics*, edited, annotated, and translated, New York 1912 (104 a. 55). Comp. thereon A. Cohen, *JQR*, N. S. IV, 475–479.

J. Holzer, *Mose Maimuni's Einleitung zu Chelek*, im arab. Urtext u. der hebr. Übs . . . mit Anmm., Berlin, 1901 (42 a. 30).

Isr. Friedländer, *Arabisch-deutsches Lexikon zum Sprachgebrauch des Maim.*, Frkf. o. M. 1902 (21 a. 119).

c. Isaac ben Malkiṣedeḳ of Siponto, twelfth century (see Gross *Mag.*, II) wrote a commentary on Zera'im, which is published in the new edition of the Wilna Talmud.

Samson ben Abraham (Rashba) of Sens, about 1150–1230, wrote a commentary on the order Zera'im (Ber. excepted) and Ṭoharoth (except Nidda), which was published at first by D. Bomberg 1523 and since then in almost all Talmud editions. He is also the author of the Sens-Tosaphoth. Comp. Heinr. Gross, *Gallia Judaica*, Paris 1897, 661 f.

Meir ben Baruch Rothenburg (Mahram), died 1293. His commentary on the orders Zera'im and Ṭoharoth [only Neg. and Ohal.] is incorporated in the newer Talmud editions. Biography by Wellesz *REJ*, LVIII–LXI.

Asher ben Jehiel (Rabbenu Asher or Rosh), of Germany, died 1327. His commentary on the Mishnah was first published in the Talmud editions Amst. II (1714 ff.) and Berlin-Frkf. o. O. I (1715 ff.), the commentary on tractate Ned. in most Talmud editions, on Ber. see *REJ*, LXV, 47–53. His fame rests upon his Talmud compendium (see below p. 165). Biography by E. Freimann, *JbJLG*, XII (1918), 237–317.

Obadiah di Bertinoro, in Italy, subsequently rabbi in Jerusalem, died 1510: in almost all Mishnah editions with commentaries since Venice 1548f.; Latin translation by Surenhuysen, see above p. 142.

Isaac ibn Gabbai; his commentary *Kaf Naḥath* is found in several Mishna editions: Venice 1609, 1614, 1625 etc.

Yom Ṭob Lipmann Heller (1579–1654), rabbi in Prague and in Cracow, his Tosephoth Yom Tob in a number of Mishna editions, at first Prague 1614–17, with additions Cracow 1642–44, Wilmersdorf 1681–84, all 4to, etc. [Autobiography Megillath 'Eba with German translation by J. H. Miro, Breslau 1836, Vienna 1862].

Jacob ben Samuel Ḥagiz (middle of seventeenth century, comp. above p. 19), commentary 'Eṣ Hayyim with the text: on Order I, Verona 1650; on the entire Mishna Leghorn 1653 f.

Elisha ben Abraham (of Grodno), commentary *Kab we-naḳi* in the Mishna editions: Amst. 1697; 1698; 1713 etc.

Shneior Pheibush ben Jacob, commentary *Melo kaph naḥath* (based on commentaries of Obadiah and Heller) in the Mishna editions: Offenbach 1737, Berlin 1832–1834 (Jost).

Isaac ben Jacob Ḥayyuth, *Zera' Yiṣḥaḳ*, Frkf. o. O. 1732, 4to.

David Ḥayyim Corinaldi, *S. Beth David*, Amst. 1739, 4to.

David Pardo, *Shoshanim L'David*, Ven. 1752, 4to.

Israel Lüpschütz, *Mishnayoth . . . 'im ha-perush Tiph'ereth Yisrael*. [Mishna with commentary T. Y.], 6 volumes, Hannover, Danzig, Königsberg 1830–50.

Nathan (ben Simon) Adler, *S. Mishnath Rabbi Nathan*, vol. I [Zera'im] Frkf. o. M. 1862, 4to.

Sheraga Pheibush Frenkel, *Liḳḳute ha-Mishna* Breslau, 1873, 4to (133 leaves).

A great number of commentaries (Obadiah di Bert., Heller, Lüpshütz etc.; for the first time Isaiah Berlin on Zera'im and Mo'ed) are found in the Wilna edition Romm 1887 (Orders I and VI), 1908 f. (Orders II-V), 13 vol. folio (comp. *JQR*, N.S. II, 265–270); besides there is here published for the first time the textually important work of Solomon Adeni (comp. above p. 80).

B. Commentaries on the Palestinian Talmud.

Joshua Benveniste, *Sede Yehoshu'a*, 3 volumes, fol., Const. 1662, 1749 [on the haggadic parts of 18 tractates].

David Fränkel, teacher of Moses Mendelssohn, *Ḳorban ha-'Eda* (supplements *Shire Ḳorban*). Mo'ed: Dessau 1743 fol.; Nashim: Berlin 1757 fol.; of the commentary on Nezikin only 3 tractates have been published (Berlin 1760?).

Elijah ben Judah Leib: Zera'im Amst. 1710 fol.; B.Ḳ., B.M., B.B.: F.o.M. 1742 fol.

Moses Margalith, *Pene Moshe*, Nashim: Amst. 1754 fol. Neziḳin: Leghorn 1770 fol.; in the edition of the Palestinian Talmud Zhitomir, also Zera'im and Mo'ed.

Nahum Trebitsch, *Shelom Yerushalayim* on Mo'ed in the edition of the Palestinian Talmud Vienna.

Elijah Wilna, *Haggahoth Yerushalmi* [notes on Zera'im, by David Luria on Mo'ed], Königsberg 1858 (36 Leaves).

A. Krochmal, *Yerushalayim ha-benuyah*, Lemberg 1867 (31 pp. and 112 leaves).

Comp. also above p. 83.

C. Commentaries on the Babylonian Talmud.

A. Jellinek, *Ḳontres ha-mepharesh*, Vienna 1877 (18), names, according to the order of the tractates, the older commentators up to Bezalel Ashkenazi. The improved reprint by A. Freimann in the *Hoffmann-Festschr.*, Hebr. part 106–129, names additional unpublished commentaries. Comp. also *JE*, XII, 28–30.

a. Saadia's commentary on Ber. was published by S. A. Wertheimer according to a Geniza fragment with a Hebrew translation (*Perush . . . 'al masseketh B.*), Jerusalem 1908 (12 pp. and 27 leaves). As for Sherira's commentaries on Ber., Shab., B.B. see J. N. Epstein, *REJ*, LXIV, 210–214.

Under the name of Gershom ben Judah, *Me'or ha-golah* (of Lorraine, later in Mayence, died 1040), there are published in the Wilna Talmud (Widow and Brothers Romm) commentaries on Taanith, B.B. and on Order Ḳodashim (except Zeb.); comp. Kohut, *Supplement to the Aruch*, 1892, 8–27. But A. Epstein, in the *Steinschneider-Festschr.* 115–143, has shown that they are not by Gershom, but represent the notes by several men (Ḥul. at all events from another hand) from the Mayence school (probably that of Isaac ben Judah). Here belongs also Pseudo-Rashi on M. Ḳ. (in the above mentioned Talmud edition) and on Ned.

Hananel ben Hushiel (about 990–1050), in Kairwan, it seems, wrote a commentary on the entire Babylonian Talmud in which he used the Palestinian Talmud quite extensively. We possess in print the commentary on Pesaḥim (J. Stern, Paris 1868), on Mak., (in: Migdal Ch.) and on several other tractates (in the Wilna Talmud, Widow and Brothers Romm, comp. Kohut, *Supplement to the Aruch*, 1892, 28–81). The rest is as yet unpublished.

Comp. A. Berliner, *Migdal Chananel, Über Leben u. Schriften R. Chananel's in Kairvan nebst hebr. Beilagen*, Leipzig 1876 (32 and 52); M. Seligsohn, *JE*, VI, 205; S. Eppenstein, *MGWJ*, 1911, 740 f. a. in Wohlgemuth's *Jeschurun*, V (1918), 580–584.

Nissim ben Jacob in Kairwan, first half of the eleventh century, *S. ha-maphteaḥ shel man'ule ha-talmud* on Ber., Shab., Erub., published by J. Goldenthal, Vienna 1847 (63 leaves) and in the Wilna Talmud (Romm) 1888. [On Nissim comp. Wohlgemuth's *Jeschurun*, V, 321–327].

b. Rashi (R. Solomon Yiṣḥaḳi, of Troyes, died 1105) wrote a most highly valuable commentary on most of the tractates containing Gemara, which is now a component part of almost all Talmud editions.

Comp. J. H. Weiss, *Toldoth Rabbenu Shlomo ben Yiṣḥaḳ*, Vienna 1882 (72 pages; p. 38 ff. the question is discussed on which tractates we do not possess Rashi's commentary); A. Berliner, *Beiträge zur Geschichte der Raschicommentare*, Berlin 1903 (50). || S. Blondheim, 'List of Extant Manuscripts of Rashi's Talmudical Commentaries': *JQR*, N. S. VIII, 55–60.

Shemaiah, father-in-law of Rashbam, commentary on Middoth, in the larger Talmud editions. On Shemaiah see A. Epstein, *MGWJ*, 1897, 257–263, 296–312.

Judah ben Nathan (Riban), Rashi's son-in-law, commentary on Mak. 19b to the end; he also wrote commentaries on almost the entire Talmud. In the Wilna edition Pseudo-Rashi on Nazir is wrongly ascribed to him. Comp. Gross, *Gallia Judaica*, 226.

Samuel ben Meir (Rashbam), Rashi's grandson on his mother's side, died about 1174, completed Rashi's commentary on B.B. (from page 29a) which had remained unfinished at the death of his grandfather. His commentary on Pes. chapter 10 is printed next to Rashi's commentary; portions of his commentary on A. Z. are found in the Hebrew supplement to *Mag.*, 1887.

c. The Tosaphists, particularly of the twelfth and thirteenth centuries in Germany and France. The *Tosaphoth* (literally: additions), as far as they are published, are placed in the ordinary Talmud editions on the outer margin of the text (Rashi being on the inner margin) and are cited by the initial words, D. H. = *Dibbur ha-mathḥil*, of the individual notes. They do not form a running commentary, but are rather detailed explanations of single passages and are related to the text of the Gemara as the discussions of the Amoraim to the Mishna (comp. Ch. Tschernowitz in *Schwarz-Festschr.*, Hebr. part 9–18). The Tosaphoth in our Talmud editions are mainly derived from the collection of Eliezer of Touques (near Trouville in France) of the thirteenth century. Among the older Tosaphists are 3 grandsons of Rashi: Isaac ben Meir (Ribam), the above named Samuel ben Meir, and Jacob ben Meir, R. T. [Rabbenu Tam]; a nephew of Jacob was Isaac ben Samuel of Dampierre, *R. Y. ha-zaḳen.* Other Tosaphists frequently mentioned are: Judah ben Isaac of Paris, named Sir Leon, Eliezer ben Nathan of Mayence (Raban), Isaac ben Asher Ha-levi (Riba), Ephraim ben Isaac of Ratisbon, Samson ben Samson of Coucy (Gross, *Gallia Judaica*, 554) and Perez ben Elijah of Corbeil (thirteenth century). Thorough information about the Tosaphists may be found in Zunz, *Zur Geschichte und Literatur*, I (Berlin 1845), 29–60; comp. also M. Seligsohn, *JE*, XII, 202–207 and P. Buchholz, 'Die Tosaphisten als Methodologen,' in: *MGWJ*, 1894, 342–359, 398–404, 450–462, 549–556.

Piske Tosaphoth. 'A German of the fourteenth century excerpted from the Tosaphoth which he had before him the results or decisions on 36 tractates. In our Talmud editions they follow the Tosaphoth of the individual tractates for each one separately, numbered according to paragraphs. The 8 tractates, Shab., Pes., Git., Keth., Ḥul., B.K., B.M., B.B., which by their contents enter largely into matters of law and religion, contain by themselves half of all those [5931] decisions, which have obtained a certain authority in practice.' (Zunz, l. c. 59).

d. Moses ben Naḥman (Ramban) (born 1194 in Gerona, died about 1270). For editions of his Ḥiddushim (Novellae) on numerous tractates see *Catalogue Brit. Mus.*, 590 f.

Menahem ben Solomon, commonly called Meiri, with his Provençal name Don Vidal Solomon, born 1249 in Perpignan, died 1306. Of his numerous Talmud commentaries only a part has been published (under the title Beth ha-beḥirah or Ḥiddushim); latterly, it seems, his commentary on Sukka by J. M. Alter, Warsaw 1910, and on Erubin, 1913. | Magen Aboth, edited by J. Last, London, 1909.

Solomon (ben Abraham) Adret (not: Addereth, see *JE*, I, 212) (Rashba), born 1235 in Barcelona, died 1310. For editions of his Ḥiddushim see *Cat. British Museum*, 713 f. [J. Perles, *R. Salomo ben Abraham ben Adereth. Sein Leben und seine Schriften*, Breslau 1863].

Asher ben Jehiel, commentary on Ber. and Ned., see above p. 148.

Yom Ṭob ben Abraham of Seville, pupil of Rashba, Ḥiddushim, see *Catalogue Brit. Mus.*, 784 f.

Nissim ben Reuben of Gerona (Ran), also Rabbenu Nissim, Middle of fourteenth century in Barcelona. Of his commentaries the very important one on Ned. is found in most of the recent Talmud editions, the others are as yet unpublished. Comp. *JE*, IX, 317 f.

Bezalel (ben Abraham) Ashkenazi, pupil of David ibn Zimra (Radbaz) (died 1573); *JE*, II, 195. *Shiṭṭa Meḳubbeṣeth* on numerous tractates, see *Cat. Brit. Museum*, 94 f. On the

Order Ḳodashim for the first time in the Wilna Talmud. He often quotes older authors and gives important textual variants, see above p. 82. *Kelale ha-talmud* see above p. 137.

Solomon Luria (Mahrshal), died in Lublin 1573. *Ḥokmath Shelomo*, first published Cracow about 1582, 4to (the only complete edition: in the later prints, much has been omitted, see *Diḳd.*, I, 23); in many Talmud editions as *Ḥiddushe Mahrshal* [biography: S. A. Horodecki, *Kerem Shlomo* Drohobycz 1896 (40)].

Samuel Edels, abbreviated Mahrsh'a, born in Posen 1555, died in Ostrog 1631. His *Ḥiddushe Aggadoth* and *Ḥiddushe Halakoth* are found in many Talmud editions [biographies: S. A. Horodecki, *Shem mi-Shemu'el*, Drohobycz 1895 (39) and (of no consequence): R. Margulies, *Toldoth Adam*, Lemberg 1912 (97)].

Meir Lublin (ben Gedaliah) (Mahram), died 1616. His commentary *Me'ir 'Ene Ḥakamim* on 17 tractates is found in most of the newer Talmud editions. [Biography by Lewinstein and Horodecki in *ha-Goren*, I (1898), 39–61].

Meir Schiff, Mahram Shif. His *Ḥiddushe Halakoth*, first published Homburg v. d. H. 1737. 41, are found in many T. editions. [Biography: Horodecki in *ha-Goren*, II, 58–66. The year of his death, 1641, has been established by M. Horowitz, *Grabsteine des Israelit. Friedhofs in F. a. M.*, 1901].

Elijah Wilna (rabbi in Vilna, died 1797; frequently referred to by modern Jews as Gaon). His critical notes in the recent Talmud editions, first published Vienna 1806–11. Biographies: J. H. Levin and Ṣebi Hirsh ben Naḥman, *'Aliyyoth 'Eliahu*, Wilna 1856 (96); S. Schechter, *Studies in Judaism*, London 1896, 89–119; *JE*, V, 133–135; S. J. Yaṣkan, *Rabbenu Eliahu mi-Wilno*, Warsaw 1900 (159).

Isaiah Berlin (named also I. Pic, after his father-in-law), rabbi in Breslau, died in 1799. His Haggahoth were first published in Talmud Dyhernfurth 1800–1804 and frequently thereafter. [Biography: A. Berliner, *Mag*, VI, 65–89; comp. *JE*, III, 79 f.].

Akiba Eger, 1761–1837, rabbi at Märkisch Friedland, later in Posen. His brief notes are first found in the Talmud edition Prague 1830–34. [Biography: L. Wreschner, *JbJLG*, I, II; *JE*, V, 52 f.].

e. An important aid for the understanding of the Babylonian Talmud are the works of Joshua Boaz; printed for the first time in Justiniani's edition (Ven. 1546–51) and considerably enlarged in later editions: *Masoreth ha-talmud*, an index of parallel passages in Talmud (improved by Isaiah Berlin, beginning with the Vienna and Prague editions 1830); *Torah 'Or* references to the Bible passages quoted in the Talmud; and *'Ein Mishpat*, references to the codes of Moses Maimonides, Moses of Coucy, Jacob ben Asher (comp. Cat. Bodl., col. 214–216, 1524).

Shabbethai ben Eliezer Susman, *Me'ir Nathib*, Altona 1793–1802, fol. (192 leaves), collected the parallel passages in the Talmud.

Arieh Loeb Yellin, *Yephe 'Einayim*, in the Wilna Talmud, references to parallel passages in Tosephta, Midrashim and Palestinian Talmud.

Joshua Lewin, *Ṣiyyun Yehoshua* [an index of all of the parallel passages in the Babylonian and in the Palestinian Talmud arranged according to tractates], Wilna 1869 f.

Aaron of Pesaro, *Toldoth 'Aharon* [index of biblical passages quoted in the Babylonian Talmud], Freib. 1583–84; Ven. 1591–92; Amst. 1652 [Jacob Sasportas has added to it an index *Toldoth Ya'aḳob* of the biblical passages quoted in the Palestinian T.].

D. Commentaries to single Tractates, also translations of Tractates with Gemara.

(According to the Hebrew alphabet. G. = with Gemara.).

Aboth. Ch. Taylor, *Sayings of the Jewish Fathers, comprising Pirqe Aboth in Hebrew and English, with notes and Excursuses*, 2d edition, Cambridge 1897 (192 and 51 pp.; the text according to the Cambridge Codex, see above p. 80). || H. L. Strack, *Die Sprüche der Väter* (*herausgegeben, übs. u. erklärt*), 4th edition, Leipzig, 1915 (40 a. 44; introduction 6–8 gives further literature).

Baba Bathra (G.). Rabbinowicz, see above p. 144.

Baba Meṣi'a (G.). A. Sammter, *Tractat Baba Mezia mit deutscher Übs. u. Erklärung*. Berlin 1876, fol. (174 pages; 2–119 double). || Rabbinowicz see above p. 144.

Baba Ḳamma (G.). Rabbinowicz see above p. 144. || Mishna: L'Empereur (Leiden 1637), comp. above p. 142 (Surenhuysen). || Ch. Tschernowitz, Sheur'im ba-talmud, *Vorlesungen über den Talmud*, I, *Einleitung in Baba Kama*, Warsaw 1913 (127 and 71) [introduction, notes on chapters 1–3]. || I. Lewy, *Interpretation des* 1-6 *Abschnittes des paläst. Talmud-tractates Nesikin*, Breslau 1895–1914 (186). [Programmes of the Jewish Theolog. Seminary in Br.; German introduction, text with Hebrew commentary]. || Vitt. Castiglioni, *Babà Kammà, Baba Metzi'a. Testo ebraico punteggiato* [with translation and notes]. Rome 1913, 1914 (102).

Berakoth. L. Chiarini, *Le T. de Babylone, traduit . . . et complété par celui de Jérusalem.* 2 vol. Leipzig 1831 (414 and 373) [only Ber.]. || E. M. Pinner, *T. Babli. Babylonischer T. Tractat Berachoth Segensprüche. Mit deutscher Übs. . . .* [Rashi, Tosaphoth, Maimonides, philological and explanatory notes], *Einl. in den T.* [comp. above p. 140, l. 11 ff.]. First [only] vol. Berlin 1842. (16 pages, 24 and 87 leaves, fol.; also with Hebrew title). || Joh. Jac. Rabe, *Der talmudische Tractat Brachoth . . . nach der Hierosolymitan.-u. Babylonischen Gemara . . . übs. u. . . . erläutert.* Halle 1777, 4to (28 a. 382). || [Heinr. Georg F. Löwe (apostate)], *Der erste Abschnitt des ersten Traktats vom Babylonischen T., betitelt: Brachoth . . . übs. nebst Vorrede u. Einl. Mit drei Anhängen.* Hamburg 1836 (44 a. 107); *Der neunte u. letzte Abschnitt des ersten Tr.* Hamburg 1839 (56). || Mor. Geller, *Talmud-Schatz*, I, Budapest [without date, about 1880; gives in translation Mishna Ber. and excerpts from the Gemara]. || J. Wiesner, *Scholien zum B. T. 1. Heft, Berachoth*, Prague 1859 (159). || Guisius, see above p. 142. || J. Rosenfeld, *Der Mischnatractat Berachot* [1–4] *übs. u. erläutert*, Pressburg 1886 (64). || S. Carlebach, Beth Yoseph Ṣebi 'al Masseketh Berakoth, Berlin 1915 (640) [aims at saving the reader laborious consultation of other commentators]. || H. L. Strack, *Berakoth, Der Mišnatraktat B. 'Lobsagungen'* [edited, translated and expounded], Leipzig 1915 (56).

Demai. Guisius, see above p. 142.

Zebaḥim (G.). B. Ugolini in his *Thesaurus antiquitatum*

sacrarum, XIX (Ven. 1756, fol.) gives the text with Latin translation.

Ḥagiga (G.). A. W. Streane, *A Translation of the Treatise Chagigah from the Babylonian T. with Introduction, Notes, Glossary*, Cambridge 1891 (16 a. 166). || J. S. Hottinger, *Discursus gemaricus de incestu, creationis et currus opere ex cod. Chagiga c.* 2 *misn.* 1 *petitus, latinitate donatus . . . illustratus*, Leiden 1704, 4to.

Ḥullin (G.). M. Rawicz, *Der talmud. Traktat 'Chulin' . . . nach der Wiener Ausgabe vom Jahre* 1865 (*ed. Schlossberg*) . . . *übertragen u. kommentiert.* I (to fol. 69b), Offenburg 1908 (333).

Yadaim. M. J. Owmann, *Lotio manuum Judaeis usitata, ex codice Mischnico . . . restituta*, Hamburg 1706.

Yoma. H. L. Strack, *Joma, der Mišnatraktat 'Versöhnungstag'* [edited, translated and explained], 3d edition, Leipzig 1912 (58). || Robert Sheringham, London 1648, see above p. 142. || M. Fried, *Das Losen* (פיס) *im Tempel*: *MGWJ*, 1901, 292–298.

Kil'aim. Guisius, see above p. 142.

Kelim. D. Graubart, 'Le véritable auteur du traité Kèlim,' *REJ*, XXXII (1896), 200–225.

Kethubboth (G.). M. Rawicz, *Der Tractat Kethuboth . . . übertragen u. kommentiert.* F. o. M., 1898. 1900 (261 and 335). [After a censored edition, comp. for instance p. 67 'Ägypter,' 333 'Sadducäer'].

Megilla (G.). M. Rawicz, *Der Traktat M. nebst Tosafat* [sic] . . .*übertragen.* F. o. M. 1883 (117) [very careless, is to be used only in comparison with the original]. || W. Rothstein, *Der Mischnatractat M. . . übs. . . . mit Anmm.*, Tüb. 1912 (20).

Middoth. L'Empereur, Leiden 1630, see above p. 142. || I. Hildesheimer, *Die Beschreibung des herodianischen Tempels im Tractate M. u. bei Flavius Josephus*, Berlin 1877 (32) 4to ['Jahresbericht' of the Orthodox Rabbinical Seminary].

Makkoth. H. S. Hirschfeld, *Tractatus Macot cum scholiis . . glossario*, Berlin 1842 (173) [without translation]. || Coccejus, comp. Sanhedrin.

Menaḥoṭh (G.). Ugolini in his *Thesaurus antiquitatum sacrarum*, vol. XIX, text and Latin translation.

Maasroth. Guisius, to chapter 2, see above p. 142.

Nega'im, in German in: J. Chr. Wagenseil, *Belehrung der jüdisch-teutschen Red- u. Schreibart*, Altdorf 1699. 4to.

Soṭa (G.). Jo. Christoph Wagenseil, *Sota. Hoc est liber Mischnicus de uxore adulterii suspecta una cum libri En Jacob excerptis Gemarae Versione Latina et Commentario . . . illustrata.* Altdorf (near Nuremberg) 1674, 4to (1375). || H. Bahr a. L. A. Rosenthal, *Der Mischnatraktat Sotah. Einl., Textausgabe u. übs.*, Berlin 1916 (44).

Sukka (G.). *Talmudis Babylonici codex Succa . . . Latinitate donavit, . . . illustravit* Frid. Bernh. Dachs . . . *Accedit Joh. Jac. Crameri . . . Commentarius posthumus.* Utrecht 1726, 4to (580). || S. Carlebach, Beth Yoseph Sebi 'al Masseketh Sukka, Berlin 1910 (554). || P. Volz, *Das Neujahrsfest Jahwes* (*Laubhüttenfest*), Tüb. 1912 (61).

Sanhedrin (G.). M. Rawicz, *Der Tractat S. . . übertragen u. mit erläuternden Anmerkungen versehen*, F. o. M. 1892 (543 a. 20) [better than the translation of Megilla]. || Ugolini in *Thesaurus antiquitatum sacrarum*, vol. XXV (Ven. 1762 fol.), text and Latin translation. || Joh. Coch (Cocceius), *Duo tituli Thalmudici S. et Maccoth . . . cum excerptis ex utriusque Gemara versa et . . . illustrata*, Amst., 1629, 4to (16 and 440); Rabbinowicz, see above p. 144. || Sam. Krauss, *The Mishnah Treatise S. with introduction, Notes and Glossary*, Leiden 1909 (12 and 61). || H. L. Strack, *Sanhedrin-Makkoth, Die M. Traktate über Strafrecht and Gerichtsverfahren* [text, translation a. commentary], Leipzig 1910 (60 and 56). || G. Hölscher, *S. and Makkot, übs. und . . . mit Anmerkungen*, Tüb. 1910 (143). || H. Danby, *Tractate S. Mishnah and Tosefta . . . translated . . . with brief annotations*, London 1909 (21 and 148).

Aboda Zara (G.). F. Chr. Ewald, *Abodah Sarah oder der Götzendienst. Ein Tractat aus dem T. . . übs. mit Einl. u. Anmerkungen.* Nuremberg 1856 (25 and 545) [includes the vocalized Mishna, but not the text of the Gemara]. Second (unrevised) edition 1868. || G. El. Edzard, *Tractatus Talmudici Avoda Sara sive de Idololatria caput primum* [secundum] *e Gemara Babylonica Latine redditum et . . . illustratum.* Hamburg 1705 [1710], 4to (48 and 352 [Chapter 2; 593] pp.). || P. Feibig in *ZDMG*, 1903, 581–604 translated Mishna a. Gem. to 3. 1, 2. || H. L. Strack,

Aboda Zara, der Mišnatraktat 'Götzendienst' herausgegeben, übs. u. erklärt, 2d edition, Leipzig 1909 (31 and 20). || W. A. L. Elmslie, *The Mishnah on Idolatry Aboda Zara, ed. with translation . . . and notes,* Cambridge 1911 (29 and 136). || N. Blaufusz, *Römische Feste u. Feiertage nach den Traktaten über fremden Dienst* (Aboda zara). Nuremberg 1909 [Programme of a Gymnasium, 40]; *Götter, Bilder u. Symbole nach . . .* , 1910 (51).

Eduyyoth. J. H. Dünner, '*Über Ursprung u. Bedeutung des Traktates Edojoth*' [sic]: *MGWJ*, 1871, 33–42, 59–87. || H. Klueger, *Genesis u. Composition der Halacha-Sammlung Edujot,* Breslau 1895 (120). [Comp. *MGWJ*, 1897, 278–283, 330–333. Rabbinowicz, *Legisl. crimin.* (see above p. 144) p. 205–212 on Ed. 1. 4–6. || D. Feuchtwang, 'Der Zusammenhang der Mišna im Tr. Ed.,' *Hoffmann-Festschr.* 92–96. || Halevy, *Doroth Ha-rishonim* I e, 216–231. || Ros., *Entst.*, II, § 43–51.

Erubin. J. Wiesner, *Scholien zum B. T.* III: *Erubin u. Pesachim.* Prague 1867, p. 1–75. || Seb. Schmidt see above p. 142.

Orla. A. Rosenthal, *Der Mischnatraktat Orlah, sein Zusammenhang u. seine Quellen,* Berlin 1913 (48).

Pe'a (G.). Joh. Jac. Rabe: *Der Talmudische Tractat Peah von dem Ackerwinkel aus der Hierosolymitanischen Gemara übs. u. mit Anmerkungen, nebst einer Abhandlung von der Versorgung der Armen bey den Juden.* Anspach 1781 (20 a. 156), 4to. || Guisius, see above p. 142.

Pesaḥim (G.). J. Wiesner, *Scholien zum B. T.*, III (Prague 1867), p. 79 to 176. || W. H. Lowe, *The Fragment of T. Babli Pesachim of the ninth or tenth Century, in the University Library, Cambridge.* Cambr. 1879, 4to (P. 1–48 elucidations to Pes. 7a and to the middle of 9a, 13a end to 16a beginning). || H. L. Strack, *Pesaḥim, Der Mišnatraktat Passahfest* [edited, translated and annotated], Leipzig 1911 (40 a. 48).

Rosh Ha-shana (G.). M. Rawicz, *Der Traktat Rosch ha-Schanah mit Berücksichtigung der meisten Tosafot . . . übertragen.* Frkf. o. M. 1886 (176) [somewhat superior to the translation of the tractate Meg.]. || Henr. Houting, Amst. 1695, 4to (with extracts from the Gemara), comp. above P. 142. || S. Carlebach, Beth Yoseph Ṣebi 'al Masseketh Rosh ha-Shanah, Berlin 1912. ||

J. H. Gunning, *Rosj-Hassjana* (in the Journal *Theologische Studien* published in Utrecht, 1890, 31–74, 179–200). [Dutch translation and interpretation of the Mishna.]

Shebi'ith. Guisius, see above p. 142.

Shabbat (G.). Mor. Geller, *Talmudschatz* II, Budapest (about 1882); renders the Mishna and gives extracts from the Gemara in translation. || J. Wiesner, *Scholien zum B. T.*, II *Sabbath*, Prague 1862 (277). || H. L. Strack, *Schabbath, der Mischnatraktat Sabbath herausgegeben u. erklärt*, Leipzig 1890 (78). || Seb. Schmidt, see above p. 142. || Is. Levy, *Der achte Abschnitt aus dem Traktate Sabbath (Babli u. Jeruschalmi) übs. u. philologisch behandelt*, Breslau 1891 (34). || G. Beer, *Mischnatraktat S. übs. u. mit Anmerkungen*, Tüb. 1908 (120).

Sheḳalim. Joh. Wülfer, *Schekalim. Tractatus Talmudicus de modo annuaque consuetudine siclum . . . offerendi . . . latinitate donatus et . . . illustratus*. Altdorf (near Nuremberg) 1680 (170), 4to. || Jo. Heinr. Otho, *Lexicon rabbinico-philologicum . . . auctum est a J. F. Zachariae*, Altona a. Kiel 1757, p. I–LIV [Mishna with Latin translation and brief notes].

Tamid. Ugolini, 'Codex misnicus de sacrificio jugi,' in: *Thesaurus antiquitatum sacrarum*, XIX (Ven. 1756 fol.), Col. 1467–1502 [text, Latin translation, notes]. Arnoldi, see above p. 142.

Ta'anith (G.). D. O. Straschun, *Der tractat Taanit des B. T. übertragen* [with notes], Halle 1883 (19 a. 185). || Lund, see above p. 142.

§ 4. Aids for the Understanding of the Language (also several Chrestomathies).

Mishna. Hananiah (Elhanan Hai) Cohen, *Sepher Saphah Aḥath, Ragionamento sulla lingua del testo misnico*, Reggio 1819–22.

Ant. Th. Hartmann, *Thesauri linguae Hebraicae e Mischna augendi particula* I, II, III, Rostock 1825–26, 4to (116).

S. Mannes, *Uber den Einfluss des aramäischen auf den Wortschatz der Mišnah*. I, A.-M., Posen 1899 (55).

N. M. Nathan, *Ein anonymes Wörterbuch zur Mišna u. Jad haḥazaḳa*, Berlin 1905 (46) (a Hebrew-Arabic dictionary, written in the middle of the sixteenth century in Yemen, א and ב].

L. Dukes, *Die Sprache der Mischna lexikographisch u. grammatisch betrachtet*, Esslingen 1846 (127). || J. H. Weiss, *Mishpat Leshon ha-Mishna*, Studies on the language of the Mishna. Vienna 1867 (18 a. 128).

M. H. Segal, 'Mišnaic Hebrew and its Relation to Biblical Hebrew and to Aramaic,' in: *JQR*, XX (1908), 647–737.

K. Albrecht, *Neuhebräische Grammatik auf Grund der Mišna*, Munich 1913 (136).

H. Rosenberg, *Das Geschlecht der Hauptwörter in der Mischna*, Berlin 1908 (78). || Sal. Stein, *Das Verbum der Mischnasprache*, Berlin 1888 (54). || F. Hillel, *Die Nominalbildungen in der Mischnah*, Frkf. o. M. 1891 (52). || H. Sachs, *Die Partikeln der Mischna*, Berlin 1897 (51). || C. Siegfried, 'Beiträge zur Lehre von dem zusammengesetzten Satze im Neuhebräischen,' in: G. A. Kohut, *Semitic Studies*, Berlin 1897, 543–556.

Abr. Geiger, *Lehr- u. Lesebuch zur Sprache der Mischnah*. Breslau 1845 (10 a. 54; 10 a. 135). [Compare H. Grätz in: *Der Orient, Literaturblatt*, 1844, No. 52; 1845, Nos. 1, 2, 4–6, 41, 42, 46, 48–50; J. Levy, ibid., 1844, No. 51].

S. A. Wolff, *Mischna-Lese oder T.-Texte religiös-moralischen Inhalts*, 2 parts, Leipzig 1866. 68 (158). || O. Lipschütz, Mishnath Shemu'el, Textbook for elementary instruction in the Mishna. I (Ber.) Hamburg 1867 (56); II (Pe'a) Berlin 1871 (86). || Ch. D. Rosenstein, Mishna Berura, Warsaw 1910 (141). [Selected sections of Mishna, Baraitha and Tosephta vocalized, with a short commentary for the instruction of the youth.]

Haim Joshua Kassovsky, 'Oṣar Leshon ha-mishna, *Concordantiae totius Mischnae*, 2 volumes, Frankf. o. M. 1927.

2. Talmud.

a. Nathan ben Jehiel (died 1106 in Rome), *Sepher he-'Aruk* [Dictionary of the Talmud] appeared first before 1480 without place and date; Pesaro 1517 etc. fol. || With additions and corrections by Benjamin Musaphia under the Title: *Sepher musaph he-'Aruk*, Amst. 1655 fol. || Isaiah Berlin, *Haphla'ah shebe-Arakin* I Breslau 1830, II Vienna 1859; S. Lindermann, *Sarid Shebe'arakin*, Thorn 1870 (83). Newly edited: M. J. Landau, *He-'Aruk. Rabbinisch-Aramäish-deutsches Wörterbuch zur Kenntniss des Talmuds, der targumim u. midraschim*; *mit Anmerkungen*,

Prague 1819.24 5 volumes. (1676 pages, excluding the introductions etc.) [To each catchword is appended the German translation, besides numerous notes in German.] *'Aruk ha-Shalem Aruch completum . . . critice illustrat* Alex. Kohut. 8 volumes and Supplement, Vienna 1878–1892 (with additional use of manuscripts; and notes in Hebrew; not reliable). Comp. *JE*, IX, 180–183.

Joh. Buxtorf (father), *Lexicon Chaldaicum, Talmudicum et Rabbinicum* . . . editum a J. Buxt. Filio. Basel 1640 fol. (2680 columns).

Mich. Sachs, *Beiträge zur Sprach- u. Altertumsforschung aus jüd. Quellen*, 2 parts, Leipzig 1852. 54 (400).

Jacob Levy, *Neuhebräisches u. chaldäisches Wörterbuch über die Talmudim u. Midraschim. Nebst Beiträgen von H. L. Fleischer.* 4 volumes, Leipzig 1876–1889 (567, 542, 736, 741 pp.). Supplements and corrections were published by M. Lattes, in: *Saggio di giunte e correzione al Lessico Talmudico*, Turin 1879 (142); *Nuovo saggio di giunte e corr. al Less. Talm.*, Rome 1881, 4to (81); *Miscellanea postuma, Terzo Supplemento al Less. Talm.*, Milan 1884–1885 (69); and by Josef Mieses, *Neuhebräisches Wörterbuch. Ein Supplement Zu J. Levy's Neuhebr. Wörterbuch*, I, א-ב, Vienna 1919 (XIX, 35).

M. Jastrow, *Dictionary of the Targumim, the Talmud Babli and Yerushalmi and the Midrashic Literature*, New York 1886–1903, 4to.

Lolli, *Dizionario del linguaggio ebraico-rabbinico*, 1. fascicle Padua 1867 (to *Aḥarith*).

G. Dalman, *Aramäisch-neuhebräisches Handwörterbuch zu Targum, T. u. Midrasch*, Frkf. o. M. 1901 (447 pages and a lexicon of abbreviations 129 pages) [too short for the Talmud]; 2nd edition, 1922.

S. J. Fünn, *Oṣar Leshon ha-mikra we ha-mishna* [Dictionary of the Old Testament, Mishna and Midrashim; with explanations of catchwords in Russian and German; supplements by S. P. Rabinowitz] Warsaw 1912–1913 (4 volumes, about 2260 pages).

Felix Perles, 'Nachlese zum neuhebr. u. aram. Wörterbuch,' in: *Schwarz-Festschr.*, 293–310. Additional matter, ibid. by J. N. Epstein, 317–327, a. L. Ginzberg, 329–360.

Imm. Löw, *Aramäische Pflanzennamen*, Leipzig 1881 (490). 'Lexikalische Miscellen,' in: *Hoffmann-Festschrift*, 119–138.

A. Jellinek, *Sephath Ḥakamim* [The Persian and Arabic words in T., Targum a. Midrash] in Benjacob *Debarim Atikim*, fascicle 2, Leipzig 1846.

S. a. M. Bondi, *Or Esther oder Beleuchtung der im T. von Babylon u. Jerusalem, in den Targumim u. Midraschim vorkommenden fremden, bes. lateinischen Wörter.* Dessau 1812 (24 a. 272) [Hebrew and German].

Ad Brüll, *Fremdsprachliche Redensarten u. ausdrücklich als fremdsprachlich bezeichnete Wörter in den Talmuden u. Midraschen.* Leipzig 1869 (58). Supplements by N. Brüll, *Jbb*, I (1874), 123–220.

Jul. Fürst, *Glossarium Graeco-Hebraeum oder der griech. Wörterschatz der jüd. Midraschwerke.* Strassburg 1891 (216); comp. Jos. Cohn, *MGWJ*, 1893. || J. Fürst, 'Zur Erklärung griechischer Lehnwörter in T. u. Midraš': *MGWJ*, 1894, 305–311, 337–342.

Sam. Krauss, *Griechische u. lateinische Lehnwörter in T., Midrasch u. Targum*, Berlin 1898 f. (41 a. 349; 687) [A very industrious effort, but it is to be regretted that faulty prints were used in part, and that it also contains otherwise much else that is uncertain]. 'Zur Griech. u. Latein. Lexikographie aus jüdischen Quellen': *Byzantinische Zeitschrift*, II (1893), 493–548.

b. A. Stein, *Thalmudische Terminologie, zusammengestellt u. alphabetarisch geordnet*, Prague 1869 (13 a. 62).

W. Bacher, *Die exegetische Terminologie der Jüdischen Traditionsliteratur*, Leipzig 1905. I: *Die bibelexegetische Term. der Tannaiten* (207). II: *Die bibel- u. traditionsexegetische Term. der Amoräer* (258).

c. G. Dalman, *Grammatik des jüdisch-palästinischen Aramäisch nach den Idiomen des p. T, des Onkelostargum . . .*, 2d edition, Leipzig 1905 (419). || Moses Schlesinger, *Das aramäische Verbum im Jerusalemischen T.*, Berlin 1889 (86) [reprint from: *Mag.* 1889].

S. D. Luzzatto, *Elementi grammaticali del Caldeo Biblico e del dialetto Talmudico Babilonese*, Padua 1865 (106). | *Grammatik der biblisch-chaldäischen Sprache u. des Idioms des Talmud Babli,* translated into German by M. S. Krüger, Breslau 1873 (123). | *Grammar of the Biblical Chaldaic language and of the idiom of the Talmud Babli* translated by J. Goldammer, New York 1876.

C. Levias, *A Grammar of the Aramaic idiom contained in the Babylonian Talmud*, Cincinnati 1900 (255).

G. Rülf, *Zur Lautlehre der aramäisch-talmudischen Dialecte. I: Die Kehllaute*, Leipzig 1879 (55). || A. Liebermann, *Das Pronomen u. das Adverbium des Babylonisch-talmud. Dialekts*, Berlin 1895 (63). || Isaak Rosenberg, *Das aramäische Verbum im Babylonischen T.*, Marburg 1888 (67). [Reprint from: *Mag.*, 1887.].

M. Lewin, *Aramäische Sprichwörter u. Volkssprüche*, Berlin 1895 (90) [pp. 14–22 lexical matter, 22–28 grammatical matter].

Max L. Margolis, *A Manual of the Aramaic Language of the Babylonian Talmud* [with chrestomathy], Munich 1910 (99 and 184).

d. The following chrestomathies ought to be mentioned: Ph. Lederer, *Lehrbuch zum Selbstunterricht im B. T. Musterstücke . . . mit Übs. u. Erläuterungen.* 3 fascicles, Frkf. o. M. 1881–1888 (96, 104, 96). || J. Goldmann, *Gemara Lemathḥilim*, Wilna 1902 (176). || N. Lewin, *Mebo ha-talmud*, 15th edition, Wilna 1913. || Ch. D. Rosenstein, *Beth Midrash*, Wilna 1907 [Lewin and Ros. are very much praised].

Ch. Tschernowitz, *Kiṣṣur ha-talmud*, I, Lausanne 1919 (39 a. 312); 2d edition, Leipzig 1921 [Ber., R. H., Yoma. All repetitions and digressions from the essential theme are omitted].

§ 5. Halakah.

P. Buchholz, 'Über die mannichfachen Kodifikationen des Halakhastoffes von ihren ersten Anfängen bis zu ihrem letzten Abschluss:' *MGWJ*, 1864, 201–217, 241–259.

The following are important for an understanding of the constituent halakic elements of the Talmud in particular:

a. The Epitomes of the Talmud.

Simon Ḳayyara[1] in the first half of the ninth century. The older recension of his Halakoth Gedoloth used in Babylon, northern France, and Germany, was printed in Venice 1584, Amsterdam 1762, Vienna 1810, Warsaw 1874 (by Traub). || The much expanded recension, used in Spain and North Africa, was edited by I. Hildesheimer with Hebrew notes, Berlin 1890 (652). Introduction and Index appeared in 1892 (162). Comp. the same author: *Die Vaticanische Handschrift der Halachoth Gedoloth.* ['Jahresbericht' of the Rabbinical Seminary 5646] Berlin 1886 (42). Comp. *JE*, VII, 461 f.

The chief sources of Simon Ḳ. were the She'eltoth of Aḥa of Shabḥa and the Halakoth Pesuḳoth of the highly respected Jehudai (ben Naḥman) Gaon. The She'eltoth are not an halakic compendium, but a collection of discourses and of themes for discourses on religious questions, arranged in the order of the annual cycle, a work of Babylonian origin (the P. T. is not used), see A. Kaminka in *Schwarz-Festschrift*, 437–453. The Editions of the She'eltoth Venice 1546; Dyhernfurth 1786; with a commentary by Isaiah Berlin, Wilna 1861 ff.; a critical edition by Kaminka is in print. Comp. also Zunz, *GV.*, 56, 96, 343, 354. || The Aramaic original of H. P. has now been found (Codex Sassoon; see *MGWJ*, 1917, 127 ff.) and will be printed in Vienna by the organization Mekize Nirdamim; compare S. Poznanski, 'L'original araméen des Halachot Pesoukot,' *REJ*, LXIII, 232–244. Hebrew translation according to an imperfect manuscript in Leon Schlossberg, *Halakoth pesuḳoth 'o Hilkoth Re'u*, Versailles 1886 (148). Another part of this translation was published by J. N. Epstein in *JbJLG.*, XII (1918), 96–131. The translator, as E. shows, is a Palestinian. The work apparently started with ordinances concerning Erubin; hence the title Re'u, comp. Exod. 16.29.

The Halakoth Keṣuboth were written by a Palestinian disciple of Rab Jehudai; printed in Ch. M. Horovitz, *Beth Nekoth ha-halakoth*, Frkf. o. M. 1881; a further fragment in L. Ginzberg, *Geonica*, II, 398 f.

See in addition Joel Müller, *Handschriftliche Jehudai Gaon zugewiesene Lehrsätze*, Berlin 1890 (18) 4to (8th 'Jahresbericht' Lehranst. f. d. Wiss. des Judth.); *JE*, XII, 590 f.; L. Ginzberg, *Geonica*, I, 75–117 (R. Aḥa; Jehudai Gaon).

On Sepher Methiboth, compiled from both Talmuds it seems in Palestine about the year 1000, see *JQR*, N. S., I, 86–99.

Isaac ben Jacob, Alfasi (because for a long time a resident in Fez) but also called Rif, born 1013 in Kala'at Hammad, died 1103 as rabbi in Lucena, Spain: *Halakoth* Const. 1509. This edition, on account of its text, is much more valuable than that of Venice which was followed by the later editions (see Rabbinovicz, Ma'amar 130 f.). Printed subsequently with the title *Sepher Rab Alphas*, Venice 1521 f.; 1552; Riva di Trento and often, fol. This work is important also for the criticism of the Talmud text.

Eliezer ben Joel Ha-levi (thirteenth century in Western Germany) *Rabiah* [Decisions, Novellae and Responsa on the Talmud], edited by Dembitzer (Cracow 1882) and by V. Aptowitzer (Berlin 1913 ff.). The *Sepher Rabiah* was, as is now universally recognized, a source, though often unnamed, for Isaac Or Zarua', Meir Rothenburg, Asher ben Jehiel, Mordecai, Haggahoth Maimuni and Arba'a Turim, see *MGWJ*, 1916, 101.

Mordecai ben Hillel, died 1298 in Nuremberg, followed closely Alfasi, see S. Kohn, *MGWJ*, 1877, 1878; L. Ginzberg, *JE*, IX, 11–13.

Asher ben Jehiel (see above p. 148). His compendium of the Talmud, known ordinarily as Asheri, is found in most editions of the Babyl. T.—His son Jacob ben Asher compiled the decisions of this work under the title *Piske ha-Rosh* (Kiṣṣur).

b. The Responsa of the Geonim.

Z. Frankel, *Entwurf einer Geschichte der Literatur der nachtalmudischen Responsen*. Breslau 1865 (96).

Joel Müller, *Maphteaḥ lithshuboth ha-geonim. Einleitung in die Responsen der babylonischen Geonen*. Berlin 1891 (300). [Hebrew].

Louis Ginzberg, *Geonica*, I *The Geonim and their Halakic Writings* (210); II *Geniza Studies* (425). New York 1909.

A. Harkavy, *Responsen der Geonim*. Berlin 1887.

c. The 'Codes,' see above p. 89.

Moses ben Maimon 1135–1204, *Mishne Torah*, in later times also named *ha-Yad ha-ḥazaḳah*, because it comprises in 14 books the whole Halakah arranged in accordance with subject-matter. Comp. Ad. Schwarz, *Der Mischneh Thorah, ein System der Mosaisch-talmudischen Gesetzeslehre*, Vienna 1905 (230). [Composition, Language, Arrangement, Attitude to Halakic Exegesis].

Moses (ben Jacob) of Coucy near Soissons, completed 1250: *Sepher Miṣwoth* (*Gadol*) Semag.

Jacob ben Asher, 1269–1343, often called *Ba'al ha-turim* after his important work: *Arba'ah Turim* whose four parts are named *Oraḥ Ḥayyim*, *Yore De'a*, *Eben Ha-'ezer* and *Ḥoshen Ha-Mishpat*.—Biography of Jacob by A. Freimann, *JbJLG*, XIII (1920), 160–211.

Joseph Karo, died 1575 in Safed in Palestine: Shulḥan 'Aruk, printed for the first time in Venice 1564–65. K. follows often the wording of the Mishneh Torah, which therefore must be compared; he omits laws pertaining to sacrifices and purity and other statutes impossible of execution after the destruction of the Temple; but just as frequently it matters little to him whether the subjects admitted are inapplicable to his own times. The oldest and most important commentary, universally recognized among Eastern European Jews: Haggahoth or Mappa (Tablecloth) by Moses Isserles. To the Sh. A. belong the commentaries, see Hoffmann, 2d ed., 38–41. It is permissible to contradict the Sh. A. when compelled by the sources and when the statute rests on presuppositions no longer adequate. See in addition Ch. Tschernowitz, *Die Entstehung des Schulchan-Aruch*, Bern 1915 (79).

§ 6. Haggada.

1. H. S. Hirschfeld, *Die hagadische Exegese*, Berlin, 1847 (21 and 546). || J. Ziegler, 'Die haggad. Exegese u. der einfache Wortsinn': *MGWJ*, 1899, 159–167, 241–250. || See above Chap. XI, § 1, 4.

N. J. Weinstein, *Zur Genesis der Agada*, II: *Die Alexandrinische Agada*, Göttingen 1901 (275). [Arbitrary hypotheses; assumes a very powerful influence of the Alexandrian religious philosophy upon Talmudic Literature, see Leop. Cohn, in: *MGWJ*, 1903, 89–96].

Z. Frankel, 'Geist der paläst. u. babylon. Haggada:' *MGWJ*, II (1853), 388–398; III (1854), 149–158, 191–196, 387–392, 453–461.

Abraham Wilna, ספר רב פעלים, Warsaw 1894 (160) [Bibliography of the Haggada]; corrections and additions: S. Buber a. S. Ḥones, מחברת יריעות שלמה, 1896 (52).

Moses ben Joseph Figo (פיגו), זכרון תורת משה, Const. 1552 fol., Prague, 1623 [an alphabetic index to the Haggadic elements of both Talmuds]. || Sheraga Pheibush Fraenkel, ספר ציון לדרש, Krotoschin 1858 (296); Cracow 1877 (156 leaves) [an alphabetic index of the Haggadic passages]. || Mordecai ben Benjamin, מפתח האגדות, Wilna 1880. || Elijah Cohen, מדרש תלפיות, Warsaw 1875 (281 leaves). [A haggadic Encyclopedia. Title after Canticles 4.4 (comp. Ber. 30a)]. || A. Hyman, בית ועד לחכמים, London 1902, 4to (272) [an alphabetic index to about 14,000 Haggadoth in the Talmuds and Midrashim].

2. Samuel Jaffe (second half of the 16th century) collected all the haggadic passages of the Pal. T., see: יְפֵה מַרְאֶה, Const. 1587, Ven. 1590, Berlin, 1725/26, Amst. 1727, all folio. With some additions by Noah Ḥayyim ben Moses Levin of Kobrin entitled ספר בנין ירושלים [place not given], 1864 (126 leaves) 4to.

Jacob ben Solomon ibn Ḥabib, of Zamora in Spain, gathered together the haggadic passages of the Babyl. Talmud (those of the Pal. Talmud only from Zera'im and Mo'ed). His עין יעקב has been printed very often: Saloniki about 1516, Ven. 1546/47; Wilna 1883, 3 folio volumes (with many commentaries); under the title בית ישראל, Ven. 1566, as עין ישראל, Prosnitz 1603, Ven. 1625, etc., in 2 folio volumes (see Cat. Bodl. No. 5518); with commentary by Abr. Schick, אגדת בבלי כו׳, Königsberg, 1848, 4 vols. 8vo—As the author worked upon manuscripts, the readings of the unmutilated editions of the עין יעקב are frequently of use for the purposes of textual criticism.

Gabr. Müller, ספר אוצר אגדות בבלי וירושלמי. I–III (א–ו). Pressburg, 1877 ff.; IV (ז–ח) Paks, 1901.

El. Susmann Sofer, ילקוט אליעזר, Pressburg, 1874. [The Hag. in T. and Midrash according to subjects.]

J. Ch. Rawnitzki and Ch. N. Bialik, ספר האגדה, 3 volumes, Cracow 1908–1910 [haggadic material from the T. and Midrash arranged according to subjects].

K. W. Perl, אוצר כל [Sayings and parables from Talmudic

literature, alphabetically arranged with notes], I, א–ג, Lublin, 1909 (311 and 36).

Aug. Wünsche, 'Die Zahlensprüche in T. und Midrasch', *ZDMG*, 1911, 57–100, 395–421; 1912, 415–459.

W. Bacher (died December 25, 1913); s. M. Liber, *REJ*, LXVII, 161–169, *Die Agada der Tannaiten*, 2 volumes, Strassburg, 1884. 1890, vol. I, 2nd edition, 1903; *Die A. der babylon. Amoräer*, 1878; *Die A. der palästinens. Amoräer*, 3 volumes, 1892–99; *Die A. der Tannaiten u. Amoräer: Bibelstellenregister* 1902 (92). | Hebrew index by M. Guttmann in Blau L., *Bacher Vilmos élte és Müködésé* (life and work of W. B.), Budapest, 1913, 117–136.| *Rabbanan. Die Gelehrten der Tradition, Beitrag zur Geschichte der anonymen Agada*, Budapest 1914 (104). | *Die Proömien der alten jüd. Homilie*, Leipzig 1913 (126), comp. V. Aptowitzer, *MGWJ*, 1916, 184–188.

Aug. Wünsche, *Der Jerus. T. in seinen haggad. Bestandtheilen . . übertragen*, Zurich, 1880; *Der Babyl. T. in seinen hagg. Bestandtheilen. . . übs.*, Leipzig 1886, s. above p. 144 α. γ.

Jo. Buxtorf, fil., *Florilegium Hebraicum*, Basel 1647 (390).

P. I. Hershon, *A Talmudic Miscellany, or, A thousand and one Extracts from the T., the Midrashim, and the Kabbala.* London 1880 (27 and 361). || Idem, *Treasures of the T., being a series of classified subjects from A to L compiled and translated from the Babylonian T.*, London 1881 (330).

R. J. Fürstenthal, *Rabbinnische* [sic] *Anthologie, oder Sammlung von Erzählungen, Sprichwörtern . . . der alten Hebräer*, Breslau 1834 (384) [only in German]. || Gius. Levi, *Parabeln, Legenden und Gedanken aus Thalmud und Midrasch.* Translated by M. Seligmann, 3rd edition, Leipzig 1904 (394). || S. Rapoport, *Tales and Maxims from the Midrash*, London 1907 (272). || Judah Seni (di Cologna, in the 16th century), יהודה יעלה, *Sammlungen von Sentenzen u. Sprüchwörtern im T. u. Midrasch.* Jerusalem [Berlin] 1890 (204 and 54). || Israel Michelstädt, מִלִּין דְּרַבָּנָן, often printed, for instance, in Frankfort o. O. 1781; Warsaw 1875, 1881. || Leop. Dukes, *Rabbinische Blumenlese* [Sayings from Ben Sira, Talmud and Midrashim, with a translation and glossary]. Leipzig 1844 (333). || M. C. Wahl, *Das Sprichwort der hebräisch-aramäischen Literatur mit bes. Berücksichtigung des Sprichwortes der neueren Umgangssprachen*, I, Leipzig 1870 (164) 4to. || Moïse Schuhl, *Sentences et proverbes du T. et du Midrasch, suivis du traité d'Aboth* [with a translation and notes], Paris, 1878 (546). || K. W. Perl, אוצר לשון חכמים, Warsaw, 1900 (336). [6,424 numbers; compares also sayings and proverbs from Latin, German, etc.]. || J. J. Weissberg, משלי קדמונים, 2nd edition, Nischyn, 1900 (85). || Moses Lewin, *Aramäische Sprichwörter u. Volkssprüche.* Frankfort o. Main 1895 (12 and 90).

M. Goldman, משלי חכמים, *Proverbs of the Sages* [with translation and annotations]. New York 1911 (287).

3. J. Bergmann, 'Geschichte u. Legende,' in: *Schwarz-Festschr.*, 89–108.

Louis Ginzberg, *The Legends of the Jews*, 4 volumes, Philadelphia 1909–1914 (424, 375, 481, 448) [I. From Creation to Jacob. II. From Joseph to the Exodus. III. To the death of Moses]. || Micha Josef bin Gorion, *Die Sagen der Juden*, 2 volumes, Frankfort o. Main 1913, 1914 (378 and 446) [I. Prehistoric age. II. The Patriarchs]; *Der Born Judas*, Leipzig 1917 ff.

Aug. Wünsche, *Schöpfung u. Sündenfall des ersten Menschenpaares im jüd. u. moslemischen Sagenkreis*, Leipzig 1906 (84).

V. Aptowitzer, *Kain und Abel in der Agada*, etc., Vienna, 1922.

B. Beer, *Leben Abrahams nach Auffassung der jüdischen Sage*, Leipzig 1859 (215). || M. Doctor, *Abram. Jugendgeschichte des Erzvaters Abraham nach der talmud. Sage.* Frankfort o. Main 1905 (62). || P. Billerbeck, 'Abrahams Leben u. Bedeutung für das Reich Gottes nach Auffassung der älteren Haggada', in the journal *Nathanael* 1899, 1900, edited by myself.

Kurrein, *Traum u. Wahrheit. Lebensbild Josefs nach der Agada*, 2d edition, Brünn, 1889 (182).

B. Beer, *Leben Moses nach Auffassung der jüd. Sage. Ein Fragment aus dessen handschriftl. Nachlasse*, Berlin 1863. || Salv. de Benedetti, *Vita e morte di Mosè. Leggende ebraiche tradotte, illustrate e comparate*, Pisa, 1879 (336).

J. S. Renzer, *Hauptpersonen des Richterbuches in T. und Midrasch*, I, *Simson*, Berlin 1902 (44).

A. Rosner, *Davids Leben u. Charakter nach T. und Midrasch* [Diss. Bern], Oldenburg, 1908 (92).

G. Salzberger, *Die Salomo-Sage in der semit. Literatur.* Berlin 1907 (129); *Salomos Tempelbau u. Thron in der semit. Sagenliteratur*, Berlin 1912 (111). || R. Faerber, *König Salomon in der Tradition* (Diss. Strassburg), Vienna, 1902 (11 and 70); *Entwicklung der Sage von Salomo u. dem Todesengel*, Frankfort o. Main 1904 (20).

B. Fischer, *Daniel u. seine drei Gefährten in T. u. Midrasch* (Temesvar) Frankfort o. Main 1906 (106).

Abr. Sarsowsky, *Die ethisch-religiöse Bedeutung der alttestamentl. Namen* [of persons] *nach T., Targum und Midraš* (Diss. Königsberg i. Pr.), 1904 (90).

4. A. Sulzbach, 'Das Mašal [parable] im Midraš', in Wohlgemuth's *Jeschurun* V (1918), 337–348.

M. Güdemann, 'Mythenmischung in der Haggada. Ein Beitrag zur jüd. Sagengeschichte, wie zur Mythologie der Ägypter, Phöniker u. Griechen': *MGWJ*, 1876. [Also in: G., *Religionsgeschichtliche Studien*, Leipzig 1876, 1–64].

M. Gaster, 'Beiträge zur vergleichenden Sagen- u. Märchenkunde', in: *MGWJ*, 1880. 1881. | Idem, 'Zur Quellenkunde deutscher Sagen u. Märchen': *Germania, Vierteljahrsschrift für deutsche Alterthumskunde*, XXV (1880), 274 ff.; XXVI (1881), 199 ff.

Sam. Back, 'Die Fabel in T. und Midraš': *MGWJ*, 1875, 1880, 1881, 1883, 1884.

Max Grünbaum, *Neue Beiträge zur semit. Sagenkunde*, Leiden, 1893 (291); *Aufsätze zur Sprach- u. Sagenkunde*, Berlin 1901 (18 and 600).

J. Schapiro, *Die Haggadischen Elemente im erzählenden Teil des Korans*, I, Leipzig 1907 (96).

J. Friedländer, *Die Chadhirlegende u. der Alexanderroman*, Leipzig 1913 (24 and 338. Alexander's expedition a. the T. 42–50). Comp. *ZDMG*, 1913, 739–751.

Ign. Ziegler, *Die Königsgleichnisse des Midrasch beleuchtet durch die römische Kaiserzeit*, Breslau, 1903 (32, 453 and 192).

Sol. Hurwitz, 'Pygmy-legends in Jewish literature': *JQR*, N. S., VI, 339–358.

M. Huber, *Die Wanderlegende von den Siebenschläfern*,

Leipzig 1910 (21, 574 and 32). Comp. W. Weyh, *ZDMG*, 1911, 289–301 (Mongolian material from Russian sources).

M. Grünwald, 'Die Kirchenväter in ihrem Verhältnis zur . . . Haggada,' in: Königsberger's *Monatsblätter für Vergangenheit u. Gegenwart des Judentums*, I, Berlin 1890–91, Parts 1–4 [Salamander, Sinai, Adam, Chiliasm, Resurrection of the dead, The Last Day] (Reprint: Jungbunzlau, 1891, 49 pp.). || M. Friedländer, *Patristische u. talmudische Studien*. Vienna, 1878 (148). [Moses and Plato; Judaism and Christianity; Justin's Dialogue with Tryphon. Comp. *Theol. Litztg.*, 1878, No. 25]. || A. H. Goldfahn, *Die Kirchenväter u. die Agada*. I: *Justinus Martyr u. die Agada*, Breslau, 1873 (54) [reprinted from *MGWJ*]. || L. Ginzberg, *Die Haggada bei den Kirchenvätern*. I: *Die H. in den pseudo-hieronymianischen 'Quaestiones'*, Amst. 1899 (Diss. Heidelberg. 132 pp.). | 'Die H. bei den K.; 1. Buch Mose', in: *MGWJ*, 1898, 1899 [also a reprint of 131 pp.]

S. Krauss, 'The Jews in the Works of the Church Fathers': *JQR*, 1893, 122–157; 1894, 82–99, 225–261.

§ 7. Further Material for the Understanding of the Old Testament (compare § 6, 3).

G. Marx (Dalman), *Traditio Rabbinorum veterrima de librorum Vis Ti ordine atque origine*, Leipzig 1884 (60).

B. Aptowitzer, 'Rabbinische Berichte über die Entstehung der LXX', in: הקדם (Petersburg), II (1908), 11–27, 102–122; III (1912), 4–17.

M. Eisenstadt, *Über Bibelkritik in der talmud. Literatur*, Berlin 1894 (55).

V. Aptowitzer, *Das Schriftwort in der rabbin. Literatur*, 5 parts, Vienna, 1906–1915. [Divergences from the masoretic text in citations in the Talmud and Midrash].

M. Friedmann, 'Die Verseinteilung der Bibel nach dem T. u. Midraš,' in: הקדם Hebr. part I (1907), 116–123, 149–155; III (1912), 30–38.

J. Cohn, 'Die Schaubrote nach Bibel u. T.,' in: *Hoffmann-Festschr.* 71–86.

Ernst Bass, *Die Merkmale der israelit. Prophetie nach der traditionellen Auffassung des T.*, Berlin 1917 (45).

Georg Aicher, *Das Alte Test. in der Mischna*, 1906 (see below p. 285 α); comp. the important review by Bacher, *JQR*, XIX, 589–606 and Blau, *MGWJ*, LI, 569–89.

Balth. Scheidt (1614–1670, Professor of Theology in Strassburg), *Nucleus Talmudico-Biblicus . . . omnia dicta Biblica quae citant vel explicant Doctores Talmud Babylonici . . . Latine reddita* [5 quarto volumes, not printed, see M. Steinschneider, *Catalog der hebr. Handschriften in der Stadtbibliothek zu Hamburg*, 1878, No. 64, 65].

P. J. Hershon, חמשה חומשי התורה לפי התלמוד I [Genesis] London, 1874 (437). || In translation: *The Pentateuch according to the Talmud*, I: *Genesis with a Talmudical commentary*, 1883 (32 a. 531).

Mor. Rahmer, *Die hebr. Traditionen in den Werken des Hieronymus. Quaestiones in Genesin*, Breslau, 1861 (74). | *Die Commentare zu den zwölf kleinen Propheten*, 1. Hälfte, Berlin 1902 (174).

P. Billerbeck, 'Der 110 Psalm in der altrabbin. Literatur,' in: *Nathanael*, 1910, 21–29, 33–42.

H. Deutsch, *Die Sprüche Salomo's nach der Auffassung im T. u. Midrasch.* I: *Einleitendes.* Berlin 1885 (108).

H. E. Kaufmann, *Die Anwendung des Buches Hiob in der rabbin. Agadah.* I [the Tannaïm] Frkf. o. M. 1893 (43). Comp. M. Lewin, *Targum u. Midrasch zum Buche Hiob in ihrem gegenseitigen Verhältnis*, Mainz, 1895 (63). || J. Wiernikowski, *Das Buch Hiob nach der Auffassung der rabbin. Litteratur in den ersten fünf nachchrist. Jahrhunderten.* I (Dissert. Breslau), Berlin 1902 (92).

S. Schiffer, *Das Buch Kohelet nach der Auffassung der Weisen des T. u. Midrasch.* I [up to the completion of the Babyl. T.] Frkf. o. M. 1884 (140).

§ 8. Theology, Liturgy, Sects, Superstition.

a. Theology.

S. Schechter, *Studies in Judaism*, I, New York, 1896 (147ff.: Dogmas, 182 ff.: History of Jewish tradition, 213 ff.: Divine retribution); II, London, 1908 (362). | *Some Aspects of Rabbinic Theology*, London, 1909.

M. Duschak, *Biblisch-talmud. Glaubenslehre*, Vienna, 1873 (25 a. 256).

Ferd. Weber, *Jüdische Theologie auf Grund des Talmud u. verwandter Schriften*, 2d edition, Leipzig 1897 (40 a. 427). (First edition 1880, as *System der altsynagogalen palästinischen Theologie*). [Industrious, but uncritical].

W. Bousset, *Die Religion des Judts. im neutest. Zeitalter*, 2d edition, Berlin 1906 (618). [Without personal knowledge of the original sources in Hebrew and Aramaic, see F. Perles, *B. s Rel. des J. im neutestl. Z. kritisch untersucht*. Berlin 1903 (133).]

Leop. Löw, 'Die talmudische Lehre vom göttlichen Wesen', 1866, in: *Schriften* I, Szegedin, 1889, 177–186. || J. Abelson, *The Immanence of God in Rabbinical Literature*, London, 1912 [tries to show that 'God is very near indeed.']

Alex. Kohut, *Die jüdische Angelologie u. Dämonologie in ihrer Abhängigkeit vom Parsismus*, Leipzig 1866 (107). || M. Schwab, *Vocabulaire de l'angélologie d'après les mss. hébreux*, Paris, 1897 (318) 4to; *Supplément*, 1899 (50) 4to. || V. Aptowitzer, 'La chute de Satan et des anges': *REJ*, LIV, 59–63. || B. Heller, 'La chute des anges': *REJ*, LX, 202–212.

Alex. Kohut, 'Was hat die talmud. Eschatologie aus dem Parsismus aufgenommen?' *ZDMG*, 1867, 552–591.

Aug. Wünsche, 'Die Vorstellungen vom Zustande nach dem Tode nach Apokryphen, T. u. Kirchenvätern': *Jbb. für protest. Theologie*, 1880, 355–383, 495–523. || S. Spira, *Die Eschatologie der Juden nach Talmud u. Midrasch*, 1889 (39 pages, Dissert. Halle). || Bernh. Templer, *Die Unsterblichkeitslehre (Psychologie, Messianologie und Eschatologie) bei den jüd. Philosophen des Mittelalters*, Leipzig a. Vienna, 1895 (on the T. see pp. 14–20).

G. Dalman, *Der leidende u. sterbende Messias der Synagoge im ersten nachchristl. Jahrtausend*, Berlin 1888 (100). || M. Löwy, 'Messiaszeit u. zukünftige Welt': *MGWJ*, 1897, 392–409. || J. Klausner, *Die Messianischen Vorstellungen des jüdischen Volkes im Zeitalter der Tannaiten*, Berlin 1904 (119); הרעיון המשיחי בישראל מראשיתו ועד חתימת המשנה, 2d edition, Jerusalem, 1926 (346). || M. Rabinsohn, *Le Messianisme dans le Talmud et les Midraschim*, Paris, 1907 (108). || M. J. Lagrange, *Le Messianisme chez les*

Juifs (150 *av. J.-C.* à 200 *ap. J.-C.*) Paris, 1909 (349) [without first-hand knowledge of the rabbinical literature].

Israel Lévi, *Le péché originel dans les anciennes sources juives*, 2me éd., Paris, 1909 (32).

W. O. E. Oesterley, *The Jewish Doctrine of Mediation*, London, 1915.

C. G. Montefiore, 'Rabbinic Conceptions of Repentance': *JQR*, 1904, 209–257.

F. Ch. Porter, 'The yeçer hara, a Study in the Jewish Doctrine of Sin': *Biblical and Semitic studies . . . Yale University*, New York, 1901, 93–156.

A. Marmorstein, *The Doctrine of Merits in Old Rabbinic Literature*, London, 1920 (199).

b. Liturgy.

Ismar Elbogen, *Der jüd. Gottesdienst in seiner geschichtl. Entwicklung*, Leipzig 1913 (619), comp. *MGWJ*, 1916, 468–476.| *Studien zur Geschichte des jüd. Gottesdienstes*, Berlin 1907 (192) [Shema', Shemone Esre, Day of Atonement], comp. *MGWJ*, 1910, 491–503. | 'Bemerkungen zur alten jüd. Liturgie', in: *Kohler-Festschr.*, 74–81. [Tamid end of 4, beginning of 5]. | 'Eingang u. Ausgang des Sabbats nach talmud. Quellen,' in: *Lewy-Festschr.*, 173–187.

K. Kohler, 'Über die Ursprünge u. Grundformen der synagogalen Literatur': *MGWJ*, 1893, 441–451, 489–497.

N. Friedmann, *Das Gebet in den Beurteilungen des T.*, Bern, 1909 (49. Dissert.).

Baruch Homa, מקור ברוך, *Die Quellen der Gebete, deren Begründer u. die Zeit ihrer Abfassung u. Ordnung*, Jerusalem, 1905 (24). || W. Jawitz, מקור הברכות, Berlin 1910 (97). || Commentaries on the Prayer-book, showing the talmudic sources: El. Landshuth, סדור הגיון לב, Königsberg, 1845; S. Baer, סדור עבודת ישראל, Rödelheim, 1868. אוצר התפלות, Wilna, 1914.

D. de Sola Pool, *The Old Jewish-Aramaic Prayer, the Kaddish*, Leipzig 1909 (121).

Emil Schwaab, *Historische Einführung in das Achtzehngebet*, Gütersloh, 1913 (169).

D. Kaufmann, 'Das Alter der drei Benediktionen von Israel, vom Freien und vom Mann': *MGWJ*, 1893, 14–18.

M. Liber, *La récitation du Schema et des Bénédictions*, Paris, 1909 (54) [reprinted from *REJ*, LVII, LVIII, some corrections *REJ*, LXIV, 303].

Ad. Büchler, *Die Priester u. der Cultus im letzten Jahrzehnt des Jerusalemischen Tempels*, Vienna, 1895 (207). Comp. *MGWJ*, 1896, 138 to 144. | 'Zur Geschichte des Tempelkultus in Jerusalem', in *Chwolson-Festschr.*, 1–41 [Distribution by lot of the offices; 8 ff. Simon the Just; 21 ff. The signals in the Temple for the offices].

Jos. Hochman, *Jerusalem Temple Festivities*, London, 1908 (128) [Bikkurim, Water Libation]. || D. Feuchtwang, *Das Wasseropfer u. die damit verbundenen Zeremonien*, Vienna, 1911 (56). [Also coming on the stone שתיה. Reprinted from *MGWJ*, 1910, 1911.]

W. Brandt, *Die jüdischen Baptismen oder das religiöse Waschen u. Baden im Judentum*, Giessen, 1910 (148); *Jüdische Reinheitslehre u. ihre Beschreibung in den Evangelien*, ibidem, 1910 (64). Comp. *REJ*, LXII, 292 to 295. || C. F. Rogers, 'How did the Jews baptize?', in: *Journal of Theological Studies* XII (1911), 437–445 a. XIII (1912), 411–414; comp. thereon J. Abrahams XII, 609–612 [Rogers is against the assumption of complete immersion, Abrahams for it].

D. Feuchtwang, 'Der Tierkreis in der Tradition u. im Synagogenritus': *MGWJ*, 1915, 241–267 (Ḳalir 258 ff.).

Herm. Vogelstein, 'Entstehung u. Entwicklung des Apostolats im Judentum': *MGWJ*, 1905, 427–449. || S. Krauss, 'Die jüdischen Apostel': *JQR*, 1905, 370–383.

c. Religions Disputations and controversies.

The religious disputations, at least most of them, are unhistorical.

Z. Frankel, 'Zur Geschichte der Religionsgespräche': *MGWJ*, IV (1855) 161 ff., 205 ff., 241 ff., 413 ff., 447 ff. || Ch. Obstler, *Die Religionsgespräche im Talmud Babli u. Jeruschalmi*, Bern (Dissert.) 1905 (76). || P. Billerbeck, 'Altjüdische Religionsgespräche', in the journal *Nathanael* edited by me 1909, 13–30, 33–50, 66–80.

M. Joel, *Blicke in die Religionsgeschichte zu Anfang des 2. christl. Jahrhunderts*. 2 volumes, Breslau, 1880, 1883 (177 a. 190).

M. Friedländer, *Das Judenthum in der vorchristl. griechischen Welt, Beitrag zur Entstehungsgeschichte des Christenthums*, Vienna, 1897 (74). | *Der vorchristl. jüdische Gnosticismus*, Göttingen, 1898 (123). | *Die religiösen Bewegungen innerhalb des Judentums im Zeitalter Jesu*, Berlin 1905 (30 a. 380).

J. Bergmann, *Jüdische Apologetik im neutestamentl. Zeitalter*, Berlin 1908 (168) [over against Christianity and the Gnostics].

M. Freimann, 'Die Wortführer des Judentums in den älteren Kontroversen zwischen Juden u. Christen': *MGWJ*, 1911, 555–585 (Papiscus, Justinus); 1912, 49–64, 164–180 (Celsus).

d. Sects.

Ed. Baneth, *Der Ursprung der Sadducäer und Boethusäer*. Berlin 1882 (71).

Isr. Taglicht, *Die Kuthäer als Beobachter des Gesetzes nach talmud. Quellen*, Erlangen (Dissert.) 1888 (45).

S. Krauss, 'Dosithée et les Dosithéens': *REJ*, XLII (1901), 27–42. Comp. Ad. Büchler, p. 220–231 a. XLIII, 50–71.

Joseph Lehmann, 'Les sectes juives mentionnées dans la Mischna de Berakhot et Meguilla': *REJ*, XXX (1895), 182–203; XXXI, 31–46.

A. Marmorstein, 'Les "Épicuriens" dans la littérature talmudique': *REJ*, LIV (1907), 181–193.

Heinr. Kraus, *Begriff u. Form der Häresie nach T. u. Midrasch* (Diss. Bern). Hamburg, 1896 (62) [מינים a. אפיקורוס].

W. Bacher, 'Le mot "Minim" das le Talmud, designe-t-il quelquefois des chrétiens?': *REJ*, XXXVIII (1899), 38–46 [a severe criticism of Friedländer's *Der vorchristl. jüd. Gnosticismus*].

M. Friedländer, 'Encore un mot sur Minim, Minout et Guilionim dans le T.': *REJ*, XXXVIII, 194–203 (a supplement to his book *Der vorchristliche jüdische Gnosticismus*). Comp. further Isr. Lévi, ibid. 204–210.

B. Kellermann, *Kritische Beiträge zur Entstehungsgeschichte des Christentums*, Berlin 1906 (91). [No. 2: The problem of the Minim.]

Concerning the Sadducees and Pharisees see § 10.

A. Marmorstein, *Religionsgeschichtl. Studien*. I *Die Bezeichnungen für Christen u. Gnostiker im T. u. Midraš*, Skotschau 1910 (83). [There is some material here, but it is 'utilized with a degree of carelessness that borders on levity.' W. Bacher.]

A. Büchler, 'Die Minim von Sepphoris u. Tiberias im 2. u. 3. Jahrh.,' in: *Cohen-Festschr.*, 271–296 [claims that these Minim were for the most part antinomistic Gnostics, that there were no Judaeo-Christians among them and that no definite allusions to Christianity could be discovered].

e. Heinr. Laible, *Jesus Christus im Thalmud.* 2d edition, Leipzig 1900 (96 a. 19).

R. Tr. Herford, *Christianity in T. and Midrash*, London, 1903 (449). See Bacher's review, *JQR*, XVII, 171–183.

H. L. Strack, *Jesus, die Häretiker u. die Christen nach den ältesten jüd. Angaben* [texts, translation and commentary]. Leipzig 1910 (128).

J. Klausner, ישו הנוצרי, Jerusalem, 1922 (468). | English translation: *Jesus of Nazareth*, New York, 1925 (434).

f. Alex. Kohut, 'Les fêtes persanes et babyloniennes mentionnées dans les Talmuds de Babylone et de Jérus.': *REJ*, XXIV, 256–271.

Isid. Lévy, 'Cultes et rites syriens dans le Talmud': *REJ*, XLIII, 183–205.

g. Superstition and mythological material.

D. Joël, *Der Aberglaube u. die Stellung des Judenthums zu demselben.* Breslau I, 1881 (116). II, 1883 (65).

Gideon Brecher, *Das Transcendentale, Magie u. magische Heilarten im Talmud.* Vienna, 1850 (233).

Leop. Löw, *Zur talmudischen Mantik*, 1866, in: *Schriften* II, Szegedin, 1890, 105–114; *Die Astrologie bei den Juden*, 1863: II, 115–131.

Sal. Thein, *Das Princip des planetarischen Einflusses nach der Anschauung des Talmuds*, 2nd edition, Vienna, 1876 (102).

S. Wolffsohn, *Oneirologie im T., oder der Traum nach Auffassung des T.* Breslau, 1874. || Ad. Löwinger, *Der Traum in der jüd. Literatur*, Leipzig 1908 (35).

Ludw. Blau, *Das altjüdische Zauberwesen*, Budapest, 1898 (167).

J. Bergel, *Mythologie der alten Hebräer*, Leipzig 1882 f. (118 a. 80).

E. Bischoff, *Babylonisch-Astrales im Weltbilde des T. u. Midrasch*, Leipzig 1907 (172).

D. Feuchtwang, 'Der Tierkreis in der Tradition u. im Synagogenritus': *MGWJ*, 1915, 241–267.

S. Funk, 'Babylonisches im babyl. Talmud': *MGWJ*, 1910, 268–273 [festivals, solar deity, dove].

§ 9. Ethics.

H. B. Fassel, *Die mosaisch-rabbinische Tugend- u. Rechtslehre*, 2nd edition, Gross-Kanischa, 1862.

J. Scheftelowitz, 'Grundlagen einer jüd. Ethik': *MGWJ*, 1912, 129 to 146, 359–378, 478–495 [Love of the neighbor; enemy; child; protection of animals]. || L. Lazarus, *Zur Charakteristik der talmudischen Ethik*, Breslau (Berlin) 1877 (48). || Mor. Lazarus, *Die Ethik des Judenthums*, Frkf. o. M. I, 1898 (25 a. 469); II, 1911 (55 a. 404).

M. Bloch, *Die Ethik in der Halacha*, Budapest, 1886 (96). || Marc Lévy, *Essai sur la morale du T.*, Brussels, 1892 (136). || Salo Stein, *Materialien zur Ethik des T. I. Die Pflichtenlehre*, Frkf. o. M. 1894 (185) [immature, see *MGWJ*, 1897, 239 f.]. || Albert Katz, *Der wahre Talmudjude*, Berlin 1893 (see below p. 281 n. 15).

S. Schaffer, *Das Recht u. seine Stellung zur Moral nach talmudischer Sitten- u. Rechtslehre*, Frkf. o. M., 1889 (132). || M. Güdemann, 'Moralische Rechtseinschränkung im mosaisch-rabbinischen Rechtssystem': *MGWJ*, 1917, 422–443 (שורת הדין a. לִפְנִים מְשׁוּרַת הדין).

H. G. Enelow, 'Kawwana, The Struggle for Inwardness in Judaism,' in *Kohler-Festschr.*, 82–107.

M. Steckelmacher, 'Etwas über die "leichten u. schweren" Gebote,' in: *Schwarz-Festschr.*, 259–268 ['light' and 'heavy' at first according to the penal measure, later with a deeper religious conception].

J. Günzig, 'Pessimistische Gedanken in T. u. Midraš', in: *Maybaum-Festschr.*, 148–156.

F. Perles, 'Zur Würdigung der Sittenlehre des Ts.,' in: F. P., *Jüdische Skizzen*, Leipzig 1912, 114–124 [Ḳiddush ha-shem, love of truth].

S. Stein, 'Das Problem d. Notlüge im T.': *JbJLG*, V, 206–224, 384 [Ned. 3.4].

H. Cohen, *Die Nächstenliebe im T.*, 3rd edition, Marburg, 1888 (35). || N. J. Weinstein, *Geschichtliche Entwickelung des Gebotes der Nächstenliebe innerhalb des Judenthums*, Berlin 1891 (48). || M. Güdemann, *Nächstenliebe. Ein Beitrag zur Erklärung des Matthäus-Evangeliums.* Vienna, 1890 (48). | 'Jüdische u. christliche Nächstenliebe': *MGWJ*, 1893, 153–164 [controversy with H. Hilgenfeld]. || K. Kohler, 'Die Nächstenliebe im Judentum', in: *Cohen-Festschr.*, 469–480.

E. Grünebaum, *Die Sittenlehre des Judenthums andern Bekenntnissen gegenüber.* [Also concerning Pharisaism and its attitude towards the founder of the Christian religion], 2nd edition, Strassburg, 1878 (36 a. 448).

M. Duschak, *Die Moral der Evangelien u. der T.*, Brünn, 1877 (58). || S. J. Moscoviter, *Het Nieuve Testament en de T.*, Rotterdam, 1884. || H. Oort, *Evangelie en T., uit het oogpunt der zedelijkheid vergeleken*, Leiden, 1881 (107). || Idem, *The T. and the New Testament.* Reprinted from the *Modern Review.* London, 1883 (57).

§ 10. Further Material for the Understanding of the New Testament.

a. Joh. Lightfoot, *Horae hebraicae et talmudicae* (Gospels, Acts, Romans, 1. Corinthians): *Opera omnia*, edited by Joh. Leusden, Franeker, 1699 fol., II, 243–742, 783–928.

Joh. Gerh. Meuschen, *Novum Testamentum ex Talmude et antiquitatibus Judaeorum illustratum.* Leipzig 1736 (1216). 4to [A collection containing: Balth. Scheid, Loca Talmudica concerning Jesus, the Apostles and explanations of the New Testament, p. 1–232; furthermore treatises by Joh. Andr. Danz, Jacob Rhenferd, Herm. Witsius, Meuschen].

Christian Schöttgen, *Horae hebraicae et talmudicae in universum Novum Testamentum.* Dresden a. Leipzig 1733 (1280), 4to. Vol. II: *Horae hebr. et talm. in theologiam Judaeorum dogmaticam antiquam et orthodoxam de Messia impensae*, 1742 (996). | *Jesus der Wahre Messias aus der alten u. reinen Jüdischen Theologie dargestellt u. erläutert*, Leipzig 1748. [Translation of II, 1–709].

Joh. Jak. Wettstein, *Novum Testamentum graecum . . . cum lectionibus variantibus . . . necnon commentario . . . ex scriptoribus veteribus hebraeis, graecis et latinis*, 2 volumes, fol. Amst., 1751, 52.

F. Nork, *Rabbinische Quellen u. Parallelen zu neutestamentl. Schriftstellen*. Leipzig 1839. (200 a. 419.) [From Lightfoot, Schöttgen, etc.]

Carl Siegfried, *Analecta Rabbinica ad N. T. et patres ecclesiasticos spectantia.* Leipzig 1875 (Congratulatory publication on the occasion of the Jubilee of the Magdeburg Domgymnasium, p. 3–11). | 'Rabbinische Analekten,' in: *Jbb. für protest. Theologie*, 1876, 476–478.

Franz Delitzsch, 'Horae Hebraicae et Talmudicae. Ergänzungen zu Lightfoot u. Schöttgen': *Zeitschrift für die gesammte luther. Theologie u. Kirche*, 1876–1878.

Aug. Wünsche, *Neue Beiträge zur Erläuterung der Evangelien aus T. u. Midrasch.* Göttingen, 1878 (566). [Partial to the Pharisees.]

Th. Robinson, *The Evangelists and the Mishna.* London, 1859 (332).

W. H. Bennett, *The Mishna as illustrating the Gospels.* Cambridge, 1884 (116).

H. L. Strack u. Paul Billerbeck, *Kommentar zum Neuen Testament aus Talmud u. Midraš*, 3 volumes, Munich, C. H. Beck, 1921 ff. [The intention was to present accurately and in convenient form the whole material hitherto known.]

b. W. van Surenhuysen, ספר המשוה *sive* Βίβλος Καταλλαγῆς *in quo secundum . . . Hebraeorum formulas allegandi, & modos interpretandi conciliantur loca ex V. in N. T. allegata.* Amst., 1713 (712), 4to.

Er. Bischoff, *Jesus u. die Rabbinen. Jesu Bergpredigt u. 'Himmelreich' in ihrer Unabhängigkeit vom Rabbinismus.* Leipzig 1905 (114). || G. Friedlaender, *The Jewish Sources of the Sermon of the Mount*, London, 1911 (30 a. 301).

G. Klein, *Den första Kristna Katekesen.* Stockholm, 1908 (350). Translation: *Der älteste christliche Katechismus u. die jüd. Propaganda-Literatur*, Berlin 1909 (273). [Deals with the

Didache. Opposes the main thesis of Bischoff's work, but the arguments are not convincing. Useful as a collection of material].

G. Dalman, *Die Worte Jesu* I, Leipzig 1898 (319): *Einl. u. wichtige Begriffe* [the Aeon, eternal life, designations of God and Jesus].

P. Fiebig, *Altjüdische Gleichnisse und die Gleichnisse Jesu.* Tübingen, 1904 (167).

M. Freimann, 'Eine missverstandene Rede Jesu [Matth. 12.1–8]': *MGWJ*, 1914, 281–289.

M. Güdemann, 'Die λόγια des Matthäus als Gegenstand einer Satyre [Mt. 5.17 a. Shab. 116b]', in: G., *Religionsgeschichtl. Studien*, Leipzig 1876, 65–97, comp. *MGWJ*, 1877, 141–144.

M. Güdemann, 'Das Judentum im neutestamentl. Zeitalter in christl. Darstellung'. *MGWJ*, 1903, 38–53, 120–136, 231–249.

M. Freimann, 'Wie verhielt sich das Judentum zu Jesus u. dem entstehenden Christentum?', in: *MGWJ*, 1910, 697–712; 1911, 160 to 176, 296–316 [the conclusion is missing].

M. Güdemann, 'Das 4. Evangelium u. der Rabbinismus': *MGWJ*, 1893, 249–257, 297–303, 345–356.

D. Chwolson, *Das letzte Passamahl Christi u. der Tag seines Todes nach den in Übereinstimmung gebrachten Berichten der Synoptiker u. des Evangelium Johannis, nebst einem Anhang: Das Verhältnis der Pharisäer, Sadducäer u. der Juden übh. zu Jesus Christus nach den mit Hilfe rabbinischer Quellen erläuterten Berichten der Synoptiker.* Petersburg, 1892 (132), large 4to. | Anastatic reprint [with additional notes and corrections]. Leipzig 1908 (11 a. 190).

Isr. Lévi, 'Le sacrifice d'Isaac et la mort de Jésus': *REJ*, LXIV, 161 to 184; LXV, 138–143, 311.

c. Mor. Löwy, 'Die Paulinische Lehre vom Gesetz': *MGWJ*, 1903, 322–339, 417–433, 534–544; 1904, 268–276, 321–327, 400–416.

J. Eschelbacher, 'Zur Geschichte u. Charakteristik der paulinischen Briefe', in: *MGWJ*, 1907, 395–428, 542–568 [Conclusion is wanting. Eschelbacher, following Rud. Steck and W. C. van Manen, maintains that 'the 4 main Epistles' are post-Pauline and endeavors to prove it from the manner in which the Old Testament is expounded].

M. Güdemann, 'Zur Erklärung des Barnabasbriefes', in: *Religionsgeschichtl. Studien*, 1876, 100–131.

d. S. Bamberger, *Sadduzäer u. Pharisäer in ihren Beziehungen zu Alexander Jannai u. Salome*, Frkf. o. M. 1907 (26) [according to Is. Halévy].

Ad. Schwarz, 'La victoire des Pharisiens sur les Sadducéens en matière de droit successoral'. *REJ*, LXIII, 51–62 (B. B. 115b; Meg. Ta'anith 5).

Rud. Leszynsky, *Die Sadduzäer*, Berlin 1912 (309). [The written Torah was to them the only norm, the Hellenization was only a means to the end of exerting influence on the government. Comp. also B. Revel, *JQR*, N. S. VII, 429–438.]

Kaufm. Kohler, 'Sadducees': *JE*, X, 630–633; 'Pharisees': *JE*, IX, 661 to 666. || J. Lauterbach, 'The S. and Ph., a study of their respective attitudes towards the Law', in: *Kohler-Festschr.* 176–198.

R. Tr. Herford, *Pharisaism, its Aim and its Methods*, London, 1912 (340). [entirely one-sided in favor of the Pharisees]. Comp. Ehrh. Bosse, *Nathanael*, 1915, p. 1–18; Julien Weill, *REJ*, LXV, 1–15.

M. Schreiner, 'Was lehrten die Pharisäer?', in: *JbJGL*, II, 55–74. || I. Elbogen, *Die Religionsanschauungen der Ph. mit besonderer Berücksichtigung der Begriffe Gott u. Mensch*, Berlin 1904 (88).

E. Schürer, 'Die Ph. u. Sadd.': *Gesch.*, 4th edition, II, 447–489.

A. Marmorstein; *Religionsgeschichtl. Studien*, II *Die Schriftgelehrten*, Skotschau, 1912 (119).

§ 11. Philosophy, Mathematics, Linguistics, Pedagogy.

a. Abr. Nager, *Die Religionsphilosophie des Thalmud in ihren Hauptmomenten dargestellt*. Leipzig 1864 (44).

M. Jacobson, *Versuch einer Psychologie des Thalmud*. Hamburg, 1878 (107). || J. Wiesner, 'Zur talmudischen Psychologie': *Mag.*, I, II (1874 f.). || R. Wohlberg, *Grundlinien einer talmud. Psychologie* (Diss. Erlangen) Berlin 1902 (57).

b. B. Zuckermann, *Das Mathematische im T. Beleuchtung*

. . . *der Talmudstellen mathematischen Inhalts.* Breslau, 1878, 4to (64). [Comp. M. Steinschneider in: *HBg*, XV (1875), 128.]

c. A. Berliner, *Beiträge zur hebr. Grammatik im T. u. Midrasch*, Berlin 1879 (59); comp. Goldziher, *ZDMG*, XXXIV, 375–384. || Z. Rabbiner, *Beiträge zur hebräischen Synonymik in T. u. Midrasch;* I: *Synonyme Nomina*, Berlin [Dissert. Heidelberg] 1899 (28 a. 65).

d. B. Strassburger, *Geschichte der Erziehung u. des Unterrichts bei den Israeliten. Von der vortalmudischen Zeit bis auf die Gegenwart.* Stuttgart, 1885 (310). || N. H. Imber, 'Education in the T.' in: *Report of the Commissioner of Education for 1894–95*, chap. XLVI, p. 1795–1820, Washington, 1896. || J. Ster, *Die talmudische Pädagogik*, Breslau, 1915 (1402) [after Herbart].

E. van Gelder, *Die Volksschule des jüd. Altertums nach talmud. u. rabbinischen Quellen*, Berlin 1872 (31). || Joseph Simon, *L'éducation et l'instruction des enfants chez les anciens Juifs d'après la Bible et le T.*, 3d ed., Leipzig 1879 (63).

Blach-Gudensberg, *Das Pädagogische im T.* Halberstadt, 1880 (26).

Sam. Marcus, *Zur Schul-Pädagogik des T.*, Berlin 1866 (55). [Vienna 1877 in 2d (unrevised) edition as second part of: *Die Pädagogik des israelit. Volkes von der Patriarchenzeit bis auf den T.*]

M. Duschak, *Schulgesetzgebung u. Methodik der alten Israeliten.* Vienna, 1872 (179). || Jos. Wiesen, *Geschichte u. Methodik des Schulwesens im talmudischen Altertume.* Strassburg, 1892 (49). || Jul. Lewit, *Darstellung der theoret. u. prakt. Pädagogik im jüd. Altertum*, Berlin 1896 (79). || Sal. Stein, *Schulverhältnisse, Erziehungslehre u. Unterrichtsmethoden im T.*, Berlin 1901 (37). || L. Wiesner, *Die Jugendlehrer in der talmud. Zeit*, Vienna, 1914 (85).

W. Bacher, 'Das altjüdische Schulwesen': *JbJGL*, VI, 48–81.

S. Frankfurter, *Das altjüdische Erziehungs-und Unterrichtswesen im Lichte moderner Bestrebungen*, 4th edition, Vienna 1910 (41).

§ 12. Jurisprudence.

a. Ch. Tschernowitz, 'Zur Erforschung der Geschichte des jüd. Rechts': *Zeitschrift für vergleichende Rechtswissenschaft*,

XXVII, 404–424. [Jewish law, likewise, had a development, one which proceeded from its innermost foundations.]

b. J. L. Saalschütz, *Das Mosaische Recht, nebst den thalmudisch-rabbinischen Bestimmungen*, 2d ed., Berlin 1853 (34 a. 879).

S. Mayer, *Die Rechte der Israeliten, Athener u. Römer.* 2 volumes. Leipzig 1862–66 (418 a. 564).

Jacques Levy, *La jurisprudence du Pentateuque et du Talmud.* Constantine, 1879 (51).

Josef Kohler (died 1919), 'Darstellung des talmudischen Rechtes', in: *Zeitschrift für vergleich. Rechtswissenschaft*, XX (1908), 161–264 [on the basis of Goldschmidt's translation; hence to the exclusion of the law pertaining to the family. Comp. V. Aptowitzer in *MGWJ*, 1908, 37–56, 185–205].

M. W. Rapoport, *Der T. u. sein Recht*, 2d ed., Berlin 1912 (148 a. 49 a. 68). [General remarks, intestate inheritance, donations, obligations. Reprint from: *Zeitschr. f. vergleich. Rechtswiss.* XIV–XVI.]

Sal. Gandz, *Recht* (=*Monumenta Talmudica* II) Vienna, 1913 ff.

On the dependence of Armenian law on the Mosaic see D. H. Müller, *Semitica* II, Vienna, 1907, in: *Sitzungsberichte der Wiener Akademie, hist.-philos. Kl.* CLIV. | V. Aptowitzer, ibid. CLVII; *Wiener Zeitschrift f. die Kunde des Morgenlandes*, XXI (1907), 251–267; *JQR*, N. S., I, 217–229.

V. Aptowitzer, *Die syrischen Rechtsbücher u. das mosaisch-talmudische Recht*, Vienna, 1909 (108).

M. M. Mielziner, *Legal Maxims and Fundamental Laws of the Civil and Criminal Code of the Talmud*, Cincinnati, 1898.

Max Eschelbacher, 'Recht u. Billigkeit in der Jurisprudenz des T.,' in: *Cohen-Festschr.*, 501–514.

A. Perls, 'Der Minhag im T.,' in: *Lewy-Festschr.*, 66–75.

Armin Abeles, 'כל ישראל ערבים זה בזה, Alle Israeliten Sind Bürgen, einer für den andern,' in: *Schwarz-Festschr.* 231–246. | 'Der Bürge nach biblischem Recht,' *MGWJ*, 1922, 279 ff.

c. J. Selden, *De synedriis et praefecturis juridicis veterum Ebraeorum*, London, 1650; Amst., 1679, 4to.

Dav. Hoffmann, *Der obere Gerichtshof in der Stadt des Heiligthums*, Berlin 1878 (47), 4to.

Heinr. Heinemann, 'Das Königtum nach bibl.-talmudischer Rechtsauffassung': *JbJLG*, X, 115–190.

S. Funk, 'Die Gerichtshöfe im nachexil. Judt.': *MGWJ*, 1911, 33–42 (number of members); 699–712 (functions). On the number of members see A. Karlin, 1913, 24–31 a. in retort Funk 501–506.

L. Fischer, 'Die Urkunden im T., zusgestellt, erklärt u. mit den Ausgrabungen verglichen': *JbJLG*, IX, 47–197. Reprint Berlin 1912 (157). The second part, 'Die Kaufverträge,' appeared in *JbJLG*, XIII (1920), 1–54.

d. Z. Frankel, *Der gerichtliche Beweis nach mosaisch-talmudischem Rechte.* Berlin 1846 (544).

J. Klein, *Das Gesetz über das gerichtliche Beweisverfahren nach mosaisch-thalmudischem Rechte*, 1885 (41).

Oscar Bähr, *Das Gesetz über falsche Zeugen nach Bibel u. T.*, Berlin 1882 (80). || J. Horovitz, *Zur rabbin. Lehre von den falschen Zeugen*, Frkf. o. M., 1914 (14 a. 90).

Z. Frankel, *Die Eidesleistung der Juden.* Dresden a. Leipzig 1840 (170). Second edition, 1847 (263).

J. Blumenstein, *Die verschiedenen Eidesarten nach mosaisch-talmudischem Rechte u. die Fälle ihrer Anwendung.* Frkf. o. M., 1883 (31) [not thorough].

e. Criminal law.

S. Mendelsohn, *The Criminal Jurisprudence of the Ancient Hebrews; compiled from the T. and other rabbinical writings, and compared with Roman and English Penal Jurisprudence.* Baltimore, 1891 (270).

J. Fürst, *Das peinliche Rechtsverfahren im jüdischen Alterthum*, Heidelberg, 1870 (48). || Moses Bloch, *Das mosaisch-talmud. Strafgerichtsverfahren*, Budapest, 1901 (71). Comp. *MGWJ*, 1902, 381–388.

H. B. Fassel, *Das mosaisch-rabbinische Strafrecht u. strafrechtliche Gerichtsverfahren*, Gross-Kanischa, 1870.

M. Duschak, *Das mosaisch-talmud. Strafrecht*, Vienna, 1869 (95).

P. B. Benny, *The Criminal Code of the Jews*, London, 1880.

J. Wohlgemuth, 'Das jüd. Strafrecht u. die positive Strafrechtsschule,' in: *Berliner-Festschr.*, 364–376.

M. Waxman, 'Civil a. Criminal Procedure of Jewish Courts,' in: *Jewish Theological Seminary of America Students' Annual*, I (New York, 1914), 259–309.

D. W. Amram, 'The Summons, a Study in Jewish a. Comparative Procedure': *University of Pennsylvania Law Review*, 1919 (18).

Is. Steinberg, *Die Lehre vom Verbrechen im T.*, Stuttgart, 1910 (139 pp., Dissert.). Reprint from: *Ztschr. f. vergl. Rechtsw.*, XXV. [The application of modern juristic concepts is not immediately admissible, comp. *MGWJ*, 1916, 429–431].

J. Ziegler, 'Die Sünde Mord in Bibel u. Midraš,' in: *Schwarz-Festschr.*, 75–88.

A. Perls, 'Der Selbstmord nach der Halakha': *MGWJ*, 1911, 287–295.

Ch. Tschernowitz, 'Der Einbruch nach biblischem u. talmud. Rechte': *Ztschr. f. vergleich. Rechtsw.*, XXV, 443–458. || Id., 'Der Raub nach biblisch-talmudischem Recht,' ibid., XXVII, 187–196.

Thonisson, *la peine de mort dans le T.* Brussels, 1886. || A. Büchler, 'Die Todesstrafen der Bibel u. der jüdisch-nachbiblischen Zeit': *MGWJ*, 1906, 539–562, 644–706.

A. Büchler, 'L'enterrement des criminels d'après le T. et le Midrasch': *REJ*, XLVI, 74–88.

A. Büchler, 'Die Strafe der Ehebrecher in der nachexilischen Zeit': *MGWJ*, 1911, 196–219.

H. Vogelstein, 'Notwehr nach mosaisch-talmud. Recht,' in: *MGWJ*, 1904, 513–533. Reprint Stettin, 1904 (41).

J. Goitein, 'Das Vergeltungsprinzip im bibl. u. talmud. Strafrechte': *Mag.*, 1892, 1893. || J. Horowitz, 'Auge um Auge, Zahn um Zahn,' in: *Cohen-Festschr.*, 609–658. || D. W. Amram, 'Retaliation and Compensation': *JQR*, N. S., II, 191–211. || J. Weismann, *Talion u. öffentliche Strafe im Mosaischen Rechte*, Leipzig 1913 (100, reprint from *Festschrift* for Adolf Wach).

S. Ohlenburg, *Die biblischen Asyle in talmud. Gewande*, Munich, 1895 (54).

J. Wiesner, *Der Bann in seiner geschichtlichen Entwickelung auf dem Boden des Judenthumes*. Leipzig 1864 (107). || M. Aron, *Histoire de l'excommunication juive*, Nimes, 1882 (168). || S.

Mandl, *Der Bann. Ein Beitrag zum mosaisch-rabbin. Strafrecht*, Brünn, 1898 (51). See *MGWJ*, 1898, 524 f.

Mos. Bloch, *Das mosaisch-talmudische Polizeirecht*. Budapest, 1879 (43).

f. Civil Law.

H. B. Fassel, *Das mosaisch-rabbinische Civilrecht*. 2 volumes. Gross-Kanischa, 1852–54 (898). | *Das mosaisch-rabbin. Gerichtsverfahren in civilrechtlichen Sachen*. Ibid., 1859 (295).

M. Bloch, *Die Civilprocess-Ordnung nach mosaisch-rabbin. Rechte*, Budapest, 1882 (108).

L. Auerbach, *Das jüdische Obligationsrecht*. I [sole] volume. Berlin 1871 (627). [P. 62–114 deal with the origin of the T.]

Jos. Marcuse, *Das biblisch-talmud. Zinsenrecht*, Königsberg, 1895 (62).

N. A. Nobel, 'Studien zum talmud. Pfandrecht,' in: *Cohen-Festschr.*, 659–668.

Isay Lewin, *Die Chasaka des talmud. Rechts*, Stuttgart, 1912 (148). [Reprint from *Ztschr. f. vergleich. Rechtsw.* XXIX. According to the author, חזקה has 'a most striking similarity' with 'Gewere' in German law.]

N. Hurewitsch, 'Die Haftung des Verwahrers nach talm. Recht': *Ztschr. f. vergleich. Rechtsw.*, XXVIII, 425–439.

Moses Bloch, *Der Vertrag nach mosaisch-talmud. Rechte*. Budapest, 1893 (108).

Joh. Selden, *De successionibus in bona defuncti ad leges Hebraeorum*, London, 1646. || A. Wolff, *Das jüdische Erbrecht*, Berlin 1888 (50). || Moses Bloch, *Das mosaisch-talmudische Erbrecht*. Budapest, 1890 (70).

L. Bodenheimer, *Das Testament . . . nach rabbin. Quellen*, Crefeld, 1847.

g. Family and the law pertaining thereto.

P. Buchholz, *Die Familie in rechtlicher u. moralischer Beziehung nach mosaisch-talmud. Lehre*. Breslau, 1867 (138). || L. G. Lévy, *La famille dans l'antiquité israélite*, Paris, 1905 (296).

Jos. Bergel, *Die Eheverhältnisse der alten Juden im Vergleiche mit den griechischen u. römischen*, Leipzig 1881 (33).

Ludw. Lichtschein, *Die Ehe nach mosaisch-talmudischer Auffassung u. das mosaisch-talmud. Eherecht*, Leipzig 1879 (172).

Z. Frankel, *Grundlinien des mosaisch-talmud. Eherechts*, Breslau, 1860, 4to (48). || M. Duschak, *Das mosaisch-talmud. Eherecht*. Vienna, 1864 (150). || A. Billauer, *Grundzüge des bibl. talmud. Eherechts*, Berlin 1910 (78, Dissert.).

E. Fränkel, *Das jüdische Eherecht nach dem Reichscivilehegesetz vom 6. Febr. 1875*. Munich, 1891 (128).

Leop. Löw, *Eherechtliche Studien*, 1860–67 (in: *Schriften* III, Szegedin, 1893, 13–334).

Ludw. Blau, 'Zur Geschichte des jüd. Eherechts', in: *Schwarz-Festschr.*, 193–209 [confirmation of the husband's death, formula of betrothal, betrothal ring].

Leop. Fischer, 'Die Urkunden im T.': *JbJLG* IX, *Eherechtliche U.*, 103–197: marriage contract, alimony, rebelliousness, bill of divorcement, repudiation of marriage, levirate.

Ad. Büchler, 'Familienreinheit u. Familienmakel in Jerusalem vor dem Jahre 70 [C. E.]', in: *Schwarz-Festschr.*, 133–162 [עיסה]. || Lewi Freund, 'Genealogieen u. Familienreinheit in biblischer u. talmud. Zeit,' ibid., 163–192.

S. Krauss, 'Die Ehe zwischen Onkel u. Nichte,' in: *Kohler-Festschr.*, 165–175 [with reference to S. Schechter, *Documents* I].

Isr. Mattuck, 'The Levirate Marriage in Jewish Law'; ibid., 210–222.

M. Mielziner, *The Jewish Law of Marriage and Divorce in Ancient and Modern Times, and its Relation to the Law of the State*. Cincinnati, 1884 (149).

W. Leiter, *Die Stellung der Frau im T.*, Amsterd., 1918 (63).

Jacob Neubauer, *Beiträge zur Geschichte des biblisch-talmud. Eheschliessungsrechtes*, Leipzig 1920 (249).

A. S. Herschberg, מנהגי האירוסין והנשואים בזמן התלמוד, in: העתיד V (Berlin 1913), 75–102.

Dav. W. Amram, *The Jewish Law of Divorce according to Bible and Talmud with some Reference to . . . Posttalmudic Times*, Philadelphia, 1896 (224). || L. Blau, *Die jüd. Ehescheidung u. der jüd. Scheidebrief*, Budapest, 1911, 1912 (80 a. 116).

K. Weissbrodt, *Gattenpflichten nach Bibel u. Talmud*, Berlin 1891 (173).

Joh. Selden, *Uxor Ebraica*, London, 1646.

J. Stern, *Die Frau im T.*, Zurich, 1879 (47).

E. Weill, *La femme juive. Sa condition légale d'après la Bible et le Talmud*, Paris, 1874.

Ch. Tschernowitz, 'Das Dotalsystem [the wife's property] nach der mosaisch-talmud. Gesetzgebung': *Ztschr. f. vergleich. Rechtsw.*, XXIX, 445–473.

Jakob Neubauer, *Beiträge z. Geschichte des bibl. talm. Eheschliessungsrechtes*, Leipzig, 1920.

S. R. Hirsch, 'Das jüd. Weib in den Überlieferungen des T.,' in: *Schriften* IV, 202–208 (Frkf. o. M., 1908).

J. Nacht, 'Euphémismes sur la femme dans la littérature rabbinique [שָׂדֶה, לֶחֶם, etc.]'; *REJ*, LIX, 36–41.

M. S. Zuckermandel, 'Die Befreiung der Frauen von bestimmten religiösen Pflichten nach Tosephta u. Mišna,' in: *Lewy-Festschr.* 145–172.

Is. Unna, 'Die Aguna-Gesetze,' in: J. Wohlgemuth's *Jeschurun*, III (Berlin 1916), 347–366. || B. Bernstein, 'Die A.-Frage im Lichte des Weltkrieges,' in: *Schwarz-Festschr.*, 557–570. [עֲגוּנָה is a woman who has no certain information as to the whereabouts of her husband or as to his death.]

S. Keyzer, *Dissertatio de tutela secundum jus Talmud.*, Leiden, 1847. || M. Bloch, *Die Vormundschaft nach mosaisch-talmud. Recht*, Budapest, 1904 (52). || Isr. Lebendiger, 'The Minor in Jewish Law:' *JQR*, N. S., VI, 459–493; VII, 89–111, 145–174.

R. Kirsch, *Der Erstgeborene nach mosaisch-talmudischem Recht*, I [position, rights], 1901 (Bern Diss.), Frkf. o. M., 1901 (55).

S. Rubin, 'Der "nasciturus" als Rechtssubjekt im talmud. u. römischen Rechte': *Ztschr. f. vergleich. Rechtswiss.*, XX (1907), 119–156.

§ 13. History.

a. Joh. v. Gumpach, *Über den altjüdischen Kalender*, Brussels, 1848 (384). || L. M. Lewisohn, *Geschichte u. System des Jüdischen Kalenderwesens*, Leipzig 1856 (81 pp. a. 7 tables). || B. Zuckermann, *Materialien zur Entwickelung der altjüdischen Zeitrechnung*, Breslau, 1882 (68). || A. Kistner, *Der Kalender der*

Juden. Vollständige Anleitung zur Berechnung für alle Zeiten, Carlsruhe, 1905 (102).

D. Sidersky, 'Étude sur l'origine astronomique de la chronologie juive,' Paris, 1914 (in: *Mémoires de l'Académie des inscriptions*, XII, 2, 595–683; comp. *MGWJ*, 1914, 382–384).

b. J. Derenbourg, *Essai sur l'histoire et la géographie de la Palestine d'après les Talmuds et les autres sources rabbiniques*. I: *Histoire de la Palestine depuis Cyrus jusqu'à Adrien*, Paris, 1867 (486).

L. Herzfeld, *Handelsgeschichte der Juden des Alterthums*, Braunschweig, 1879; 2d ed. 1894 (394).

Jos. Lehmann, 'Quelques dates importantes de la chronologie du 2e temple [A. Z.]': *REJ*, XXXVII (1898), 1–44.

Isr. Lévi, 'Les sources talmudiques de l'histoire juive': *REJ*, XXXV, 213 to 223. [For pre-Christian times they are 'très souvent de simples agadot.' Demonstrated by the example of Alexander Jannai.]

F. Rosenthal, 'Das Sikarikongesetz:' *MGWJ*, 1893, 1–6, 57–63.

H. P. Chajes, 'Les juges juifs en Palestine de l'an 70 à l'an 500': *REJ*, XXXIX (1899), 39–52.

A. Schlatter, *Die Tage Trajans u Hadrians*, Gütersloh, 1897 (100). Comp. W. Bacher in *REJ*, XXXVI, 197–204.

S. Krauss, 'Das Erdbeben v. J. 115 [C. E.] in Palästina': *MGWJ*, 1914, 290–304.

Sam. Krauss, 'Die römischen Besatzungen in Palästina:' *Mag.*, 1892, 227–244; 1893, 104–133.

A. Büchler, *The Political and Social Leaders . . . of Sepphoris in the Second and Third Centuries*, London, 1909 (92). | *The Economic Conditions of Judaea after the Destruction of the Second Temple*, London 1912 (68). | *Der galiläische 'Am ha-'Areṣ des 2. Jahrh.*, Vienna, 1906 (338). Comp. *MGWJ*, 1908, 739 ff.; 1910, 352–354; Em. Schürer, *Theolog. Literaturzeitung*, 1906, No. 23.

Bondi, 'Der jüdische krieg gegen Hadrian' (after Is. Halevy), *JbJLG*, XIII, 255–280.

M. Auerbach, 'Zur polit. Geschichte Palästinas im 3. u. 4. nachchristl. Jahrh.': *JbJLG*, V, 155–181.

H. Kottek, 'Der Kaiser Diokletian in Palästina': *JbJLG*, I, 213–223.

L. Lucas, *Beiträge zur Geschichte der Juden*, I. *Zur G. der J. im 4. Jahrhundert*, Berlin 1910 (134). Comp. *MGWJ*, 1910, 364–372.

c. H. Kottek, 'Gesetz und Überlieferung bei den Juden Babyloniens in vortalmud. Zeit': *JbJLG*, V, 280–303. [These Jews had been practising the commandments of the oral teaching, תקנות דרבנן as well. Follows Halevy II.]

Is. Unna, 'Babylonien um das Ende der Tannaitenzeit,' in: *JbJLG*, I (1903), 269–277.

S. Funk, *Die Juden in Babylonien*, 200–500, Berlin 1902, 1908 (148 a. 22 pp.; 160).

Felix Lazarus, *Die Häupter der Vertriebenen* [רישי גלותא]. *Beiträge zu einer Geschichte der Exilsfürsten in Babylonien unter den Arsakiden u. Sassaniden.* Frkf. o. M. 1890, (183) (=Brüll's *Jbb.*, X).

M. Judilowitz, חיי היהודים בזמן התלמוד, Wilna, 1906 (87 leaves) [Nehardea, with notes by Harkavy].

L. Bank, 'Rigla, Riglè, Schabbata derigla': *REJ*, XXXIII, 161–186.

S. Funk, 'Beiträge zur Geschichte Persiens zur Zeit der Sasaniden,' in: *Schwarz-Festschr.*, 425–436.

d. S. Krauss, 'Talmud. Nachrichten über Arabien': *ZDMG*, 1916, 321 to 353 [names, political conditions, commerce and trade, linguistic matter, religious ideas].

J. Barth, 'Midraschische Elemente in der muslimischen Tradition,' in: *Berliner-Festschrift*, Berlin 1903, 33 ff.

A. Cohen, 'Arabisms in Rabbinic Literature:' *JQR*, N. S., III, 221–233 (14 words referred to by Levi [see above p. 124] as Arabic).

Abr. Geiger, *Was hat Mohammed aus dem Judenthume aufgenommen?* Bonn, 1833 (216); Leipzig 1902 (213).

J. Gastfreund, *Mohammed nach T. u. Midrasch*, 3 parts (Berlin), Vienna, 1875, 77, 80, (32, 32 a. 28).

M. Rachmuth, 'Die Juden in Nordafrika bis zur Invasion der Araber': *MGWJ*, 1906, 22–58.

Max Radin, *The Jews among the Greeks and Romans*, Philadelphia, 1915 (422. Hereon *JQR*, N. S., VII, 628–633). || Jean Juster, *Les Juifs dans l'Empire romain*, 2 volumes, Paris, 1914 (510 a. 338, treats in particular of the legal position of the Jews and their economic life).

S. Krauss, 'Griechen u. Römer,' in: *Monumenta Talmudica*, vol. V, *Geschichte*, part 1, Vienna, 1914 (194).

S. Klein, *Jüdisch-palästin. Corpus Inscriptionum und synagogeninschriften*, Vienna-Berlin 1920 (106).

§ 14. Geography.

Ad. Neubauer, *La géographie du T.* Paris, 1868 (40 a. 468 pp.).—Criticised severely but pertinently by J. Morgenstern (died April 3, 1887), *Die französische Academie u. die 'Geographie des Talmuds,'* Berlin 1870 (35); Id., *Die französische Academie u. die 'G. des T.' Zweite vollständige Auflage* (as a matter of fact an entirely new work of supplementation). Berlin 1870 (96).

H. Hildesheimer, *Beiträge zur Geographie Palästinas.* Berlin, 1896 (93).

Hirschensohn, שבע חכמות שבתלמוד I [nothing more has appeared], Lemberg, 1883 (240; an industrious alphabetic compilation).

Is. Goldhor, אדמת קדש . . . לגבולותיה, Jerusalem, 1913 (332) [elucidates the talmudic data by surveying].

Sapir, הארץ, Jaffa, 1911.

Sam. Klein, *Beiträge zur Geographie u. Geschichte Galiläas*, Leipzig, 1909 (112 [in connection with the Baraitha of the 24 divisions of the priests, Palest. Taan. 68d]. | *Zur Palästinakunde*, Berlin, 1913. | ארץ ישראל, Vienna, 1922 (150, Hebrew). | Also papers in Luncz, *Jerusalem*, X; *Mitteilungen und Nachrichten d. deutschen Palästina-Vereins*, 1908, 33 ff.; 1912, 19 f.; *Zeitschrift des deutschen Palästina-Vereins*, 1910, 26–40; 1912, 38–43; *MGWJ*, 1910, 14–27; 1915, 156–169; 1917, 133–149; 1920, 123–131; 181–196; 1921, 370 ff.; 1923, 202–205, 270–273.

S. Krauss, 'Les divisions administratives de la Palestine à l'époque romaine': *REJ*, XLVI (1903), 218–236.

Paul Berto, 'Le temple de Jerusalem': *REJ*, LIX, 14–35, 161–187; LX, 1–23 [according to Josephus a. the Mishna].

Abr. Berliner, *Beiträge zur Geographie u. Ethnographie Babyloniens im T. u. Midrasch.* Berlin, 1883 (71).

W. Bacher, 'Rome dans le T. et le Midrasch:' *REJ*, XXXIII, 187–196.

Israel S. Horowitz, ארץ ישראל ושכנותיה (encyclopaedic work comprising all names of places in Palestine and Syria mentioned in Bible, Talmud, etc.) I,י—א, Vienna 1923 (372, large 4to).

§ 15. Natural Sciences and Medicine.

a. Natural Sciences.

Joseph Bergel, *Studien über die naturwissenschaftlichen Kenntnisse der Talmudisten.* Leipzig 1880 (102).

M. Z. Taksin, ידיעות הטבע שבתלמוד, Warsaw, 1907 (68).

L. Lewysohn, *Zoologie des Talmuds.* Frkf. o. M., 1858 (400). [The author lacked philological training.]

Imm. Löw, 'Aramäische Lurchnamen,' 7 essays, in: *Ztschr. f. Assyriologie*, XXVI (1911): lizards; *Harkavy-Festschr.*: snakes; *Cohen-Festschr.*: chameleon, crocodile, tortoise; *Florilegium Vogüé:* frog a. toad, salamander. | 'Aram. Fischnamen', in: *Nöldeke-Festschr.*, 549 to 570.

M. Duschak, *Zur Botanik des Talmud.* Budapest, 1870 (136).

Imm. Löw, *Aramäische Pflanzennamen.* Leipzig 1881 (490). [Very careful and erudite.] || *Der biblische 'ezob*, Vienna, 1909 (30. *Wiener Akad. Philos.-histor. Kl.*, CLXI). 'Die Meerzwiebel [חצב],' in: *Lewy-Festschr.;* 'Karpas': *Ztschr. f. Assyriologie*, XXIX; 'Erwe u. Wicke,' ibid. XXX; 'Asphodelos:' *Schwarz-Festschrift*, 311.

b. Medicine.

M. Steinschneider, 'Schriften über Medizin in Bibel u. T. u. über jüdische Ärzte': *Wiener Klinische Rundschau*, 1896, No. 25, 26. Additional bibliography by J. Preuss: *ZHBg*, I (1896), 22–28.

Max Grünwald, *Die Hygiene der Juden*, Dresden, 1911, 12 (735 and 64).

R. J. Wunderbar, *Biblisch-talmudische Medicin oder Darstellung der Arzneikunde der alten Israeliten.* Riga-Leipzig 1850–60. 2 volumes.

Jos. Bergel, *Die Medizin der Talmudisten. Nebst einem Anhange: Die Anthropologie der alten Hebräer.* Leipzig 1885 (88).

Isr. M. Rabbinowicz, *Einl. in die Gesetzgebung u. die Medizin des Thalmuds*. Leipzig 1833 (272). [Translation of: La médecine, s. p. 144 γ.]

W. Ebstein, *Die Medizin im Neuen Test. u. im T.*, Stuttgart, 1903 (338).

J. Preuss, *Biblisch-talmud. Medizin*, Berlin 1911 (735) [688–704 Bibliography]. Comp. Imm. Löw, *MGWJ*, 1912, 107–115.

Leop. Löw, *Zur Medizin u. Hygiene* (steam baths, physicians, cupping, caesarean operation) 1860–66 (in: *Schriften* III, Szegedin, 1893, 367–406).

Joach. Halpern, *Zur Geschichte der talmud. Chirurgie*. Breslau, 1869.

J. L. Katzenelson, *Die normale u. die pathologische Anatomie in der althebr. Literatur u. ihr Verhältnis zur altgriech. Medizin*, St. Petersburg, 1889 (162. Russian). German translation by R. Kirschberg in: *Historische Studien aus dem pharmakolog. Institut zu Dorpat*, V (1896), 164–296.

A. H. Israels, *Collectanea Gynaecologica ex Talmude Babylonico*. Gröningen, 1845.

M. Rawitzki, 'Die Lehre vom Kaiserschnitt im T.': Virchow's *Archiv für patholog. Anatomie*, LXXX (1880), 494–503. Compare on the other hand and in addition to this: LXXXIV (L. Kotelmann), LXXXVI and XCV (Rawitzki), as well as: *Mag.*, 1881, 48–53; 1884, 31–35.

D. Schapiro. *Obstétrique des anciens Hébreux, d'après la Bible, les Talmuds et les autres sources rabbiniques, comparée avec la tocologie gréco-romaine*. Paris, 1904 (167).

Gabriel Nobel, *Zur Geschichte der Zahnheilkunde im Talmud*. Leipzig 1909 (66, Diss.).

E. Rosenbaum, *Une conférence contradictoire . . . sur l'anatomie et physiologie des organes génitaux de la femme à l'école de Rami, fils de Samuel, et de Rabbi Yitshac, fils de Rabbi Yehoudou, à la fin du 2me siècle. Extraite du T.* [Nidda]. Frankfort o. Main, 1901 (89).

A. Rosenzweig, *Das Auge in Bibel u. T.*, Berlin 1892 (36).

L. Kotelmann, *Die Ophthalmologie bei den alten Hebräern*, Hamburg, 1910 (436).

§ 16. Antiquities.

a. S. Krauss, *Talmudische Archäologie*, 3 volumes, Leipzig 1910–1912 (720, 722 and 491). | Idem, *Synagogale Altertümer*, Berlin, 1922.

b. M. Weinberg, 'Die Organisation der jüdischen Ortsgemeinden in der talmud. Zeit': *MGWJ*, 1897, 588–604, 639–660, 673–691.

S. Krauss, 'Die Versammlungsstätten der Talmudgelehrten', in: *Lewy-Festschr.* 17–35. || Ad. Büchler, 'Learning and Teaching in the Open Air:' *JQR*, N. S., IV, 485–491.

W. Bacher, 'Zur Geschichte der Ordination': *MGWJ*, 1894, 122–127. || L. Löw, 'Die Horaa': *Schriften* IV (Szegedin, 1898), 158–166; 'Der Titel Rabbi u. Rabban,' ibid., 210–216. || A. Marmorstein, 'La dignité de gérousiarque de la synagogue,' *REJ*, LXI, 288–292.

c. Jos. Perles, *Die jüdische Hochzeit in nachbiblischer Zeit.* Leipzig, 1860 (24). [Reprinted from: *MGWJ*, 1860.]

Jos. Perles, *Die Leichenfeierlichkeiten im nachbiblischen Judenthume*, Breslau, 1861 (32). [Reprinted from: *MGWJ*, 1861.]

F. I. Grundt, *Die Trauergebräuche der Hebräer*, Leipzig, 1868 (60). || Siegfried Klein, *Tod u. Begräbnis in Palästina zur Zeit der Tannaiten*, Berlin, 1908 (101). Comp. *REJ*, LX, 110–113.

J. L. Palache, 'Das Weinen in der jüd. Literatur': *ZDMG*, 1916, 251–256 (mourning, repentance, prayer).

J. Rabbinowicz, *Der Todtenkultus bei den Juden*, Frankfort o. Main, 1889 (66).

d. J. Lehmann, 'Assistance publique et privée d'après l'antique législation juive': *REJ*, XXXV, *Actes et confér.*, I–XXXVII. || A. van Iterson, *Armenzorg bij de Joden in Palestina van* 100 *v. Chr.*-200 *n.* Chr., Leiden, 1911 (126). || K. Kohler, 'Zum Kapitel der jüdischen Wohltätigkeitspflege,' in: *Berliner-Festschrift*, 195–203.

e. Slaves.

M. Mielziner, *Die Verhältnisse der Sklaven bei den alten Hebräern nach biblischen u. talmud. Quellen*, Copenhagen, 1859 (68); English translation, *The Institution of Slavery among the Ancient Hebrews*, Cincinnati, 1894. || Zadoc Kahn, *L'esclavage selon la Bible et le T.*, Paris, 1867 (138); German translation: *Die Sklaverei nach Bibel u. T.*, Prague, 1888 (133). || J. Winter, *Die Stellung der Sklaven bei den Juden in rechtlicher u. gesellschaftlicher Beziehung nach talmud. Quellen*, Breslau, 1886 (66). || R. Grünfeld, *Die Stellung der Sklaven bei den Juden nach biblischen u. talmud. Quellen*, I, 1886 (38). || M. Olitzki, 'Der jüdische Sklave nach Josephus u. der Halacha': *Mag.*, 1889, 73–83. || Tony André, *L'esclavage chez les anciens Hébreux*, Paris, 1892 (197).

Dav. Farbstein, *Das Recht der unfreien u. der freien Arbeiter nach jüdisch-talmud. Recht, verglichen mit dem antiken, speziell mit dem röm. Recht*, Frankfort o. Main (Dissert. Bern) 1896 (97). || S. Rubin, 'Ein Kapitel aus der Sklaverei im talmud. u. röm. Rechte,' in: *Schwarz-Festschr.*, 211–229, 572–574 [part of a larger work].

S. Rubin, *Das Talmudische Recht.* I. Abteilung, I. Buch: *Die Sklaverei* (acquisition of slaves; their status; manumission), Vienna, 1920 (137).

f. Industry and Technology.

S. Kalischer, 'Die Wertschätzung der Arbeit in Bibel u. T.,' in: *Cohen-Festschr.*, 579–608.

Franz Delitzsch, *Jüdisches Handwerkerleben zur Zeit Jesu*, 3d edition, Erlangen, 1879 (83). || S. Meyer, *Arbeit u. Handwerk im T.*, Berlin, 1878 (46).

M. B. Schwalm, *L'industrie et les artisans juifs a l'époque de Jésus.* Paris, 1909 (63).

Chr. Schöttgen, *Antiquitates triturae et fulloniae ex antiquorum reliquiis*, Utrecht, 1727 (97 and 68).

Paul Rieger, *Technologie u. Terminologie der Handwerke in der Mišnah*, I: *Spinnen, Färben, Weben, Walken*, Berlin, 1894 (48).

Gust. Löwy, *Die Technologie u. Terminologie der Müller u. Bäcker in den rabbin. Quellen* (Dissert. Bern), Leipzig 1898 (51).

J. Krengel, *Das Hausgerät in der Mišnah*, I. Frankfort o. M., 1899 (68).

M. Winter, *Die Koch- u. Tafelgeräte in Palästina zur Zeit der Mišnah*, Berlin, 1910 (88).

g. Agriculture and Hunting.

H. Vogelstein, *Die Landwirtschaft in Palästina zur Zeit der Mišnah.* I: *Der Getreidebau.* Berlin, 1894 (78).

Martin Salomonski, *Gemüsebau u. Gewächse in Palästina zur Zeit der Mischnah*, Berlin, 1911 (71).

Felix Goldmann, 'Der Ölbau in Palästina in der tannait. Zeit,' in: *MGWJ*, 1906, 563–580, 707–728; 1907, 17–40, 129–141. Reprinted Pressburg, 1907 (79).

S. Klein, 'Weinstock, Feigenbaum u. Sykomore in Palästina,' in: *Schwarz-Festschr.*, 389–402.

J. Taglicht, 'Die Dattelpalme in Palästina,' in: *Schwarz-Festschr.*, 403–416.

A. Sch. Herschberg, 'Çemer u. Pisṭa zur Zeit der Mišna u. des T.s': הקדם, II (1908), 57–80; III (1912), 7–29.

S. Alexander, *Beiträge zur Ornithologie Palästinas auf grund der alten hebräischen Quellen*, I. *Geflügelzucht* (Dissertation Würzburg), Berlin 1915 (47).

h. Dwellings and Clothing.

Arthur Rosenzweig, *Das Wohnhaus in der Mišnah*, Berlin, 1907 (77).

Adolf Brüll, *Trachten der Juden im nachbiblischen Alterthume*, I. Frankfort o. M., 1873 (90).

Adf. Rosenzweig, *Kleidung u. Schmuck im biblischen u. talmud. Schrifttum*, Berlin, 1905 (130).

M. Mainzer, *Über Jagd, Fischfang u. Bienenzucht bei den Juden in der tannäischen Zeit*, Frankfort o. M., 1910 (78) [reprinted from *MGWJ*, 1909].

Siegfr. Schemel, *Die Kleidung der Juden im Zeitalter der Mischnah*, Rostock, 1914 (95. Dissert.).

S. Carlebach, 'Haarverhüllung des jüd. Weibes,' in: *Hoffmann-Festschr.*, 454–459 a. Hebr. 218–247 [attempts to show as against Rosenzweig that covering the head was a Jewish religious law and did not originate in non-Jewish influences].

Jac. Nacht, 'The Symbolism of the Shoe' [particularly according to Jewish sources]: *JQR*, N. S. VI, 1–22.

i. Books.

Leop. Löw, *Beiträge zur jüd. Alterthumskunde* I: *Graphische Requisiten u. Erzeugnisse bei den Juden*, Leipzig, 1870, 71 (243 and 190). || Ludw. Blau, *Studien zum althebr. Buchwesen*, Budapest, 1902 (203) [form, arrangement, manufacture, sale].

Leop. Fischer, 'Die Urkunden im T.': *JbJLG*, IX, 45–197.

k. Measures, Coins, Weights.

H. J. Scheftel, ערך מלין לשעורי תורה שבכתב ושבעל פה, Berdiczev, 1904 (75 leaves small fol.) [coins, measures, weights, dates in the O. T. and in the Talmuds, comp. *ZHBg*, IX, 135–137].

B. Zuckermann, *Talmudische Münzen u. Gewichte*, Breslau, 1862, 4to (40).

Eliezer Lambert, 'Les changeurs et la monnaie en Palestine:' *REJ*, LI, 217–244; LII, 24–42.

L. Herzfeld, *Metrologische Voruntersuchungen zu einer Geschichte des ibräischen resp. altjüdischen Handels*, Leipzig 1863–65 (95 and 103). || B. Zuckermann, *Das jüdische Maasssystem u. seine Beziehungen zum griechischen u. römischen*, Breslau, 1867 (58 pp. and 4 tables).

Lauterbach, 'Weights and Measures': *JE*, XII, 483–490.

l. Adf. Rosenzweig, *Geselligkeit u. Geselligkeits-Freuden in Bibel u. Talmud.* I. Berlin 1895 (52).

Jos. Friedmann, *Der gesellschaftliche Verkehr u. die Umgangsformen in talmud. Zeit*, Berlin, 1914 (65)..

S. Krauss, 'Baden u. Badewesen im Talmud': *Hakedem* I (1907), 87–110, 171–194; II, 32–50.

Ad. Büchler, 'Das Ausgiessen von Wein u. Öl als Ehrung bei den Juden': *MGWJ*, 1905, 12–40.

Aug. Wünsche, *Der Kuss in Bibel, T. u. Midrasch*, Breslau, 1911 (59. Chapters 2 and 3 appeared previously in *Lewy-Festschr.*)

A. S. Herschberg, יופי והתיפותה של האשה בזמן התלמוד, in: העתיד, IV, 1–56; V, 102–4.

Löw, 'Der Kuss,' *MGWJ*, 1921, 253ff.; 323ff.

PART II

INTRODUCTION TO THE MIDRASHIM

PART II

INTRODUCTION TO THE MIDRASHIM[1]

CHAPTER XV

Introductory Remarks

§ 1. Character of Midrash

After the monarchy there followed in Israel, not, as is maintained on many sides, the period of priestly rule, but rather the times of the reign of the Law. After the return from Babylon, the Torah became more and more the norm in accordance with which the entire life of Israel was regulated in its externalities and the center of all spiritual life. When Haggai[2] admonishes the Jews that what is of moment in their relations to God is the right disposition, he impresses his instruction on their memory by connecting it with passages of the ceremonial law,[3] on which occasion he takes it for granted that the priests are the recognized teachers of this law. Ezra, the student of the law (*sopher*, not 'scribe'), bent all his efforts to have the extant Law of Moses actually obeyed in practice. The memory of the external splendor of the monarchy grew less and less vivid, the prospect of an abiding restoration of the ancient splendor became more and more nebulously distant; for just a few decades, under the Hasmoneans, there was national independence in a commonwealth small and insignificant as compared with the past, and in the year 70 C.E. Jerusalem and with it the sanctuary of the Temple became a ruin. Is it to be wondered at that the written Law, the only sacred possession of the nation which remained from pre-exilic times (Ark, Urim and Thummim etc. had disappeared), was now to the Jews their one and all and that the entire spiritual activity of Jewry assumed the character of searching and studying the Scriptures?

The written 'Torah of Moses' was not a complete code of

laws, it was not intended for the conditions in the first centuries after the Babylonian captivity, much less for the time when the Jewish state had ceased to exist wholly. Hence there was a need to accommodate the Torah to later times and to complete it in not a few points. This was done partly by a continuous process of lawmaking, partly by Midrash, exposition.[4]

This activity which has for its object the regulation of life through the law is called the halakic; the fixed norm resulting therefrom as well as a single proposition is called halakah.[5] The collection of such propositions which became authoritative is the Mishna of Judah ha-Nasi;[6] another collection is the Tosephta.[7] Much halakic matter is likewise found in the Baraithoth[8] and in the tannaitic Midrashim.[9]

The Torah (here in the wider sense betokening the collection of the holy Scriptures of the Old Testament[10]), moreover, meant to the Jews the sum and substance of all that is good and beautiful, of all that is worth knowing. Hence it ought to be possible to apply it to all conditions of life, it should comfort, exhort and edify, and it must be shown further that it contained everything even though germinally.[11]

It is again through Midrash that Holy Writ was made to do this service; but this midrashic activity is now ordinarily expressed by the word haggadah.[12] The Haggadah in part followed closely the biblical text; frequently, however, the latter served as a peg upon which to hang expositions of the most divergent sort. 'The Haggadah, which is to bring heaven nearer to the congregation and then to lift man heavenward, approves itself in this profession on the one side as glorification of God and on the other as consolation to Israel. Hence the chief contents of the addresses are made up of religious truths, maxims of morality, colloquies on just retribution, inculcation of the laws which mark off national coherence, descriptions of Israel's greatness in past and future, scenes and legends from Jewish history, parallels drawn between the institutions of God and those of Israel, praises of the Holy Land, edifying accounts and all kinds of consolation.'[13] These addresses used to be delivered in synagogue or academy, feasibly also in private dwellings or in the open, principally on Sabbaths and festivals, but also on important public or private occasions (war, famine; circumcision, weddings, funerals etc.).[14]

§ 2. Committing the Midrash to Writing.

Not alone the Halakah was taught, but also the Haggadah. This is shown by the expression, frequently recurring in the Palest. Talmud, 'our teachers of the Haggadah', *rabbanan d'aggadta*.[1] It follows furthermore from what we hear[2] of Jacob bar Aḥa finding 'in the Haggadah Book of the School.'[3] Comp. also the expression *saddar 'aggadta*, to discourse on the Haggadoth seriatim.[4] As to the interdict on writing, we have discussed it above.[5] From the first third of the third Christian century on the existence of Haggadah books is attested on many sides. However, the purely haggadic Midrashim which have come down to us date from later times. The 'tannaitic Midrashim' ascend in their more ancient elements to the second century.[6]

It is exceedingly difficult to ascertain the date of composition. The greater part of the important works are no longer available in their earliest form; copyists and printers have frequently gone about the text carelessly and even arbitrarily, as is shown e. g. by glosses, omissions and disfigured proper names. Here and there damage has been done by censorship. L. Zunz's work, *Die gottesdienstlichen Vorträge der Juden*,[7] should be pronounced epoch-making in this field, though by no means final. Before a real history of the Midrash literature may be written, it would be necessary to produce critical editions of all important Midrashim on the basis of manuscripts. Up to date only a small beginning has been made. The numerous editions by Buber, it is true, are eminently superior to those which preceded them in time, but in no way do they answer to the demands of strict criticism. So far only two editions deserve serious consideration.[8]

The strictly productive midrashic activity ceased very soon after the completion of the Babylonian Talmud; thereafter came the period of assembling which lasted until the end of the Gaonate (1040 C.E.) and even beyond that date.[9] Slowly but surely the Midrash was superseded by the more modern sciences: history, theology and grammatical exposition, and on the other side by the counterpart of science: Cabalah.

§ 3. Remarks on the Structure of the Midrashim.

A distinction must be made between expositional Midrashim and homiletical Midrashim.

A. The expositional Midrashim comment on the Scriptural text according to the order of the verses or join thereto their tales, parables and the like. The oldest, the 'tannaitic Midrashim,' are mainly halakic in content. The others, so already Genesis Rabba, have this distinctive mark that the individual parashas (sections) are equipped with proems which were derived from haggadic discourses.

B. The homiletical Midrashim handle individual texts, for the most part the beginnings of Scriptural lections. These lections are either: (a) the Pentateuchal pericopes according to the triennial Palestinian cycle whereon rests the division of the Pentateuch into 154–175 Sedarim—we call such homilies Tanḥuma homilies because of their employment in the Tanḥuma Midrashim; but they are found also in Exod. Rabba, Levit. R., Num. R. (from ch. 15 on)[1]—or: (b) those sections of the Pentateuch and the prophetical books which were designated according to the Pesiḳtha cycle for the festivals and special Sabbaths (four Sabbaths before Passover, the Sabbaths of mourning and consolation from the 17th of Tammuz to the conclusion of the Jewish calendar year)—we call them Pesiḳtha homilies, comp. Pesiḳtha Kahana a. Pesiḳtha Rabbathi.

Each homily, or, as the case may be, each parasha, pisḳa, opens with a number of proems (*pethiḥa* from *pathaḥ*), i. e. by joining the text to a verse, mostly outside the Pentateuch, preferentially from the Hagiographa. The proems are either simple or composite. Simple are those proems in which the opening verse receives a continuous exposition which either wholly or at least in its last part has reference to the theme.[2] At times we find merely fragments or else just one verse is adduced and it is left for the hearer (reader) to find out its application. We call those proems composite when the opening verse is followed by diverse expositions on the part of different haggadists, each independent in itself. The last exposition or at least its conclusion must lead over to the theme proper.[3] The authors of the homiletic Midrashim strove to bring together in each section as many proems as they could. In the Pesiḳtha Kahana edited by Buber, the average discourse has four Pethiḥoth, the 11th and the 25th seven each. In Genesis Rabba the number varies between 1 and 7; the 53d parasha has 9, probably because Gen. 21.1ff. was read on New Year's Day and therefore frequently expounded.[4] The Midrash on Lamentations abounds especially in introductions.[5]

Among the earliest it is related of Meir[6] that he was wont to construct his discourses of halakic and haggadic matter as well as of parables. Tanḥum of Nave, i. e. in all probability Tanḥuma bar Abba[7], had a halakic question preface a haggadic discourse.[8] It came to be a peculiarity of the younger Midrashim, for which various explanations have been offered,[9] to open a haggadic discourse with the discussion of a simple halakic problem.[10] In the Pesiḳtha Kahana halakic introductions are still absent.[11]

The proems are followed by the exposition. In the homiletic Midrashim, such as Pesiḳtha, Tanḥuma, Levit. R. etc., the actual exposition covers only a few (some three or four) verses; the longest haggadic elucidation is as a rule attached to the first significant verse. The greater number of the discourses close with citations of Scriptural verses having reference to the future glory of Israel.[12]

Chapter XVI

The Tannaitic Midrashim Mekiltha, Siphra, Siphre[1]

The authors of the sayings contained in these works are almost wholly Tannaim; but the final compilers were Amoraim. As has been shown by D. Hoffmann in particular, two parallel tendencies may be discerned: the views of the academy *be rab*,[2] i. e. of the school of Akiba, and then those of his contemporary and opponent Ishmael.[3] The expert may easily recognize the Midrashim of the school of Ishmael in the first place by the names of the teachers cited, e. g. Josiah and Jonathan, which occur neither in the other tannaitic Midrashim nor in the Mishna or Tosephta; secondly, by certain technical terms.[4] Akiba quite frequently applies word-analogy, *gezerah shawah*; Ishmael does so only when the word would otherwise seem superfluous and therefore appears to have been designedly used to point to a deduction.[5] Then we find with Akiba the method of Inclusion and Exclusion,[6] whereas Ishmael proceeded according to the rule *kelal u-ferat*.[7] Akiba found scope in all sorts of linguistic peculiarities, the duplication of expressions, even particles and letters, for arriving at new ordinances and deductions, whereas Ishmael rejected all such forced interpretations.[8]

§ 1. Midrashim of the School of Akiba.

a. Siphra, 'The Book,' or Torath Kohanim, on Levit., contains but little haggadic matter.[1] The name Siphra is due to the fact[2] that in the schools a beginning was made with the third book of the Torah and not with the first. As the basic element we may consider the exposition by Judah ben El'ai;[3] the final compiler was Ḥiyya the Elder, pupil and friend of Rabbi.[4] It is not likely that the Midrash of the School of Ishmael was drawn upon except indirectly.[5]—In earlier times the Siphra was divided into nine large sections. At present fourteen divisions are recognized, and it is customary to cite after them (adding at the same time chapter and verse).[6] The subdivisions are called in part parashas (indicated by Roman figures), in part peraḳim (sing. pereḳ, Arabic figures); these subdivisions are again subdivided into mishnayoth. Frequently citations are also made by folio and column of the edition by Weiss.

b. Siphre on Deut. 12–26, i. e. on the strictly legal part of Deuteronomy.[7]

c. The Mekiltha of Simeon ben Joḥai.[8] L. Ginzberg[9] seeks to prove that Simeon ben Joḥai was the first author, while Hezekiah son of Ḥiyya was the final compiler. Both hypotheses are opposed by S. Horovitz,[10] it seems with good reason.

d. Siphre Zuṭa on Num., cited by Jewish writers of the Middle Ages also as Midrash shel-panim aḥerim a. Wishalleḥu zuṭa.[11] Especially characteristic are the following points: certain Tannaim are named here who occur in the other halakic Midrashim not at all or only sparingly; mishnayoth which deviate considerably from Rabbi's Mishna; differences, otherwise unknown, between the Shammaiites and Hillelites; here and there the terminology. S. Horovitz is inclined to pronounce Siphre Zuṭa as coming from the school of Eliezer ben Jacob II.

§ 2. Midrashim of the School of Ishmael.

a. Mekiltha. The word signifies properly: measure, form, rule for deducing the Halakah from Scripture, Hebr. *middah;* then straightway: Midrash.[1] The name of the M. on Exod. from the school of Ishmael is found in Aruk and Rashi; in older times this book was comprised within the collective term Siphre. The M. sets in at Exod. 12, the first legal piece in Exod., and extends in the main to 23.19, where the chief legal portions of Exod. end; hence it appears that the author aimed to construct an halakic Midrash. However, since he indulges in a running exposition, the greater part is haggadic.[2] Two small pieces legal relating to the Sabbath 31.12–17 a. 35.1–3 form the conclusion. The M. is divided into nine tractates *massektoth*.[3]

b. Siphre on Num.; because it sets in with the legal matter of Num. 5, it is also called *wishalleḥu.* Haggadic elucidations occur.[4]

c. Siphre on Deut., disconnected pieces in the first part of the book,[5] mostly haggadic.[6]

c. There existed at one time also a Mekiltha of Ishmael on Levit., from which passages are adduced especially in the Talmuds.[7]

D. Hoffmann[8] has compiled from the Ms. of the Midrash ha-gadol in the State Library at Berlin the tannaitic Midrashim on Deut. which are found therein. The greatest part coincides, if we abstract from numerous and important textual differences, with our Siphre. This book affords new proof that Ishmael's Mekiltha on Deut. contained also halakic matter.[9]

§ 3. Bibliography.

Ad § 1: a. Siphra. Editions: Venice 1545 fol.; Venice 1609–1611 (title S. Ḳorban Aḥaron) with commentary by Aaron ibn Ḥayyim; Bucharest 1860 with commentary by M. L. Malbim (see above p. 93); Vienna 1862 fol. with valuable commentaries by Abraham ben David a. the editor I. H. Weiss; Warsaw 1866 fol. with commentary by Samson of Sens. M. Friedmann, *Sifra, der älteste Midrasch zu Levitikus. Nach Handschriften . . . u. mit Anmerkungen*, Breslau 1915 (15 a. 144). Only as far as 3.9. Otherwise comp. Wolf, *B. H.*, II, 1387 ff.; III, 1209; IV, 1030 f.; Frankel, *MGWJ*, 1854, 387 ff., 453 ff.; Geiger, *Jüd. Zeitschrift*, XI (1875), 50–60; *JE*, VIII, 555 a. (S. Horovitz) XI, 330–332.

b. Siphre (on Num. a. Deut.). Editions: Venice 1545 fol., Dyhernfurt 1811 (part 1) a. Radawel 1820 (part 2) with commentary by Abr. Lichtschein; Vienna 1864 with commentary by M. Friedmann (part 2, which was to have contained a circumstantial introduction, has not appeared); Wilna 1866 with notes by Elijah Wilna. | H. S. Horovitz, Sifre 'al Sefer Bemidbar we-Sifre Zutta, *Siphre d'be Rab*, I: *Siphre ad Numeros adjecto Siphre zutta cum variis lectionibus et adnotationibus*, Leipzig 1917 (21 a. 336); comp. *MGWJ*, 1917, 339 f. || Otherwise comp. Wolf, *B. H.*, II, 1389; IV, 1030 f. || On Mekiltha a. Siphre see Abr. Geiger, *Urschrift u. Übersetzungen der Bibel*, Breslau 1857, 434–450, a. (especially with a view to Weiss a. Friedmann) *Jüd. Zeitschrift*, IV (1866), 96–126; IX (1871), 8–30; also *JE*, VIII, 555 f. a. XI, 352 f.

d. Siphre zuṭa. The portions probably belonging here may be found in Horovitz, *Siphre*, 225–336. See also N. Brüll in *Graetz-Festschrift*; S. Horovitz in *MGWJ*, 1906 to 1909 a. *JE*, XI, 333 f.

Ad § 2. a. Mekiltha. Editions: Constantinople 1515 fol.; Venice 1545 fol.; Wilna 1844 fol. with notes by Elijah Wilna; Vienna 1865 with commentary by I. H. Weiss; Vienna 1870 with commentary by M. Friedmann. || H. Almqvist, *Mechilta Bo* [12. 1–13, 16], *Pesachtraktaten med noter . . . inledning ock glossar*, Lund 1892 (158 a. 128); the same, *Mechilta Bo . . . översatt*, Lund 1892 (147). | J. Winter a. A. Wünsche, *Mechilta, ein tannaitischer Midrasch zu Exod. . . . übersetzt u. erläutert*, Leipzig 1909 (391). || In addition comp. Wolf. *B. H.*, II, 1349 ff.; III, 1202; IV, 1025; Z. Frankel, *MGWJ*, 1853, 390 ff.; 1854, 149 ff., 191 ff.; also *JE*, VIII, 444–447, 554 f.

S. Buber, Liḳḳutim mimidrash 'Elle ha-Debarim Zutta ha-nimṣa'im etc., Vienna 1885, prints on p. 1–10 Yalḳuṭ excerpts from a Midrash Debarim zuṭa no longer extant; on p. 10–27, from cod. Munich Hebr. 229, the parasha Debarim after a recension of Midrash Debarim Rabba ascertained through citations by many authors and differing from the printed one.

CHAPTER XVII

The Homiletic Midrashim

§ 1. Pesiḳtha (deRab Kahana).

The oldest Midrash which goes by the name of Pesiḳtha, hence ordinarily known simply as Pesiḳtha, but also as Pesiḳtha deRab Kahana, had been known for a long time merely from citations, particularly in Aruk and in Yalḳuṭ. Zunz[1] attempted to reconstruct its contents. Subsequently four manuscripts became known or available, and Buber's edition based on them has confirmed that Zunz's attempt was on the whole successful; however, over against Geiger who overestimated Zunz's exposition, Buber has published 135 corrections.[2] This Pesiḳtha consists of some 32 homilies, which grew out of discourses for festivals and distinguished Sabbaths.[3] The work seems to be a composite of two collections, of which one began with New Year's Day (Tishri 1), while the other consisted of discourses on the 11 (12) haphtaras following Tammuz 17.[4] Where the first collection began may be inferred from the fact that in Aruk[5] two passages belonging to the New Year's homily are cited as found 'at the head of the pisḳas;' as to the beginning of the second collection, it must have been the homily on the first of the three haphtaras with messages of evil,[6] since this one opens with the words *R. 'Abba bar Kahana pathaḥ*. According to the explanation now current, though hardly justified, the designation of the work as *pesiḳtha de Rab Kahana*, found in Meshullam ben Moses (a generation before Rashi) and other authorities, was got at by abbreviating the opening just referred to.[7] As a matter of fact, codex Carmoly, which to be sure contains much spurious matter,[8] sets in with the discourse on this Sabbath, and codex de Rossi (Parma) 261, which is headed Midrash of Haphtaras, contains just the homilies pertaining to these eleven Sabbaths.[9] Hence the order adopted by Buber in accordance with codex Luzzatto and the Oxford manuscript, so as to have the Hanukkah festival constitute the beginning, is not the original one. Nevertheless it deserves to be mentioned that the sequence in Pesiḳtha Rabbathi strangely coincides with that in Buber's Pesiḳtha as regards a number of points, especially in placing the Hanukkah festival first.[10]

An estimate of the date of this Pesiḳtha depends on our opinion as to its literary connections. Zunz[11] was of the opinion that the Pesiḳtha is dependent on Gen. R., Levit. R. and Midrash Lamentations and so held that it was written approximately in the year 700. Buber[12] contended that the Pesiḳtha was older, and Theodor,[13] in my judgment, has proved that the Midrashim Levit. R. and Lamentations are rather dependent upon the Pesiḳtha; entire homilies of the Pesiḳtha have passed over into Levit. R., Tanḥuma and Pesiḳtha Rabbathi. It still requires to be ascertained how old the cycle *D. Sh. Ḥ., N. W.'.,'.R. Ḳ., Sh. D. Sh.* is, i. e. the custom to read on the twelve Sabbaths before Tabernacles the haphtaras Jer. 1.1; 2.5; Isai. 1.21; 40.1; 49.14; 54.11; 51.12; 54.1; 60.1; 61.10; 55.6; Hosea 14.2.[14] Theodor has advanced the conjecture that this cycle originated with the Gaon Mar Rab Kahana in Pum Beditha (who, however, flourished not earlier than 800). In all likelihood we possess the Pesiḳtha no longer in the form in which it emanated from its first author; quite the other way, it has been subjected here and there to additions and modifications; which is not to be wondered at if we remember in particular that the work represents a collection of discourses for festivals and special Sabbaths.

The name Pesiḳtha is related to Pasuḳ, Paseḳ, Pisḳa and means 'section.' 'Accordingly, originally each individual section alone received the name Pesiḳtha or Pisḳa, followed by the title which was expressed, as we may gather from the oldest writers, especially R. Nathan [in Aruk], by means of the preposition *d'*. . . Hence the whole work was called Pisḳoth, i. e. Pisḳas. When citing from this work without naming the section, one would apply the general name Pesiḳtha to the sum of the matter, hence to the whole book.'[15]

§ 2. Wayyiḳra Rabba.

Wayyiḳra Rabba, Levit. R., generally counted among the older Midrashim, consists in its 37 parashas of just as many homilies: 25 on the sabbath lections of the Sedarim cycle;[1] five homilies equal, with but minor differences, as many of the Pesiḳtha Kahana.[2] As to the remaining 7 beginnings, the reason why they are set down may be found perhaps in a different division of the Sedarim. Levit. R. itself offers a remarkable instance of different division: on 2.3 it is said that Ḥanina bar Abba (Aḥa?) found (not 2.1, but) 2.3 as the commencement of a Seder. Both Midrashim share a certain originality in the structure of the proems; they also resemble one another with regard to the concluding formula. Characteristic of Levit. R. is the use of proverbs. According to Zunz[3] and Weiss[4] Pesiḳtha Kahana is dependent upon Levit. R.; but Lauterbach[5] maintains the opposite.[6]

§ 3. Tanḥuma or Yelammedenu.

Tanḥuma or Yelammedenu is the name for a homiletic Midrash on the whole of the Pentateuch known in a number of collections. The second name is derived from the halakic introduction *Yelammedenu Rabbenu* 'may our master instruct us.' As for the name Tanḥuma, the explanation is either that several discourses open with the phrase: 'So did R. Tanḥuma bar Abba introduce the discourse,' or[1] that this Amora[2] himself laid the foundation for these homilies. As a matter of fact, no other teacher has so many proems handed down in his name as Tanḥuma. The name Tanḥuma is found e. g. in Rashi and in Yalḳuṭ, the name Yalammedenu especially in Aruk and in Yalḳuṭ. Originally this Midrash contained just one homily for each Seder or each sabbath lection. The arrangement is characteristic: halakic beginning, several proems, exposition of the first verses of the Pentateuchal section, messianic conclusion. By omitting a certain number of homilies and replacing them by others of identical form (such homilies in all probability must have circulated in a large number anonymously) it was possible for several works, greatly diverging from one another, to arise out of one original collection (Yelammedenu). The author of the Yalḳuṭ had before him at least two collections; the one he calls Tanḥuma, the other Yelammedenu.[3]

§ 4. Pesiḳtha Rabbathi.

Pesiḳtha Rabbathi is differentiated from the older Pesiḳtha by the appellation 'the Great.' Like the other it is a collection of homilies for the festivals and special Sabbaths; but in No. 1 it has a different starting-point, probably the Sabbath Bereshith before the Ḥanukkah festival (Nos. 2–8). The homilies 10–15 are destined for the Sabbaths before and after Purim, Nos. 16–19 for the Passover festival, 20–25 for the festival of Weeks, 27–39 for the Sabbaths preceding Tabernacles, 39–44 New Year, 45 Sabbath after New Year; 46–48 lead up to the Day of Atonement. The homilies 15–18 a. 33 are equal to Pesiḳtha Kahana 5–8 a. 19; No. 14 (Para) equals largely Pes. K. 4. Otherwise both works go apart in contents. Not less than 28 homilies[1] set in with the phrase Yelammedenu Rabbenu and with 'So did R. Tanḥuma open up'; neither is found in Pes. K. According to Zunz[2] the work was 'certainly not composed before the second half of the ninth century.' The reasons adduced by him are from internal evidence; then from the circumstance that the Sheeltoth by Aḥa of Shabḥa which date from 750 C.E. have been made use of; lastly from the testimony of the book itself[3] which makes 777 years to have elapsed from the destruction of the Temple, hence the year 845 must have been passed. Both Isr. Lévi[4] and W. Bacher[5] accept the date proposed by Zunz, at the same time maintaining that the book was written in Italy: *b.'r.i* No. 28[6] is identified with Bari. On the other hand, Friedmann (hardly rightly) is of the opinion that Aḥa is dependent upon Pes. R. and that the number 777 has been interpolated; he maintains that our book was used by the compiler of Levit. R. and that even in Gen. R. there are found sentences for which Pes. R. was basic. The printed text is disfigured by lacunae and glosses. Friedmann follows the Breslau edition, although at least codex Parma 1240[7] might readily have been accessible. One should therefore reserve judgment concerning Friedmann's view that the homilies 21–24, 26–28, 34–37 originated with other authors. It is true that homily 26 is probably of a different origin (it does not set in with a biblical verse and is differentiated by its manner of presentation).[8]

§ 5. Debarim Rabba, Bemidbar R., Shemoth R.

a. Debarim Rabba, Deut. R., is divided in the prints according to the sabbath pericopes of the annual cycle into 11 sections.[1] In reality Deut. R. consists of 27 homilies (among them 2 fragments), each complete in itself, relating to texts of the triennial cycle; the exceptions are best explained by the supposition that the basic order of Sedarim differed from the one which alone had been known to us. The homilies set in with an halakic introduction *halakah* (*'adam miyyisra'el*); then one or several proems, which here already present themselves as original homiletic structure; exposition of the opening part of the Scriptural section; a conclusion with consolatory promises. Large pieces at the end of Deut. R. are supplements with material derived from the Midrash on the Passing away of Moses.[2] It is quite clear that the sources were the Palest. Talmud, Gen. R. and Levit. R. According to Zunz, the work was composed about 900; the author of the Aruk and Rashi do not cite our Midrash; it is frequently adduced in Yalḳuṭ as *'Elle ha-Debarim Rabba.*[3] It is remarkable that writers of the thirteenth and the following centuries cite portions of Deut. R. as Tanḥuma; the two works have little in common as regards the contents; the printed Tanḥuma on Deut. has no halakic introductions and only three complete homilies constructed according to rule (14.22; 25.17; 33.1), and these are derived from Pes. K. (Nos. 11, 3, 32).[4]

b. Bemidbar Rabba, Num. R., or[5] Bemidbar Sinai Rabba, in 23 sections, consists of two heterogeneous parts. The first (1–14 approximately three fourths of the whole) is a recent haggadic composition on Num. 1–7; in sections 1–5 one may still recognize, despite the ample expansions, the homilies of the Tanḥuma Midrashim; in section 6 ff. on the sabbath pericope Naso there stands out still more clearly the aim to produce a Midrash treating the whole of the text, 'In room of the brief explanations or allegories of the ancients, instead of their constant appeal to authorities, we read here compilations from halakic and haggadic works, intermixed with artificial, often playful applications of the Scriptures and for many pages we find no source named.'[6] This part is probably not older than the twelfth century. In it alone are found the large amplifications which came in part from Pesiḳtha Rabbathi, in part from writings of later, in particular French, rabbis.[7] The Midrash on Lamentations has likewise been used.[8]

The second part, sections 15–23, relating to Num. 8–35, is disposed in the printed editions according to the sabbath pericopes of the annual cycle, only the parasha *Shelaḥ Leka* (Num. 13–15) has two sections. This part is, as was recognized by Benveniste,[9] essentially the Midrash Tanḥuma. At the beginning of the halakic introductions the prints of Num. R. have *halakah*; but according to the testimony of A. Epstein, the Paris Ms. Hebr. 150 has the older formula Yelammedenu Rabbenu.[10]

c. Shemoth Rabba, Exod. R., has 52 sections. In the first 14 a running exposition of the single verses of each Seder; from section 15 on (Exod. 12.1) homilies and fragments of homilies with proems and expositions of the first verse in each case. Accordingly we should distinguish two parts. For the first part some older expositional Midrash (a continuation of Gen. R.?) will have served as source; certain expressions remind us of the tannaitic Midrash. In the second part many homilies are derived from the Tanḥuma Midrash;[11] nevertheless the author must have commanded still other sources, as the Pesiḳtha Kahana.[12] Twice in the printed editions there is simply a reference to a homily collection;[13] it is possible, however, that these 'references' are abbreviations by a well-read copyist. Certainly a late Midrash; according to Zunz[14] probably of the eleventh or twelfth century.[15]

§ 6. Smaller Homiletical Midrashim.

a. Aggadath Bereshith, a collection of 28 homilies on Gen., according to the triennial cycle.[1] Each homily has three sections: the first connects itself with Gen.; the second with a text from the Prophets, which is to be looked upon as haphtara of this Seder; the third with a passage of the Psalms (perhaps read on the same Sabbath). The beginning (Gen. 1.1 to 6.4) and the last discussion of a verse of the Psalter are missing. The matter is mainly derived from Midrash Tanḥuma (Buber's text); the book is not cited by ancient writers.[2]

b. Midrash Hashkem or M. Wehizhir, M. on Exod. to Num. (also Deut. ?) according to the annual cycle. The predominating halakic part of the matter is derived from Sheeltoth, Halakoth Gedoloth, also the Baraitha on the Structure of the Tabernacle; the haggadic matter specifically from Tanḥuma. The Munich Ms. Hebr. 205, defective at the head, opens with a haggadic piece Exod. 8.16, which is also found in Tanḥuma of the earlier editions (at the same place) and from the initial word of which, *hashkem*, this Midrash derives its name; it reaches as far as Num. 5.11 ff. The other name is due to the circumstance that almost all Pentateuchal sections begin with *wehizhir ha-Ḳ.B.H.* (and God warned or admonished Israel). Zunz conjectures that the work was composed in the tenth century in the south of Europe. L. Grünhut[3] has collected citations from ancient writers. J. M. Freimann is wrong in naming Hephez Alluph as author.[4]

c. Pesiḳtha Ḥadatta, New Pesiḳtha, a more concise Midrash for the festivals.[5] Sources: Gen. R., Pirḳe R. Eliezer, Book Yeṣira etc.[6]

d. Midrash Wayekullu named after Gen. 2.1 *wayekullu*. Only known from citations[7] in writers of the twelfth century. These citations relate to Gen., Levit., Num., Deut.; hence the Midrash seems to have comprised the entire Pentateuch. Tanḥuma (or Yelammedenu of the Yalḳuṭ) served essentially as a source.[8]

e. Midrash Abkir, known from more than fifty excerpts in Yalḳuṭ and citations by Tobiah ben Eliezer (1097 ff.) and others, probably covered only Gen. and Exod. Its name is derived from the formula *'Amen beyamenu ken yehi raṣon* with which all its homilies closed.[9] The language is pure Hebrew; matter and mode of presentation are reminiscent of younger haggadic works. As in Pirḳe R. Eliezer, there are many references to angels.[10] The whole work was known by Azariah de Rossi (died 1578) and Abraham ibn Aḳra.[11]

CHAPTER XVIII

The Oldest Expositional Midrashim

§ 1. Bereshith Rabba.

Genesis Rabba, *Bereshith Rabba*,[1] i. e. probably: great Midrash on Gen., presumably in order to distinguish it from a shorter and older Midrash which may basically ascend to Oshaia.[2] A tradition widely spread ascribes the composition of this Midrash to the Palestinian Amora of the first generation, Oshaia or Hoshaia, the first proem begins with his name.[3]

Gen. R. offers partly simple explanations of words and sentences, partly, in frequently loose association, briefer or more extended haggadic expositions and demonstrations, such as were customary in public discourses; often sententious sayings and parables are woven in. Quite frequent are foreign words, esp. Greek, among them some which do not seem to occur elsewhere in Jewish literature; many times narratives are introduced and they are designated by the Greek term *δρᾶμα*. A characteristic of Gen. R. is the frequent *'athmaha* (astonishment, query, mostly just simple interrogative particle),[4] also in the three parashas 95–97 discovered by Theodor! The language is almost throughout neo-Hebraic; Aramaic occurs principally in narratives and popular matter. The Aramaic is of the Galilean variety as in the Palestinian Talmud. Halakic discussions are rare.[5]

The whole work is divided into parashas (at present: 101) and receives over against the tannaitic Midrashim its specific stamp through the proems which, however, are in part of later date; Theodor counts some 230 in 1–96. Much else has been likewise added by later copyists (supplementers);[6] many still later additions, in the more recent manuscripts and the previous editions, are made to emerge into view through Theodor's critical edition. A peculiar condition attaches to the last sections, it is only of late that an insight into the matter has been given and even so only as to the main point.[7]

In almost all manuscripts (barring Vat. Hebr. 30) the exposition of chapter 49 (last words of Jacob) appears in a younger recension which in part is derived from Tanḥuma homilies; this recension alone is cited in Aruk a. in Yalḳuṭ.[8]

When we abstract from the additions specified above, Midrash Gen. R. cannot have been compiled much later than the Palestinian Talmud. It cannot be demonstrated that the latter was made use of. Quite inconclusive are the arguments with which S. Maybaum[9] supports his theory that Gen. R. was not compiled before the end of the seventh century, and possibly even as late as the second half of the eighth century. The haggadic explanations Gen. 16. 12 a. 25. 18 in no wise prove that at that time the Arabs were dominant in Palestine or that the Omayyad dynasty had fallen; according to Midrash Lam. 1.5[10] commanders from other nations, among them *Dukus d'Arabya*, hence an Ishmaelite, fought on the side of Vespasian's army.

In the majority of printed editions, Gen. R. is divided into 100 parashas; manuscripts and editions vary between 97 and 101,[11] but almost all witnesses are uniform with regard to the first 94.[12] The basis is the division according to the small parashas, pethuḥoth and sethumoth, of which Genesis has 43 + 48, in part also that according to the Sedarim of the triennial Palestinian cycle of sabbath lections. In the first part of the book the fulness of material leads to breaking up: the sabbath pericope Bereshith Gen. 1.1–6.8 has 29 parashas occupying approximately one fourth of the Midrash (perhaps, however, the increase in bulk is to be explained by the assumption of later expansion); a number of these parashas treat only a few verses and some even just one verse.[13]

§ 2. Midrash on Lamentations.

Midrash Lamentations, *M. 'Ekah* (after the initial word of Lamentations), Aggadath Eka (Hananel), Megillath Eka (Aruk) a. Eka Rabbathi (Rashi, Yalḳuṭ); the last name designated at first only the Midrash on the first chapter. One of the oldest Midrashim of Palestinian provenance, as is indeed shown by the great number of Greek foreign words. The opening consists of 36 proems which make up more than a fourth of the work and which by no means need be supposed as coming from a later compiler. The great number may be accounted for by the fact that from early times it was the custom to deliver discourses on Lamentations both on the ninth of Ab (the day on which Jerusalem was destroyed) and on the eve thereof.[1] Apparently it is from just this sort of discourses that the greater part of the exposition, arranged according to the sequence of verses, proceeded. The exposition exhibits the same character as that in Gen. R.: side by side with plain interpretations haggadic pieces, which often are only loosely connected and by which the treatment of the single sections produces the impression of a lack of uniformity; here and there repetitions. The authorities named are not younger in date than those of the Palestinian Talmud. Numerous passages are essentially identical with the latter.[2] Zunz's conjecture that Midrash Lamentations was compiled 'not earlier than the second half of the seventh century' rests upon a supposed allusion to Arab dominion; but according to the correct reading[3] it is Seir, not Ishmael, that is named by the side of Edom.[4]

CHAPTER XIX

Midrashim on the Five Megilloth

§ 1. The so-called Rabboth.

a. M. Eka.[1]

b. M. Shir Ha-shirim, M. on the Song of Songs, also called Aggadath Ḥazitha because the book opens with the verse Prov. 22. 29 *ḥazitha 'ish mahir.* Allegorical interpretation[2] of the Song which had been proclaimed most holy by Akiba. The treatment of the single passages is entirely disproportionate: proems, and even complete sermons are taken from older homilies. Frequent repetitions. Main sources: Palest. Talm., Gen. R., Pesiḳtha K., Levit. R.; likewise passages of the Mishna and Baraithoth are adduced. The proems at the head conclude with one and the same sentence from Seder Olam.[3]

c. Midrash Ruth, expositions and haggadic compilations according to the order of the verses of the text, in 8 sections. At the head is found an introduction with 6·proems and a longish working out[4] of the idea that wherever an Old Testament narrative begins with *wayehi bime* it points to a time of tribulation. Proems are found also in front of the sections 3, 4, 6, 8. At the head of 2 a. 4 there are longer expositions of I Chr. 4.21–23 a.[5] I Chr. 11.13. Main sources: Palest. Talm., Gen. R., Pesiḳtha K., Levit. R. M. Ruth has certain matter in common with M. Ḳoh.[6] Of other long pieces we may signalize the sixfold interpretation of 2.14 as referring to David, Solomon, Hezekiah, Manasseh, the Messiah, Boaz.[7]

d. Midrash Ḳoheleth follows the text verse by verse (only a few verses are left without comment). Four sections which, in accordance with the old list of Sedarim, begin 1.1; 3.13; 7.1; 9.7. The author draws largely upon the proems found in the older Midrashim (Gen. R., Midrash Eka a. Song of Songs, esp. Pesiḳtha K. a. Levit. R.) which start from a verse of Ḳoheleth. The long piece 12.1–7 is a composite of the proem to Levit. R., section 18 a.

the 23d proem in Midrash Lamentations. The Haggadoth of the Palest. Talm. are frequently drawn upon; there are also found borrowings from the Babyl. Talmud. The late date of this Midrash becomes most clear from the fact that the tractate Aboth[8] and even several of the smaller Tractates (Proselytes, Slaves, Fringes, Phylacteries a. Mezuza[9])[10] are referred to by name. Contrast the basic passage (proem to Levit. R. parasha 22). Repetitions are not infrequent. Four times (2.24; 3.13; 5.17; 8.15): 'In all passages in which in this scroll eating and drinking is referred to, the meaning is the enjoyment which is afforded by Torah and good deeds.' 2.4–8 is an example how skilfully the author combines allegorical exposition with simple explanation and moulds the material gathered from diverse sources into a whole.[11]

e. Midrash Esther, more rarely called Megilla, exposition of the Scroll of Esther which is recited on Purim. The beginnings of the six sections (1.1, 4, 9, 13; 2.1, 5) are marked as proems intended by the author; four coincide with the closed paragraphs *sethumoth* of the traditional text of Scripture. It was likewise the intention that 3.1 should open a section, as is evidenced by the preceding proems. The exposition likewise makes the impression of something unfinished: at chapter 7 it grows scanty and ceases altogether at the end of chapter 8. The matter admitted is for the most part very ancient (we must remember that the book of Esther was begun to be expounded in the academies at an early period[12]). Sources used: Palest. Talm., Gen. R., Levit. R., Pirḳe R. Eliezer. In chapter 6 there is found a long interpolation from Josippon (dream and prayer of Mordecai, prayer of Esther and her appearance before the king). Nevertheless, there is no reason to conclude from that or from the fact that the Midrash is not cited in Rashi, Aruk, Yalḳuṭ that it was composed at a late date.[13]

§ 2. Other Midrashim on the Megilloth.

a. S. Buber. *Midrasch suta. Haggadische Abhandlungen über Schir ha-Schirim, Ruth, Echah u. Koheleth nebst Jalkut zum Buche Echah . . . nach Handschriften . . . u. mit einer Einl.*, Berlin, 1894 (172). Whereon see *MGWJ*, 1895, 562–566.—It is to be regretted that Buber dealt with his text arbitrarily, nor are the parallel passages indicated satisfactorily.—The Song, Ruth, Lament., Ḳoh. according to codex de Rossi 541; another recension of Lament. according to cod. 261; p. 145–171 the excerpts of the Yalḳuṭ from M. Eka a. from Eka Zuṭa.

The same Midrash on the Song according to the same Ms. and the fragment de Rossi 626 was edited by S. Schechter: *Agadath Shir Hashirim*, Cambridge, 1896 (112; appeared previously in *JQR*, V, VI), with instructive notes. Schechter is of the opinion that the author manifestly made use of M. Yelammedenu and that he wrote somewhere about the end of the tenth century. See in addition *JE*, XI, 292 f.

A third Midrash on the Song was edited by L. Grünhut: *Midrasch Schir-Ha-Schirim* . . . [according to a Ms. of the year 1147], *mit Einl.*, Jerusalem 1897 (38 a. 104). Whereon Bacher, *REJ*, XXXV, 230–239. This Midrash was made use of by writers from the eleventh to the beginning of the fourteenth century.

b. S. Buber, *Sifre d'Aggadta Megillath Esther, Sammlung agadischer Commentare zum Buche Esther* [M. Abba Gorion, M. Panim aḥerim, Leḳaḥ Ṭob]. *Nach Handschriften mit Erklärungen u. einer Einl.*, Wilna 1886 (14 a. 112). Comp. in addition N. Brüll, *Jahrbücher*, VIII, 148–154.

The Midr. Abba Gorion on Esther, cited already by Rashi, was printed also in *Beth Ha-midraš*, I. See in addition Zunz, *GV.*, 279. Translated in *Israels Lehrhallen*, II.

S. Buber *'Aggadath Esther. Agadische Abhandlungen zum Buche Esther* [according to two Yemenite Mss.] *herausgegeben u. mit Anmerkungen*, Cracow 1897 (12 a. 84). The compiler made use of Alphasi and Maimonides, also of Targum sheni, and wrote not earlier than the fourteenth century.

M. Megillath Esther. The text in *Beth Ha-midraš*, I, 18–24; translation in *Israels Lehrhallen*, II, 139–148.

Mordecai's Dream a. Esther's Prayer. Text in *Beth Ha-midraš*, V, 1–8; translation in *Israels Lehrhallen*, II, 149–163.

CHAPTER XX

Other Expositional Midrashim[1]

a. Midrash Samuel, *M. Shemu'el* or *'Aggadath Shemu'el*, haggadic expositions of verse in the Book of Samuel, compiled throughout from older writings, for which reason not all parts of the text are taken into consideration. From the Babylonian Talmud only one citation,[2] it is also to be noted that of the Amoraim only those of Palestine are mentioned; hence compiled in Palestine.[3]

b. Midrash Jonah consists in the editions of two parts. The first is essentially found also in Yalḳuṭ on Jonah,[4] and both seem to have drawn from the same source. Chapter 10 is almost entirely taken over from Pirḳe R. Eliezer, a few points also from Palest. a. Babyl. Talm. The second part, which sets in at 2.11 ('and the Lord spoke unto the fish'), comes from the Zohar;[5] it is not found in cod. de Rossi used by H. M. Horovitz.[6]

c. Midrash Tehillim, M. on the Psalter, or, after the opening words, *Shoḥer ṭob* Prov. 11.29, consists, as was recognized by Zunz,[7] of two wholly disparate portions. The first comprises Psalms 1–118 (only these are found in the Mss. and in the first print) and possibly a part of 119.[8] It is not a uniform work by a single compiler; for the Mss. diverge considerably, and we find not a few repetitions. There must have been still available remains of the old haggadic collections on the Psalter[9] when later haggadists formed Midrashim on biblical books in greater number. From the most diverse sources homilies and comments on single verses were collected until gradually there arose a tolerably connected Midrash.[10] Hence it is impossible to name a definite date for this Midrash as for many others. Zunz pointed quite generally to the last centuries of the gaonic period. The phraseology and the manner of the haggadic comments speak in favor of Palestine as place of composition; in favor of this assumption we may note that the Amoraim mentioned are throughout Palestinians or at least (they are but few) occur also in the Palestinian Talmud. It deserves to be pointed out that in the course of exposition frequently regard is had to Ḳere and Kethib, full and defective spelling. Again and again the numerical value of a letter or word is utilized; we find likewise the breaking up of words (gematria a. notaricon).[11]—The second part comprising Psalms 119 ff., in the first edition Saloniki 1515 standing by itself, is found in none of the manuscripts and is for the most part (Ps. 122, 124–130, 132, 137) literally reproduced from the Yalḳuṭ. For Ps. 123 a. 131 Buber has compiled from Pesiḳtha Rabbathi, Num. R. a. Babyl. Talm. a substitute Midrash.[12]

d. Midrash Mishle, M. on the Book of Proverbs, first to cite it was Hananel (died 1050). To a large extent more a commentary than a Midrash.[13] Some parts are left without any comment.[14] Older Midrashim served as sources, also the Babyl. Talm., but not the Palest. (which, however, does not signify that Buber is right when he maintains that it was composed in Babylonia). The tractate Hekaloth which cannot possibly have been written before the ninth century also was made use of.[15]

e. Midrash Iyyob, attested as extant e. g. by Yalḳuṭ Ha-Makiri. The preserved excerpts and citations have been collected by S. A. Wertheimer.[16]

CHAPTER XXI

Other Haggadic Works

§ 1. Narrative Haggada.

With reference to the time taken into consideration we may designate as comprehensive writings:

a. Megillath Taanith.[1]

b. Seder Olam, from the twelfth century on (for the first time in Abraham ben Jarhi) in contradistinction to the work named Seder Olam Zuṭa which deals with the chronology of the exilarchs: Seder Olam Rabba; ascribed by tradition to the Tanna Jose ben Ḥalaphta, probably compiled in early Amoraic times, but subsequently enlarged or revised, takes in the time from Adam to the end of the house of Herod (in chapter 30, briefly, the period to Bar Kokeba is included).[2]

c. Pirḳe R. Eliezer, or[3] Baraitha deRabbi Eliezer, a description of the workings of God in creation and in the oldest history of Israel with leanings on Gen., Exod., Num. The aim of the author, which at the head is expressed by Eliezer ben Hyrcanus,[4] was to declare the glory of God, Ps. 106.2. Chapters 3–11: Creation; 12–23: Adam to Noah (announcement of the ten descents, *yeridoth*, of God to the earth; the three pillars upon which the world rests: Torah, worship, beneficence); 24 f.: the corruption of mankind and the confusion of tongues; 26–39 Abraham to Jacob; 40–48: Moses to the theophany after the sin with the goden calf; 49 f.: the descendants of Amalek (Haman, Titus) with remarks on the Scroll of Esther; 51: the future redemption; 52: seven miracles; 53 f.: punishment of Miriam for slandering Moses. This very conclusion proves that the book remained unfinished. The case is established by further considerations such as the following. In the first place at the end of the chapters sentences of the Eighteen Benedictions are applied, but that is not carried to a finish. Secondly, in chapter 14 ten manifestations of God are mentioned; but the book concludes with the eighth.

The book was prob. written in Palestine, some time about the beginning of the ninth century; thus the allusion to Arab dominion is accounted for.[5] Of matters of detail we may note the remarks on the calendar chap. 6–8[6] and the numerous references to Jewish customs.[7]

d. Yosippon, a history of the Jews, intermixed with much fiction, from the fall of Babylon to the destruction of the Temple in Jerusalem;[8] written in Italy, prob. in the second half of the ninth century, it received in the course of time considerable amplification both in the manuscripts and in the printed editions.[9]

e. Sepher ha-yashar, [10] from Adam to the time of the judges, but the latter is only briefly told, written in southern Italy in the eleventh (twelfth ?) century.[11]

On the other hand, the following works deal with specific times:[12]

f. Midrash Wayyissa'u, the combats of the sons of Jacob with the Amorites and Esau, with reference to Gen. 35.5; 36.6. The antiquity of these stories is attested by the Book of Jubilees chap. 34, 37 f. a. the Testament of Judah, 2 ff.[13]

g. Dibre ha-yamim shel Mosheh, the life of Moses in pure Hebrew, in part made up of Bible verses; the legends by which the story is embellished contain matter which in part at least is quite old, since similar matter is met with in Josephus' *Antiquit.* II, 9, § 2 ff. (What is the relation to Sepher Ha-yashar?).[14]

h. Midrash of the Passing away of Aaron, *M. Peṭirath 'Aharon* according to Num.20.[15]

i. Midrash of the Passing away of Moses, *M. Peṭirath Moshe.* Three recensions.[16]

k. Book of Zerubbabel, *Sefer Zerubabel.*[17]

l. Megillath Antiochus, or the Book of the Hasmoneans *Sefer Beth Ḥashmonai*, written in the ninth or perhaps earlier in the eighth century, legendary account of the times of the Maccabees leading up to the institution of the Festival of Lights. The language imitates the biblical Aramaic. Saadia is the first to mention it.[18]

m. Midrash *'Elle Ezkerah* (Ps. 42.5) describes the execution of 10 noted Tannaim: Rabban Simeon ben Gamaliel II, the high priest Ishmael, Akiba, Hananiah ben Teradion, Judah ben

Baba, Judah ben Dama, Huzpith, Hananiah ben Hakinai, Jeshebab, Eleazar ben Shammua. The unhistorical character becomes evident when we consider that these ten men, as we know for a certainty, did not die at one and the same time. Somewhat divergent enumerations of the ten *haruge malkuth* in M. Eka 2.2 a. Midr. Ps. 9.13. The opening is taken from M. Konen, the dialogue of Ishmael with the angels, prob. from Hekaloth.[19]

n. *'Eser Galuyyoth* Midrash on the ten captivities.[20]

o. Midrash Wayyosha', exposition of Exod. 14. 30–15. 18 in the diction of the more recent haggada. Much is taken literally from Tanḥuma, likewise use has been made of the Dibre ha-yamim shel Mosheh.[21] On 15. 18: Armilus, who slays the Messiah from the tribe of Joseph and is in turn to be put to death by the Messiah ben David. God gathers Israel, sits in judgment to punish the wicked and brings on a new world full of bliss and glory.[22]

p. Midrash of the Ten Commandments, *M.'Asereth ha-dibberoth.* In the introduction the starting-point is Ps. 106.2 with a leaning on Pirḳe R. Eliezer.[23]

q. Midrash Espha, after Num. 11.16: 'Gather unto Me seventy men of the elders of Israel,' known almost entirely from a few excerpts in Yalḳuṭ on Num.[24]

r. Midrash al-yithhallel (Jer. 9.22). Stories from the life of the wise Solomon, the mighty David and the rich Korah.[25]

s. Numerous *ma'aseh* Books in Hebrew a. Judeo-German.[26]

§ 2. Ethical Midrashim.

a. Derek Ereṣ Rabba, D. E. Zuṭa.[1]

b. Tanna debe Eliyyahu. This book, which has been named 'the jewel of haggadic literature', owes its division and a part of its matter to the story in the Talmud[2] how the prophet Elijah taught Rab Anan (a pupil of Rab) Seder Eliyyahu Rabba a. S. El. Zuṭa. Of the passages cited in various tractates of the Talmud with the formula Tanna debe Eliyyahu, seven recur in the book as we have it. To judge from chronological data in chapters 2, 6, 31, the work must have been composed in the second half of the tenth century, probably (at least in the present form) in southern Italy. It purports, as is enunciated immediately at the head when expounding Gen. 3.24, to exhort people in the direction of right conduct, *derek 'Ereṣ*, and to glorify the study of the Law. The matter is made up on the one hand of comments on legal prescriptions, on the other hand of narratives. In the latter the prophet is presented as speaking, and his discourse is enlivened by parables, sententious sayings, prayers, exhortations. The author's liberality of mind shows itself in such an utterance as:[3] 'I call heaven and earth to witness that, whether a person be non-Jew (*Goi*) or Jew, man or woman, bondman or bondwoman, according to the deed which he does, the Holy Spirit rests upon him.'[4]

c. M. *Ma'aseh Torah*, a collection of doctrines and maxims after the numbers from 3 to 10.[5]

d. Alphabet of Ben Sira. Two lists, alphabetically arranged, of twenty-two proverbs each, one Aramaic, the other Hebrew, with haggadic commentary.[6]

e. M. Temura, this ethico-haggadic booklet, composed according to Jellinek in the first half of the thirteenth century, seeks 'to demonstrate that alternations and contrasts are necessary in the world.' In chap. 2 Ishmael and Akiba are introduced as teaching; the last (third) chapter expounds Ps. 136 with reference to Ḳoh. 3.1–8.[7]

§ 3. Mysticism (also Symbolism of Letters and Numbers).[1]

a. The Book Yeṣira. Linguistic and cosmogonic speculations, the former on the letters, the latter under gnostic influences. Before the date and provenance of the book (one may perhaps think of the sixth century) can be ascertained, a critical edition is required. The first print, Mantua 1562, contains two recensions, of which the commentaries of Saadia and Shabbethai Donnolo apply themselves to the longer, while the shorter and in later times almost solely printed was commented upon by Jacob ben Nissim, Judah ben Barzillai, Moses ben Naḥman.[2]

b. M. Tadshe (according to the verse Gen. 1.11 commented on at the head) or Baraitha de Rabbi Pinḥas ben Jair (P. named twice in the text and as author at the end), principally symbolism of numbers.[3]

c. Alphabet (or Othiyyoth) of R. Akiba.[4]

d. M. Ḥaseroth witheroth, M. on words written with or without vowel letters.[5]

e. The great and small Hekaloth, first cited by Hai Gaon.[6]

f. M. Ḳonen: 'Descriptions of heaven and earth, of hell and paradise.'[7]

g. Book Raziel.[8]

CHAPTER XXII

Collective Works and Commentaries which go by the Name of Midrash

a. Yalḳuṭ Shim'oni, ordinarily just *Yalḳuṭ*, a midrashic thesaurus on the whole of the Old Testament, compiled from more than fifty works, of which several are no longer extant; valuable also because of correct readings which it offers for those works which are extant. Of particular value in this regard is the first edition Saloniki.[1] As it appears, the author, or his associate, used in different parts of the work different manuscripts. In the editions named the sources of the excerpts are noted at the head of each excerpt, while in the later editions they are placed on the margin. The work consists of two parts: the Pentateuch with 963 paragraphs and the other books with 1085. The order of the Old Testament books follows the talmudic,[2] except that Esther precedes Daniel; hence: Isaiah after Ezekiel; Hagiographa: Ruth, Psalms, Job, Proverbs, Ḳoheleth, Song, Lamentations, Esther, Daniel, Ezra-Nehemiah, Chronicles. The single sections are of altogether unequal length. Probably composed in the first half of the thirteenth century (not earlier, since both Deut. R. a. M. Abkir are made use of). The name of the author was Simeon; the epithet Darshan was prob. applied to him after his death; according to the title-pages of the editions (beginning with that of Venice) he was a native of Frankf. o. M. Rapoport,[3] A. Levy,[4] D. Cassel[5] and others would have this Simeon Darshan a brother of Menahem ben Ḥelbo, hence the father of Joseph Ḳara; in which case he would have lived earlier, in the second half of the eleventh century. But this supposition has been rightly controverted by Abr. Geiger,[6] R. Kirchheim[7] and partic. by A. Epstein.[8] This Yalḳuṭ is older by a century than the Y. ha-Makiri soon to be mentioned: Exod. R., Num. R. and the M. Ḳoh. a. M. Esther occasionally referred to as Rabboth were unknown to it.[9]

b. Yalkuṭ ha-Makiri. Makir ben Abba Mari (ben Makir ben Todros) prob. lived in Spain; certainly before the end of the fourteenth century, for one of the extant Mss. (in Leiden) belongs to the beginning of the fifteenth century. His work, compiled from older writings, comprised the prophetic writings proper and the three major poetical Hagiographa. He was able to use M. Yelammedenu (Tanḥuma) in a form with which neither of the two printed Tanḥ.-Midrashim squares. Therein, as likewise in the partially exceedingly important variants which it offers to the text of its sources otherwise known, lies for us the value of Makir's effort.[10]

c. Midrash ha-gadol, on the Pentateuch, compiled in Yemen, at a time subsequent to the death of Maimonides, since his Yad ha-ḥazaḳa is frequently cited; particularly valuable because of the excerpts from tannaitic Midrashim now lost.[11]

Only on account of their title we mention here:

d. Yalḳuṭ Reubeni, *Yalḳuṭ Reubeni 'al ha-Torah* (also named Y. R. gadol, in contradistinction to the same author's Y. R., an index to kabbalistic books, printed for the first time Prague 1660) by R. ben Höschke (Hoschke; Polish diminutive of Joshua) Cohen, rabbi in Prague, died 1673. This Yalḳuṭ, printed Wilmersdorf 1681, in a better edition Amsterdam 1700 (see Cat. Bodl. 6824; Cat. Ros. 962 f.), a collection of kabbalistic comments on the Pentateuch, is without scientific value. See *JE*, VI, 479.

e. The New Yalḳuṭ, *Yalḳut Ḥadash*, likewise kabbalistic, anonymous (by Israel of Belczicz?), for the first time Lublin 1648. Cat. Bodl. 3554–3557.

f. Bereshith Rabba major. Moses ha-darshan of Narbonne, first half of the eleventh century, often cited by Rashi and his grandson Jacob Tam, wrote commentaries (*Yesod*) on biblical books and compiled Midrashim; according to the Spanish Dominican Raimundus Martini (of the thirteenth century) he was the author of the M. Bereshith Rabba major, according to Epstein also of M. Tadshe. The trustworthiness of Martini's citations (in *Pugio fidei*) has often been called in question, particularly by S. M. Schiller-Szinessy.[12] On the other side it has been defended by Zunz,[13] Jellinek,[14] E. B. Pusey,[15] Ad. Neubauer,[16] A. Epstein.[17]

g. Leḳaḥ Ṭob, after Prov. 4. 2, at the same time alluding to the name of the author Tobiah ben Eliezer. This man was not born in Germany, but was a native of Castoria in Bulgaria; he wrote his book prob. in the year 1079, and then he re-wrote it in 1107 a. 1108 with additions and corrections.[18] Leḳaḥ Ṭob extends over the Pentateuch and the Megilloth, 'half commentary, half haggada, for the most part from older works.'[19]

h. Sekel Ṭob. The author used the Yelammedenu, but not Buber's Tanḥuma.[20] His book, although it can hardly be named a Midrash, is mentioned here solely in order that it may not appear to have been forgotten.[21]

i. Samuel ben Nissim Masnuth, at the latest in the first third of the thirteenth century, named, it is true, his *Ma'yan Gannim*, a commentary on Job,[22] Midrash Sepher Iyyob, but so he named similarly his commentaries on Daniel and Chronicles. He drew upon both Talmuds and many Midrashim, also the Rabboth (but not Deut. R.).

CHAPTER XXIII

Midrash Collections and Translations

§ 1. Midrash Collections.

Ad. Jellinek, *Sammlung kleiner Midraschim u. vermischter Abhandlungen aus der älteren jüdischen Literatur. Nach Handschriften u. Druckwerken gesammelt u. nebst Einleitungen* [in German] *herausgegeben*, I–IV, Leipzig 1853–57; V, VI, Vienna 1873. 1877.

Ḥayyim M. Horowitz, *Sammlung kleiner Midraschim*, I, Berlin (Frankf. o. M.) 1881: Pereḳ R. Eliezer ben Hyrcanus, three recensions of M. Jonah,[1] Aggadath Ḳarne Remim, a story of Abraham, dissertation on the ten kings, M. Megillath Esther, Aggada from the book Ha-ma'asim.—The same author, *Bibliotheca Haggadica*, 2 fascicles, Frankf. o. M. 1881.—The same, *Uralte Tosefta's*, I–III, Mayence 1889; IV, V, Frankf. o. M. 1890.—The same, *Sammlung zehn kleiner, nach Zahlen geordneter Midraschim*, Frankf. o. M. 1888.[2]

S. A. Wertheimer, *Kleinere Midraschim*, Jerusalem, 4 fascicles (to 1897).—The same, *Leḳeṭ Midrashim* Jerus. 1903.—The same, *Oṣar Midrashim* 2 fascicles, Jerus. 1913. 14.

L. Grünhut, *Sammlung älterer Midraschim u. wissenschaftlicher Abhandlungen*, 6 fascicles, Jerusalem 1898–1903.

J. D. Eisenstein, *Bibliotheca Midraschica. A Library of Two Hundred Minor Midrashim* [with introd. a. Hebrew notes]. New York 1915 (605) 4to.

§ 2. Translations.[1]

a. Blasius Ugolini[2] printed in his *Thesaurus antiquitatum sacrarum* (Venice, fol.) the following Midrashim in the original with a parallel Latin translation: Mekiltha a. Siphra, vol. XIV (1752); Siphre, XV (1753), col. 1–996; Lekaḥ Ṭob on Levit., Num., Deut. as Pesiktha, XV, col. 997–1226, a. XVI (1754).

b. Aug. Wünsche published in Leipzig under the summary title 'Bibliotheca Rabbinica. Eine Sammlung alter Midraschim zum ersten Male ins Deutsche übertragen' with introductions a. brief notes: Gen. R., 1881; Exod. R., 1882; Levit. R., 1884; Num. R.; 1885; Deut. R., 1882; Song of Songs, 1880; Ruth, 1883; Lamentations, 1881; Ḳoheleth, 1880; Esther, 1881; Mishle, 1885; Pesiḳtha Kahana, 1885. [The reader should not omit to give heed to the important additions a. corrections by J. Fürst a. D. O. Straschun at the end of each of these publications!]—Wünsche translated furthermore: *Midrash Tehillim*, 2 volumes, Trier 1892 f.—Lastly the same scholar published: 'Aus Israels Lehrhallen,' 5 volumes (vol. V in two parts), Leipzig 1907–1910. I, II: *Kleine Midraschim zur späteren legendarischen Literatur des A. T. s.* III: *Kleine M. zur jüd. Eschatologie u. Apokalyptik.* IV: *Kleine M. zur jüd. Ethik, Buchstaben u. Zahlensymbolik.* V a: *M. Šemuel.* V b: *Neue Pesiqtha u. M. Tadše.* With the exception of M. Samuel, the texts of almost all these Midrashim are found in Jellinek's *Beth Ha-midrash.*[3]

NOTES

PART I

NOTES TO CHAPTER I, P. 3

[1] Aboth 2.4; 3. 7; Meg. 28b הַשְׁנֵה הֲלָכוֹת.

[2] Yeb. 37a הִלֵּל שָׁנָה. Frequently with ל: Ḥul. 63b לעולם יִשְׁנֶה אדם לְתַלְמִידוֹ דרך קצרה, 'one should always teach his pupil in the briefest manner;' B. M. 44a 'thus you taught us in your youth,' שְׁנִיתָ לָנוּ; 'Erub. 54b, 'Moses taught him his portion,' שנה לו; B. M. 33b, 'this proposition was taught (laid down) in the times of Rabbi', נשנית משנה זו. In the sense 'to teach' we meet in post-tannaitic times also with the Hif'il הִשְׁנָה: Bacher, *Terminologie*, I, 193 f.; II, 225 f.

[3] In the sense of oral law the word was probably sounded originally as מִשְׁנָה, comp. מִשְׁנֵה התורה Deut. 17.18. For the transition into מִשְׁנָה comp. מִקְנֶה and מִקְנָה, מִקְוֶה and מִקְוָה (the latter form alone in New Hebrew, pl. מִקְוָאוֹת).

[4] Aboth 3.7.

[5] Tos. Ber. 2.12 'a בַּעַל קֶרִי (comp. Deut. 23.11) לא יציע את המשנה, may not discourse on the oral law.'

[6] Ber. 2.1 זמן מקרא, 'the time of reading (the Shema'),' Soṭa 7.2, מקרא בכורים, 'the recitation of Deut. 26.5 ff. on the occasion of offering the first-fruits.'

[7] E. g. Ḳid. 49a, in the name of R. Meir, איזו היא מ' הלכות.

[8] Yeb. 50a משנה שאינה צריכה, 'a superfluous statement, paragraph.' A single point of law dealt with in the official Mishna code (as above under 4 or 5) is spoken of as דְּבַר משנה: Sanh. 33a, 6a; Keth. 84b, 100a, 'when a judge has erred in a statement of law so as to run counter to the Code, a new trial may be ordered', טעה בדבר משנה חוזר.

[9] So read for חונה of the printed editions, see Midr. Ps. 104.22 and Buber ad loc.

[10] Pal. Hor. 3.48c. Similarly Midr. Ḳoh. 2.8; Midr. Cant. 8.2 and Ḳoh. 6.2; at the same time the Mishna collection of Akiba is referred to. On the Mishna of Levi bar Sisi, see chap. XIII, §7.

[11] Bacher, *Terminologie*, II, 238–240.

[12] Meg. 28ab. Bacher, *Tradition und Tradenten*, 619 and *ZDMG*, 1913, 6.

[13] Soṭa 22a.

[14] B. B. 87a; Ḥul. 110a.

15 See Friedmann, *Mechilta de-Rabbi Ismael*, Vienna, 1870, Introd., p. 40; Halevy, II, 88 ff., 128, 500; D. Hoffmann, *Jahrb. d. Jüd.-Literar. Gesellsch.*, VII, 306; J. N. Epstein, *Der geonäische-Kommentar zur Ordnung Tohorot*, Berlin, 48–50. On וְתַנָּא תוּנָא, 'the Tanna teaches,' see Epstein, *Schwarz-Festschr.* 319–322.

16 See D. Hoffmann, p. 312, No. 9,10.

17 Bacher, *Terminologie*, II, 241.

18 For the expression comp. Pal. Ned. 10, 42b, ארעא ברייתא 'the extraneous country (i. e. situated outside of Palestine).' The Hebrew phrase משנה חיצונה is late, Numb. R. 18 (fol. 184d, ed. Venice); in the older parallel passage, Midr. Cant. 6.9, we read תּוֹסָפוֹת.

19 Pal. Nidda 3, 50dα.

20 Bab. Keth. 12a.—Sometimes Mathnitha is used outright for Baraitha: Bacher, *Tradition u. Tradenten*, 235 f.

21 *MGWJ*, 1916, 153.

22 Ibid., 155.

23 Ibid., 156.

24 See S. Horovitz, *Lewy-Festschrift*, 194.—See in general L. Ginzberg, *Jew. Enc.*, II, 513–516.

25 A small beginning has been made by M. Stieglitz in his dissertation, *Die zerstreuten Baraitas der beiden Talmude zur Mischna Berachot*, Bern, 1908 (31 pp.).

26 St. determ. of גְּמָר, hence masc.

27 Shabb. 31a. Comp. also Ḥag. 15b גמר תורה מִפּוּמֵיהּ דאחר, 'he studied Torah at the mouth of Aḥer.' The verb is likewise used of the ratiocinative deduction of one opinion from another. Frequently statements of the oral law are introduced with the formula: גָּמְרִי (pl. of the part.) 'they learn,' i. e. it has been handed down.

28 Ḥul. 103b it is said of Rab Ashi that גְּמָרֵיהּ אִיעֲקַר לֵיהּ, 'his knowledge slipped from his memory.' Note that Shabb. 147b in exactly the same connection the word used is תלמודיה.

29 It has become customary to construe the noun as a feminine, the concluding ā being taken for the femin. ending.

30 So Levy, I, 343.

31 Erub. 32b three Amoraim address to R. Naḥman b. Jacob the question: קְבַעִיתּוּ לֵיהּ בגמרא, 'Have you given it a place in the Gemara?' It is true, the word may have here its primary meaning, 'scope of study.' Proceeding, however, from this passage, the Geonim, including Sherira, employ the term in

the sense which has now become current. See also Amram Gaon (856 C. E.): גמרא דארץ ישראל; *Halakoth Gedoloth*, ed. Venice, 138b: גמר בשחיטת חולין. See further M. Lattes, *Saggio di giunte . . . al Lessico Talmudico*, 1879, 85–87; *Nuovo saggio*, 1881, 30; W. Bacher, 'Gemara,' in *Hebrew Union College Annual*, 1904, 26–36 and *Terminologie*, II, 28–33.

[32] Comp. תַּנְחוּם, 'consolation,' from נָחַם 'to console.

[33] So frequently in the combination תַּלְמוּד לומר, 'there is a point of instruction on the part of Scripture in that it says' (then follows the scriptural passage subjected to the desired interpretation). In explaining the term, S. Krauss (*REJ*, LXVII, 177) compares the expression Ber. 4a למד לשונך לומר איני יודע, where similarly לומר is combined with למד. Another frequent expression is: בא הכתוב ללמד, 'Scripture comes to tell us,' Bacher, *Terminologie*, I, 95. Hence often also: מאי תלמודא, 'What point is implied in the scriptural word?' Sanh. 59b, etc.; יש תלמוד, B. Ḳ. 104b. 'ת comes to be the equivalent for *locus probationis*.

[34] In this sense the term ascends to the tannaitic literature. See Bacher, *Terminologie*, I, 202. Comp. Sherira (ed. Lewin, p. 51, 1.7) תלמוד הוא חכמת הראשונים דסברין ביה טעמי משנה, 'Talmud is the wisdom of the ancients, in which they develop the reasons for a mishnic (halakic) statement.' A related term is Midrash (see above §1), with this difference, however, that Midrash takes its point of departure from a scriptural passage.

[35] Ḥag. 10a: There is no peace, says Samuel with reference to Zech. 8.10, for him who abandons the Talmud for the Mishna; Joḥanan, Samuel's younger contemporary, adds, Even for him who abandons one Talmud for another (the Palestinian for the Babylonian). For further examples see Bacher, *Terminologie*, II, 235.

[36] Possibly so already Ezra 7.10. The noun Midrash is met with for the first time II Chron. 13.22, where in regard to king Abijah reference is made to מִדְרַשׁ הנביא עדו, and 24.27, which names מ' ספר המלכים (ספר probably a gloss; LXX just τὴν γραφήν, Lucian γραφὴν βιβλίου, see Field, *Hexapla*, I, 749b) as a source for the history of king Jehoash of Judah; but the exact meaning of the word in both these passages is uncertain.

[37] Yoma 8.9.

[38] E. g. Aboth 1.17: 'Not learning מדרש but doing מעשה is the groundwork.' Hence Midrash frequently as a synonym of 'Talmud,' e. g. Pal. Pes. 3, 30b.

[39] E. g. Keth. 4.6: זה מדרש דרש 'thus did he expound' (the exposition follows as object).

40 E. g. Pal Yoma 3, 40c: כל מ' ומ' כענינו, 'a scriptural exposition must in each case be in keeping with the general subject of the passage;' Gen. R. c. 42 on 14.1: 'This interpretation 'מ we took with us out of the Babylonian exile, that whenever there occurs in Scripture the expression ויהי בימי, a time of distress is had in mind.'

41 Shab. 16.1; pl. בָּתֵּי מִדְרָשׁוֹת Pes. 4.4. The oldest occurrence in Ben Sira 51.23.

42 E. g. Midrash Ruth. For further particulars see chap. XV ff.

43 א here is not femin. ending.

44 Comp. Bacher, *Terminologie*, I, 25–28, 103–105; II, 41–43, 107.

45 So הלך אחר בית דין יפה, 'to follow a competent court of justice,' Sanh. 32b; הולכין אחר (ה)רוב, 'one follows the majority,' Keth. 15a.

46 B. M. 5.8, Rabban Gamaliel acted thus, not because that was the accepted norm הלכה, but because he wished to exercise rigor so far as his own person was concerned. B. B. 130b (Nidda 7b): אין לְמֵדין הלכה לא מפי תלמוד ולא מפי מעשה עד שיאמרו לו הלכה למעשה, 'neither theoretical discussions (on the part of the Tannaim) nor (a scholar's) action (on a single occasion) make for the deduction of a norm, so long as it is not expressly remarked that the Halakah is to be followed in practice.'

47 Pea 3.6; Shebi'ith 9.5 (not in the Munich codex); Yeb. 4.12.

48 Comp. also Bacher, *Terminologie*, I, 42 f.; II, 53–56; J. Wellesz, *REJ*, LXIV, 286 f.

49 For the importance of Minhag (custom, current practice) comp. B. M. 7.1: Everything depends upon the custom of the country; Pal. B. M. 7.11b הַמִּנְהָג מְבַטֵּל את ההלכה. See art. 'Custom,' *Jewish Encycl.*, IV, 395–398; M. L. Bamberger deals with the rise of spurious Minhagim in an article in Wohlgemuth's *Jeshurun*, V (1918), 664–672.

50 אַחֲרֵי רַבִּים לְהַטּוֹת, Exod. 23.2! see B. M. 59b; Sanh. 3b; Ḥul. 11a. See further 'Eduy. 1.5 אֵין הֲלָכָה אֶלָּא כְּדִבְרֵי הַמְּרוּבִּין, Tos. Ber. 4.15, הלכה כדברי המרובים. Ch. Tschernowitz, הַכְרָעָה במחלוקת יחיד ורבים, in *Lewy-Festschrift* Hebrew part, pp. 1–9, endeavors to show that the principle holds good only when there has been an actual counting of votes and that it matters very much who the opponent is.

51 Comp. אַדְלָקָה, אַבְדָּלָה, etc. The vocalization אֲגָדָה rests on error.

52 See *JQR*, IV (1892), 406–429, and in expanded form, *Agada der Tannaiten*, 2d ed., I, 450–475. Bacher's explanation is disputed by Ch. Tschernowitz, *Die Entstehung des Schulchan-Aruch, Beitrag zur Festlegung der Halacha*, Bern, 1915, p. 10.

[53] E. g. מַגִּיד הַכָּתוּב שֶׁ, 'the scriptural word teaches that;' also with omission of הכתוב, which word, however, is to be supplied mentally as subject: מגיד ש. Quite synonymous is the expression בא הַכָּתוּב לְלַמֶּדְךָ שֶׁ, more briefly לְלַמֶּדְךָ שֶׁ, as also מְלַמֵּד שֶׁ.

[54] Concerning Haggadah see Zunz, *Gottesdienstliche Vorträge*, Berlin, 1832; Z. Frankel, *MGWJ*, II, 388 ff.; III, 149 ff., 191 ff., 357 ff., 437 ff.; Hamburger, II, 921–934; Bacher, 'Die H. als einer der drei Zweige der jüd. Traditions-wissenschaft,' *Agada der Tannaiten*, 2d ed., I, 475–489.

NOTES TO CHAPTER II, § 1, P. 8

[1] Jer. 25.11; 29.10 ff.; comp. Dan. 9.2; II Chron. 36.21 ff.; Ezra 1.1.

[2] Jer. 29.13.

[3] Ezekiel, the author of Isaiah 40 ff.; comp. also צוֹפַיִךְ, Isai. 52.8.

[4] See V. Ryssel, *Theologische Studien u. Kritiken*, 1887, 149–182.

[5] Ezra 7.6, comp. 7.11; Neh. 8.1, 4, 13; 12.26, 36.

[6] Ezra 7.10.

[7] Ib., 8.16.

[8] שׂוֹם שֶׂכֶל Neh. 8.4 ff.

[9] Comp. Deut. 17.11.

[10] See A. Kuenen, *Over de Mannen der Groote Synagoge*, Amsterdam, 1876 (in German translation in Kuenen, *Abhandlungen zur biblischen Wissenschaft*, 1894, 125–160) and the writer's article 'Grosse Synagoge,' in *Protestantische Realencyclopädie*, 3d ed., XIX, 221–223.

[11] Moses Brück, *Rabbinische Ceremonialgebräuche in ihrer Entstehung u. geschichtlicher Entwicklung*, Breslau, 1837, ix ff.; Moses Bloch, ספר שערי תורת התקנות, *Die Institutionen des Judenthums nach . . . den thalmudischen Quellen*, 3 volumes, Vienna and Budapest, 1873–1906.

[12] Of Joshua it is also said that when he distributed the land he stipulated certain conditions, תְּנָאִים, B. Ḳ. 80b, Pal. B. B. 15aα (Bab. Erub. 17a inexactly תקנתא).

[13] So concerning Erub and the ritual washing of the hands, Erub. 21b.

[14] B. Ḳ. 82a.

[15] The eleventh in Meg. 31b. See S. Zeitlin, *JQR*, N. S. VIII, 61–74; for criticism and rejoinder ib., X, 367–371.

[16] R. H. 31b; Soṭa 40a. See Derenb., 304 ff.

[17] Comp. Aboth 1.1.

[18] Pe'a 2.6; 'Eduy. 8.7; Yad. 4.3—in the two latter places of statutes which, considering the subject-matter, cannot possibly have originated in the times of Moses.

[19] See Simeon Peiser, *Naḥalath Shim'oni*, Wandsbeck, 1728, fol. 47a–49b; J. Levy, *MGWJ*, 1855, 355 ff.; L. Herzfeld, *Geschichte des Volkes Jisrael*, III (Nordhausen, 1857), 227–236; O. H. Schorr in *Heḥaluṣ*, IV (1859), 28 ff.; Weiss, I, 72–76; Hamburger, *Supplement*, II, art. 'Sinaitische Halakha'; W. Bacher, *Tradition u. Tradenten*, 33–46 (=*Kohler-Festschrift*, 56–70).

[20] Ed. Hamburger, p. 24 f.

[21] Similarly Joseph ibn 'Aḳnin, p. 15 (in the work listed below, ch. XIV § 1), only that the latter has in the place of הערלה בחו"ל something else from codex P.—Benjamin B. Guth, ספר שטה מקובצת החדש, I (New York 1910), presents in the Appendix a new enumeration of 67 examples found in the Talmuds and of 21 occurring in mediaeval authors.

[22] Comp. *MGWJ*, 1907, 307.

[23] From Lev. 11.33 יטמא; see Soṭa 5.2.

[24] Ḥagiga 1.8.

[25] See D. Hoffmann, *D. Buch Leviticus*, Berlin, 1905, p. 4. On עין תחת עין see Aḥad Haam, על פרשת דרכים, I, 110 f.

[26] See below, ch. IV, § 4, note 57.

[27] *Die erste Mishna*, Berlin, 1882, 3.

[28] See the writer's *Einleitung in das Alte Testament*, Munich, 1906, §§ 7–15.

[29] R. Jose in A. Z. 9a.

[30] Ḥul. 28a; comp. Siphre Deut. 12.21 (§ 75).

[31] *Schriften*, I (Szegedin 1889), 1–13, 241–317. Löw's attitude was dictated by opposition to traditional Judaism and his argumentation is rather antiquated. See Hoffman, 'Die Überlieferung der Väter und die Speisegesetze' in *Carlebach-Festschrift*, 31–88; then the monograph by Kraatz, *Die mündliche Lehre und ihr Dogma*, part 1, Leipzig, 1922, and the review by M. Guttmann in *MGWJ*, 1922, 238 f., who remarks: 'Weiss, in the first edition of his *Dor* and elsewhere, had adduced instructive examples which point unconditionally to the existence of an oral lore. Kraatz, however, goes further. The whole question is subjected to a searching analysis and the thesis, luminously presented in the opening pages of his work, is substantiated by additional examples.' See also S. Funk, *Die Entstehung des Talmuds* (Göschen Series, No. 479), p. 8 ff.; specifically on the subject of the ritual mode of killing animals Hoffmann, *Das Buch Deuteronomium* (Berlin, 1913), p. 167 f. and H. Hildes-

heimer, 'Der biblische Ursprung der Schächt-Vorschriften,' *Israelitische Monatsschrift* (Wissenschaftliche Beilage zur 'Jüdischen Presse'), 1905, No. 4. See in addition Grätz, III (5th ed.), p. 671 top.

[32] Ed. Mangey, II, 629. The fragment is preserved in Eusebius' *Praeparatio Evangelica*, VIII, 7, 6.

[33] Comp. also *De justitia*, *Mang.* II, 360 f.

[34] *Antiq.* XIII, 10, 6.

[35] *Antiq.* X, 4, 1; comp. Mat. 15.2; Mark 7.3, 5.

[36] *Antiq.* XIII, 16, 2.

NOTES TO CHAPTER II, § 2, P. 12

[1] *Einblicke in die Geschichte der Entstehung der talmudischen Literatur*, Vienna 1884, p. i.

[2] Ibid., p. 2.

[3] He cites Temura 14b, Sopherim 16.2; Giṭ. 60b.

[4] See the Prologue.

[5] *Blicke in die Religionsgeschichte zu Anfang des zweiten christl. Jahrh.*, I (Breslau, 1880), p. 59 dubiously, but p. 61 and 64 unreservedly.

[6] Nor does M. Friedmann, *Mechilta*, Vienna, 1870, Introd. p. 38.

[7] Op. cit., p. 64.

[8] Shab. 115a.

[9] Op. cit., p. 5.

[10] Ḳoheleth 12.12; Pal. Sanh. 10.28a.

[11] Temura 14b = Giṭ. 60b.

[12] כותבי הלכות כשורף התורה.

[13] דברים שבעל פה אי אתה רשאי לאומרן בכתב וכו'.

[14] תנא דבי ישמעאל.

[15] Pal. Kil. 9.32b. אשגרית עיניי בכל ספר תילים אגדה.

[16] Sanh. 57bα בספר אגדתא דבי רב; Bacher, *Agada der babyl. Amoräer*, p. 2.

[17] Temura 14b = Giṭ. 60a מעייני בספרא דאגדתא.

[18] Ber. 23aγ.

[19] ברית כרותה היא הלמד אגדה מתוך הספר לא במהרה הוא משכח, Pal. Keth. 5.9a.

[20] Pal. Shab. 16.15c: "May the hand that wrote the Haggada collection be cut off," see Soph. 16.10 and Midr. Ps 22.4.

[21] The context suggests that we should read סְפָרֵי. Z. speaks of the Haggadists, whom he calls masters (students) of witchcraft. But even so the expression points to the existence of haggadic writings which evoked his disapproval. Z. carried in his mind the phrase סִפְרֵי קוסמים with which the tannaitic Halakah is wont to designate the Bibles of the Judeo-Christians (so Bacher, *Agada d. Tannaiten*, II, 297; *Agada d. palästin. Amoräer*, III, 502).

[22] Pal. Maasroth 3.51a.

[23] So Origen, In Matth. Comment. ser. § 28 (Migne, XIII, 1636): ex libris secretioribus qui apud Judaeos feruntur; In Matth. 17.2 *εἴτε ἐκ παραδόσεων εἴτε καὶ ἐπιβάλλοντες εἴτε καὶ ἐξ ἀποκρύφων*; Jerome on Jer. 29.21: ipsa ... fabula non recipitur nec legitur in Synagogis eorum; then on Ezek. 1.10: Legi et cuiusdam Catinae, quem Syri *Λεπτόν*, i. e. acutum et ingeniosum vocant, brevem disputatiunculam. S. Krauss had suggested that this C. is identical with the Zeira just mentioned, since he was also called "the Little one with the burnt thighs," קטינא חריך שקיה, B. M. 85a; Sanh. 37a; Ber. 46a. Bache (*Agada d. palästin. Amoräer*, III, 801), however, considers this conjecture entirely unfounded. See once more S. Krauss in the Hebrew Festschrift dedicated to M. Bloch, p. 85, n. 7.

[24] See Midr. Gen. R. on 1.31 (טוב מות), 3.21 (כָּתְנוֹת אור), 46.27 (וּבְן־דן v. 27); Pal. Taanith 1.64a (משא דומה Isai. 21.11: משא רומי). Contrast Ad. Blumenthal, *Rabbi Meir*, 1888, 24, 134 f.

[25] Tanḥuma, וארא, on וְאַל־יִשְׁעוּ Exod. 5.9 (ed. Mantua, 1563, fol. 27d).

[26] כתוב באגדתך ופרשה, Ḥul. 60b.

[27] מעייני באגדתא.

[28] Shab. 89a.

[29] Ber. 23a (comp. above p. 14).

[30] זוגא דסרבלא.

[31] B. M. 116a; B. B. 52a; Shebu. 46b.

[32] Taan. 2.8; Erub. 62b a. frequently.

[33] Comp. Zunz, *Gottesdienstl. Vorträge*, 127 f.; Grätz, III (third ed.), notes 1 and 26; Derenbourg, 439–446; Wellhausen, *Die Pharisäer u. die Sadducäer*, Greifswald, 1874, 56–63; Joseph Schmilg, *Über Entstehung u. historischen Werth des Siegeskalenders Megillath Taanith*, Leipzig, 1874 (52 pp.); Joel Müller, *MGWJ*, 1875, 43–48, 139–144; M. Brann, ib., 1876, 375–384, 410–418, 445–460; B. Ratner, ס' היובל (Festschrift in honor of Sokolow), Warsaw, 1904, p. 500–509; Lauterbach, *Jew. Encycl.*, VIII, 427 f. The editions are enumerated in Cat. Bodl., col. 3723–3726. See also Steinschneider, *Geschichtsliteratur*, 8–9, 172–173.

[34] Yeb. 49b; comp. also the Haggadist Levi, Pal. Taan. 68a, l. 45; Gen. R. 98, whereon Lewi Freund in the *Schwarz-Festschrift*, 187–190.

[35] Siphre Deut. 33.27 (§ 356); Pal. Taan. 68a, 1.40; Aboth derabbi Nathan B, ch. 46; Soph. 6.4.

[36] *JQR*, N. S., VIII, 385–423.

[37] Pes. 62b.

[38] So! see Bacher, *Agada d. palästin. Amoräer*, I, 60.

[39] Siphre Deut. 11.22 (Friedm. 84aγ).

[40] As the Yalḳuṭ reads.

[41] *Midrasch Tannaim zum Deuteronomium*, Berlin, 1908, p. VII f.

[42] This is the reading in Midrash ha-gadol.

[43] Comp. also Aboth derabbi Nathan B, ch. 27 (p. 56) והיו עוסקים בהלכות חסידים, and see Schechter (n. 26).

[44] *Halakoth gedoloth*, ed. Hildesheimer, 615.

[45] *Hist. Eccles.* VI, 25.

[46] See Leszinsky, *MGWJ*, 1911, 401, n. 1.

[47] See Zunz, *Gottesdienstl. Vorträge*, 62; Bab. Ber. 8b.

[48] See Pal. Meg. 4.74d. Comp. also A. Berliner, *Thargum Onkelos*, II (Berlin 1884), 88 ff.

[49] Bab. Yoma 38b; Pal. Sheḳ. 5.49a β.

[50] Shabb. 6b, 96b, comp. B. M. 92a. On Isi see Bacher, *Agada d. Tannaiten*, II, 378.

[51] Comp. Yeb. 72b.

[52] A better reading, given in the Tosaphoth in the name of R. Ḥananel is תריסר גווילי 'twelve pieces of parchment.'

[53] Ḥul. 95b.

[54] In the Babyl. Talm.: Ilpha.

[55] פִּנְקָסָא πίναξ.

[56] See Bab. Men. 70a; Pal. Maas. 2.49d.

[57] Shab. 156a.

[58] Ber. 19a.

[59] Mak. 16a. For נפק כו' comp. also Pes. 19a; Ḥag. 19a; Yeb. 36a, 105a; Keth. 81b; B. M. 20b; B. B. 172b; A. Z. 68a; Zeb. 58a; Ḥul. 6a, 31b.

[60] Shab. 19b.

[61] B. M. 85b.

[62] Pal. A. Z. 1.39c: Rab read in A. Z. 1.2 אידיהן, Samuel עידיהן; Rab read Erub. 5.1 מאברין, Samuel מעברין; Rab read Ber. 8.6 שיאותו Samuel שיעותו. See Chajes, מבוא התלמוד. On the other hand, Frankel (Additamenta to the

Hodegetica, p. 16 and 218) calls attention to such variants as סני and סכי (Bekoroth 44a on 7.3), בעולם and בעולה (Me'ila 15b on 4.2) which imply divergence due to graphic similarity. An intermediate position is taken by Halberstam (כבוד הלבנון, X, 7).

[63] B. M. 80b.

[64] See *MGWJ*, 1916, 68 f.

[65] See Bacher, *Tradition u. Tradenten*, 255–266 (pp. 255–262 the names of many).

[66] A. Perls, *MGWJ*, 1914, 311.

[67] E. g. Ber. 47a, Shab. 15a, Bekor. 5a, Eduy. 1.3.

[68] Pal. Ḳid. 1.61aγ.

[69] A Palestinian Amora of the fifth generation, comp. Bacher, *Agada d. palästin. Amoräer*, III, 436.

[70] Tanḥuma (Verona, 1595), וירא, 9a, also כי תשא, 41cγ, comp. Pesiḳtha Rabb. 5 (Friedm. 14b).

[71] Num. R. on 7.72 (Par. 14). Similarly Abin Pal. Pe'a 17a, Pal. Ḥag. 76d (Bacher, *Agada d. palästin. Amöräer*, III, 412).

[72] Meg. 18b.

[73] אפי הילכתא.

[74] קְצָרָא, Ned. 41a.

[75] To whose father Jacob and the men of Kairwan Sherira's Epistle was addressed!

[76] Vienna, 1847.

[77] 3, 67.

[78] Pinner, *Berachoth*, introd., 3b, 4a, 8a, 10a.

[79] Commentary on Aboth (Vienna, 1854), 6a, 8b, 9a.

[80] Ed. London, p. 48b, 201b, 204a.

[81] *Hodegetica*, 216–218.

[82] *Dor*, II (Vienna, 1876), 216 f.; III (1883), 243–248.

[83] II, 796 f.

[84] II, 10–13.

[85] *Toledoth Yisrael*, VI (Cracow, 1907), 340 ff.

[86] On Shab. 13b, Erub. 62b, B. M. 33a, etc.

[87] Bloch, *Einblicke*, p. 117. On Meg. 32a the Tosaphoth say: The Talmud teachers were in the habit of reciting the Mishnayoth in a specific chant, for the reason that the Mishnayoth, even after Rabbi, were not committed to writing and so impressed themselves upon the memory with greater ease.

[88] I, 73; II, 53.

[89] עץ חיים, first edition, Verona, 1650.

[90] Zolkiew, 1836.

[91] Vienna, 1830. See also *Kerem Ḥemed*, V (1838), 61–63 and Luzzatto's Hebrew Letters, Przemysl, 1882, No. 139 and 144.

[92] IV (4th ed.), n. 35.

[93] *Graphische Requisiten u. Erzeugnisse bei den Juden*, II (Leipzig, 1871), 112–115, 166 f.; comp. *Schriften*, I, 10.

[94] In the work cited above (n. 1).

[95] *Exercitationes Biblicae*, Paris, 1669, 294 f.

[96] *Sepher ha-yuḥasin*, ed. Constantinople, 1566; Cod. Oxford Bodl., No. 2521, 2; Cod. Halberstam-Epstein, now in the Library of the Israelitisch-theologische Lehranstalt in Vienna.

[97] Cod. de Rossi 217 in Parma; Oxford Bodl., 2198; Vienna, see Catalogue by J. Goldenthal, III, 21; Paris, 585; the Aleppo Codex, which in Lewin's edition is placed in parallel column with the Yuḥasin text.

[98] חפש מטמונים, Berlin, 1845 (reproducing Cod. Berlin Orient. Quarto 685) and אגרת רב שרירא גאון, Mainz, 1873.

[99] *Scherirae quae dicitur epistola*, Breslau, 1861 (with Latin translation).

[100] *Mediaeval Jewish Chronicles*, I, Oxford, 1887.

[101] London, 1910. See the unfavorable review in *Jahrb. d. Jüd.-Liter. Gesellschaft*, VIII, 350–354.

[102] *Epître historique du R. Scherira Gaon, Antwerp*, 1904 (pp. 42 and 90).

[103] Haifa, 1921. See Lewin, *Jahrb. d. Jüd.-Liter. Gesellschaft*, VII, 226–292; VIII, 318–354; M. Steinschneider, *Geschichtsliteratur der Juden*, I, Frankf. a. M., 1905, 18.

[104] Novella 146: τὴν δὲ παρ' αὐτοῖς λεγομένην δευτέρωσιν ἀπαγορευόμεθα παντελῶς ὡς ταῖς μὲν ἱεραῖς οὐ συνειλημμένην βίβλοις.—Further literature on the "Interdict on Writing:" Lebrecht, *Handschriften u. erste Ausgaben des babylonischen Talmud*, I, Berlin, 1862; J. M. Rabbinowicz, *Législation civile du Talmud*, II (Paris, 1877), p. XLV–LVII; A. Sammter, *Baba Mezia mit deutscher Übersetzung u. Erklärung*, Berlin, 1876 (folio), 121–124.

NOTES TO CHAPTER II, § 3, P. 20

[1] Frankel, 215 f.

[2] Nazir 1.4; 4.5; Mak. 1.8.

[3] So particularly in Aboth and at the end of several tractates, e. g. Soṭa

9.15; A. Z. 2.6 it appears that the patriarch Judah II, Rabbi's grandson, and his court are meant (comp. Pal. Giṭ. 48d).

[4] Comp. the significant observations by D. Hoffmann, *Jahrb. d. Jüd.-Liter. Ges.*, VII, 303–316.

[5] See Hoffmann, p. 309, and previously *Magazin*, 1882, 156 f.

[6] See below ch. IX, § 2a.

[7] This follows from the very opening of the Mishna, Ber. 1.1; the words ואכילת פסחים are wanting, but this plus is expressly designated in the Gemara as the Palestinian reading.

[8] According to B. M. 44a, Rabbi taught in his youth: Gold is acquired by means of silver, i. e. gold, as the more precious metal, is specie, while silver represents merchandise, and specie is acquired by means of merchandise. The reverse was taught by Rabbi in his old age. The current text of the Mishna 4.1 and the Babylonian Talmud read according to the latter formulation; on the other hand, the Cambridge, Parma, Budapest codices (according to the Sepher Ha-'iṭṭur, ed. Venice, I, 6a, also the accurate codices known to the author of this work) and the Palestinian Talmud follow the former. Similarly A. Z. 4.4 the manuscripts just named as well as other codices, likewise the Palestinian Talmud abide by the earlier formulation ושל ישראל, while the later is found almost alone in the Munich Ms. 95 and the first Bomberg edition; see Babyl. Talm. 52b.

[9] הלכה כסתם משנה, Yeb. 42b.

[10] הִלְכְתָא כְּתַנָּא קַמָּא.

[11] וחכמים אומרים.

[12] Except e. g. Pes. 3.6, where the opinion of the sages is followed by that of Eleazar ben Zadok. It must not be supposed, however, that the closing opinion is always normative, see, e. g., B. M. 4.4.

[13] Comp. Eduy. 1.4–6. See in addition J. Bassfreund, "Zur Redaktion der Mischna," *MGWJ*, 1907, esp. pp. 427 ff. (to be used with caution).

[14] אשריך כלים

[15] Kelim 30.4.

[16] Hor. 13b.

[17] Yoma 16a.

[18] See Pe'a 2.6.

[19] Yoma 14b.

[20] Zeb. 67b, 68a.

[21] See *REJ*, XXXII, 200 ff.

[22] *Magazin*, 1884, 89–92.

[23] Sanh. 86a: אמר ר׳ יוחנן סתם מתניתין ר׳ מאיר, סתם תוספתא ר׳ נחמיה, סתם ספרא ר׳ יהודה, סתם ספרי ר׳ שמעון, וכולהו אליבא דר״ע.

[24] Sanh. 3.4; Tosephta M. Sh. 2 (ed. Zuckerm., 88, 89).

[25] Comp. in addition (1) such statements as כשהיה ר״ע מסדר הלכות לתלמידים, "when Akiba ordered Halakoth for his pupils," Tos. Zabim 1.5 (ed. Zuckerm., 676) or ר״ע שהתקין מדרש הלכות והגדות, Pal. Sheḳ. 5. 48c; (2) certain passages in Epiphanius, which, however, are inexact or corrupt, esp. *Haeres.* XXXIII, 9 (I, 459 in Holl's edition): Αἱ γὰρ παραδόσεις τῶν πρεσβυτέρων δευτερώσεις παρὰ τοῖς Ἰουδαίοις λέγονται. Εἰσὶ δὲ αὗται τέσσαρες. μία μὲν ἡ εἰς ὄνομα Μωυσέως φερομένη (מִשְׁנֵה תוֹרָה, Deuteronomy; according to Professor Blau, rather the statutes known as הלכה למשה מסיני, see above, p. 9) δευτέρα δέ τοῦ καλουμένου Ῥαββὶ Ἀκιβά, τρίτη Ἀδδᾶ ἤτοι Ἰούδα (Rabbi's Mishna), τετάρτη τῶν υἱῶν Ἀσαμωναίου (these words refer perhaps to the ordinances of John Hyrcanus, or, as Professor Blau thinks, in general to those of the בית דין של חשמונאים; possibly, however, we have here a corruption of Hoshaiah; but against this supposition militates a further passage in Epiphanius, cited by Schürer, I, 123 (4th ed.), n. 24: τῶν δὲ υἱῶν Ἀσσαμωναίου ἐν χρόνοις Ἀλεξάνδρου καὶ Ἀντιόχου; it is, of course, strange that the Hasmoneans appear in the fourth position, the chronological order being maintained otherwise), and *Haeres.* XV, 2 (I, 209 in Holl's edition): Δευτερώσεις δὲ παρ' αὐτοῖς τέσσαρες ἦσαν μία μὲν εἰς ὄνομα Μωυσέως τοῦ προφήτου (φερομένη), δευτέρα δὲ εἰς τὸν διδάσκαλον αὐτῶν Ἀκίβαν οὕτω καλούμενον ἢ Βαρακίβαν (read Ραβ(ι)'Ακ.), ἄλλη δὲ εἰς τὸν Ἀδδᾶν (cod. Ἀνδὰν; ἢ Ανναν (perhaps for Αννασι=הַנָּשִׂיא) τὸν καὶ Ἰούδαν, ἑτέρα δὲ εἰς τοὺς υἱοὺς Ἀσαμωναίου; (3) the passages in which the משניות גדולות of Aḳiba, Ḥiyya, Hoshaiah and Bar Ḳappara are spoken of, e. g. Midrash Cant. 8.2, Midrash Ḳohel. 6.2, 12.7.

[26] Aboth 3.8; comp. also 3.7b.

[27] P. 21.

[28] משנה ראשונה.

[29] Sanh. 3.4.

[30] *Die erste Mischna und die Controversen der Tannaim*, Berlin, 1882. On pp. 15–26 a list of all the portions of our Mishna for which there is an indicium that they date from those times.

[31] *Magazin*, 1886, 1–20 and *Hoffmann-Festschrift*, 346–361. He bases himself upon the Seder Tannaim we-Amoraim and on a remark by Jerome on Isaiah, Book III, chapter 8 (see below chapter XIII, § 2 under 'Shammai'). But the props are too weak to sustain the structure.

32 I c, 204 ff. Halevy's contention is characterized by Lerner (l. c., 359 f.) as "frankly grotesque" and "fantastic."

33 *Entstehung*, I, § 26–31.

34 E. g. Yoma 6.1 (the two goats) and Neg. 14.5 (the two birds for the cleansing of the leper).

35 I, § 32–56.

36 II, § 11–24.

37 II, § 31–42.

38 II, § 69–84.

39 II, § 76.

40 III, § 17–27

41 § 28–37.

42 § 51c.

43 III, § 52–60.

44 § 52.

45 § 60cd.

46 With Rabbi and the close of the Mishna Rosenthal deals in § 66–80.

47 § 78.

48 § 76bc.

49 § 72.

50 § 78.

51 § 74.

52 § 75.

53 See above, p. 9 f.

54 Comp. J. Z. Lauterbach, "Midrash and Mishnah, a study in the early history of the Halakah," *JQR*, N. S., V, 503–527; VI, 23-95, 303–323. The Gaon Ṣemaḥ, likewise, regarded the form of Midrash as the earlier, see Lauterbach, VI, 315.

55 Pes. 70b.

56 Chap. XIII, § 2.

57 VI, 68 ff., 75 ff.

58 Eduy. 8.4.

59 VI, 37, 62.

60 VI, 89, 83.

61 VI, 92 f.

62 Siphra, Ṣaw, 11, ed. Weiss, 34d f.

63 A few examples will suffice. In M. Sh. 5.10–14 we find an exposition of Deut. 26.13-15. In Yeb. 8 we read several regulations concerning maimed

persons and castrates in accordance with Deut. 23.2; in immediate sequence the law touching the exclusion of Ammonites and Moabites from the Israelitish community and the admission of Egyptians and Edomites is taken up as in Deut. 23.4 ff. Soṭa 8 deals with the allocution of the priest anointed for warfare and in general expounds Deut. 20.2–9; then follows in 9 the law concerning the heifer whose neck is broken in expiation of a murder by an unknown criminal, Deut. 21.1–9. B. M. 2.10 mention is made of the ass succumbing under its burden = Exod. 23.5; the subject is entirely foreign to the context, and its introduction was entrained by the reference to the animal gone astray = Exod. 23.4. In Mak. 2 the regulations concerning unpremeditated manslaughter = Deut. 19.4 ff., and the cities of refuge = Deut. 19.2 ff., which are in no wise related to the subject-matter of the tractate, are introduced at this point simply because the matter in ch. 1 concerns the punishment with stripes which is meted out to false witnesses, Comp. Deut. 19.19. The tractate Shebuoth is composed of the exposition of two biblical passages, Levit. 5 (chapters 1–5) and Exod. 22.5–14 (chapters 6–8). Comp. L. Blau in Königsberger's *Monatsblätter für Vergangenheit u. Gegenwart des Judentums*, I (1891), 97–101. A. Z. 3.3, Deut. 13.18 is cited; the section which follows immediately deals with Rabban Gamaliel in the bath-house of Aphrodite for the reason that the identical verse is adduced; comp. in addition the words of Aḳiba in section 5 showing up the scriptural context. The tractate Bekoroth deals with the first-born according to Levit. 27.26 f.; hence in Bekor. 8.10 the regulations concerning property which does not revert in the year of jubilee in accordance with Levit. 27.17–24 and in Bek. 9 concerning the tithe of cattle, comp. Levit. 27.32. The biblical passage which underlies the tractate Arakin is Levit. 27.2 ff.; hence Arak. 8 treats of devoted things, comp. Levit. 27.28 f., and Arak. 9 of the redemption on the year of jubilee of a field previously sold = Levit. 25.18–28, as well as of walled cities = ib., 29 ff. Nega'im 12.5–7 is a running commentary on Levit. 14.35 ff. Comp. in addition D. Hoffmann, *Die erste Mischna* (Berlin, 1882), 7–12; Rosenthal, *Entstehung*, I, § 57–70 and p. 155–157; G. Aicher, *Das A. T. in der Mischna*, Freiburg, 1906, 154 ff.

64 Comp. M. Sh. 5 (Zuckerm. p. 96); Sukka 3 (p. 196 f.); Soṭa 6, 7, 11 (p. 305, 309, 315 f.); Sanh. 14 (p. 437, 12); Shebu. 1.3 (p. 446, 449 f.); Para 1 (p. 630).

65 So for that matter, as we are reminded by Professor Blau, the very opening of the first tractate (Berakoth) where the Shema' section, though presupposed, is not adduced; hence the query in the Gemara as to the starting-point of the Tanna.

66 Examples: Bikk. 2; Giṭ. 4, 5 (comp. Tosaphoth 48b top); Soṭa 1, 5, 9; Men. 3, 4; Bekor. 4; Arak. 2, 3; Me'ila 4; Nidda 6; Maksh. 2.

67 Meg. 1 (thirteen statements beginning with אין בין, almost all of which are repeated elsewhere in the Mishna in their appropriate places; see L. Ginzberg, *Hoffmann-Festschrift*, 311–345, who suspects that we have here "probably a Shammaiitic Mishna dating from a period when the Halakoth were strung together according to an external principle such as אין בין is"); Hor. 3; Ḥul. 1; Para 1.

68 M. Sh. 5 (modifications ordained by the high priest Joḥanan); Sheḳ. 7 (seven ordinances of the law court); Keth. 13 (Ḥanan and Admon); Eduy.

69 E. g. Shab. 2.6f. (three transgressions, three words); B. M. 4.7f. (five peruṭoth, five-fifths). See Rosenthal, *Entstehung*, I, § 86 and II, p. 145f. (Number Mishna).

70 Comp. Rosenthal, I, 78 f.

71 E. g. Shab. 2.3 the subject, so readily memorized, כָּל־הַיּוֹצֵא מִן־הָעֵץ (all that comes from a tree) receives two predicates of which only the first belongs into this tractate.

72 So by means of כַּיּוֹצֵא בוֹ (in similar manner, with the identical intent) Shab. 1.3; Ḥalla 3.4, 9.

73 See above p. 21.

74 *Magazin*, 1890, 323. Professor Blau believes that beside the pedagogic another principle was at play. He recalls the fact that in the Scriptures the prophetic books are arranged likewise according to size; moreover, the same mode of arrangement may be witnessed in the literature of antiquity generally and also in the Koran.

NOTES TO CHAPTER III, P. 26

1 The Aramaic סדר answers to Hebrew ערך. Hence שֵׁשׁ עֶרְכֵּי הַמִּשְׁנָה Pesiḳtha de-Rab Kahana 7a and Midrash Cant. 6.4. ש' סדרי המשנה occurs but once: Numb. R. 12.17.

2 The usage ascends to the Tosaphists. See Blau, *Freie Jüdische Lehrerstimme* (Vienna), 1917, 7f. and *Magyar Zsido Szemle*, 1918, 48–50.

3 Lit. 'a web.' For the development of meaning comp. Latin *textus*.

4 E. g. Shab. 3b, B. M. 23b bottom, A. Z. 7 a.

5 Midrash Ps. 104; Mishna cod. Cambridge, fol. 32a. Otherwise: מַסְּכוֹת ib. fol. 69a; מַסֶּכְתִּיּוֹת Midrash Cant. 6.9.

[6] Order I = Volume 1; II = Volumes 2–4; III = Volumes 5, 6; IV = Volumes 7–9; V = Volumes 10, 11; VI = Volume 12.

[7] Plur. of נֶזֶק, comp. פֶּסֶל, פְּסִילִים. As to נְזָקִין see Levy, III, 367, A. Berliner and H. Hirschensohn in *Ha-misderona*, I, 19 f., 41.

[8] Comp. Isai. 33.6. This name is met with in the Parma Ms., the Palestinian Talmud, Tosephta, Midrash Numb. R. (section 13), Maḥzor Vitry (introduction to Aboth, Berlin 1891, 461), Aggadoth Ha-talmud, Jerahmeel and the Latin Ms. Paris 16, 558, *Extractiones de Talmud*, which contains an account of the disputation between Jehiel and Nicholas Donin.

[9] When we come across occasionally (so in the disputation between Jehiel and Donin at Paris in the year 1240) the statement that there are only four Orders, the reason is that both the first and the sixth Order possess each but one tractate with Gemara (Berakoth and Nidda), hence Berakoth was looked upon as belonging to Mo'ed (so indeed did Meiri find it in the Mss.), just as Nidda was probably drawn to Nashim. Comp. Is. Loeb, *REJ*, XVI, 282–286 and below p. 366, n. 1 concerning cod. Munich 95. Comp. also what Rabba bar Abuha says to Elijah B. M. 114b and Rashi ad loc. But the number six is as old as Ḥiyya, B. M. 85b = Keth. 103b; comp. Funk, I, 137. By תלתא סדרי (e. g. in Meiri) are meant the three Orders Mo'ed, Nashim, Neziḳin, because these are the ones which specifically deal with laws valid to this day (*Zeitschr. f. hebr. Bibliographie*, 1906, 141, 152).

[10] E. g. Mo'ed: Sukka 4b; Neziḳin: Ber. 20a, Taan. 24; Ṭoharoth: B. M. 114b.

[11] He finds them hinted at in Isai. 33.6: Shab. 31a; comp. Midr. Numb. R. on 7.19 (section 13), on Esther 1.2 and Ps. 19.8.

[12] *Wissensch. Zeitschr. f. jüd. Theologie*, II, 487.

[13] *Hodegetica*, 254.

[14] So Ber.: B. Ḳ. 30a; Terum.: Pes. 30a; Erub.: ib., 79a and Pal. Shabb. 19. 16d; Yoma: Yoma 14b; R. H.: Taan. 2a; Keth. Ned. Nazir Soṭa: Soṭa 2a; B. Ḳ. B. M.: A. Z. 7a; Sanh. (including Makkoth): Pal. Mak. 8.31b; Mak. Shebu.: Shebu. 2b; Eduy.: Ber. 28a and under the name Beḥirtha, ib. 27a and Ḳid. 54b; Aboth: B. Ḳ. 30a; Menaḥoth: Men. 7a; Kerith.: Sanh. 65a; Tamid: Yoma 14b; Middoth: ib. 16a (see above p. 21); Kelim: Kelim 30. 4 (see above p. 21); Ahiloth Neg.: Pal. M. Ḳ. end; Para: Yoma 43b; Nidda: Pal. Ber. 2. 5b; Ṭebul Yom: ib., 3. 6c; Uḳṣin: Hor. 13b (above p. 21). Of the 'Minor Tractates,' Ebel Rabbathi: M. Ḳ. 24a, 26b, Keth. 28a; Derek Ereṣ: Pal. Shab. 6.8a bottom. See Geiger, 485 f.; Frankel, 255; A. Berliner in *Ha-misderona*, I, 20f., 40f.; Aptowitzer in *Ha-ṣophe* (ed. Blau), IV, 19f.; comp.,

however, L. Ginsberg, in *Journal of Jewish Lore and Philosophy*, I, 34, n. 34. Considering that the names of the greatest number of tractates are Hebrew, S. Landauer holds that the names Yoma, Baba,Uḳṣin are not original.

[15] So 'Beṣa' more frequently than 'Yom Ṭob;' 'Sheḥiṭath Ḳodashim' is the older name for 'Zebaḥim' and 'Mashkin' for 'Mo'ed Ḳaṭan.'

[16] See B. K. 102a, Judah b. Ezekiel ib. 30a, Raba in B. M. 10ab; Midrash Cant. 5.11 (=Levit. R. on 15.25): 'N. has 30 chapters, Kelim has 30 chapters.' So also cod. Kaufmann and the Parma Ms.

[17] For the same reason Kelim, in the Tosephta, is divided into three Gates.

[18] So in the Parma and Kaufmann codices. Comp. Pal. Mak. 1.31b בכל סנהדרין and J. Lewy, *Interpretation des P. Talmudtraktats Nesikin*, p. 23δ. Observe the identical opening אלו הן Sanh. 7. 4, 9.1, 11.1; Mak. 2.1, 3.1.

[19] In his Introduction to the Mishna.

[20] Midr. Cant. 6.9.

[21] On the number of tractates see also Isaiah Berlin in the preface to his edition of the Sheeltoth, Dyhernfurth, 1786.

[22] The law concerning vows Numb. 30.2–17 pertains specifically to women, and Nazir 9 mention is made of the Nazirate vow of women and slaves.

[23] See the Table in Appendix I.

[24] R. H. Taan. see Taan. 2a; Nazir Soṭa s. Soṭa 2a; Mak. Shebu. s. Shebu. 2b.

[25] *Wissensch. Zeitschr. f. jüd. Theologie*, II, 489–492.

[26] See above, p. 25.

[27] For Seder IV observe what has just been said touching the three Baboth and on Makkoth. In Seder V, the division of Tamid into 7 chapters is not the original one.

[28] The order of the tractates in the middle of the first Seder according to the Vienna codex of the Tosephta is: Terum., Shebi'ith, Kil'aim (11, 10, 9 chapters). In the Erfurt Ms. of the Tosephta, likewise, the order of the tractates in Zera'im follows their compass in a manner more manifest than in the Mishna.—As to the prophetic books in the Canon being similarly arranged according to size see above Chapter II, § 3, n. 74 and *Protest. Realencyclopädie*, 3d ed., IX, 755.

[29] See above, p. 24. See also Zuckermandel, *Der Wiener Tosefta-Codex* Magdeburg, 1877, 4–9.

[30] See Frankel, 264 f.

[31] Bikkurim with 3 chapters.

[32] Aboth with 5 chapters.

[33] Tamid with 7 chapters.

[34] In Ber. Rashi read ch. 4 תפלת השחר after ch. 2 היה קורא. Many Mss. of Pes. place ch. 10 after ch. 4 for the reason that it was customary to study ch. 10 in front of 5–9. In Meg., the printed editions of the Babylonian Talmud have the third ch. בני העיר in the fourth place. In Giṭṭin, Rabbenu Asher and a number of French Mss. place ch. 7 מי שאחזו ק' in front of ch. 6. In B. B., Cod. Hamburg 19 presents ch. 5 המוכר את הספינה after ch. 6 and ch. 7 אומר לחבירו בית כור after ch. 8 יש נוחלין. The well-known ch. 10 of Sanh. כל ישראל ('All Israel has a share in the world to come') in Mishna and Palest. Talm. is eleventh in the Babyl. Talm. The tenth chapter of Menaḥ. in Mishna ר' ישמעאל אומר is sixth in the Babyl. Talm. See also Chapter IV.

NOTES TO CHAPTER IV, P. 29

[1] Rashi read ch. 4 תפלת השחר after ch. 2 היה קורא (see Tosaphoth of Asher b. Jehiel הרא"ש Ber. 17b מי).

[2] דמי = דום 'be suspicious,' or still better from דָּמָה 'be like, similar,' Piel דִּמָּה (because the affirmative and the negative are equally possible). D. Hoffmann, *Magazin*, 1893, 145, takes it that דמאי is nothing else than דמעי (see below n. 5) 'something that still contains דֶּמַע = תְּרוּמָה.' Ibn Ezra, in his poem on the tractates of the Mishna, pronounces *dammai*; comp. the opposite *waddai* 'that of which it is certain that the tithe has been given.'

[3] Not merely suspended, so at least according to the understanding of the Mishna, see D. Hoffmann, *Das Buch Deuteronomium*, I (1913), 226 ff.

[4] This formula, introduced by Hillel, read as follows: "I, So and So, deliver to you, the judges in place So and So, (the declaration), that I may call in the debt which is owing to me at any time I choose." With this reservation declared, the sabbatic year had no effect on canceling the debt and thus the temptation was done away with to refuse to make a loan with a view to the approaching of the seventh year. See Schürer, II, 427, 60; M. Lerner, *Hoffmann-Festschrift*, 535–355.

[5] דֶּמַע denotes in Samaritan as חֵלֶב in Hebrew 'that which is best, most excellent;' in the Mishna the heave which belongs to the priests is called דֶּמַע, hence the verb דִּמַּע 'to turn something into Terumah,' מְדֻמָּע 'equivalent to the heave.'

[6] 4.1: When one squeezes olives upon his body (to anoint himself there-

with), they are free from the tithe; but when the oil which has been pressed out is gathered up in the hand, the tithe must be given (for the reason that the hollow hand constitutes a small vessel).

[7] According to the rabbinic explanation, Levit. 27.30–33 deals likewise with the second tithe.

[8] 3.1. No one may say to another person: "Take up these fruits to Jerusalem, that we may divide them" (because in that case a debt would be paid with the tithe). But one may say: "Take them up, that together we may eat or drink them in Jerusalem" (in the present instance the words amount to an invitation). It is also permissible to make gifts of them with no return in money.

[9] One may act with cunning מערימין (to escape paying the surcharge) by saying to one's grown son or daughter or to one's Hebrew bondman or bondwoman; "Here is money; redeem for thyself this second tithe." (This transaction is regarded in the light of a redemption effected by a person other than the owner.) But it is not permissible to say so to minor children or to Canaanite slaves (because these persons cannot by law acquire property). § 5. A person finding himself on the threshing-floor without money (and nevertheless desirous of avoiding the payment of the surcharge) may say to his neighbor: "These fruits are presented to you as a gift," and then immediately: "Suffer these fruits to be treated as profane (redeemed) for the money which I have in my house."—Similar easing of one's duty on the part of a 'clever' person (פִּקֵּחַ) may be found in Nazir 2.5 and Shabbath 16.3; comp. also Temura 5.1 (מערימין).

[10] In many editions of the Mishna (as early as Naples, 1492), in the Kaufmann codex (but not in the Cambridge manuscript) and in the majority of the editions of the Talmud, likewise in the Munich Ms. of the Talmud, there follows here a fourth chapter, concerning the position of the hermaphrodite *androginos*, but it does not belong to the Mishna, having been taken over from the Tosephta and then amplified.

[11] All four names appear Tosephta Shab. 1.1.

[12] Erub. 9.2; Pal. Shabb. 1.2dγ; 11.13aβ; from כַּרְמְל?

[13] *Shabb.* 101aα.

[14] Shabb. 6a; Erub. 101b.

[15] Comp. Ed. Baneth, *Mishnajoth*, Erubin, ch. 9, n. 14; Maimonides on Shabb. 1.1.

[16] Agriculture 7; preparation of food 4; of clothing 13; obtaining meat and preparation of skins (leather) 7; writing and blotting out 2; building and

pulling down 2; extinguishing or kindling a fire 2; striking with the hammer 1; carrying from one domain to another 1. As to numbers 1 to 11 comp. the words of Ben Zoma Berak. 55a (Bacher, *Agada der Tannaiten*, I, 2d ed., 428, n. 4). We have to do here with the primitive labors and necessities of mankind (comp. Gen. 3.19 and 20): (1) bread; (2) clothing): (1) 1–11; (2) 12–24. Numbers 25–33 concern preparations for 'writing' (tanning of skins belongs here likewise), comp. Kethub. 103b (Hiyya) and see thereon Bacher, ibid., II, 521. After bread and clothing, writing is named as the first in the labors of civilization, since according to the ancient Jewish view it was created in the same day with man (Aboth 5.6). The groups which follow (building, extinguishing and kindling fire, striking with the hammer) are the first labors of primitive man (Gen. 4.17: בֹּנֶה; then v. 22: the crafts). 'Carrying' appears as last labor. According to this grouping, which may be considered as the original, the 39 classes of labor have no immediate connection with the labors in constructing the Tabernacle. We are dealing rather with a fanciful combination on the part of the latter Tannaim.—See also M. Benedikt, מגן אבות Petrikow, 1903 fol. (108).

[17] The owner is permitted to salvage but little himself. However (16.3), "he may say to others, 'come, salvage for yourselves.' And when those addressed are prudent, they may after the Sabbath settle with the owner." Thus the owner receives back his goods (formally given away) and those have, at least as a matter of form, assisted in the rescue without counting on payment. Honest folk will refrain from turning another man's losses to their profit; see the commentaries.

[18] In this connection the reader will recall how Jesus was pursued by the Pharisees on the score of his healings on the Sabbath day: Matth. 12.10 ff.; Mark 3.1 ff.; Luke 6.6 ff., 13.10 ff., 14.1 ff.; John 5.1 ff., 9.14 ff.

[19] In many Mss. (so Munich 95 and 6, Vaticanus 109) ch. 10 עַרְבֵי פסחים is inserted after chs. 1–4; this transposition merely serves the convenience of the student, as it was customary to take up this chapter ahead of 5–9.

[20] Adar is the last month of the ecclesiastical year, it comes immediately before Nisan.

[21] Comp. Mark 11.15; El. Lambert, 'Les changeurs et la monnaie en Palestine du Ier au IIIe siècle de l'ère vulgaire d'après les textes talmudiques,' in *Revue des Etudes Juives*, LI (1906), 217–244 and LII, 24–42.

[22] So Cambridge and Kaufmann codices, the Gaon Sherira.

[23] Tosephta.

[24] This chapter interrupts the context. According to D. Hoffmann, *Die*

erste Mischna, p. 19, the following parts most probably belong to the tractate in its oldest form; 1.1 as far as פלהדרין, 2–7; 3.1, 2 from הורידו to הטבילה. 4,6,8,9 as far as גורלות; 4. 1–3; 5. 1,3,4 as far as עירה, 5 to ויורד, 6 up to the first החיצון; 6. 2,3 as far as ישראל להוליכן, 4,5,6 up to שתחשך, 7 to השרפה, 8 up to the first למדבר; 7. 1,3,4. Comp. J. Derenbourg, *Revue des Etudes Juives*, VI, 41–80.

[25] 4.6: 'R. Eliezer, son of Hyrcanus, permits on the festival picking up a splinter lying in the yard and using it for a toothpick . . . The sages, however, say that such wood may be picked up only for fuel.'

[26] So the usual pronunciation; more properly מַלְקִיּוֹת.

[26a] Comp. Julian Morgenstern, "Two ancient Israelite agricultural festivals," *Jewish Quarterly Review*, New Series, VIII, 31–54.

[27] Comp. J. Levy in the Hebrew periodical *Oṣar Neḥmad*, III, 175 ff.

[28] This chapter, opening with the words בני העיר, is the third in the Palestinian Talmud, in the Cambridge codex, in many editions of the Mishna (Riva, 1559; Amsterdam, 1646), in the Mss. of the Babylonian Talmud Munich No. 140 and Oxford, Bodleian (Neubauer's Catalogue) No. 366. The same order of chapters meets us also in the Tosephta and in Alphasi. On the other hand, in the printed editions of the Babylonian Talmud and in the Munich codex 95 (of the year 1343) the chapter הקורא את המגלה עומד designated above as fourth is placed ahead.

[29] Concerning עריות 4.9 and Hagiga 2.1 see Ad. Büchler in *Monatsschrift*, 1894, 108 ff., 145 ff. and for a contrary view S. H. Margulies, 1895, 63–79.

[30] In the liturgy the intervening festival days are called חולו של מועד. The ancient teachers said for the full festival days יום טוב and for intervening days מועד (e. g. Pes. 4.7). This expression is used in the Mishna throughout this tractate. The epithet קטן serves to distinguish the name of the tractate from that of the whole Order (J. Derenbourg in *Revue des Etudes Juives*, XX, 136 f.); occasionally, however, it is dispensed with, so in the gaonic commentary on the Order Ṭoharoth edited by Epstein, p. 15.

[31] So cod. Kauffmann and Cambridge, Aruk; so also certain Spanish and French Jews, see *Monatsschrift*, 1912, 498, 627.

[32] A second festival day is kept only outside Palestine; see Beṣa 4b, Sukka 46b; Hirsch, *Choreb*, § 177, 258; Bodenschatz, *Kirchliche Verfassung der Juden*, II, 166.

[33] An ordinary person may sew according to his wont, but a tailor must make his stitches irregular.

[34] After a discussion of Eccles. 1.15 there follows quite abruptly: "The

dissolution of vows hangs in the air and has no foundation in Scripture. The ordinances concerning the Sabbath, the festival offerings and the misappropriation of consecrated property are like mountains suspended by a hair; for there is little about these in Scripture, yet the ordinances are many. On the other hand, the regulations concerning (civil and criminal) law, the sacrificial worship, purity and impurity, incest have much support in Scripture; these therefore (according to another reading: הן והן these as well as those) are essential parts of learning."

[35] A. Schwarz, "Die erste halakhische Kontroverse," *Monatsschrift*, 1893, 164 ff., 201 ff. Against him D. Feuchtwang, 1894, 385 ff., 433 ff. Comp. also A. Sidon, "Die Kontroverse der Synedrialhäupter" in *Gedenkbuch . . . David Kaufmann*, Breslau, 1900, 355–364; S. Zeitlin, "The Semikah Controversy between the Zugoth," *Jewish Quarterly Review*, N. S., VII, 499–517. See furthermore L. Löw, *Gesammelte Schriften*, V, 82 ff.; M. L. Lilienblum, *Woszchod*, 1882, part 3; Bornstein, התקופה, IV, 396, footnote; all of whom take סמיכה in the sense of ordination. M. Eschelbacher reviews in *Monatsschrift*, 1919, 372, a novel but certainly impossible explanation by Leszinsky.

[36] So according to the current interpretation.

[37] So codd. Cambridge and Kaufmann after the opening words חמש עשרה נשים.

[38] See the important essay by Büchler in the *Bloch-Festschrift*, Hebrew part, 21–30; comp. further the same author, *Der galiläische Am ha'areṣ*, p. 71, end of note. In addition to the references adduced we may also point to Mishna Demai 6. 6.

[39] Comp. D. Kaufmann, "Zur Geschichte der K.," *Monatsschrift*, 1897, 213–221; E. N. Adler, *Jew. Enc.*, VII, 472–478; S. Krauss, *Talmudische Archäologie*, II, 44; M. Gaster, "Die K. bei den Samaritanern," *Monatsschrift*, 1910, 174 ff.; L. Fischer, *Die Urkunden im Talmud*, I, 66–121.

[40] According to cod. Kaufmann, 14 chapters, see *Monatsschrift*, 1907, 62 f.

[41] On Mark 7.1–13 see J. H. A. Hart, *Jewish Quarterly Review*, 1907, 615–650. In the place of קונם שֶׁאֵינִי the correct reading is שֶׁאֲנִי, comp. Ned. 8.7, see H. Laible, *Monatsschrift*, 1916, 29–40 (ש not 'that' but 'that which').

[42] נִדְרֵי זֵרוּזִין vows of spurring on, by which buyers and sellers seek to operate upon one another; נ' הֲבָאי hyperbolical vows, resting upon an exaggeration or an untruth not seriously intended; נ' שְׁגָגוֹת vows based upon error or forgetfulness; נ' אֳנָסִין vows the fulfilment of which has been inhibited by force majeure.

[43] In more exact phraseology גֵּט אִשָּׁה in contradistinction to גֵּט שִׁחְרוּר.

[44] According to Asher ben Jehiel, chapter 7 מי שאחזו should precede chapter 6 האומר התקבל. So also Masoreth ha-talmud, Saloniki 1523, and, it seems, the majority of French copies; for Tosaphoth 62b האומר know of the order as we have it only from the Palestinian Talmud. The current order is vouched for by Moses ben Naḥman in his Novellae; he refers to Alphasi, Hai Gaon and Samuel ben Hophni.

[45] A document folded together and sewed up which should have a witness's signature in every one of its folds without but in which some of these folds are blank, comp. Giṭ. 8.10.

[46] 9.10: "The school of Shammai taught: A man shall not divorce his wife except he has found in her something scandalous דְּבַר עֶרְוָה, since we read in Deut. 24.1, 'because he hath found some unseemly thing עֶרְוַת דָּבָר in her.' The school of Hillel said: Even for burning his food, basing themselves on the word דָּבָר, 'anything.' Akiba said: Even when he has found another woman more beautiful than she, recalling the words of Scripture, 'if she find no favour in his eyes'." Jos. Derenbourg considers this passage to have been interpolated, *Monatsschrift*, 1880, 178; he is rightly opposed by Ben Seeb, *Jüdisches Literaturblatt*, 1880, 115. Comp. in addition S. A. Wolff, *Mischna-Lese*, part 2 (Leipzig, 1868), p. 102 ff. According to Blau (31 ff.; 48, n. 4), 'burning one's food' is not to be taken literally, it is merely a forceful expression dictated by opposition. Dr. Klein calls my attention to Berak. 62a (referred to in my own work, *Jesus etc.*, 39*, n. 7 toward the end) and he is inclined to see in the expression a euphemism for marital intercourse, adducing examples from Scripture (Prov. 30.20 אכלה) and midrashic literature which show that 'eating, food' was a quite common expression for תשמיש.—Comp. in addition Matth. 19.3 and Giṭ. 90b: Eleazar ben Pedath said: He who divorces his first wife, the altar itself sheds tears over him (Mal. 2.13 f.).

[47] 2.4. The opinion of Eliezer and Joshua concerning the female sex.

[48] According to Berak. 28a, בו ביום has reference everywhere to the day in which Gamaliel II was deposed and Eleazar ben Azariah made Nasi. Comp Yad. 4 (Grätz in *Literaturblatt des Orients*, 1845, No. 46, col. 729; L. A. Rosenthal, *Entstehung*, 2d ed., II, § 43 ff.—Contrast Geiger (*Lesestücke aus der Mischna*, Breslau 1845, p. 37): 'On the same day on which the previous precepts were presented').

[49] See above, p. 27.

[50] 7.7 אין מגדלין, see Sam. Krauss, 'La défense d'élever du menu bétail en Palestine et questions connexes,' *Revue des Etudes Juives*, LIII, 14–55.

[51] 6.1: When one hires men to do an urgent piece of labor which if deferred

in execution would entail loss, and the laborers drop their work, it is permissible, when no laborers are to be had (for the same price), to hire other laborers at the expense of those originally hired, or even to make them feigned promises (או מַטען).

[52] D. Hoffmann, *Magazin*, 1879, 116f., conjectured that this chapter הבית והעליה properly belongs to B. B. This conjecture is substantiated by the fact that in a gaonic responsum two passages are cited as occurring in B. B., though they are found in B. M. 10, see L. Ginzberg, *Geonica*, II, 66, n. 6.

[53] In the Hamburg Ms. 19 the fifth chapter המוכר את הספינה (in print 73a) is placed after ch. 6 המוכר פירות, and ch. 7 האומר לחבירו בית כור (in print 102b) after ch. 8 יש נוחלין.

[54] Concerning this vaulted jail see Levy, II, 322a.

[55] In the Babylonian Talmud, this chapter, called חֵלֶק or כל ישראל occupies the eleventh, and the eleventh אלו הן הנחנקין the tenth place. The commentary on חלק which, according to L. Heller, is responsible for this transposition, was written by a disciple of Rashi's, see Dikd., p. 260. Rashi had before him the current sequence, see Mak. 2a התם קאי.—On Sanh. 10.1 see Guttmann, *Magazin*, 1898, 289–303.

[56] 11.3 the much cited, but often misunderstood statement: חֹמֶר בְּדִבְרֵי סוֹפְרִים מִבְּדִבְרֵי תוֹרָה "It is more culpable to go counter in teaching to the ordinances of the scribes than to those of the Torah itself" (Jost), see Maimonides ad loc.

[57] 3.10: 'Forty less one.' Deut. 25.2 f. reads: "The judge shall cause him to be beaten according to the measure of his wickedness, by number. Forty stripes he may give him, he shall not exceed; lest . . ." The Mishna evolves its number by combining במספר: ארבעים which it takes as 'by number 40, i.e. close to 40.' Comp. II Cor. 11.24 and Josephus, *Antiquities*, 4, 8, 23 (§ 248) πληγὰς τεσσαράκοντα μιᾶ λειπούσας λαμβάνων. So (39) is the Halakah according to Maimonides and Obadiah di Bertinoro. Judah ben El'ai, however, demands "full forty, the fortieth between the shoulders." It may be noted that the Septuagint likewise joins במספר to ארבעים.

[58] 3.16: רצה הקב"ה לְזַכּוֹת את ישראל, i. e. "it pleased God to give Israel the opportunity of acquiring merits."

[59] Levit. 5.4 להרע או להיטיב i. e. negatively and affirmatively. The two subordinate species (which, like the other subordinate species, are not taught in the written Torah itself but have been ordained by the Sopherim) arise by reference to the past, inasmuch as those expressions point in the first instance to the future. For particulars see Shebu. 3.

60 Not עֲדָיוֹת.

61 Ber. 28a.

62 Ber. 27a; Ḳid. 54b.

63 In this case and the next בן probably signifies 'from the place.' On כפר סגנא see Büchler, *Der galiläische 'Am ha'areṣ*, 79, n. 1; Klein, *Schwarz-Festschrift*, 391, n. 22.

64 Where was this place situate which sounds like the biblical גדגד (Num. 33.32) or גדגדה (Deut. 10.7)? It cannot be בית גדגד Ṭohar. 6.6, for there the correct reading is גלגל, see Klein, *Magazin*, 1921, 370 f. See further Giṭ. 5.5. Joḥanan בן גודגדה (Büchler, l. c., 149).

65 8.4 the only halakic statements of the Mishna in the Aramaic language, comp. J. Z. Lauterbach, *Jewish Quarterly Review*, N. S., VI, 62—75

66 On this usage of זָר see Isai. 43.16; Deut. 32.16 etc.—The appellations 'Abodath kokabim u-mazzaloth' (worship of the stars and constellations) and 'Obed k. u-m.' (worshiper of stars etc.; idolater) or, as the abbreviation according to the initial letters runs, 'Akkum' עכו"ם, are found neither in the oldest editions of the ritual code *Mishne Tora* by Moses Maimonides and of the *Shulhan Aruk* (ranking codification of Jewish law) nor in the manuscripts and those editions of the Mishna and the Talmuds which are free from censorship, but are solely an invention of the censors!! The whole article עכו"ם in Levy, III, 646 is to be deleted! The original readings are: נָכְרִי, גוֹי, עבודה זרה etc. Comp. also David Hoffmann, *Der Schulchan-Aruch und die Rabbinen über das Verhältniss der Juden zu den Andersgläubigen*, 2d ed., Berlin, 1894, 129–134.

67 פֶּרֶק chapter,

68 On 3.11 see J. Guttmann, *Magazin*, 1898, 303 ff., 337 ff.: this saying by R. Eleazar of Modiim is pointed against the Judeo-Christians.

69 3.8 places in sequence Priest, Levite, Israelite, Mamzer (bastard, offspring of prohibited intercourse), Nathin (descendant of the Gibeonites, Josh. 9.27 ויתנם, comp. Ezra 2. 43; 8.20), Proselyte, Freed Slave. But all this only other things being equal. When, however, the bastard is a scholar and the high priest an ignoramus (עַם הָאָרֶץ), then the former has precedence.

70 Older name שְׁחִיטַת קָדָשִׁים, B. M. 109b. Quite arbitrary is the appellation קָרְבָּנוֹת in the 1521 edition of the Tosephta joined to Alphasi.

71 According to Levit. 7.18 that sacrifice of which the sacrificer has the intention to partake at a time later than that which is allowed by law, is called Piggul.

72 In the Babylonian Talmud this chapter רבי ישמעאל אומר occurs

erroneously as sixth chapter, so that chapters 6–9 stand in the seventh to the tenth place.

73 Not חוּלִּין.

74 Codex Kaufmann, Geonim, Sherira, Rashi, Alphasi.

75 They may not be killed in the temple court, A. Z. 7.9; B. Ḳ. 7.2.

76 From 5.3; When one kills a cow, then her young and then the young of that, he receives (because of two transgressions by means of two actions) 80 stripes. But when after the old cow he first kill the young of the young cow and then the young cow itself, he receives only 40 (since only one transgression has been committed).

77 See below chapter XII, §1.

78 4.6: 'When a person accepts payment in order to render decisions in a judicial quality, his decisions are invalid; similarly when a person accepts payment in order to appear as a witness his testimony is invalid.'

79 The fact that the tithe of cattle is discussed at this place goes to show among other things that our Mishna rests to a large extent on scriptural exegesis (see above p. 24): Levit. 27.26 f. treats of the firstborn of cattle. Comp. further Bekor. 8.10 with Levit. 27.17–24.

80 Or כְּרִיתוֹת?

81 M. Ḳ. 28a; Pal. Bikkurim 2.64c; Pal. Sanh. 11.30b middle. E. Fink, 'Über die כָּרֵת-Strafe,' in Wohlgemuth's *Jeschurun*, IV (1917), 383–399.

82 Chapters 6 and 7 form in the Cambridge Ms. a single chapter.

83 The place where the great Sanhedrin met. According to Schürer, 4th ed., II, 263 f., the 'chamber close to the Xystus' on the western border of the Temple mount. Contrast W. Bacher in Hastings' *Dictionary of the Bible*, IV, 39 and S. Krauss, *Jew. Enc.*, XII, 576.

84 Comp. Zeb. 8 concerning the mingling of sacrificial blood with other blood, water, etc.

85 J. N. Epstein, *Der gaonäische Kommentar zur Ordnung Tohoroth*, Berlin 1915, p. 59f. Ordinarily the name Ṭoharoth is reserved for the fifth tractate of this Order of the Mishna.

86 The first chapter may be regarded as a sort of introduction to the whole Order Ṭoharoth, see Halevy, Ic (1918), 231–235.

87 אֲבוֹת הַטֻּמְאָה: A chief impurity (אב הט' Pes. 1.6, lit. father of impurity) defiles also persons, vessels, etc. that come in contact with it, thus rendering them וְלַד הַט' or רִאשׁוֹן לַט' (lit. born of, child of impurity, something that has come to be impure, first degree of impurity). The ולד הַט' defiles by contact articles of food and drink, likewise the hands, but not persons and vessels.—

A corpse defiles also without contact anything that may be found along with it in the same room and renders that which is touched by itself אַב הַטֻּמְאָה; hence with Rashi and others (but not with Maimonides) it is called אֲבִי אָבוֹת הַטֻּמְאָה.

88 But Tosephta and Palest. M. Ḳ. 2.81b, Kaufmann codex, Munich codex 95 (twice) etc. אֲהִילוֹת 'Roofings over.'

89 The biblical law is formulated in the first instance with reference to the sojourn in the wilderness. In the Mishna Tent denotes everything which is above the corpse (or a part of the dead body), e. g. the branches of a tree.

90 עַם־הָאָרֶץ (John 7.49 (ὁ ὄχλος οὗτος ὁ μὴ γινώσκων τόν νόμον) those ignorant of the law (hence also not living according to the law); then also as a singular: one who is ignorant of the law, whereof then the plural עַמֵּי הָאָרֶץ, comp. *Jahrbuch der Jüd.-Liter. Gesellschaft,* VIII (1910), 336–338. Pes. 49b Eleazar ben Pedath says: 'One may pierce through an 'Am ha-areṣ even on the Day of Atonement when it falls on a Sabbath;' in the same place Joḥanan: 'One may tear an 'Am ha-areṣ as one tears a fish.' Aug. Rohling, *Die Polemik und das Menschenopfer des Rabbinismus,* Paderborn, 1893, 95, in blind hatred of Jews, takes these expressions as literally referring to 'piercing through and killing' and renders 'Am ha-areṣ as 'non-Jew!' Contrast the saying of Akiba which is characteristic of the corresponding hatred of the man ignorant of the law for the scholars in the same passage of the Talmud: 'When I was an 'Am ha-areṣ I was wont to say: Would that I had a scholar תלמיד חכם that I might bite him like an ass.'—A. Büchler, *Der galiläische 'Am ha-'Areṣ des zweiten Jahrhunderts,* Vienna, 1906 (338 pp.; see the review by Em. Schürer, *Theologische Literaturzeitung,* 1906, No. 23); D. Chwolson, *Beiträge zur Entwicklungsgeschichte des Judentums von ca.* 400 *v. Chr. bis ca.* 1000 *n. Chr.*, Leipzig, 1910, p. 1–54: 'Der 'am ha-areç in der alten rabbinischen Literatur.'

91 Codices Cambridge and Kaufmann, Geonim, Aruk read מִקְווֹת; singular מִקְוָה Isa. 22.11.

92 The rendering 'Bath of purification' is not appropriate, since in this connection the matter of purification (which must be effected quite apart from this bath) is not as important as the observance of the regulations of the traditional law.

93 Mnemonic words: יד שחט דם (from the initials of the seven words).

94 Short for נְטִילַת כְּלִי לִתֵּן עַל הַיָּדַיִם, comp. Tosephta Ber. 4.8 (p. 9, line 8 ff.).

95 3. 2. This as a precaution against storing the Holy Scriptures by the

side of the heave (equally holy, belonging to the priests) and accordingly against damage by mice. Comp. Levy II, 163 f.; Franz Delitzsch, *Zeitschrift für lutherische Theologie*, 1854, 280–283.

[96] In 4. 6 ספרי המירס is the best attested reading according to the Cambridge Ms.; Pal. Sanh. 10.28a (also L. Ginzberg, *Yerushalmi Fragments*, I, 262, New York 1909); Maimonides on Yadaim 4.6; Aruk sub מירום ad Ḥullin 60b. What is meant is Homer, comp. Grätz, *Kohelet*, 166; Perles, *Revue des Etudes Juives*, III, 142 ff.; M. Perles, *Blicke in die Religionsgeschichte*, I (Breslau, 1888), 73 ff.; Kohut, *Jewish Quarterly Review*, III, 546 ff.; M. Friedmann in הַגֹּרֶן III (Berdyczew, 1902), 30–39; IV (1903), 5–26; S. Buber in his edition of the Midrash Ps. 1.1; the 'gaonic commentary on the Order Ṭoharoth' edited by J. N. Epstein, Berlin, 1915, p. 52, says in the present passage in Yadaim expressly: All these uncanonical books ספרים חיצונים of Greek wisdom are called in their language הומרוס.

NOTES TO CHAPTER V, § 1, P. 65

[1] In the collection of responsa Shaare Ṣedeḳ, Saloniki 1792, III, 2, 9.

[2] Berlin, 1885 ff. At least 8 times.

[3] Mafteaḥ.

[4] In his Dictionary. Add also Lewin, גִּנְזֵי קֶדֶם 'Haifa 5682, p. 10, line 17 (from a Geniza Ms.: a commentary by Hai Gaon on Shabbath 75).

[5] See הַקֶּדֶם II, 35.

[6] Beginning of Ḥullin, s. v. הכל.

[7] So the Responsa edited by Harkavy (at least 5 times), Isaac Alphasi, Judah bar Barzillai frequently in his Commentary on the Book Yeṣira (Berlin, 1885); so also the Leiden Ms. of the Pal. Talmud 370 a (but also just Talmud, ibid. 1b, 193b).

[8] See *Revue des Etudes Juives*, LVIII, 183 f.

[9] Sepher ha-ḳabbala.

[10] Introduction to his Commentary on the Mishna.

[11] So Sherira; according to Halevy about 290.

[12] W. Bacher, רבנן דקיסרין in *Magazin*, 1901, 298–310.

[13] See also W. Bacher, 'Zur Geschichte der Schulen Palästinas im 3. und 4. Jahrhundert. Die Genossen חַבְרַיָּא' in *Magazin*, 1899, 345–360, 572 (the חֲבֵרִים of Amoraic times are the unordained members of the schools).

[14] תני שמואל.

15 See Is. Lewy, *Interpretation des paläst. Talmud-Tractates Nezikin*, introduction, p. 20 f.

16 See the List in Appendix IV after Bacher in *Jew. Encycl.*, XII, 6 f.

NOTES TO CHAPTER V, § 2, P. 66

1 110b.

2 See the Table in Appendix I.

3 See L. Ginzberg, *Yerushalmi Fragments from the Genizah*, I, New York, 1909 (372 pp., 4to).

4 Frankel, *Introduction*, 45a f.; S. Buber, *Magazin für die Wissenschaft des Judentums*, 1878, 100–105.

5 In particular S. M. Schiller-Szinessy, *Occasional Notes*, and Schorr החלוץ, XI, 33–46.

6 In the introduction to his Commentary on the Mishna.

7 See the collection by S. Buber in ירושלים הבנויה, Jerusalem, 1906 (50 pp.)

8 In Luncz's *Jahrbuch*, Jerusalem, VII, 148–157.

9 Judah ben Barzillai (twelfth cent.) adduces in his Commentary on the Book Yeṣira (Berlin, 1885, p. 59) under the caption בירושלמי a passage which is found in Midrash Gen. R. on Gen. 18.17 (as demonstrated by Brüll, *Jahrbücher*, IX, 154).

10 *Magazin*, 1911, 419–425 and 1916, 108 f.; הצופה (ed. Blau), VI, 179–186.

11 On Babyl. Nidda 66a they cite the Palest. Gemara for chap. 7.

12 See the introduction to his Commentary on the Mishna.

13 Orient. Qu. 554, fol. 78a: 'פי׳ גמר עקצין בגמרא דבני ירוש.

14 See above p. 20 and below p. 80.

15 Szinérváralja 1907 (Ḥul., Bekor.), 1908 (Zeb. Arak.).

16 See in particular B. Ratner in the weekly העולם, Cologne, 1907; Chief Rabbi Ritter of Rotterdam in *Der Israelit*, Frankf. o. M. 1907, No. 25,27,29,31, 33,35,44,46 and 1908, No. 6; D. Simonsen in *Israelitische Monatsschrift* (Berlin), 1907, No. 12; W. Bacher in הקדם, 1907 (in comparing the contents of the new text with the one long known he shows up on the one hand a remarkable mass of literal or almost literal agreements and on the other hand here and there linguistic points to which exception may be taken) and *Zeitschrift für hebräische Bibliographie*, 1907, 23–29; Porges, ibid., p. 157 f.; M. Liber, *Revue des Etudes Juives*, LVI, 141–143; V. Aptowitzer, *Magazin*, 1910, 564–570. See further Ratner, הקדם, I, 89–108; Ritter, הקול, II, Warsaw 1908, Nos. 15–25 W. Rabinowitz, היונה, I (Odessa, 1907), 15–18 and תל תלפיות, XIX (1910), Nos. 9–10.

NOTES TO CHAPTER V, § 3, P. 69

[1] The Geonim almost exclusively use the Babylonian Talmud. Citations in gaonic writings from the Palestinian Talmud have been collected by J. Reifmann and S. Buber in הכרמל, I (Wilna 1861), 279–283, 558–570. Comp. also *Zeitschr. f. hebr. Bibliogr.*, XIII, 70, 71 (Siddur Rab Amram, Halakoth Gedoloth; Saadia). In the 17 Responsa 129,130,139,208,213,233,247,257,259, 261,330,349,361,389,434,466,512 (ed. Harkavy) passages are adduced just from 9 tractates (only once in each case from 6): Yoma, R. H., Taan. (twice), Meg., Ḥag., Yeb., Keth. (8 times), B. M. (twice), Shebu. Sam. Poznański, 'Die Geonim u. der jerus. T.,' הקדם, I (1907), 135–148; II (1908), 24–51, 114–116. Whether the Palest. Talm. is cited in the Sheeltoth of R. Aḥai (A. Kaminka, הקדם, II, 20–23 comes to a negative result) we shall be able to say when once we possess a critical edition of the Sheeltoth.—In the Halakoth Gedoloth (ed. Hildesheimer, p. 21) a passage found in Pal. Berak. 2.1 is cited from תלמוד דמערבא. A series of other passages in the Halakoth Gedoloth rest on the Palest. Talm. (see Hildesheimer's Index, p. 10 f.).—Much use was made of the Palest. Talm. in southern Italy, so in the Pesiḳtha Rabbathi (prob. of the tenth cent.); see *Monatsschrift*, 1911, 735 f.—On several occasions Hananeel follows the Palest. Talm. against the Babylonian; see O. H. Schorr, החלוץ, V, § 42,43 (according to Marx, *Jewish Quarterly Review*, New Series, I, 438).

[2] Comp. the Responsum by Hai Gaon in Sepher ha-eshkol by Abraham ben Isaac of Narbonne (ed. B. H. Auerbach, II, 49, Halberstadt, 1867; Ratner's suspicion in Ahabat etc. on Sukka, p. 78 against the authenticity of that which is said in Eshkol is unfounded, since it is substantiated by Carmoly's Ms.), the anonymous Responsum in ספר המכריע by Isaiah di Trani I (No. 42, Leghorn 1779, 32a), which seems to ascend to Sherira; Isaac Alphasi, end of Erubin; Shiṭṭa meḳubbeṣeth by Bezalel Ashkenazi on B. M. 45b; the methodology of the Talmud, Yad Mal'aki by Malachi Cohen (Leghorn, 1767), beginning of second part. Concerning Maimonides see B. Ratner, *Ahabath Ṣiyyon Wirushalaim* on Ber. 2d, p. 38.

NOTES TO CHAPTER VI, P. 70

[1] B. M. 85a.

[2] See Hilprecht and Clay, *Business Documents of Murashu Sons, of Nippur*, Philadelphia, 1898 (clay tablets from the times of the Persian kings Artaxerxes I and Darius II).

[3] Comp. Is. Halevy, lc. 89–143.

[4] כַּלָּה means 'bride,' and the selection of this appellation was probably suggested by the fact that the Midrash likens the Torah to a bride: Simeon ben Laḳish in Midrash R. Exodus on 31.18 points by way of homily כְּכַלָּתוֹ. Comp. B. B. 12a אין פותחין בכלה פחות מעשרה. S. Krauss would explain כלה as equivalent to כְּלִיל 'crown, wreath, *corona*, circle of people.'

[5] B. M. 97a.

[6] B. B. 157b.—On the other hand, Halevy, II, 523 ff., endeavors to show that the fixation of the text did not take place in the Kalla months but in special convocations (וַעַד) of all the scholars of Babylonia.

[7] See Lauterbach, *Jewish Quarterly Review*, New Series, VIII, 110–112 against Bacher, *Terminologie*, II, 31f.

[8] Comp. Isr. Lewy, *Interpretation . . . Nesikin*, Publications of the Breslau Seminary, 1895, p. 3.

[9] See ibid. and S. Horovitz, *Monatsschrift*, 1919, 126.

[10] סוֹף הוֹרָאָה B. M. 86a.

[11] Note L. Löw, *Schriften*, V, 67: "The statement that the Talmud was closed at the end of the fifth century hangs in the air. The work on the Talmud was discontinued in the middle of the eighth century for the reason that independent literary productions such as the Halakoth Pesuḳoth and Gedoloth had begun to usher in a new epoch and because the rise of Karaism was prejudicial to the talmudic system."

[12] For the first time we find the Tannaite Judah ben El'ai indulging in mnemonic Simanim.

[13] Comp. N. Brüll, *Jahrbücher*, II, 58–67; J. Brüll, דורש לציון *Die Mnemotechnik des Talmuds*, Vienna, 1864 (53 pp.).

[14] See the list in Pinner, *Traktat Berachoth*, Berlin 1842, introduction, fol. 22. N. Brüll, 62 ff., has collected much from *Diḳduḳe Sopherim*, I and II and from ancient authors. Concerning the Simanim of the Babylonian Naḥman bar Isaac (died 356) comp. Bacher, *Agada der babylonischen Amoräer*, 134. David Pardo, למנצח לדוד, Saloniki, 1765, folio, contains among other matters an explanation of the Simanim in the Talmud. Similarly does A. Hyman, *Toldoth Tannaim weamoraim*, London, 1910, introd., p. 17–28, offer a collection and interpretation of the סימני הש"ס.

[15] Namely, in the Order Zera'im 10: all with the exception of Ber.; in Mo'ed 1: Sheḳalim (the editions and manuscripts reproduce on this tractate the Palest. Talmud); in Neziḳin 2: Eduy., Aboth; in Ḳodashim 2½: Middoth, Ḳinnim, and in part (see Appendix I) Tamid; in Ṭoharoth 11: all except Nidda.

[16] Comp. the statement of Raba (died 352; Taan. 24ab, Sanh. 106a; the same is said by Papa, a disciple of Raba, Ber. 20a): "In the days of Judah bar Ezekiel they were wont to discuss only the Order Neziḳin, ואנן קא מְתַנֵּינַן שיתא סדרי, but we discuss all six Orders." In the passages adduced we read: 'We discuss the tractate Uḳṣin in 13 gatherings.'

[17] So also Halevy, II, 524 f.

[18] *Ha-misderona*, II (Jerusalem 1888), 97–112.

[19] הַכֶּרֶם, 1887, 144–154.

[20] III, 111–130; II, 568.

NOTES TO CHAPTER VII, § 1, P. 73

[1] Comp. Zunz, *GV*, 108 f.; D. Hoffmann, *Die erste Mishna*, 27 ff.; *JE*, I, 82; M. Jung, *Kritik sämtlicher Bücher Aboth in der althebr. Literatur* (Dissert.), Leipzig, 1889 (64).

[2] Also to c, e, f, g: בנין יהושע, Dyhernfurth, 1788 fol.

[3] *Tractatus de patribus Rabbi Nathane auctore*, London, 1654, 4to.

[4] According to cod. Hebr. Munich 222 in *Neweh Shalom* I, Munich 1872 (comp. *HBg*, XII, 75 f.).

[5] *Aboth deRabbi Nathan*, Vienna, 1887 (36 and 176); the second recension after cod. Hebr. Vatic. No. 303 (comp. *MGWJ*, 1887, 374–383); in addition on p. 150–166 a diverging fragment after cod. Vat. 44.

[6] *Rabbi Nathans System der Ethik und Moral*, Frankf. on M., 1905 (143).

[7] Comp. Zunz, *GV*, 95 f.; L. Blau, *JE*, XI, 426–428, and (following J. Müller) Hamburger, *Suppl.*, I, 104.

[8] *Masechet Soferim, e. Einl. in das Studium der althebr. Graphik, der Masora u. der altjüdischen Liturgie.* Nach Handschriften herausgegeben u. commentiert (German commentary), Leipzig, 1878 (38 +304+[Hebr.] 44).

[9] Berlin, 1893, p. 686–717.

[10] Arye L. Spira (Shapira), נחלת אריאל ומעון אריות, Dyhernfurth, 1793 fol.; Jacob Naumburg, נחלת יעקב, Fürth 1793 (contains also a commentary on c-g and on מַסֶּכֶת גֵּרִים; Isaac Elijah Landa, Suwalki, 1862 fol. etc.

[11] J. G. Chr. Adler, *Iudaeorum codicis sacri rite scribendi leges*, Hamburg, 1729 (24), 4to.

[12] The name occurs as early as M. Ḳ. 24a, 26b; Keth. 28a.

[13] Comp. Zunz, *GV*, 90; N. Brüll, 'Die talmudischen Traktate über Trauer um Verstorbene,' in *Jahrbücher*, I, 1–57; Hamburger, *Suppl.*, I, 51–53

(follows Brüll); Lauterbach, *JE*, XI, 180–182.—Publications: M. Klotz, *Der talmud. Tractat E. R. . . . nach Handschriften bearbeitet, übersetzt u. mit erläuternden Anmerkungen*, Part 1, Berlin, 1890, (90). Ch. M. Horowitz, *Uralte Tosefta's*, II, III (Mainz 1890) published Semahoth zutarti and several portions of Ebel tractates.

[14] Comp. Zunz, *GV*, 89 f.; V. Aptowitzer, *REJ*, LVII, 239–244.

[15] חמשה קונטרסים, *Commentarios quinque doctrinam talmudicam illustrantes* . . . edidit N. N. Coronel, Vienna, 1864 (contains also e and f).—Baruch Toledano has edited the פירוש מסכת כלה רבתי by Abraham ben Nathan ibn Jarḥi, Tiberias 1906 (28+51 leaves), see *MGWJ*, 1908, 304–306.

[16] Shab. 6.8a end.

[17] On this tractate see Zunz, *GV*, 110 f.; S. Krauss, *REJ*, XXXVI, 27–46; 205–221; XXXVII, 45–64 (whereon Bacher, XXXVII, 299–303); L. Ginzberg, *JE*, IV, 526–528.—Publications: M. Goldberg, *Der talmud. Traktat Derech Erez Rabba*, neu ediert, mit Anmerkungen, Part 1, Breslau 1888. The text is found also in Maḥzor Vitry, p. 724–735.

[18] The epithet Zuṭa 'small' is late and misleading.

[19] Comp. Zunz, *GV*, 111 f., *Die Ritus des synagogalen Gottesdienstes*, Berlin, 1859, p. 86; L. Ginzberg, *JE*, IV, 528 f.

[20] See Abrahams in *Steinschneider-Festschr.*, 1896, 72–75; *JQR*, X, 660 f. —Publications: J. Harburger, מסכת ד' א' זוטא. *Eine Sammlung der reinsten u. kernhaftesten Sitten-u. Anstandslehren der ältesten Rabbinen* . . . mit Übersetzung u. Anmerkungen, Bayreuth, 1839 (56). Abr. Tawrogi, *Der thalmud. Tractat Derech Erez Sutta* . . . kritisch bearbeitet, übersetzt u. erläutert, Königsberg i. Pr. 1885 (52). Another text in Maḥzor Vitry 721–723. Comp. also Halakoth Gedoloth (ed. Hildesheimer, 644–652) and on the citation רצונך שלא תמות מות עד שלא תמות N. Brüll, *Jahrbücher*, II, 128 f.

[21] Comp. Zunz, *GV*, 112. S. Schechter, *Aboth de R. Nathan*, p. 112 f., n. 19 on the second recension, supplies the end from a Ms. Epstein. A translation may be found in *Israels Lehrhallen*, IV.

NOTES TO CHAPTER VII, § 2, P. 74

[1] *Septem libri Talmudici parvi Hierosolymitani*, Frankfurt o. M., 1851 (44).—e, f, g had been published previously by H. J. D. Azulai in מראית העין, Leghorn, 1805 fol. (another recension of a still earlier date in שמחת הרגל, Leghorn 1782, 4to) and by Judah Nagar in חני יהודה, Pisa, 1816 fol.

[2] Bodenschatz, *Kirchliche Verfassung der heutigen Juden* (1748), IV, 19–24; *JE*, VIII, 531 f.

[3] Bodenschatz, IV, 14–19; L. Blau, *JE*, VIII, 21–28; Aug. Wünsche, *PRE*, 3d ed., XIX, 510–513.

[4] Bodenschatz, IV, 9–14; *JE*, V, 521 f. (comp. II, 75 f. Arba Kanfot and XI, 676–678 Tallit).

[5] Comp. L. N. Dembitz and S. Krauss, *JE*, XI, 402–408.

[6] Comp. Isr. Taglicht, *Die Kuthäer als Beobachter des Gesetzes nach talmud. Quellen* . . . (Dissert.), Erlangen 1883 (45). *JE*, X, 672–674; Schürer, 4th ed., II, 18–23. English translations: by Nutt, *The Samaritan Targum*, p. 68–72 and by J. A. Montgomery, *The Samaritans*, p. 196–203.

[7] Zunz, *GV*, 90; Emil G. Hirsch, *JE*, X, 220 to 224; Schürer, 4th ed., III, 150–188.

Comp. in addition N. Brüll, 'Verschollene Boraitas u. Midrashim,' *Jahrbücher*, II, 124 to 129 (B. of the tractate Nidda, B. of the 24 obstacles to repentance); Ch. M. Horowitz, תוספתא עתיקתא, Mainz, 1890.

NOTES TO CHAPTER VIII, P. 75

[1] So according to the ordinary pronunciation, comp. מַסֶּכְתָּא Tractate. We might, if at all the name is to be taken as a singular, prefer Tosaphta (or possibly Tosiphta); but in all likelihood as a title the word must have been read as a plural, Tosephatha, like Pesiḳatha; see Brüll, *Jahrbücher*, IV, 164. In the sing. we find תוספתא עתיקתא in contrast with 'new teaching' אוֹרָיְתָא חֲדַתָּא Pal. Shabb. 8.11a; Pesiḳtha Rabb. 14 fol. 63a (Friedm.); Pal. Pes. 10.37c.

[2] But it is short of 4 tractates: Aboth in the fourth Order; Tamid, Middoth, Ḳinnim in the fifth. See Appendix I.

[3] Sanh. 86a: סתם תוספתא ר' נחמיה. See above p. 22.

[4] Epistle, ed. Neubauer, p. 13; ed. Lewin, p. 34.

[5] Neg. 8.6; Zuckerm. 628.

[6] Comp. Rosenthal, *Entstehung*, I, 17, 46, 99 ff., 142 ff.; D. Hoffmann *JbJLG*, III, 307.

[7] Ibid., 316–321.

[8] Ibid., 316 f.

[9] *Hodeg.*, 304–308; Introd. to the Palest. Talmud, 23–27.

[10] *MGWJ*, 1874, 1875 and in Hebrew works: *Die Tosifta des Tr. Sabbath in ihrem Verhältnisse zur Mischna*, Karlsruhe 1879 (143); *Die Tos. des Tr.*

Erubin . . ., ibid., 1882 (40 a. 120); התוספתא לפי סדר המשניות, *T. juxta Mischnarum ordinem recomposita et commentario instructa.* I, Ordo Seraim, Wilna, 1890 (25a. 431); התוספתא, *die Tosefta zum Tr. Chullin neugeordnet u. mit e. Commentar*, Frankf. o. M., 1901 (82); *Die Tosifta des Traktates Nesikin geordnet u. kommentiert*, ibid., 1912 (40 a. 121).—In a letter to me (December 1920) Schwarz writes that 'there existed several תוספתות out of which our Tosephta was compiled.'

[11] *Die Erfurter Handschrift der Tosefta*, Berlin, 1876 (117); *Der Wiener Tosefta-Codex*, Magdeburg, 1877 (15); *Tosefta-Varianten*, Trier, 1881 (40). || *Tosefta, Mischna u. Boraitha in ihrem Verhältnis zueinander, oder palästinens. u. babylon. Halacha*, 2 volumes, Frankf. o. M., 1908, 1909 (30 a. 484; 508); Supplement, 1910 (34). *Gesammelte Aufsätze*: I, Zur Halachakritik, 1911 (210); II, Zur Tosefta u. Anderes, 1912 (202).

[12] Tos. Baba Ḳamma, p. xi ff.

[13] J. H. Dünner, *Die Theorien über Wesen u. Ursprung der Tosephta kritisch dargestellt*, Amst., 1874 (95). Weiss, II, 217–224. D. Hoffmann, 'Mischna u. Tos.,' *Magazin*, 1882, 153–163. N. Brüll, 'Begriff u. Ursprung der Tos.' in *Zunz-Festschrift*, 92–110. J. Z. Lauterbach, *JE*, XII, 207–209. H. Malter, *JQR*, N. S., II, 75–95 (in favor of Zuckerm.). See also Blau, *REJ*, 1914, 1–23.

Editions. The Tosephta was first printed in the ספר רב אלפס, Venice, 1521f., then, similarly with Alphasi's work, Venice 1522 and frequently; furthermore in various editions of the Talmud, e. g. Vienna, 1870 (with the variant readings of the Vienna Ms.) and Wilna, 1880 (with numerous commentaries: תנא תוספאה by Samuel Abigdor b. Abraham, חסדי דוד by David Pardo, Elijah Wilna on the Order Ṭoharoth, etc.). M. S. Zuckermandel, *Tos.*, Pasewalk, 1880 (690), a supplement containing a survey, indices and glossary, Trier, 1882 (94); the editor based himself on the Erfurt codex, he also collated the Vienna Ms. and the first editions, but not with sufficient reliability. Many years ago Krengel (in Bohemian Leipa) announced that he was preparing a critical edition. Lev. Friedländer, *La Tosephta* . . ., Pressburg, 1889, 1890, I, *Seraim* (32 a. 386), II, *Naschim* (16 a. 248), with the commentaries חֵשֶׁק שְׁלֹמֹה a. קֶשֶׁר בּוֹגְדִים (supposedly with variants from a Spanish Ms.).— Biagio Ugolini edited in his *Thesaurus antiquitatum sacrarum* 31 tractates of the Tos. with his own Latin translation, in vol. XX the first Order, in XVII and XVIII Mo'ed, in XIX Ḳodashim, Venice, 1755–1757 fol. H. Laible, *Der T.-Traktat Berachoth . . . übersetzt*, Rothenburg o. T., 1902 (32). Quite unsatisfactory is the edition (text, translation and commentary) by O. Holtzmann, Giessen, 1912. H. Danby, *Tractate Ṣanhedrin Mishnah and Tosefta translated . . . with brief annotations*, London, 1919 (148) (each section of the Mishna is here followed by the corresponding one of the Tosephta in smaller type). E. A. Rousselle, *Historisch-kritische Einführung in den Tosephtatraktat Pesachim* (Heidelberg Dissertation), 1916 (54). The author endeavors to demonstrate two older recensions (Akiba and Nehemiah) and a proper Tosephta layer or final redaction.

NOTES TO CHAPTER IX, § 1, P. 77

[1] A few points relevant to the present discussion may be found in M. Jastrow, 'The History and the Future of the Text of the Talmud,' *Publications of the Gratz College*, I (Philadelphia 1897), 77–103.

[2] N. Brüll, *Jahrbücher*, VIII, 59f.; S. Horovitz-Breslau, *MGWJ*, 1919, 122 to 125.

[3] *Tradition u. Tradenten*, 589.

[4] B. Ḳ. 59a, Ḥul. 119b, Tem. 11a.b, Nidda 29a.

[5] E. g. Sukka 14b, Giṭtin 14a and several passages in Tem. 1–7.

[6] E. g. ולית הלכתא כוותיה 'the Halaka is not according to him', Pes. 86b, 104b.—As to additions which go back to Jehudai Gaon see N. Brüll, *Jahrbücher*, II, 121f., 73ff.; on those of the Tarbiṣae (the younger students devoted to knowledge) ibid., 78–85. V. Aptowitzer, הצופה מארץ הגר, IV, 17f., lists Responsa and Commentaries in which attention is drawn to additions and explanatory matter on the part of the Geonim; in particular he discusses the many additions in Ber. In B. M., many additions are found which go back to Jehudai Gaon (in the Mss., especially in the older ones, these are introduced with the word פירוש 'explanation'; see Kerem ḥemed, VI, 249ff.)

[7] דבר על אודות התלמוד אם יכול הוא להתרגם כל צרכו, Vienna 1885.

[8] See Al. Marx, *JQR*, N. S., I, 279 to 282.

[9] See above p. 4f.

[10] *Oeuvres*, IX, 167 f.

[11] Brüll, *Jahrbücher*, IV, 70.

[12] At the end of the twelfth century French scholars addressed an inquiry to Babylonia whether at Passover leaven is forbidden במשהו (no matter how small the quantity) or only בששים (1 among 60) and received a reply from Samuel ben Ali that in copies ascending to the times of Rab Ashi (died 427) he text Pes. 30a beginning read במשהו כרב, i. e. 'במשהו according to Rab;'

see V. Aptowitzer, *Rabiah*, II, 77; *ZHBg*, XIX, 36 f.

[13] Not Saloniki.

[14] *ZHBg*, XIV, 80; XV, 180 f.

[15] Only a few fragments: *ZHBg*, XII, 16–19.

[16] A noteworthy example is Palest. Taan. 63d, 64a with reference to the five causes on account of which Israel was redeemed from Egypt; the passage is to be rectified in accordance with Deut. R. 2: *REJ*, IX, 256–259.

[17] In March 1246 the Dominican Raymond Martini together with the Bishop of Barcelona and three other Dominicans, received the commission to inspect the manuscripts which the Jews were ordered by James I of Aragon (1213–1276) to bring forward, and to delete anything offensive to the Christian religion; see A. Touron, *Histoire des hommes illustres de l'ordre de St. Dominique*, I (Paris, 1743), 492: *Pugio fidei*, ed. Carpzov, Leipzig, 1687, introd. 105. The rescripts of James, dated August 1263 and March 1264, have been reprinted in *REJ*, LXI (1911), 1f., 7f.

[18] In Ms. Berlin Orient. Fol. 567, fol. 185, the passage dealing with Jesus in Maimonides' Epistle to Yemen is indicated by an original blank; similarly in the same Ms. a few omitted utterances of an anti-Christian character by Maimonides in his Mishna Commentary on A. Z.

[19] Sanh. 98b.

[20] See also Isr. Levi, *Le péché originel dans les anciennes sources juives*, Paris 1909 (32).

[21] See Sepher ha-'ittim in N. Coronel's זכר נתן, Vienna, 1872, fol. 132b, 134a; J. Schorr's edition, Berlin, 1903, 267. Alex. Marx, *ZHBg*, XIII, 173; XV, 127, pronounces the report as legendary, though it is quite possible that Natronai brought with him a copy.

[22] *JQR* (1906), 401, 770.

[23] *Hilkoth malweh weloweh*, 15.2.

[24] *Milhamoth Jhwh. B.* Ḳ. 85b.

[25] *MGWJ* (1911), 739.

NOTES TO CHAPTER IX, § 2, P. 79

[1] On requisitions of Jewish manuscripts in France ca. 1250 see the documents registered by Ulisse Robert, *REJ*, III (1881), 214; comp. also p. 216 (rescript of Louis the Saint of the y. 1269) a. p. 223 (edict by Philip le Beau of the y. 1299).—Isid. Loeb registers a number of papal manifestations against

the Talmud in *REJ*, I (1880), 116f. (a hitherto unpublished bull of Alexander IV. of Sept. 3, 1257), 298. Comp. also A. Berliner, *Censur u. Confiscation hebräischer Bücher im Kirchenstaate*, Frankf. o. M., 1891 (65).

[2] Such committals to the flames took place e. g. in Paris after the disputation between R. Jehiel and Nicholas Donin in the y. 1240 (comp. Lewin, *MGWJ* (1869), 97ff.; F. Lebrecht, *Handschriften*, p. 36δ, Isid. Loeb in *REJ*, I, 293–296 and the pathetic elegy שאלי שרופה by R. Meir Rothenburg); in Rome and then also in other cities of Italy at the order of Pope Julius III, 1553 ff. On account of this order a great many printed books, likewise, were destroyed, especially in Venice; see D. Kaufmann, *JQR*, XIII, 533–538. H. Grätz, *MGWJ* (1885), 529–541, presents a history of the persecutions of the Talmud from Donin to the Frankists, (1757, numerous copies of the Talmud were burned by the order of the bishop of Kamienez).—On the other hand, it deserves mention that king Sigismund Augustus of Poland issued a protective edict (July 24, 1568) in favor of the Talmud and Jewish religious writings: *JbJLG*, XI, 189.

[3] *Handschriften u. erste Ausgaben des Babylon. Talmud.* First Division: Berlin, 1862 (114 pp. 4to); comp. *HBg*, V, (1862), 120–122; VI (1863), 15f., 56.

[4] *Diḳd.* I, IV, VIII, IX, XI. Comp. also *HBg*, VI, 39–42.

[5] Comp. S. M. Schiller-Szinessy, *Occasional Notices of Hebrew Manuscripts*, I, Cambridge 1878, Appendix, p. 1–12.

[6] Comp. Isr. Markon, הַקֶּדֶם, I (1917), Hebr., p. 41–49.

[7] *Lewy-Festschrift*, Hebr., p. 193 to 211.

[8] See S. Krauss, *MGWJ* (1907), 54–66, 142–163, 323–333, 445–461.

[9] See D. Kaufmann, *MGWJ* (1898), 38–46.

[10] See M. Steinschneider, *Catalogus codicum hebraeorum bibliothecae Lugduno-Batavae*, Leiden, 1858, 341–343; Lebrecht, *Handschriften* etc., p. 52f.; esp. S. M. Schiller-Szinessy, *Occasional Notices of Hebrew Mss.*, No. I. Description of the Leiden Ms. of the Palestinian Talmud (16).

[11] This commentary is printed in the edition Szitomir 1866.

[12] See p. 81.

[13] M. Lehmann has edited Ber. according to this Ms., see p. 83.

[14] M. Schwab, *REJ*, LXII, 82.

[15] Made use of by Luncz; variants in Ginzberg's publication.

[16] Described *JQR* (1897), 117–119 and made use of by Ginzberg, p. 223 f.

[17] שרידי הירושלמי. *Yerushalmi Fragments from the Genizah*, I, New York, 1909 (372 large 4to), p. 1–307.

[18] P. 1–307.

[19] 309–343.

[20] 374–372. The second volume with detailed descriptions of the manuscript fragments and with comments has not appeared as yet.

[21] תלמוד בבלי כו'. *Der babylonische Talmud nach der einzigen vollständigen Handschrift München Codex Hebraicus 95 mittels Facsimile-Lichtdrucks vervielfältigt, mit Inhaltsangaben für jede Seite u. einer Einl. versehen.* Leiden, 1912. 577 leaves large folio and 43 pp. (4to) introduction. The missing portions Pes. 119a–121b and 58a–67b (of the editions) have been supplied from cod. Munich 6, the missing portions Keth. 84a–78a and Men. 76b–77a according to cod. hebr. Vatic. 113 or 118, by faithful reprint in the Introduction. This publication has led Lazarus Goldschmidt to indite a libel against me and privately to spread it broadcast. Since all my efforts to demonstrate publicly the merits of my case by other means proved futile, I challenged Goldschmidt to sue me by the statement in the introduction to my edition of the Munich codex: 'Certainly any one who knows me or at least the manner in which his (Goldschmidt's) publications originated, has from the beginning been convinced of the flimsy character of his barefaced falsehoods and slanders.' The courts then (February 8, 1913 Amtsgericht Berlin Mitte; February 25, Landgericht I, Strafkammer 9) dismissed Goldschmidt's complaint and passed sentence to the effect that I was justified in repelling his attacks and in my position as a public teacher was indeed in duty bound to do so and that I have not transgressed the permissible measure of criticism or refutation by the use of the above mentioned expressions. In deference to requests which came to me from many quarters and in order to preclude in the future any misuse of the libel I herewith make known the issue of the case.

[22] See *Diḳd.* I, introduction, p. 36; Lebrecht, 54 f.

[23] Rabbinovicz, *Diḳd.* I, introd., p. 38, thinks that this codex was written long before the 6th millennium, i. e. long before 1240 C. E., whereas Steinschneider in his Catalogue of the Munich manuscripts queries 'possibly beginning of the 15th cent.?'—one of the numerous indications how precarious it is to estimate the date of Hebrew Mss.

[24] *Der Traktat Nezikin . . . In photolithographischer Facsimile-Reproduktion . . . u. mit textkrit. Scholien versehen* von L. Goldschmidt, Berlin, 1914 (16 and 1492 pages large folio).

[25] See *ZHBg*, XII, 108.

[26] Comp. P. de Lagarde, *Semitica*, I, Göttingen 1878, 69–71; *Verzeichnis der Handschriften im preuss. Staate*, I Hannover, 3 Göttingen, vol. III (Berlin

1894), p. 383 f. Prof. Rahlfs informs me in a personal communication that the text differs largely from the current one.

[27] Comp. Lebrecht, p. 51 f.; *Diḳd.* VIII, preface No. 15.

[28] Made use of by Rabbinovicz, see *Diḳd.* IV, preface No. 7.

[29] *Diḳd.* IV, preface No. 9.

[30] *Diḳd.*, ibid., No. 11.

[31] *Diḳd.*, ibid., No. 12.

[32] S. Schechter and S. Singer, *Talmudical Fragments in the Bodleian Library*, Cambridge, 1896, have edited Ker. according to this codex together with two leaves from No. 2674 containing Pal. Ber. (see above p. 80).

[33] See H. Loewe in *JQR* (1906), 456–474 (collation with the Venice ed.).

[34] Edited by W. H. Lowe, Cambridge, 1879 (100 a. 8 pp. 4to).

[35] Comp. *Diḳd.* IX, preface No. 17–19.

[36] Erroneously designated in *HBg*, VIII (1856), 96 as commentary by R. Hananel, see *HBg*, XIV (1874), 60.

[37] Vol. I, Rome, 1756 fol.; comp. Lebrecht, 68 ff.

[38] Concerning 20 of these Mss. (108–123,125,156,171,487) see *Diḳd.* XI, preface No. 20–39 and S. Ochser, *ZDMG* (1909), 365–393, 626, 822 f.

[39] Comp. *Diḳd.*, I, introd., p. 39.

[40] Comp. M. Margolis, *The Columbia College MS. of Meghilla* (Babyl. Talmud), New York, 1892 (14); Julius M. Price, *The Yemenite Ms. of Megilla . . . examined and edited*, Toronto, 1916 (12 a. 52).

[41] *Talmud Babylonicum ad codices ms. editionesque veterrimas correctum et completum.* מסכת ברכות. Petropoli, 1909 (136 pp. 4to).

[42] ספר ראבי"ה, ed. Dembitzer, Cracow, 1882; ed. Aptowitzer, I, Berlin 1913; II, in print.

[43] אוֹר זָרוּעַ Zhitomir, 1862; Jerusalem, 1887 to 1890.

[44] ספר אהבת ציון וירושלים. *Varianten u. Ergänzungen des Jerusalemit. Talmuds nach alten Quellen u. handschriftlichen Fragmenten edirt*, Wilna, 12 parts, 1901–1917: Order 1; Shabb.; Pes., Sukka, Beṣa, R. H., Taan., Meg.

[45] See V. Aptowitzer, *MGWJ* (1910), 160–172, 278–288, 417 f.; comp. also the suggestive reviews by W. Bacher in *REJ*, XLIII, XLVI, L, etc.

[46] Comp. M. Margolis, *Commentarius Isaacidis quatenus ad textum Talmudis investigandum adhiberi possit, tractatu 'Erubhin ostenditur*, New York, 1891 (72).

[47] See Rabbinovicz, מאמר, p. 131 f.

[48] ספר דקדוקי סופרים. *Variae lectiones* in Mischnam et in Talmud Babylonicum quum ex aliis libris antiquissimis et scriptis et impressis tum e

codice Monacensi praestantissimo collectae, annotationibus instructae. Munich.

[49] Przemysl, 1897.

NOTES TO CHAPTER IX, § 3, P. 83

[1] Here are listed only the older editions or those which are otherwise notable on account of their text. For other editions see chap. XIV.

[2] מַאֲמָר עַל הַדְפָּסַת התלמוד, Munich 1877 (132 pp. Appendix to *Diḳd.* VIII). See also M. Schwab, *Les Incunables hébreux*, Paris, 183. On the printers' family Soncino see Cat. Bodl., col. 3053–3–58; F. Sacchi, I *tipografi Ebrei di Soncino*, I (all that has appeared), Cremona, 1877; and the standard work by Giacomo Manzoni, *Annali tipografici dei Soncino*, Bologna, 1883–86. See also A. Berliner, 'Beiträge zur hebr. Typographie Daniel Bombergs,' *JbJLG*, III, 293–305.

[3] See p. 81.

[4] Not: 1503/4.

[5] A few variants in Zera'im.

[6] The Zhitomir edition has several commentaries.

[7] Sharply criticised by R. Kirchheim, המגיד, 1875, p. 220 ff.

[8] Cod. Hebr. Vatic. 133. See above p. 80, No. 5.

[9] As far as Kil'aim.

[10] As shown by S. Seeligmann, *ZHBg* (1908), 16–19.—What Chwolson (ראשית מעשה הדפוס בישראל, Warsaw, 1897) mentions as Kethuboth of Guadalaxara is actually the Fez Ḳiddushin.

[11] See *ZHBg*, XIV (1910), 80; XV, 180 f.

[12] 7 twice: Ber.; Ket., Giṭ., Ḳid.; B. Ḳ., B. M.; Ḥul. See Lebrecht, *Handschriften*, 89–92; Rabbinovicz, *Ma'amar*, 7 to 28; *ZHBg*, VIII (1904), 143 f.; XII (1908), 14.—Ber. was printed first, 1484.

[13] P. 35, 38.

[14] On the title page of the Constantinople edition of D. Ḳimḥi's Hebrew Grammar.

[15] P. 43.

[16] *HBg*, V (1862), 122.

[17] See *ZHBg*, XI, 152 f.

[18] See Rabbin. 61–65, 129 and Zedner, *HBg*, X (1870), 141 f.

[19] Rabb., 65–70.

[20] Notes for a history of the censorship of Hebrew books will be found in M. Steinschneider's article, 'Jüdische Typographie u. jüd. Buchhandel,' in Ersch and Gruber's *Allgem. Encyclopädie II*, vol. 28, p. 30; Zunz, 'Die Censur hebräischer Werke,' *HBg*, I (1858), 42–44 (=*Schriften*, III, 239–241, Berlin 1876); the same, *Die Ritus des synagogalen Gottesdienstes*, Berlin, 1859, 147–149, 222–225; M. Steinschneider, *HBg*, VI (1863), 68–70. Especially important: M. Mortara, 'Die Censur hebräischer Bücher in Italien u. der Canon purificationis (ספר הזקוק),' *HBg*, V (1862), 72–77, 96–101. G. Sacerdote, 'Deux Index expurgatoires de livres hébreux,' *REJ*, XXX (1895), 257–280; W. Popper, *The Censorship of Hebrew Books*, New York 1899 (156); N. Porges, 'Der hebräische Index expurgatorius,' *Berliner-Festschrift*, 273–295. Joseph Jacobs, *JE*, III, 642–652. Lists of censors have been given by Steinschneider, *HBg*, V, 125–128; Ad. Neubauer, *Catalogue of the Hebrew Mss. in the Bodl. Library*, p. 1099. Comp. also Fr. Heinr. Reusch, *Der Index der verbotenen Bücher*, I, Bonn 1883 and A. Berliner's publication referred to above, p. 000.

[21] See above p. 275 top.

[22] Comp. Steinschn., *Cat. Bodl.*, No. 1409; Rabb., 75; *REJ*, LXIII, 300–303.

[23] Comp. Max Freudenthal, 'Zum Jubiläum des ersten Talmuddrucks n Deutschland,' *MGWJ* (1898), 80ff., 134ff., 180ff., 229ff., 236, 278ff.; 1900, 282f. Documents with regard thereto have been published by B. Pick in *Hoffmann-Festschr.*, 175–190.

[24] The parts printed already in Amsterdam are here printed once more, 1721–22.

[25] P. 98.

[26] See W. Bacher, *Theol. Literaturzeit.*, 1910, No. 6; A. Marx, *JQR*, N. S., 279–85.

[27] In the year 5391 of Creation (1631 C. E.) a Jewish Assembly of Elders n Poland issued a circular letter which read as follows: "Having learned that many Christians have taken great pains to master the tongue in which our books are written, we enjoin you under the threat of the great ban to publish in no new edition of the Mishna or the Gemara anything that refers to Jesus of Nazareth. . .If you will not diligently heed this letter, but run counter thereto and continue to publish our books in the same manner as heretofore, you might bring over us and yourselves still greater sufferings than in previous times. . .We therefore command you that when you publish a new edition of these books the passages referring to Jesus of Nazareth be omitted and the space be filled out by a small circle. The rabbis and teachers will know how

the youth is to be instructed by word of mouth." After Ch. Leslie, *A Short and Easy Method with the Jews*, London, 1812, 2 f. Also in Des Mousseaux, *Le Juif*, Paris, 1869, 100. However, the authenticity of this document is a matter of debate, *JbJLG*, III, 92 f.

[28] See above p. 278, n. 2.

[29] Comp. Rabb., Ma'amar, p. 24.

[30] Rabb., 25.

[31] Rabb., 85.

[32] However, in this edition several words and sentences which are missing in other recent prints have been restored.

[33] Rabb., 88. See in addition Eisenmenger, *Entdecktes Judenthum*, II, 636; Popper, 27–29.

[34] Of suchlike I possess the following four: a. קבוצת ההשמטות, sine loco et anno (102). Reprinted Cracow 1893: ספר חסרונות והוא קבוצת ההשמטות (92). b. Eliezer Moses ben Menahem Mendel, ספר הֲשָׁבַת אֲבֵדָה, [Lemberg?] 1858 (32 pp.; on pp. 1–10 gaps due to censorship are collected). c. קונטרס למלאות חסרונות הש"ס, Königsberg, 1860 (108, 36). d. קונטרס אומר השכחה, 1861 fol. (20 leaves).

[35] So the leaves printed, Amst., 1708 by Simeon Shammash and his brother Isaac, on one side only, which were intended to be pasted in with the edition Frankf. o. O. and of which the Jewish Theological Seminary of America in New York City possesses a copy (*ZHBg* (1904), 127). Still further material may be obtained from *Diḳd.*—On the part of Christians: Chr. Schottgen, *Horae hebraicae et talmudicae*, II (Dresden, 1742), 839–871; H. L. Strack, *Jesus, die Häretiker u. die Christen nach den ältesten jüd. Angaben*, Leipzig, 1910 (88 a. 40).

NOTES TO CHAPTER X, § 1, P. 87

[1] Hirsch, p. 5, says that "the Talmud is the sole spring from which Judaism has flowed, the ground upon which Judaism rests, and the soul of life which shapes and sustains Judaism. As a matter of fact Judaism, as it is embodied in the phenomenon of the Jewish people so consequential to world history, and as it manifests itself in mental and moral faculties and virtues which even its enemies dare not deny, is in every respect a product of the talmudic teaching and of the education and culture guided and nursed by it: the conscious walk amidst all the change of times and of fortunes, the patient and confident

perseverance despite bitterest and most trying suffering, the power of religious conviction which makes for ready self-sacrifice . . .; the sense of duty which is exemplified in obedience faithful to prince and magistrates, in wishing well and doing well by one's compatriots of another faith . . .; the mental interest and the mental endowment . . .; the personal virtues of moderation, of industry, of benevolence, of thrift and at the same time of liberality; the . . . virtues of morality which even to this day causes a Jewish name to be accounted a rarity in the list of gross crimes against life, chastity and property; the virtues of family life, of happy relations among husbands and wives, among parents and children, of children to parents and to brothers and sisters; the communal life . . .; all these average peculiarities of the Jewish character which certainly do not discredit it, . . . have been formed solely by the Talmud, so much so that since the modern age has more or less alienated itself from the Talmud there has been a noticeable impairment of these very qualities."

[2] *Le Judaisme ou la vérité sur le Talmud*, Mühlhausen, 1859; German translation: *Das Judentum oder die Wahrheit über den T.*, Basel, 1860 (151).

[3] *Der T. Zwei Reden.* Vienna, 1865 (33). *Der Talmudjude.* [4] *Reden.* Vienna, 1882–83 (58).

[4] *Der T.*, Vienna, 1866 (20).

[5] *The T.*, appeared first in the *Quarterly Review*, CXXIII, No. 246 (October 1867); reprinted in *Literary Remains*, London, 1874, 1–58.

[6] *Über den T., Vortrag.* Würzburg, 1875 (44).

[7] *Meine in Veranlassung eines Processes abgegebenen Gutachten über den T.*, Breslau, 1877 (33).

[8] ימין צדקי, Warsaw, 1881.

[9] *Über die Beziehung des Talmuds zum Judentum u. zu der sozialen Stellung seiner Bekenner*, Frankf. o. M., 1884 (38).

[10] *Der T.*, Marburg, 1887 (14).

[11] *Der Geist des T.*, Budapest, 1887 (240).

[12] חיי היהודי על פי התלמוד, Warsaw, 1889, 2d ed., 1893 (160).

[13] *Was lehrt der T.? Rede.* Frankf. o. M., 1892 (47).

[14] *Zwei Reden über den T.*, Trier, 1892 (47).

[15] *Der wahre Talmudjude*, Berlin, 1893 (165), German adaptation of Ssuwalski's publication.

[16] *Gutmeinung über den T. der Hebräer.* Verfasst von Kar Fischer, k. k. Zensor, Revisor u. Translator im hebräischen Fache zu Prag. (From a manuscript of the year 1802.) Vienna 1883 (112). On Fischer see *MGWJ* (1918).

[17] *Der Thalmud.* Zurich, 1879 (40).

[18] *Gutmeinung*, p. 15–24.

[19] *Populärwissenschaftl. Blätter zur Belehrung über das Judentum*, V (1885), 203–206; VI (1886), 206–208, 230–232.

[20] *Beiträge z. Geschichte der hebr. u. aram. Studien*, Munich, 1884.

[21] *Inhalt des Talmuds u. seine Autorität*, nebst einer geschichtlichen Einleitung. Pressburg, 1857 (201).

[22] *Der T. vom Standpunkte des modernen Judentums.* Berlin, 1881 (52).

[23] Johann Andrea Eisenmengers . . . *Entdecktes Judenthum*, Oder Gründlicher u. Wahrhaffter Bericht, Welchergestalt die verstockte Juden die Hochheilige Dreyeinigkeit, Gott Vater, Sohn u. Heiligen Geist, erschrecklicher Weise lästern u. verunehren, . . . die Christliche Religion spöttlich durchziehen . . . Dabey noch viele andere . . . Dinge u. Grosse Irrthümer der Jüdischen Religion u. Theologie, wie auch Viel lächerliche u. kurtzweilige Fabeln u. andere ungereimte Sachen an den Tag kommen; Alles aus ihren eigenen, u. zwar sehr vielen, mit grosser Mühe u. unverdrossenem Fleiss durchlesenen Büchern, mit Anziehung der Hebräischen Worte, u. deren treuen Übersetzung in die Teutsche Sprach, kräfftiglich erwiesen . . . Allen Christen zur treuhertzigen Nachricht verfertigt. 2 voll. 4to Frankf. o. M., 1700 (998 a. 1108 pp.).

[24] On Eisenmenger's book and person see J. Schudt, *Jüdische Merckwürdigkeiten* (1714 ff.) I, 426–438; III, 1 to 8; IV, Continuation 1, 285–287; a. Contin. 3, 4 f., and especially: Anton Theod. Hartmann, *Johann Andreas Eisenmenger u. seine jüdischen Gegner in geschichtlich literarischen Erörterungen kritisch beleuchtet.* Parchim, 1834 (40). For other opinions on Eisenmenger by Joh. Franz Budde, O. G. Tychsen, Joseph Bamberger, Chr. B. Michaelis see K. de Cholewa Pawlikowski, *Der T.*, Regensburg, 1866, 331–333. Comp. in addition: L. Löwenstein, 'Der Prozess Eisenmenger,' Magazin, 1891, 209–240.

[25] *Der Talmudjude*, Munich, 1871; 6th ed., 1877 (124)—a piece of plagiarism from Eisenmenger's work, spiteful and mendacious. The same author, *Franz Delitzsch u. die Judenfrage*, 2d ed., Prague, 1881 (155 pp.).—On Rohling see H. L. Strack, *Das Blut im Glauben u. Aberglauben der Menschheit*, 8th ed., Munich, 1900, 109–120.

[26] *Blicke in's Talmudische Judenthum.* Nach den Forschungen [!?] von Dr. Konrad Martin, Bischof von Paderborn, dem christl. Volke enthüllt, Pad., 1876 (96).

[27] *Christianus in Talmude Judaeorum sive rabbinicae doctrinae de Christianis secreta*, St. Petersburg, 1892 (130).

[28] E. g. Ernst Friedrich Hess, *Juden-Geissel*, Frieslar, 1589; Fr. S. Brentz, *Jüdischer Abgestreiffter Schlangenbalg*, Nuremberg, 1614.

[29] *Der Juden Thalmud fürnembster Inhalt und Widerlegung*, Goslar, 1609.

[30] Dr. Justus, *Judenspiegel*, 4th ed., Paderborn, 1883 (88); the same author, *Talmudische 'Weisheit.' 400 höchst interessante märchenhafte Aussprüche der Rabbinen*, Paderb., 1884 (67). On the author, Ahron Brimann, see H. L. Strack, *Das Blut*, 114 f.

[31] *Rohling's Talmudjude beleuchtet*, Leipzig, 1881; 7th ed., 1881 (120).

[32] *Zur Judenfrage nach den Akten des Prozesses Rohling-Bloch*, 3d ed., Leipzig, 1886 (199 pp.). The matter put together one-sidedly, but well; useful also because the author parallels that which is pointed out as offensive in Jewish literature by corresponding utterances of Roman Catholic, specifically Jesuit authorities.

NOTES TO CHAPTER X, § 2, P. 88

[1] See above, p. 20, 21.

[2] F. Perles, *Jüdische Skizzen*, Berlin, 1912, p. 108: "In this lecture hall more than 1500 masters mentioned by name, great and small, make their appearance. The keenest dialectic reasoning confronts us in their discussions; but we miss in them the calm, clarified development of a thought. Also esthetically considered the Talmud has a formlessness which is almost repellant. Abruptly one passes from one subject to another. Unessential matters are frequently treated at too great a length. Without stops runs the flood of speech and counterspeech with the least inkling as to where a question or an exclamation begins, where a statement or an ironical rejection is in hand."

[3] Only three times: Pe'a 3.6; Shebiith 9.5; Yeb. 4.13 והלכה כדברי.—Nidda 1.3: The Halakah is as R. Eliezer. Keth. 77a: Joḥanan said: In all places in which Rabban Simeon ben Gamaliel teaches in our Mishna the Halakah is according to him barring three instances . . . Ḥul. 75b: Ulla said: Wherever Simeon Shezuri teaches in our Mishna the Halakah is according to him. A. Z. 49a (bis): Rab Judah said in the name of Samuel: The Halakah is as Jose.—Details on this subject in the methodology composed by Malachi Kohen, *Yad Mal'aki*, Part I, Leghorn, 1767; Berlin, 1856.

[4] See above, p. 77.

[5] See chap. XIV, § 5c.

[6] See D. Hoffmann, *Der Schulchan-Aruch*, 2d ed., Berlin, 1894, 38f.

NOTES TO CHAPTER X, § 3, P. 89

[1] For the first time, probably, we meet with a statement to this effect in the foreword of Maimonides' 'Guide of the Perplexed:' אין משיבין על הדרוש. However, the Gaons Sherira and Hai had denied authority to the Haggadah (אין סומכין על דברי אגדה): see Aboab's introduction to Menorath ha-maor, Eshkol, ed. Auerbach, II, 47 and Moses ibn Danan's Kelale ha-Talmud (Ms.), VII, chap. 18. Yom Tob Lipmann Heller says on Ber. 5.4: אין למדין הלכה ממדרש רבות. A different significance attaches to the words of Mar Samuel, Palest. Pe'a 2.17a: אין למדין לא מן ההלכות ולא מן ההגדות ולא מן התוספות אלא מן התלמוד.

[2] Siphre, Deut. 11.22 (§ 49).

[3] Ḥagiga 14a.

[4] 'Der alte Widerspruch gegen die H.', *Maybaum-Festschrift*, 164–172.

[5] Palest. Hor. 3.48c, with reference to Eccles. 6.2.

[6] *Über die Beziehung*, etc., p. 4f.

[7] From this 'of the character of those' it follows that 'results' may be found also outside the 'Codes.' Nor does Hirsch say that everything in the Codes is a 'result.'

[8] *Über den Talmud*, Würzburg, 1875.

[9] *Die Schrift des Lebens*, II, Strassburg, 1877, p. 223, 464, 69, 436. See also p. 458f., 410.

[10] *Judaism, its Doctrines and Duties*, 10th ed., Cincinnati, 1886, p. 5f.

[11] 'Zur Charakteristic des Talmuds,' *Weltbewegende Fragen*, II, 1, Leipzig 1869, 349 to 416.

[12] *Jüdische Skizzen*, Berlin, 1912, p. 110f., 112f.

NOTES TO CHAPTER XI, § 1, P. 93

[1] See above p. 9f., 23f.

[2] Is. Unna in Wohlgemuth's *Jeschurun*, VI (1919), 459–467, where Levit. 1.13, 5; 2.11 are cited as examples.

[3] In his commentary התורה והמצוה on Midrash Siphra, Bucharest 1860.

[4] Literature: L. Dobschütz, *Die einfache Bibelexegese der Tannaim mit besonderer Berücksichtigung ihres Verhältnisses zur einfachen Bibelexegese der Amoraim*, Breslau, 1893 (51). Hamburger, II, 181–212 (article 'Exegese'). H. Almquist, *Mechilta Bo. Pesachtraktaten*, Lund, 1892, introd., 21–37. D. Hoffmann, *Einleitung in die halachischen Midraschim*, Berlin, 1887, 3–5.

Georg Aicher, *Das Alte Testament in der Mischna*, Freiburg, 1906 (17 a. 181) (see L. Blau, *MGWJ* (1907), 569 to 589; W. Bacher, *JQR* (1907), 598–606).

H. S. Hirschfeld, *Halachische Exegese*, Berlin, 1840 (484); *Die haggadische Exegese*, Berlin, 1847 (21 a. 546). M. Mielziner, *Introduction to the Talmud*, 1894, 117–264 (hermeneutics, terminology, methodology). M. L. Malbim compiled in the introduction to his commentary on the Siphra (see above) 613 rules of exposition. Hayyim Jacob ben Ṣebi (of Oshmiany), Wilna, 1877 (78), enumerates the halakic rules and indicates the passages in which they are treated of in the Talmuds and the older commentaries.—Comp. also S. Waldberg, ספר דרכי השנויים, Lemberg, 1870 (83 leaves).

NOTES TO CHAPTER XI, § 2, P. 93

[1] See above p. 10, 24 and chap. XIII, § 2.—The 7 Middoth have been handed down in Tosephta Sanh. 7 end (ed. Zuck. 427): introduction to Siphra, at the end (ed. Weiss, fol. 3a); Aboth deRabbi Nathan, ch. 37. Comp. H. Grätz, *MGWJ*, I, 156–162; Z. Frankel, *Über palästin. u. alexandrin. Schriftforschung*, Breslau, 1854, 15–17; Derenb. 187f.; G. Aicher, *Das A. T. in der Mischna*, Breslau, 1906, 141–148: J. Z. Lauterbach, *JE*, XII, 32f.

[2] A more accurate pronunciation would probably be קַל 'Lightness.' The current pronunciation avoids a confusion with קוֹל 'voice.'

[3] Examples: B. B. 9.7; Sanh. 6.5; Aboth 1.5. With reference to Gen. R. 92 י' ק"ו בתורה (Torah = O. T.) the commentaries note that one may find easily 40 ק"ו in the O. T.—Comp. Andr. Georg Wähner, *Antiquitates Ebraeorum*, I (Göttingen 1743), 425–449; M. Mielziner, *The Hebrew Review*, I (Cincinnati, 1880), 41–53; Adolf Schwarz, *Der hermeneutische Syllogismus in der talmud. Litteratur*, Vienna, 1901 (192). Comp. Wachstein, *MGWJ* (1902), 53–62. Bacher, *Terminologie*, I, 172–174; II, 189f.

[4] גִּזְרָה? Ezek. 41.13 by the side of בנין.

[5] Examples: Ar. 4.4 concerning the dedication of persons, Levit. 27.7, 'And if it be from sixty years old and upward ששים שנה ומעלה, if it be a male, then thy valuation shall be fifteen shekels', is interpreted to the effect that if the man be precisely 60 years old the higher valuation of fifty shekels is still in force, and then from the employment of the identical word שנה in the preceding context the inference is drawn that likewise there by 'twenty years' etc. is meant not the mere attaining to this age, but the passing beyond it שנה שנה לגזרה שוה. Pes. 66a: Hillel said: The expression מוֹעֲדוֹ, its appointed

season, occurs with the Passover offering Num. 9.2 and with the Tamid offering Num. 28.2. The deduction is therefore to be made therefrom that just as the Tamid offering sets aside the Sabbath (the command to rest on the Sabbath) so does also the Passover offering set aside the Sabbath. Mek. on Exod. 21.27 (Friedm. 85b) 'לַחָפְשִׁי יְשַׁלְּחֶנּוּ he shall let him go free.' He shall give him a bill of manumission. Eliezer said: Here we meet with the verb שַׁלַּח, and so also further below (Deut. 24.1). As further below a bill (גֵּט, the bill of divorcement is meant) is spoken of, so also here a bill is intended. Other examples: A. Z. 3.6 (Lev. 11.10 a. Deut. 7.26); Besa 1.6; Ḳidd. 57a; Pes. 120b (as Exod. 12.12 'in that night' denotes 'before midnight,' so also 12.8); Mek. on Exod. 21.20 (Friedm. 83b).—See Wähner, *Antiqq. Ebr.*, I, 463–478. M. Plungian, ספר תל־פיות מאמר על הגז"ש הנמצאות בתלמוד בבלי, Wilna, 1849 (68); Hirschfeld, *MGWJ* (1879), 368–374. Adolf Schwarz, *Die hermeneutische Analogie in der talmud. Litteratur*, Karlsruhe, 1897 (193). Comp. L. Blau, *REJ*, XXXVI, 150–159. Ad. Schwarz, 'Latente δὶς λεγόμενα', *MGWJ* (1916), 348–368 (discusses 16 enthymematic ג"ש inferences). Bacher, *Terminologie*, I, 13–16; II, 27.

6 אָב for short instead of בֵּית אָב.

7 Bacher.—Examples: Siphre Deut. 17.2. כִּי יִמָּצֵא 'if there be found' is followed in verse 6 by 'at the mouth of two witnesses, or three witnesses.' This detail is made to apply by means of Binyan Ab to the other passages (Deut. 18.10; 22.22; 24.7) in which ימצא occurs in the same sense. Shab. 22a: It is taught: 'He shall pour out the blood, and cover it' (Levit. 17.13). Exactly as he pours it out [with the hand], so shall he cover it; he may not bury it in the ground with his foot; for the commandments are not to be treated with disrespect. [This last sentence is then applied further: it is unlawful to count money at the light of the Hanukkah lamp etc.] Rab Joseph said: אבוהון דכולהון דם the father of all these regulations is the blood, i. e. all the others are made to follow from that which is the rule with the covering of the blood.—Ad. Schwarz, *Die hermeneutische Induktion in der talmud. Literatur* (1. *Der Analogieschluss*; 2. *Der Induktionsschluss*). Vienna, 1909 (256). Comp. V. Aptowitzer, *MGWJ* (1911), 185–189; Bacher, *Terminologie*, I, 9–11; II, 21f.

8 Example: Mek. on Exod. 21.27 (Friedm. 85b): 'He shall let him go free for his tooth's sake.' One might infer therefrom that the master is obligated to let him go free on account of a milk-tooth. For that reason 'eye' (verse 26) is placed by the side thereof. Just as the eye does not grow again, so also a tooth is meant which does not grow again. One might still think that manu-

mission results only on account of the two specifically mentioned members, the eye and the tooth. Whence the proof that an injury of other members (which do not grow again) leads to manumission? Join both verses and apply the rule Binyan Ab. The tooth is not like the eye, and the eye is not like the tooth; but they resemble in that when they are injured no restitution is possible and that they are principal members which do not grow again. Hence, just as the slave is let go free on account of them, so also on account of all principal members which do not grow again.—Ad. Schwarz, *Die hermeneutische Antinomie in der talmud. Literatur*. Vienna, 1913 (211). Comp. V. Aptowitzer, *MGWJ* (1916), 174–181.

[9] See Shebu. 26a.—Adolf Schwarz, *Die hermeneutische Quantitätsrelation in der talmud. Literatur*, Vienna, 1916 (271). Bacher, *Terminologie*, I, 80f.; II, 83–85.

[10] יָצָא with בְּ of the price: is given out for . . ., is worth . . ., amounts to the same.—Bacher, *Terminologie*, I, 75f.; II, 81.

[11] Ad. Schwarz, *Der hermeneutische Kontext in der talmud. Literatur*, Vienna, 1921 (208); Bacher, *Terminologie*, I, 142f.

[12] Palest. Pes. 6.33a top (comp. also Tos. Pes. 4, Zuck., p. 162): Hillel is reported to have argued against the family Bathyra by means of Hekkesh, Ḳal wa-ḥomer and Gezera shawa.

[13] Bacher, *Terminologie*, I, 46; II, 57f. According to Rashi, B. Ḳ. 63bγ, ה' is the comparison of two neighboring verses.

NOTES TO CHAPTER XI, § 3, P. 95

[1] See p. 112.

[2] Siphre Num. 15.31 (112). Thus he rejects there the straining of the absolute infinitive הִכָּרֵת in front of the finite verb תִּכָּרֵת

[3] Ishm. 1 = H. 2; I. 3 = H. 3 a. 4; I. 4–11 are formed by cutting up H. 5; (see Bacher, Terminologie, I, 80f. The 11th rule of Ishmael (see also Bacher, *Terminologie*, I, 56 חדש, 57 חזר) has not met with general acceptance, see S. Horovitz, *Siphre*, introd., p. VII); I. 12 = H. 7. This Middah is referred to Ḥul. 63a as one of the '13 Middoth according to which the Torah is expounded,' but without naming Ishmael. The 6th Middah of Hillel is omitted. Joḥanan had pointed out (Shebu. 26a) that Ishmael was especially given to the employment of the Rule of the General and Particular.

[4] *Jeschurun*, VII (Frankf. o. M. 1861), 485ff. Comp. D. Hoffmann,

Israelit. Monatsschrift, Berlin, 1892, No. 5. According to H. Hausdorff-Baltimore, *JbJLG*, V, 382–384, he who gainsays it 'undermines the foundation of the Jewish religious structure'.

[5] In Wohlgemuth's *Jeschurun*, VI (Berlin 1919), 459.

[6] Already in the Mekiltha of Rabbi Simeon ben Johai on Exodus, edited by D. Hoffmann, Frankf. o. M., 1905, 117 (on 21.1) Ishmael enumerates the 13 Middoth according to which the Torah is expounded with the remark that they were delivered to Moses on Sinai.

[7] Comp. Weiss I, 9f.—Example: Mek. on Exod. 12.5 (Friedm. 4b): Akiba said: We read in Scripture (Deut. 16.2): 'Thou shalt sacrifice the Passover-offering unto the Lord צאן ובקר of the flock and the herd;' but elsewhere we read (Exod. 12.5): 'ye shall take it from the sheep, or from the goats מן הכבשים ומן העזים.' How are both verses to be maintained? Apply the rule: 'When two verses etc.' With a view thereto Scripture says (Exod. 12.21): 'Draw out, and take you lambs צאן according to your families, and kill the Passover lamb.' Hence lambs for the Passover-offering, not cattle. Ishmael said: Cattle for the Ḥagiga-offering. Comp. Siphre Deut. 16.2 (§ 129); Babyl. Men. 8. 6 a. Gemara 82b.

[8] Text with German translation in Pinner, *Berachoth*, fol. 17–20. Comp. besides Jeshu'ah ישועה Ha-levi (second half of the 15th century) הליכות עולם, § 212–254 (printed e. g. in Const. L'Empereur, *Clavis Talmudica*); Aaron ibn Ḥayyim in his commentary on Siphra, ס' קרבן אהרן, Venice, 1609ff., fol., 5–37a. Philip Aquinus (Wolf., *B. H.*, III, 928 ff., 645), *Veterum Rabbinorum in exponendo Pentateucho modi tredecim* (reproduced in D. Mill, *Catalecta Rabbinica*, Trajecti ad Rh. 1728 a. in Crenius, *Opuscula*, IV, Rotterdam, 1694, 419 to 448): Wähner, *Antiqq. Ebr.*, I, 422–425, 483–491 (No. 3), 497–503 (No. 4–6), 509 to 523 (No. 7–13); Bodenschatz, *Kirchliche Verfassung der heutigen Juden*, III, 237–246 (with examples); Derenb. 389–391; Weiss, II, 104ff.; M. Petuchowski, *Der Tanna Rabbi Ismael*, Frankf. o. M., 1894, 81–93; Ferd. Weber, *Jüdische Theologie*, 2d ed., Leipzig, 1897, 110 ff.; Mielziner, *Introduction to the Talmud*, 130–176. A Midrash on these Middoth has been edited by D. Hoffmann in the *Berliner-Festschrift*, Hebrew part, p. 55–71 (comp. *ZHBg* (1903), 173f.) A. Freimann enumerates 54 Hebrew commentaries on the 13 Middoth in *Schwarz-Festschrift*, 109–119. On the time when the Middoth and midrashic interpretation originated see the quite noteworthy publication by Moses Salomon, נתיב משה, Vienna, 1896 (31), especially p. 11, n. 1.

With regard to the other exegetical norms of Ishmael see Bacher, *Tannaiten*, I, 244–250 a. *Terminologie*, I, 43 (concerning the principle 'From that contained in a negative statement one may infer that which is the rule for the positive, and vice versa.')

NOTES TO CHAPTER XI, § 4, P. 95

[1] Ed. S. Schechter, I, Cambridge, 1902.

[2] Manuscript of the State Library at Berlin. The 32 Middoth according to the text of these two sources were published by Königsberger in the *Feilchenfeld-Festsschrift*; also reprinted under the title ל"ג בעומר, Berlin, 1907.

[3] See further Jeshu'ah Ha-levi, *Halikoth Olam*, 255–289; Wähner, *Antiqq. Ebr.*, I, 396–421; Pinner, *Berachoth*, introduction, fol. 20f.; Ṣebi Hirsch Katzenellenbogen, ספר נתיבות עולם, Wilna, 1822, with additions by Straschun, 1859; Wolf Einhorn, ספר מדרש תנאים, Wilna, 1838, 4to (94 leaves; comp. also his introduction to his commentary on Midrash Rabba, Wilna, 1853); J. Reifmann, משיב דבר Vienna, 1866 (72); Isr. Hildesheimer, in *Bericht über die öffentl. Rabbinatsschule zu Eisenstadt*, Halberstadt, 1869, offers the text according to ספר הכריתות with Hebrew commentary; Bacher, *Tannaiten*, II, 293–298 (discusses the relation to the rules of Ishmael a. Akiba); M. Schwab, *Le Talmud de Jérusalem traduit*, 2d ed., I, p. lxvii f.; H. Almqvist, *Mechilta Bo*, introd., 37–39; B. Königsberger, *Monatsblätter für Vergangenheit u. Gegenwart des Judentums*, I, Berlin, 1890 f., 3–10, 90–94, prints the text of the first eleven sections. Leo Bardowicz, *Die Abfassungszeit der Boraitha der 32 Normen für die Auslegung der heil. Schrift*, Berlin, 1913 (110): the compilation dates from gaonic times; No. 14 a. 28 are met with for the first time in amoraic, No. 9 a. 11 in gaonic times; B. Halper, *JQR*, N. S., VI, 220–223, assents in the main: No. 9 a. 11 are met with for the first time in Saadia, but then quite frequently. On the other hand, V. Aptowitzer (*MGWJ* (1916), 181 to 183, a. *Schwarz-Festsschrift*, 121–132) characterizes the thesis of Bard. as 'radical, and entirely without foundation.' S. Krauss (*Schwarz-Festschrift*, 572) points out that Rashi, Abraham ben David and Zacuto read in the title of the Baraitha not האגדה נִדְרֶשֶׁת but התורה נ׳, and concludes that the 32 Middoth 'apply quite as much to halakic interpretation' (Note that Judah Hadassi likewise has: Haggadah). See, however, our remarks in the individual sections.

[4] Ḥul. 89a.

[5] Tos. Shebu. 1. 7 (Zuck. 446), comp. Shebu. 26a a. Ḥag. 12bγ. Pes. 22b Simeon העמסוני or Nehemiah הע׳ is mentioned as Akiba's predecessor in this mode of exposition, see Bacher, *Tannaiten*, I, 62f.

[6] B. Ḳ. 117b.

[7] Gen. 1.1 'God created the heaven את השמים'; Gen. R.: including the sun, moon a. planets. Exod. 18, 18 'Thou wilt wear away גַּם־אתה, and this people that is with thee;' Mek. (Friedm. 59b): אתה i. e. Moses, גם i. e. Aaron. Exod. 19.9 'that the people may hear when I speak with thee, and may also believe thee וְגַם־בך יאמינו for ever;' Mek. (Friedm. 63b): also the prophets that will rise after thee. Halakic. Ar. 1.4: When a woman condemned to death is with child, the execution is not to be postponed until she is delivered. Gemara 7a cites in support thereof Deut. 22.22 ומתו גַּם שניהם then they (the adulterers) shall both of them die, i. e. the man and the woman with the embryo. Comp. further: Deut. 26. 13 גם, M. Sh. 5.10: Num. 18.28 גם, Terum. 1.1.

[8] Gen. 7.23: 'And Noah only אַךְ was left' is interpreted in Gen. R. to mean that Noah was not left unhurt, but rather that as he groaned by reason of the cold he spat blood. Eliezer (ben Hyrcanus) thinks that once Noah failed to feed the lion in due time and was therefore wounded by the animal. Comp. also Gen. 26.29 רק טוב, Gen. R. 64. Halakic example. Deut. 16.15 והיית אַךְ שמח 'and thou shalt be altogether joyful.' Sukka 48b: That includes the eve of the last festival day. Perhaps also that of the first festival day? This one is excluded by אך.

[9] I Sam. 17.36 'Thy servant smote both גַּם אֶת־ the lion and גַּם the bear.' The three particles גם, את, גם indicate that three further beasts, hence altogether five, are meant. Comp. Bacher, *Tannaiten*, II, 210, 448. Differently in the Halakah: אֵין ר' אַחַר ר' אֶלָּא לְמַעֵט, one addition on the top of another signifies exclusion. Men. 89a, Siphra on Levit. 7.12; Siphre Num. 19.5 (§ 124).

[10] E. g. Num. 12.2 רַק אַךְ.—As regards Halakah the rule is אֵין מ' אַחַר מ' אֶלָּא לְרַבּוֹת, one exclusion on the top of another signifies amplification, comp. B. B. 14, where I Kings 8.9 אֵין בארון רק שני לחות האבנים (there was nothing in the ark save the two tables of stone) is interpreted: there were in the ark also the fragments of the first tables. Comp. further Meg. 23b; B. Ḳ. 86b on Deut. 19.4 f.; Sanh. 15a (Levit. 17); Palest. Pe'a 6.19d (Levit. 19.9) a. Palest. Yeb. 12.12b (Levit. 23.42). Mak. 2.3, likewise, Meir decides on the basis of this rule: גֹּלֶה.

[11] See Hillel 11 a. Bacher, *Terminologie*, I, 174.

[12] See Hillel 2, 3.

[13] The Baraitha mentions two examples: I Chr. 17.5 where we must supply אֶל־מִשְׁכָּן after וּמִמִּשְׁכָּן and II Sam. 13.39 where נֶפֶשׁ should be inserted after וַתְּכַל. Siphre Deut. 21.11 (§ 211): 'and seest among the captives אֵשֶׁת יפת תאר a woman of goodly form,' even though she be a married woman

אעפ״י שהיא אשת איש. The same Ḳid. 21b end. Midrash Leḳaḥ Ṭob on Deut. 21.11: 'In all passages where we meet with אשת there follows of necessity a complement, e. g. אשת כסילות Prov. 9. This shows that in the present passage (where no complement in the genitive follows) the meaning is: even though she be a married woman.' Ps. 68.31 גער חַיַּת קָנֶה עֲדַת is interpreted by Jose b. Ḥalaphta in Pes. 118b to mean: נעור חיה וקְנֵה לְךָ עֵדָה; comp. Bacher, *Tannaiten*, II, 187, 407. Prov. 18.5 see Yoma 87a.

[14] Gen. R. 89 Judah (b. El'ai) says: 'Strictly speaking there were to come over Egypt 14 years of famine' (Gen. 41.3, 6); Nehemiah rejoins: 'Strictly speaking 28 years were determined upon: for Pharaoh saw in his dream 14 years and he repeated this number in his communication to Joseph.' Sanh. 1.6 it is proved from the duplicated הָעֵדָה Num. 34.24 f. that a lesser court of justice should consist of 23 members (עֵדָה = 10 according to Num. 14.27. To 2 x 10, 3 more are required for another reason). Ḥul. 115b, Baraitha: 'Thou shalt not seethe a kid in its mother's milk,' Exod. 23.19; 34.26; Deut. 14.26; Once to forbid eating, once to forbid benefiting and once to forbid seething. Akiba in the Mishna, Ḥul. 8.4, on the other hand, would have it that by the threefold repetition of the word 'kid' it is indicated that fowl עוף, game חַיָּה and unclean beasts do not come under the prohibition on biblical ground. Mek. on Exod. 16.25 (Friedm. 50a): 'Moses said: Eat that to-day; for to-day is a Sabbath unto the Lord; to-day ye shall not find it in the field.' Zereḳa said: From the circumstance that 'to-day' is repeated three times it follows that one must eat three meals on the Sabbath; comp. Shab. 117b. Mek. on Exod. 22.7 f. (Friedm. 92a), because אלהים is repeated three times, Josiah finds therein proof for the regulation that in civil suits three judges pass sentence; comp. Sanh. 3b.

[15] E. g. II Chr. 30.18f. Mak. 3.10 the words במספר: ארבעים Deut. 25.2 f. are joined together (see above p. 261, n. 57). Mek. Exod. 13.3 (Friedm. 19b), Jose Ha-gelili proves by joining ולא יֵאָכֵל חָמֵץ to הַיּוֹם of the following verse that in Egypt Israel partook of unleavened bread only on that day; comp. Abr. Geiger, *Nachgelassene Schriften*, IV, 30. Siphra Levit. 19.10 (Weiss 87d), by connecting, against the context and the athnaḥ, לא תְלַקֵּט with the following לֶעָנִי the deduction is arrived at that the owner must not be partial to one poor man over others by helping him glean; comp. Giṭ. 12a. Siphra Levit. 19.32 (Weiss 91a) the question how it may be proved that the aged must not molest their fellowmen is answered by joining זָקֵן (which word has an athnaḥ) to the following ויראת מאלהיך: 'O old man, thou shalt fear thy God.' Ḥul. 60b ליי׳ is joined closely to לחטאת (a sin-offering to be offered for the

Lord). Comp. Aptowitzer, *Schwarz-Festschr.*, 128–130. Bacher, *Terminologie*, I, 131.

[16] Comp. Hillel 7.—Sanh. 74a the proposition is discussed that when one is threatened with death one may commit any sin save idolatry, incest and murder. With reference to the two latter sins Judah Ha-nasi had remarked: That is exactly as 'when a man riseth against his neighbor, and slayeth him' Deut. 22.26. 'What do we gather from the comparison to the murderer? That which furnishes instruction receives instruction in turn. Exactly as in the case of the betrothed damsel (22.25) so it is likewise permissible when confronted by a murderer to save him (that is pursued) by the life (we should say: by the death) of the pursuer הַצִּיל בְּנַפְשׁוֹ. And let us compare (מַקִּישׁ) the betrothed damsel (i. e. the committal of rape with such a one) to the murderer: as we are enjoined to suffer death rather than commit murder, so we should suffer death rather than rape a betrothed damsel (according to the reading יֵהָרֵג ואל יעבור, see Yoma 82aγ).' Bacher, *Terminologie*, I, 95; II, 97.

[17] Comp. Hillel 5.—Mek. on Exod. 12.43 (Friedm. 16b): Some sections begin with the General and conclude with the Particular; with others it is the reverse. 'Ye shall be unto Me a kingdom of priests' (Exod. 19.6) is the Particular; 'these are the words which thou shalt speak' (ibid.) is the General. This is the statute of the law' (Num. 19.2) is the General; 'that they bring thee a red heifer' (ibid.) is the Particular. 'This is the ordinance of the Passover' (Exod. 12.43) is the General; 'no alien' is the Particular. With the General and (then) the Particular there is in the General only that which is in the Particular. Bacher, *Terminologie*, I, 81, 112.

[18] E. g. Deut. 32.2 the Torah with the rain. This rule is not applied in the Halakah. Bacher, *Terminologie*, I, 3, 198.

[19] See Ishmael 13.

[20] E. g. Mal. 2.16 'the God of Israel,' which expression does not occur elsewhere in the post-exilic prophets Haggai, Zechariah and Malachi. An halakic example: Siphre Num. 15.18 (§ 110) 'בבאכם אל הארץ In your coming into the land.' Ishmael: The expression for Israel's coming into the land is here different (נשתנה הכתוב) from what it is in other passages of Scripture. Elsewhere we read: 'and when ye come' or 'when the Lord will bring thee.' The divergent expression here is to teach thee that Israel was obligated to set apart Ḥalla (Num. 15.20; see above p. 33) immediately after their entrance into the land. Bacher, *Terminologie*, I, 70.

[21] Gen. 2.8, description of the Paradise, is to be supplemented from Ezek.

28.13; Num. 3, where there are no prescriptions concerning the priests' divisions, from I Chron. 24.19. Bacher, *Terminologie*, I, 156.

[22] E. g. Deut. 23.11 'that which chanceth by night,' because the accident had in mind is likely to occur most frequently by night. Siphre on Deut. 20.5f. (§ 194f.): 'What man is there that hath built a new house, and hath not dedicated it? let him be absolved from military service.' Though Scripture speaks here only of building it has in mind likewise inheriting, buying, or receiving as a gift. 'He that hath planted a vineyard, and hath not used the fruit thereof, shall be absolved from military service.' Though Scripture speaks here only of planting it has in mind likewise inheriting, buying, or receiving as a gift. Bacher, *Terminologie*, I, 39.

[23] Ps. 97.11 'light' is to be supplied in the second and 'gladness' in the first half of the verse. Mek. on Exod. 21.18 (Friedm. 82b): 'If one smite the other with a stone, or with his fist.' R. Nathan says: 'He compares the stone to the fist and the fist to the stone. As the stone must be ponderous enough to kill, so also the fist; and as the fist becomes known, so must also the stone become known. When therefore the stone is mingled among other stones and when even one stone is too small to cause death, the slayer goes free.' Bacher, *Terminologie*, I, 23, 55.

[24] Deut. 33.7 does not refer to Judah, but to Simeon. Siphre on Num. 18.15 (§ 118, Friedm. fol. 38b): 'Howbeit the first-born of man shalt thou surely redeem, and the first-born of unclean beasts shalt thou redeem.' From the wording one might infer: 'of all unclean beasts;' but we read Exod. 13.13: 'every firstling of an ass thou shalt redeem with a lamb,' accordingly of an ass, not of other unclean beasts. Or may we perchance so understand it: 'Only the firstling of an ass thou shalt redeem with a lamb, but that of all other unclean beasts with garments and utensils?' No; for we read in still another passage (Exod. 34.20): 'and the firstling of an ass thou shalt redeem with a lamb.' This duplication (comp. No. 10) teaches that one may redeem only with a lamb, and not with garments and utensils. For what purpose, then, is it said 'Howbeit . . . shalt thou surely redeem, etc.' (Num. 18.15)? If the significance עִנְיָן is not that (first-born) unclean beasts are redeemed, then apply it so that unclean beasts may be dedicated for the purpose of repairing the Temple and then again redeemed. Bacher, *Terminologie*, I, 143.

[25] Comp. Ps. 92.13 where the righteous is compared to the fruit-bearing (but shadeless) palm-tree and to the shady cedar (which, however, bears no eatable fruit). Ar. 9.7 (comp. Levit. 25.31 a. Gemara 33a): Houses in villages have the advantages of houses in walled cities and the advantages of fields:

they may be redeemed, and, moreover, they may be redeemed at once, and they may be redeemed during all the 12 months like houses, and they revert in the year of the jubilee to their owners and money is deducted (for the time during which they have been used as is the case with fields). As to הִקִּישׁ see Bacher, *Terminologie*, I, 45.

[26] Ps. 38.2 supply אַל in front of תְּיַסְּרֵנִי. Mek. on Exod. 23.1 (Friedm. 98b). The words אַל־תָּשֶׁת יָדְךָ עִם־רָשָׁע לִהְיֹת עֵד חָמָס are interpreted by Nathan as if they read: אל־תשת ידך עם־רשע להיות עד ואל־תשת ידך להיות עד חמס, comp. Sanh. 27a. As to הוֹכִיחַ see Bacher, *Terminologie*, I, 40.

[27] Only in the Haggadah. Siphre on Deut. 11.12 (§ 40): 'A land which the Lord thy God careth for.' Rabbi said: Doth He care for this land only, and not for all lands? We certainly read Job 38.26: 'to cause it to rain on a land where no man is, on the wilderness, wherein there is no man.' What then does this word signify, 'a land which the Lord thy God careth for?' Because of this His caring He cares for other lands beside theirs. Similarly Ps. 121 reads: 'Behold, He that keepeth Israel doth neither slumber nor sleep.' Does He keep only Israel, and not rather all beings? For we read Job 12.10: 'In His hand is the soul of every living thing, and the breath of all mankind. What does therefore the word 'He that keepeth Israel' signify? For the sake of this keeping He keeps all things beside them. Similarly I Kings 9.3 reads: 'Mine eyes and My heart shall be there continually.' Are they only there? For we read Zechar. 4.10: 'The eyes of the Lord run to and fro through the whole earth' a. Prov. 15.3: 'The eyes of the Lord are in every place, keeping watch upon the evil and upon the good.' What does the word 'Mine eyes and My heart shall be there continually' signify? As if it were possible that they should be only there! Rather, for the sake of being there they are everywhere.

[28] Comp. Josh. 2.1 the specific stressing of Jericho.

[29] Shab. 70a: The prohibition Exod. 35.3 to kindle fire on the Sabbath is implied already in 35.2 (whosoever doeth any work therein shall be put to death). Why is it stressed (יצתה)? In order to compare therewith and to say to thee: Just as one becomes guilty (חַיָּב obligated to bring an offering) by kindling fire, which is a main piece of labor, so also one becomes guilty by performing any other single main piece of labor.

[30] B. Ḳ. 60a (on Exod. 22.5 כי־תצא אש ומצאה קצים וְנֶאֱכַל גדיש). R. Jonathan said: Judgment comes only when there are transgressors in the world, and it begins with the rigteous. For we read: 'If fire break out, and catch in thorns.' Accordingly, fire breaks out when there are thorns. And it begins with the righteous. For we read: 'so that the shocks of corn are

consumed,' not 'it consumes the shocks of corn.' Bacher, *Terminologie*, I, 122.

31 E. g. to the 40 days Num. 13.25 correspond the 40 years Num. 14.34. This rule is the 27th and מַעַל the 28th (not the other way as in most prints), see Bacher, *MGWJ* (1896), 20; comp. *Terminologie*, I, 124f.

32 In later terminology לשון נופל על לשון. E. g. Num. 21.9 נְחַשׁ נְחֹשֶׁת. Bacher, *Terminologie*, I, 111f.

33 *γραμματεία* from *γραμματεύς* 'notarius' or directly formed from *γράμμα* with an easing metathesis of consonants (not equal to *γεωμετρία*).

34 Midrash Lam. beginning: Ben Azzai said, By the first word איכה of Lamentations it is implied that the Israelites were not carried into captivity until they denied the One א God, the ten י commandments, the law of circumcision given after twenty כ generations and the five ה books of the Torah. The number 318 (servants of Abraham) Gen. 14.14 is made in Pesiḳtha K. 70b to stand for אליעזר Eliezer; the Epistle of Barnabas finds therein an allusion to the cross T=300 and Jesus IH=18. In the same Pesiḳtha 176a, also Yoma 20a, it is observed that the numerical value of הַשָּׂטָן is 364 (for 364 days in the year Satan has dominion over Israel, but not on the Day of Atonement). The numerical value of כּוּשִׁית is tantamount to יְפַת מַרְאֶה, Targ. Onkelos Num. 12.1. Shab. 70a on Exod. 35.1 אלה הדברים: 'Words, the words, these are the words.' These are the 39 classes of labor which were specified to Moses on Sinai (as forbidden on the Sabbath). The plural דברים signifies 2, the article adds something (hence 2+1), and אלה has the numerical value of 36. Nazir 4b (=Taan. 17a; Sanh. 22b): The Nazirate lasts ordinarily 30 days. Matthena said: How is this to be proved? We read Num. 6. 5 קדש יהיה 'he shall be holy;' יהיה has the numerical value of 30.

35 E. g. Jer. 51.1 כַּשְׂדִּים=לֵב קָמָי according to the alphabet את בש גר. Comp. Bacher, *Terminologie*, I, 127 f.; 27 f.; C. Levias, *JE*, V, 589–592.

36 *νοταρικόν* (from 'notarius,' tachygraph).

37 E. g. Num. 22.32 ירט is explained in Siphra (Weiss 12d) as יָרְאתָה רָאֲתָה נָטְתָה. In the letters of the word נמרצת I Kings 2. 8, according to Shab. 105a a. Midrash Ps. 3.3, are implied the imprecations employed by Shimei: נוֹאֵף adulterer, מוֹאָבִי Moabite, רוֹצֵחַ murderer, צוֹרֵר oppressor, תּוֹעֵבָה abomination. The school of Ishmael interprets Shab. 105a=Men. 66b כַּרְמֶל as כר מלא a full cushion (ears which are as full of corn as a cushion is full of feathers). Akiba breaks up for halakic purposes יקימנו Num. 30.14 (Ned. 87b); for haggadic purposes בצלצח I Sam. 10.2 'in a bright protection' (Yalḳuṭ on Sam. § 109). Comp. Bacher, *Terminologie*, I, 125–127; II, 124; M. Seligsohn,

JE, IX, 339 f. On R. Ishmael with reference to Levit. 20.14 (Siphra ed. Weiss 92c) see L. Blau, *REJ*, LVII, 148. Likewise נ' denotes elliptic phraseology according to which a positive clause implies also the corresponding negative clause, e. g. Mek. on Exod. 20.12 (Friedm. 70a): If you do not honor your parents, your days will be shortened.

[38] I Sam. 3.3 the words 'in the temple of the Lord' go with 'was not yet gone out,' although 'and Samuel was laid down to sleep' intervenes. With regard to Levit. 1.15 'And the priest shall pinch off the head of the pigeon, and make it be consumed in smoke on the altar, and the blood thereof shall be drained out on the side of the altar' it is said Zeb. 65a: Does it occur to you to believe that only after making it be consumed in smoke he drains out? Rather the clause is intended to say that just as being consumed in smoke takes place on the top of the altar so also does the draining. With reference to Exod. 16.20 'and it bred worms, and rotted' we read Mek. ad locum (Friedm. 50a): This is מִקְרָא מְסוֹרָס, a scriptural word upside down. Does it first breed worms, and then rot? No, first the rotting and then the worms. Comp. Bacher, *Terminologie*, I, 168 and on מקרא מסורס I, 136; II, 144.

[39] Num. 7 (votive gifts) should precede Num. 1. Another term is עִרּוּב פָּרָשִׁיּוֹת. B. Ḳ. 107a: Ḥiyya bar Joseph says that Exod. 22.8 in the section concerning stuff left for keeping we must assume a transposition of sections and that כי הוא זה goes with the section concerning loans 22. 24. The school of Ishmael taught אין מוקדם ומאוחר בתורה. Comp. Bacher, *Terminologie*, I, 167f., 146.

NOTES TO CHAPTER XI, § 5, P. 98

[1] Siphre on Num. 25.1 (§ 131 beginning). See Bacher, *Tannaiten*, I, 236, 309.

[2] Yeb. 63b with reference to Gen. 9.6, 7. Comp. Bacher, *Terminologie*, I, 133; II, 142f.

[3] A. Rosenzweig, *Die Al-tiḳri-Deutungen*, Breslau, 1911 (54 pp. previously published in *Lewy-Festschrift*, 204–253). Still other Middoth are enumerated by Sherira (Neubauer 18f.; Lewin 48f.).

Ed. Biberfeld, 'Zur Methodologie der talmud. Bibelexegese,' *JbJLG*, I, 224–232 (אשר provided that); VI, 243–251 a. XI, 77–87 (פשט a. דרוש); VIII, 355–370 (אין מקרא יוצא מידי פשוטו).

[4] Shebu. 3.5 as regards Levit. 5.4.

[5] הָפְדֵה לא נפדתה Lev. 19.20 implies that the bondwoman was half-free (Kerithoth 2.4). Anonymous explications of an absolute infinitive preceding the finite verb: B. M. 2.9: Deut. 22.1 הָשֵׁב תְּשִׁיבֵם; B. M. 2.10: Exod. 23.5 עָזֹב תַּעֲזֹב. B. M. 31.10 further cases of an absolute infinitive preceding a finite verb are made to yield halakic regulations: Exod. 22.25 חָבֹל תַּחְבֹּל; Num. 35.21 מות יוּמַת; Deut. 13.16 הַכֵּה תַכֶּה; 15.8, 10 f., 14; 22.4, 7; 24.13.

[6] Gen. 4.10 דְּמֵי אָחִיךָ is interpreted Sanh. 4.5 to mean: 'his blood and the blood of his seed.'

[7] Soṭa 5.1 in ונטמאה Num. 5.29.

[8] נטמאה Num. 5.14, 29.

[9] See above p. 285 top.

NOTES TO CHAPTER XII, § 1, P. 99

[1] A distinction is made between biblical commandments which are directly prescribed in the Torah מִדְּאוֹרָיְתָא and rabbinic commandments מִדְּרַבָּנָן.

[2] In support of this view of his that boiling fowl with milk is forbidden only by the rabbis (not in the Bible) Akiba finds evidence in the Torah. Thus he maintains Ḥul. 8.4 that, since the word 'kid' occurs three times, each time something different is excluded, viz. fowl, game, unclean animals; see above p. 291 (n. 14).

[3] While the beginning of this Mishna contradicts the opinion of Akiba, the conclusion accords with a view of Akiba expressed elsewhere (Ned. 7.1). Accordingly—so believes the speaker here in the Talmud—Akiba must be accepted as the author of the conclusion of the Mishna Ḥul. 8.1, while the beginning originated with the sages who, in opposition to Akiba, hold that it is forbidden in the Bible to boil fowl in milk.

[4] If they were wholly heterogeneous the messenger, having received his commission with reference to a distinct category would not be prompted to ask for instructions.

[5] Meat including fowl; for only fish and locusts are expressly excluded.

[6] גְּזֵרָה ordinance, in particular a rabbinical one. It is an established principle that for the purpose of making effective rabbinic ordinances further rabbinic preventive ordinances are not admissible. Comp. Beṣa 2b, 3a; Levy I, 320; Bacher, *Terminologie*, II, 26f.

[7] Ḥalla (the heave of the dough) given in Palestine is, for the reason that it is considered as heave (comp. Num. 15.20 with Levit. 22.10–13), exactly

as is the heave, forbidden to a non-priest. In order to protect this prohibition, it is equally made unlawful, but only by the rabbis, for non-priests to eat Ḥalla even outside Palestine. For this reason it may be eaten in the presence of a non-priest at table, which must in no wise be done in the case of the heave forbidden in the Bible.

[8] Namely, that the rabbis are powerless to issue a preventive measure with a view to a prohibition which is rabbinical.

[9] Hence—Abaye reasons—it is not possible to draw with Rab Joseph an inference from Ḥalla 4.8 that the rabbis are powerless to issue a preventive measure with a view to a rabbinic prohibition.

[10] Hence—so Abaye further maintains against Rab Joseph—it does not follow from the rabbinical prohibition to serve fowl and cheese together that it is forbidden *in the Bible* to eat fowl and milk.

[11] See chap. XIII, § 10.

[12] Meat and cheese (or milk).

[13] While the Torah forbids only boiling. Accordingly, in any case, whether one thinks about 'fowl with milk' as Rab Joseph or as Abaye, the eating of cold meat with cold milk is forbidden only by the rabbis. Hence when serving is forbidden it amounts to a rabbinic prohibition on the top of another rabbinic prohibition.

[14] Which would be tantamount to boiling.

[15] The vessel which stood over the fire is called 'the first vessel;' that into which is dished out 'the second vessel.'

NOTES TO CHAPTER XII, § 2, P. 100

[1] Ḳid. 11b, B. B. 92b.

[2] Documents in which a debtor's property has been assessed by the court and then awarded to the creditor.

[3] Legal documents to the effect that one has obligated himself to support his wife's children on marrying her.

[4] Legal document to the effect that the woman has been released by the deceased husband's brother through the act of ḥaliṣa (see above p. 43).

[5] מֵאוּן protest. When a fatherless minor girl has been married off by her mother and brothers, she may, before she attains to majority (puberty), make a declaration in the presence of three persons that she does not wish this husband. The court certificate relating thereto enables her to contract another marriage without requiring a bill of divorcement, Yeb. 13.1.

[6] גלוסקמא, so, with ג (not ד), Palest. Talm.: γλωσσόκομον.

[7] Whether the bill was given in trust to him by the creditor or by the debtor or, after payment on account, by both.

[8] Ad Calendas Graecas. The bill must not be delivered to either of them without evidence.

[9] From בָּרַר 'make clear,' something like 'documents of clarification.'

[10] From בָּרַר 'single out, select.' According to the Palest. Talm. M. Ḳ. 3.82aγ (B. B. 10. 17cγ): compromises קומפרומיסין.—On the triumviral court see Sanh. 3.1; Shulḥan Aruk, Ḥoshen Mishpaṭ 13.2.

[11] And someone claimed that he had lost it. Bills of divorcement, when lost before delivery to the woman, should be returned to the loser only when it may be assumed that the person who drew up the bill has not changed his mind, comp. B. M. 1. 7.

[12] And it is not known which place is referred to.

[13] נפק דק ואשכח, see above p. 16.

[14] On תְּנַן a. תָּנוּ רַבָּנַן see above chap. I, § 2 (p. 3 f.).

[15] See above notes 4 a. 5.

[16] Hence when first one bill is rolled, then the second bill is wound about it and the third about the second.

[17] Hence without further statement, merely: 'I have found three bills.'

[18] B. M. 25a.

[19] The number should be stated by the (alleged) loser.

[20] It is not to be thought of that the three creditors X, Y, Z should have lost their bills at the same time in the same place. Hence the debtor is the loser.

[21] How could it happen that the three creditors should lose each his bill at the same time in the same place?

[22] By the same scribe.

[23] But has not yet reached legally the debtor's hands.

[24] In the following there are discussed objections against the general validity of the proposition that a Symphon is inoperative so long as it remains in the hands of the creditor.

[25] The conception is that the promissory note is not torn but is nevertheless found lying among torn bills, whereby its validity becomes uncertain. By the Symphon resting therewith and referring to the promissory note the payment is evidenced. But only in this special case is a Symphon, which is still in the creditor's possession, valid.

[26] B. B. 10.7.

[27] The bill of either of the two Joseph ben Simeon (that is, when

the debtor in question is not accurately described on the Symphon and the one bill).

[28] Shebuoth 7.7.

[29] The creditor's orphans.

[30] Accordingly, in this case, a certificate of payment (Symphon) found among the creditor's bills would have evidential force. According to Saphera again only in the special case when the promissory note, by reason of being next to torn bills, had been impaired in its significance.

[31] Sanh. 31b.

[32] When the creditor says that he has not yet been paid and proceeds to prove it by the fact that he has not surrendered the Symphon, nevertheless, as follows from the quotation above, the Symphon of receipt derives evidential force that payment has been made from the fact that the witnesses acknowledge their signatures.

[33] Answer: The Symphon which is still with the creditor becomes a receipt valid in law not by the signatures in themselves, but by the fact that the subscribed witnesses declare that they witnessed the payment of the promissory note. Hence the gloss in the Munich codex: על פי חותמיו.

[34] As above.

[35] Witnesses who affirm that the document was produced in court.

[36] עלין is here taken to mean: 'thereon' (concerning the payment made).

NOTES TO CHAPTER XIII, § 2, P. 107

[1] So also Halevy; comp. J. Bondi, *Jahrb. d. Jüd.-Liter. Ges.*, V (1907), 245–277.

[2] Recognized likewise by D. Hoffmann, *Magazin*, VIII (1881), 125–127.

[3] Comp. Abr. Kuenen, *Gesammelte Abhandlungen zur biblischen Wissenschaft*, Freib., 1894, 49-81; Schürer, 4th ed., II, 254–258. In defence of the traditional view D. Hoffmann, *Der oberste Gerichtshof in der Stadt des Heiligthums*, Berlin 1878, 4to, and: 'Die Präsidentur im Synedrium' in *Magazin*, 1878, 94–81. Isr. Jelski, *Die innere Einrichtung des grossen Synedrions zu Jerusalem*, Breslau, 1894, 38, 46–64, 81, thinks that the great Sanhedrin had two presidents, a political who was the high priest, and one for religious matters; the 5 x 2 authorities in Aboth 1.4ff. are not 5 pairs, but 10 successive Aboth beth din, i. e. learned presidents of the Synedrion. But it is in no wise proved that Jose ben Joezer etc. actually had an office like that. Comp. also

Is. Loeb, 'Sur le chapitre Ier des Pirke Abot,' *Revue des Etudes Juives*, XIX (1889), 188–201.

[4] Also Soṭa 9.9. See above p. 43, n. 35 concerning the controversy between them.

[5] See on him in addition Eduy. 8.4. Siphra Shemini, Par. 8.5 (ed. Weiss 55b).

[6] This reading is more correct than Nittai.

[7] Pal. Ḥag. 2. 77d narrates almost the same of Judah ben Tabai without, however, mentioning Jesus. See H. Strack, *Jesus, die Häretiker u. die Christen nach den ältesten jüd. Angaben*, Leipzig, 1910, 8.

[8] טָבַי, a better reading than Ṭabbai, is abbreviated from טוֹבִיָּה.

[9] See in addition Taan. 3.8 and in the Midrashim: Mekil. on Exod. 23.7 (ed. Friedm. 100 a); Siphra Beḥuḳḳothai 1.1 (ed. Weiss 110c); Siphre Deut. 21.22 (§ 221).—Landau, *MGWJ*, 1858, 107–122, 177–180; Derenb. 96–111; R. Leszynsky, *REJ*, LXIII, 216 to 231, and on Simeon ben Shaṭaḥ Hamb. II, 460 f.

[10] Landau, *MGWJ*, 1858, 317–329; Derenb. 116 to 118, 149 f., 463 f.; Hamb. II, 1113 f.; Schürer, 4th ed., II, 422–424.—Shemaiah and Abtalion occur also in Mekiltha on Exod. 14.15 (Friedm. 29b).

[11] *Antiqu.* 14, 9, 4.

[12] Ibid., 15, 1, 1 *πωλλίων ὁ φαρισαῖος καὶ Σαμαίας ὁ τούτου μαθητής* and 15, 10, 4 *οἱ περὶ πωλλίωνα τὸν φαρισαῖον καὶ Σαμαίαν.*

[13] Comp. Jos. Lehmann, 'Le procès d'Hérode, Saméas et Pollion,' *REJ*, XXIV (1892), 68–81.

[14] Pes. 66a.

[15] Pal. Pes. 6. 33a.

[16] Halevy, I c, 78–89.

[17] Comp. Schürer, 3d ed., I, 428, 595; 4th ed., II, 17.

[18] For the Prosbul see p. 31, n. 4; for the 7 Middoth above chap. XI, § 2.—Hillel is mentioned in the Mishna: Shebiith 10.3; Ḥag. 2.2; Git. 4.3; B. M. 5.9; Eduy. 1. 1–4; Aboth 1.12–14; 2.4–7; 4.5; 5. 17; Arak. 9.4; Nidda 1.1. In the Midrashim: Siphra Shemini Par. 9.5 (Weiss 56a); Tazri'a Neg. 9.16 (bis, Weiss 66d, 67a); Behar Par. 4.8 (W. 108d). Siphre Num. 19.1 (§ 123); Siphre Deut. 15.3 (§ 113), 34.7 (§ 357). Several times הלל הזקן.

Z. Frankel, *Hod.* 37–40; Weiss, I, 155 ff.; J. Brüll, *Introd.*, I, 33ff.; Derenb. 176–192; Abr. Geiger, *Das Judenthum u. seine Geschichte*, 2d ed., I (Breslau 1865), 99–107; J. Trénel, *Vie de Hillel*, Paris, 1867; Alex. Kisch, *Hillel der Alte. Lebensbild eines jüdischen Patriarchen*, Prague, 1889; Hamb. II, 401–412;

G. Goitein, *Magazin*, 1884, 1–16, 49–87; Bacher, *Tannaiten*, I, 4–14 and *Jew. Encycl.*, VI, 397–400; Halevy, I c, 89–143 (also concerning Babylonia, Hillel's native country); Rosenthal, *Entstehung*, II, 1–16; Sal. Stein, *JbJLG*, XII, 132–164. Beginning with the times of Judah ha-Nasi the claim was made that Hillel was descended from David, see Isr. Lévi, *REJ*, XXXI (1895), 202–211; XXXIII, 143 f.—A. Löwenstamm, מאמר קדש הלולים, Amst., 1818 (on Hillel's three answers in tract. Shab. 31).

Gothofr. Engelhard Geiger, 'Commentatio de Hillele et Schammai,' in: Ugolini, *Thesaurus antiquitatum sacrarum*, XXI, col. 1181–1212; Franz Delitzsch, *Jesus u. Hillel*, 3d ed., Erlangen, 1879 (40); Schürer, 4th ed., II, 424–428; H. L. Strack, 'Hillel,' *PRE*, 3d ed., VIII, 74–76.

[19] The name which occurs I Chr. 2.28 is apparently shortened from שְׁמַעְיָה.

[20] Shammai in the Mishna: M. Sh. 2.4, 9; Orla 2.5; Sukka 2.8; Ḥag. 2.2; Eduy. 1.1–4, 10, 11; Aboth 1.12, 15; 5.17; Kelim 22.4; Nidda 1.1.—Comp. Hamb. II, 1061 f.; *Jew. Encyc.*, XI, 230. In the Midrashim: Mekil. on Exod. 13.10 (Friedm. 21b); Siphre on Deut. 20.19 (§ 203).

[21] On Isai. Book 3, chap. 8 (Vallarsi, IV, 123).

[22] Tos. Ber. 7.24; Bab. Ber. 63a; Pal. Ber. 9.13d.

NOTES TO CHAPTER XIII, § 3, P. 109

[1] The division into generations serves the purpose to show in a clear manner which Tannaim or Amoraim developed their main activity essentially as contemporaries. The two groups of the second generation are frequently counted as two distinct generations.

[2] On Isai. Book 3, chap. 8.

[3] See esp. Eduy. 1.12–14. According to Moses Maimonides, Ter. 5.4 is the only case in which the opposite takes place.

[4] Orla 2.5.

[5] 2.12.

[6] Bacher, *Tannaiten*, I, 22.

[7] See Shab. 1.4; Zabim 5.12; M. Lerner, *Magazin*, 1882, 113–144, a. 1883, 121–156.

On the two Schools Frankel, 45–55; Brüll, 45–49; Bacher, *Tann.*, I, 14–25 and T. T., 54–71; Ad. Schwarz, *Die Controversen der Schammaiten u. Hilleliten*, I, Vienna, 1893 (109. On this work see D. Feuchtwang, *MGWJ*, 1895, 370–379); S. Mendelsohn, *Jew. Enc.*, III, 115 f.; Schürer, 4th ed., II

396, 426 f.; Halevy, I c, 548 to 607 (H. applies the expressions Beth Sh. and Beth H. also to the times of the two teachers themselves); Rosenthal, *Entstehung*, II, 16–48.

The differences are mentioned in the Mishna: Ber. 1.3; 8.1–8; Pea 3.1; 6.1 f., 5; 7.6; Demai 1.3; 6.6; Kil. 2.6; 4.1, 5; 6.1; Shebiith 1.1; 4.2, 4, 10; 5.4, 8; 8.3; Ter. 1.4; 5.4; Maas. 4.2; M. Sh. 2.3f., 7–9; 3.6 f., 9, 13; 4.8; 5.3, 6 f.; Ḥalla 1.6; Orla 2.4.—Shab. 1.4–9; 3.1; 21.3; Er. 1.2; 6.4, 6; 8.6; Pes. 1.1; 4.5; 8.8; 10.2, 6; Sheḳ. 2.3; 8.6; Sukka 1.1, 7; 2.7; 3.5, 9; Beṣa 1.1–3, 5–9; 2.1–6; R. H. 1.1; Ḥag. 1.1–3; 2.3 f.—Yeb. 1.4; 3.1, 5; 4.3; 6.6; 13.1; 15.2 f.; Keth. 5.6; 8.1, 6; Ned. 3.2, 4; Nazir 2.1 f.; 3.6 f.; 5.1–3, 5; Git. 4.5; 8.4, 8f.; 9.10; Soṭa 4.2; Ḳid. 1.1.—B. M. 3.12; B. B. 9.8 f.; Eduy. 1.7–14; 4.1–5; 5.—Zeb. 4.1; Ḥul. 1.2; 8.1; 11.2; Bek. 5.2; Ker. 1.6.—Kelim 9.2; 11.3; 14.2; 18.1; 20.2, 6; 22.4; 26.6; 28.4; 29.8; Ohal. 2.3; 5.1–4; 7.3; 11.1, 3–6, 8; 13.1, 4; 15.8; 18.1, 4, 8; Para 12.10; Toh. 9.1, 5, 7; 10.4; Mikw. 1.5; 4.1; 5.6; 10.6; Nidda 2.4, 6; 4.3; 5.9; 10.1, 4, 6–8; Maksh. 1.2–4; 4.4 f.; 5.9; Zabim 1.1 f.; Ṭebul Yom 1.1; Yad. 3.5; Uḳṣin 3.6, 8, 11.—ב"ש alone: Ber. 6.5; Demai 3.1; Kil. 8.5; Ter. 4.3; Orla 2.5, 12; Beṣa 2.6 (= Eduy. 3.10); Miḳw. 4.5.—In the Midrashim ב"ש and ב"ה are mentioned: Mek. on Exod 13.10 (Friedm. 21b). 22.7 (Fr. 91b). Siphra Ḥoba Par. 13 (ed. Weiss 28c); Ṣaw chap. 8.6 (Weiss 33b); Tazri'a 1.5 (W. 58c); 3.1, 6 (W. 59a.b); Meṣora' Zabim Par. 4.3 (W. 78a); Ḳedoshim Par. 3.7 (W. 90a.b); Emor chap. 15.5 (W. 102c); Behar 1.5 (bis, W. 106b). Siphre Num. 15.37 (§ 115 זְקֵנֵי in front of ב"ש and ב"ה). Siphre Deut. 6.7 (§ 34); 16.4 (§ 131); 16.16 (§ 143); 18.4 (§ 166); 22.5 (§ 234); 24.1 (§ 269).

8 Aboth 3.1; Eduy. 5.6; Neg. 1.4. Siphra Tazri'a Neg. Par. 2.6 (Weiss 1b). Par. 3.4 (W. 62d); Siphre Num. on 5.12 (§ 7) a. 12.10 (§ 105). Frankel 56 f.; Brüll 49; Derenb. 483 f.; Hamb. II, 32; S. J. Kämpf, *MGWJ*, V (1856), 146–158; S. Mendelsohn, *REJ*, XLI (1900), 31 to 44 and *JE*, I, 302.

9 Hillel, Shammai and several other ancient teachers are named by their mere name, which was considered as a special distinction. Rabban רַבָּן ('our teacher'; the suffix came to be meaningless) is the honorific title of several descendants of Hillel: G. I, Simeon b. G. I, G. II, Simeon b. G. II a. (Aboth 2.2) G III.; then of Joḥanan ben Zaccai. The later teachers are called Rabbi in Palestine and Rab or Mar in Babylonia. גדול מרב רבי וגדול מרבי רבן (greater than Rab is Rabbi and greater than Rabbi is Rabban). More specific information may be found in Sherira's second letter (in Lewin's edition of the famous epistle p. 125–127 better than under 'Abaye' in Aruk). In the older Midrashim anonymous haggadic utterances are cited by means of רַבָּנָן

אָמְרֵי (our teachers say); the Tanḥuma Midrashim have רַבּוֹתֵינוּ. Of later date is the form minus the suffix רַבָּנִין see Bacher, *REJ*, LXV, 32–39. The Tannaites who are distinguished by the honorific name Abba are not called Rabbi, see Lewy, *Mischna des Abba Saul*, n. 51.

[10] Acts 22.3, comp. 5.34 ff.—In the Mishna: Pe'a 2.6; Orla 2.12; R. H. 2.5; Shek̦. 6.1; Yeb. 16.7; Giṭ. 4.2 f.; (Aboth 1.16?).

[11] Soṭa 9.15.

[12] So S. J. Kämpf, *MGWJ*, 1854, 39 ff., 98 ff. In the sole passage Shab. 15a end a Simeon is mentioned who must have been Hillel's son and Gamaliel's father. On the family of Gamaliel see also Zipser, *Ben Chananja*, 1866, Appendix 4.—On Gamaliel: Frankel, 57–59; Brüll, 50–52; Derenb., 239–246; Hamb. II, 236 f.; Bacher, *JE*, V, 558–560; Schürer, 4th ed., II, 429 f. Hollander, *Die Institutionen des Rabban Gamaliel* (in *Bericht über die öffentl. Rabbinatsschule in Eisenstadt*), Halberstadt, 1869, 1–16 (of the German part).

[13] Keth. 1.5; R. H. 1.7. Frankel, 60 f.; Brüll, 52 f. Comp., however, D. Hoffmann, *Der oberste Gerichtshof in der Stadt des Heiligtums*, Berlin, 1878, 40.

[14] Comp. Keth. 105a.—Frankel, 61–63; Brüll, 53–55.

[15] See Keth. 13.1–9. According to the Baraitha 105a Ḥanan the Egyptian is not identical with Ḥanan b. Abishalom.

[16] See Shab. 2.1; Nazir 5.4; B. B. 5.2 a. A. Z. 7b.

[17] Not: Ḥanina.

[18] Aboth 3.2a; Shek̦. 4.4; 6.1; Eduy. 2.1 f.; Zeb. 9.3; 12.4: Men. 10.1; Neg. 1.4; Para 3.1. Midrashim: Siphra Saw Par. 1.9 (Weiss 29b); Tazri'a Neg. Par. 2.6 (Weiss 61b). Siphre Num. on 6.26 (§ 42). Frankel, 59 f.; Brüll, 52; Bacher, *Agada d. Tannaiten*, I, 55–58; Schürer, 4th ed., II, 434 f.; Halevy, I c, 174–180.

[19] Name of uncertain etymology. The spelling הקנה is much better attested than הקנא.

[20] Aboth 3.5. On his short prayers Ber. 4.2. Comp. also Meg. 28a; B. B. 10b. Frankel, 99; Brüll, 94; Hamb., II, 852; Bacher, *Tannaiten*, I, 58–61.

[21] Vita 38; see also chapters 39, 44, 60; Jewish War, 4, 3, 9. Mishna: Er. 6.2; Ker. 1.7. Comp. Frankel, 63 f.; Brüll, 55–57; Derenb., 270–272, 474 f.; Hamb. 1121; Midrash Tannaim on Deut., ed. D. Hoffmann, Berlin, 1909, p. 176 on Deut. 26.13.

[22] So cod. Kaufmann; perhaps more correctly with Ms. de Rossi 138 צָדוּק, comp. Σαδδουκ in Ezek., Ezra-Neh. LXX a. Σαδδουκαῖοι.

[23] Aboth 4.5; Ter. 10.9; Pes. 7.2; Suk. 2.5; Ned. 9.1; Eduy. 3.8; 7.1–4; Bekor. 1.6; Kelim 12.4 f.; Mik̦w. 5.5.

[24] Comp. Bacher, *Tannaiten,* I, 47–50; 54; Frankel, 70 f.; Brüll, 68 f.; Derenb., 342–344; *JE,* XII, 629 f.; Schürer, 4th ed., II, 434.

[25] The name Zaccai occurs as early as Ezra 2.9 and is probably abbreviated from זְכַרְיָה.

[26] Sanh. 32b. See *MGWJ,* 1893, 304.

[27] R. H. 31b.

[28] See R. H. 4.1, 3 f.; Sukka 3.12; Soṭa 9.9; Men. 10.5; Eduy. 8.3, 7; Soṭa 40a.—Further mention of R. Joḥanan in the Mishna: Shab. 16.7; 22.3; Sheḳ. 1.4; Sukka 2.5; Keth. 13.1f.; Soṭa 5.2, 5; 9.15; Sanh. 5.2 בן זכי; Kelim (2.2 we ought prob. to read Joḥanan ben Nuri, see *REJ,* XXXII, 208) 17.16; Yad. 4.3, 6. In the Midrashim: Mek. Ex. 19.1 (Friedm. 61a); 20.25 (Fr. 74a); 21.6 (Fr. 74a); 21.37 (88b); 22.6 (91b, ben Zaccai to be supplied as also 21.6). Siphra Wayyiḳra Ḥoba Par. 5.1 (Weiss 19c); Shemini Par. 7.12 (W. 54b); Ḳedoshim 10.8 (W. 92d); Emor Par. 10.10 (W. 100c); Chap. 16.9 (W. 102d). Siphre Num. 19.1 (Friedm. § 123); Deut. 16.20 (§ 144); 20.3 (§ 192); 31.14 (§ 305); 34.7 (§ 357). Comp. Landau, *MGWJ,* 1851–52, 163–176; Frankel, 64–66; Brüll, 57–59; Derenb., 266f., 276–288, 302–318; Hamb. II, 464–473; Joseph Spitz, *Rabban Jochanan ben Sakkai,* Leipzig, 1883 (48, Dissert.); Grätz, 4th ed., IV, 11–16; Ros., *Entstehung,* II, 25–30; Bacher, *Tannaiten,* I, 25–46 a. *JE,* VII, 214–217; Halevy, I c, 41 ff.; Schürer, 4th ed., II, 432 to 434; H. Reich, *Zur Genesis des Talmud. Der T. u. die Römer,* Vienna, 1892, 37–68; A. Schlatter, *Jochanan ben Zakkai, der Zeitgenosse der Apostel,* Gütersloh, 1899 (75; against him L. Blau, *MGWJ,* 1899, 548–561).

[29] See Frankel, 73–75; Brüll, 71–75; Bacher, *Tannaiten,* I, 67 to 72; Halevy, I c, 181–185.

[30] Yeb. 49b.

[31] A teacher of the same name lived in the second half of the second Christian century, see p. 115. In many passages it is difficult to decide which of the two is meant.

[32] Aboth 3.9, 10; Mek. Ex. 18.21 (Friedm. 60a).

[33] E. g. Ber. 33a, Taan. 24b.—M. Friedländer, *Ben Dosa u. seine Zeit oder der Einfluss der heidnischen Philosophie auf das Judenthum u. Christenthum in den letzten Jahrhunderten des Alterthums,* Prague, 1872 (93; may be used only with criticism); Hamb. II, 130 f.; Bacher, *Tannaiten,* I, 283 f.; S. Mendelsohn, *JE,* VI, 214–216.

[34] Shab. 1.4, see above p. 109.

[35] Pe'a 2.6, see above p. 21.

[36] Pe'a 2.6.

[37] Yoma 1.6.

[38] Cod. Cambridge constantly Hananiah.

[39] Bekor. 6.7, etc. Midrashim: Mek. Ex. 20.3 (Friedm. 67b); Siphra Wayyiḳra Nedaba chap. 9.3 (Weiss 9b), Emor Par. 3.12, 15 (W. 95c); Frankel, 128 f.; Brüll, 131 f.; Bacher, *Tannaiten*, I, 368 f.; *JE*, VI, 214; Halevy, I c, 185–190.

[40] Taan. 21a.

[41] See p. 96.—Brüll, 94 f.; Bacher, *Tannaiten*, I, 61–64; *JE*, IX, 148.

NOTES TO CHAPTER XIII, § 4, P. 110

[1] See Pal. Ber. 4. 7cd.

[2] Bab. Ber. 28a.

[3] See Derenb. 334–340 and Bacher, *Tannaiten*, I, 84 ff.

[4] Halevy, I e, 199–202.

[5] Ber. 28b end.

[6] See *JQR*, 1898, 654–659 and H. Strack, *Jesus, die Här. u. die Christen*, Leipzig, 1910, 21. Prof. Marx has also found the reading ולנוצרים in the Oxford Ms. of Amram's Siddur written in Rhodes 1426, see his *Untersuchungen zum Siddur des Gaon R. Amram*, p. 15.

On Gamaliel II, see Landau, *MGWJ*, 1851–52, 283–295, 323–335; Frankel, 69f.; Brüll, 62–68; Derenb., 306–313, 319–346; Hamb. II, 237–250; A. Scheinin, *Die Hochschule zu Jamnia u. ihre bedeutendsten Lehrer mit besonderer Rücksicht auf Rabbi Gamaliel II.*, Halle, 1878 (77); H. Reich, *Zur Genesis des Talmud*, Vienna, 1892, 115–135; Grätz, 4th ed., IV, 11 f. a. n. 4; Bacher, *Tannaiten*, I, 78–100 and *JE*, V, 560–562; Halevy, I e, 71–78 (Taan. 29a concerning the deliverance of G. which, according to Grätz, 4th ed., IV, note 18 and others, should be made to refer to G.'s son Simeon) and 271 ff. (concerning the quarrel which led to his deposition). A. Sulzbach, 'G. u. Josua,' in Wohlgemuth's *Jeschurun*, IV (1917), 75–90; Ṣchürer, 4th ed., II, 435–437.

[7] Frankel, 71; Brüll, 69 f.

[8] See Bacher, *Tannaiten*, I, 325.

[9] 'Αρχῖνος. The Mss. have partly as most of the editions הרכינס, partly ארכינס.—Aboth 3.10; Frankel, 71 f.; Brüll, 70 f.; Derenb., 368, 370; Hamb. II, 155.

[10] 'Υρκανός, הורקנוס Aboth 2.8.

[11] More than 320 times.

[12] Sanh. 32b.

[13] Bek. 5b; *REJ*, LX, 107 f.

[14] B. Ḳ. 83b, 84a.—On Eliezer see Frankel, 75–83; Brüll, 75–82; Derenb., 319 ff., 366 ff.; Hamb. II, 162–168; Grätz, 4th ed., IV, 41 ff. a. n. 5; Ros., *Entstehung*, II, 31–42; Bacher, *Tannaiten*, I, 100–160; Ch. Oppenheim, *Beth Talmud*, IV (Vienna 1885), 311 ff., 332 ff., 359 ff.; Zarkes in Suwalski's כנסת הגדולה, IV (1891), 65–71; Wassertrilling, 'Die halachische Lehrweise des El. b. H.,' *Jüd. Literaturblatt*, 1877, No. 22 f., 26; Halevy, I e, 293–296, 372–386; Schürer, II, 437–439; S. Mendelsohn, *JE*, V, 113–115.

[15] *R. Eliezer ben Hyrcanos*, Leipzig, 1877 (39 pp.; Latin).

[16] See Pal M. Ḳ. 3.81d; Bab. B. M. 59b and J. Bassfreund, *MGWJ*, 1898, 49–57.

[17] Aboth 2.8.

[18] More than 140 times.

[19] Comp. Frankel, 83–90; Brüll, 82–86; Derenb., 319 ff., 416 ff.; Hamb. II, 510–520; Grätz, 4th ed., IV, 47–50 a. n. 6; Bacher, *Tannaiten*, I, 129–194; Halevy, I e, 307–318, 386–392; Ros., *Entstehung*, II, 31–42; Schürer, 4th ed., II, 437 f. On his colloquy with the sages of Athens: L. J. Mandelstamm, *Horae Talmudicae*, I, Berlin, 1860, a. Br. Meissner, *ZDMG*, 1894, 194 f. Furthermore: M. Güdemann, *Religionsgeschichtliche Studien*, Leipzig, 1876, p. 131–144 (J. b. H. and Christianity), comp. Brüll, *Jahrbücher*, III, 180.

[20] Aboth 2.8.—R. Jose the Priest: Aboth 2.12; Frankel, 90; Brüll, 87; Bacher, *Tannaiten*, I, 72–4; *JE*, VII, 243 f. Simeon ben Nethanel: Aboth 2.13; Frankel, 90; Brüll, 87; Bacher, *Tannaiten*, I, 80, 93, 108. R. Eleazar ben Arak: Aboth 2.14; Frankel, 91; Brüll, 87; Hamb. II, 155 f.; Bacher, *Tannaiten*, I, 74–77; *JE*, V, 96 f.

[21] Not: Eliezer.

[22] Aboth 3.17. Frankel, 91–94; Brüll, 88–91; Derenb. 327 ff. a. in *MGWJ*, 1893, 395–398; Hamb. VI, 156–158; Bacher, *Tannaiten*, I, 219–240; *JE*, V, 97 f.; Halevy, I e, 362 –368 (El. after the death of G. II. Nası at Lydda); Schürer, 4th ed., II, 439 f.

[23] Not Eliezer.

[24] Frankel, 97–99; Brüll, 91–93; Bacher, *Tannaiten*, I, 50–54; *JE*, V, 120.

[25] Named above p. 110.

[26] See p. 115.

[27] Brüll, 60; Bacher, *Tannaiten*, I, 50, 54, 377.

[28] See p. 111.—Aboth 4.19. Frankel, *Additamenta*, p. 6; Brüll, 98f.; Bacher, *Tannaiten*, I, 375–378; Halevy, I e, 199–202.

29 Ber. 28b; Brüll, 97 f.

30 Bacher, *Tannaiten*, I, 64–66.

31 Aboth 3.11. Frankel, 127 f.; Brüll, 130; Bacher, *Tannaiten*, I, 194–219; *JE*, V, 102 f.

32 Aboth 4.4; also Pirḳe R. Eliezer 23, 52, 54. The date according to Bacher, *Tannaiten*, 2d ed., I, 444.

33 Kil. 6.4; Keth. 5.8. In the Mishna, in addition to Aboth 3.12, also Shebu. 2.5; Eduy. 2.4, 6; A. Z. 2.5; Yad. 4.3 (cod. Cambridge also M. Ḳ. 3.8; Eduy. 5.3). Both he and his school are mentioned very frequently in Mek., Siphra, Siphre (see the references in Hoffmann, *Einleitung*, p. 87 f.).

34 Against Akiba who deduces from the absolute infinit. Num. 15.31 הכרת תכרת הנפש ההיא that idolaters will be cut off both from the present world and from the future.

35 The commandment Josh. 1.8 to study the Torah constantly is not to be taken literally, since Deut. 11.14 work in the field is expressly commanded.—On the 13 hermeneutic rules which are ascribed to him see chap. XI, § 3.—On Ishmael: Frankel, 105–111; Brüll, 103–116; Derenb., 386–395; Hamb. II, 526–529; Grätz, 4th ed., IV, 56–58 a. n. 7; Bacher, *Tannaiten*, I, 240–271; M. Petuchowski, *Der Tanna Rabbi Ismael*, Frankf. o. M., 1894 (116); D. Hoffmann, *Einleitung in die halachischen Midraschim*, Berlin, 1887; Almquist, *Mechilta Bo*, introd., esp. 39 ff., 98 ff.; *JE*, VI, 648–650; Schürer, 4th ed., II, 440–442.

36 See p. 264, n. 90.

37 Men. 29b.

38 See p. 22.

39 See chap. XVI, § 1.

40 On Akiba comp. Landau, *MGWJ*, 1854, 45–51, 81–93, 130–148; Frankel, 111–123; Brüll, 116 to 122; Derenb., 329 ff., 395 ff., 418 ff.; Is. Gastfreund, תולדות רבי עקיבא, Lemberg, 1871 (30 leaves); Hamb. II, 32–43; Grätz, 4th ed., IV, 50–56 a. n. 7, 8; Bacher, *Tannaiten*, I, 271–348; L. Ginzberg, *JE*, I, 304–310; Halevy, I e, 455–467, 620–629 (A. and the War), 659–664; Witkind, חוט המשולש, Wilna, 1877, 9–60; Sam. Funk, *Akiba. Ein palästinensischer Gelehrter aus dem zweiten nachchristl. Jahrhundert*, I, Jena, 1896 (36 pp. Dissert.); J. Hirsch, *Die religionsgeschichtl. Bedeutung R. Akibas*, Prague, 1912; L. Stein, *R. A. u. seine Zeit*, Berlin, 1913 (110); Almquist, *Mechilta Bo*, introd., esp. p. 39 ff., 100 ff.; Schürer, 4th ed., II, 442–444; Paul Billerbeck, 'R. A., Leben u. Wirken eines Meisters in Israel,' in H. Strack's journal 'Nathanael,' 1916–1918.

41 Above p. 109.

[42] Ed. Martianay IV, 207: [Judaei] solent respondere et dicere: Barachibas et Simon et Helles [Hillel] magistri nostri tradiderunt nobis, ut bis mille pedes ambulemus in Sabbatho.

[43] On Isai. 8.11.

[44] The corresponding Greek may have been τέρπων. The name טרפון is exceedingly rare. Simeon ben Ṭ. (p. 114), Shebu. 47b Baraitha, may have been a son of R. Ṭ.—There is prob. no reason for identifying τρύφων, mentioned by Justin Martyr, with R. Ṭ., see Freimann, *MGWJ*, 1911, 565 ff., but apparently the two bore the identical name (on the Dialogus cum Tryphone Judaeo see S. Krauss, *JQR*, V, 123–134). Of the name τρύφων says Reland (in Ottho, *Historia doctorum Misnicorum*, ed. Amst., p. 129): 'quod nomen in Oriente, Syria imprimis et Aegypto usitatissimum fuit, uti ex nummis apparet.'—ר' אבין בריה דר' תנחום בר טריפון, Pal. Bikk. 2. 64c does not seem to be mentioned elsewhere.

[45] See S. Klein, 'Die Beschlüsse zu Lod' in Wohlgemuth's *Jeschurun* V (1918), 522–535.

[46] Shab. 111a.—In addition to Aboth 2.15 f. Ṭ. in the Mishna: Ber. 1.3; 6.8; Pe'a 3.6; Kil. 5.8; Ter. 4.5; 9.2; Maas. 3.9; M. Sh. 2.4, 9; Shab. 2.2; Er. 4.4; Pes. 10.6; Sukka 3.4; Beṣa 3.5; Taan. 3.9; Yeb. 15.6f.; Keth. 5.2; 7.6; 9.2 f.; Ned. 6.6; Nazir 5.5; 6.6; Ḳid. 3.13; B. Ḳ. 2.5; B. M. 2.7; 4.3; Mak. 1.10; Eduy. 1.10; Zeb. 10.8; 11.7; Men. 12.5; Bek. 2.6–9; 4.4; Ker. 5.2f.; Kelim 11.4, 7; 25.7; Ohal. 13.3; 16.1; Para 1.3; Miḳw. 10.5; Maksh. 5.4; Yad. 4.3. In the Midrashim: Mek. on Ex. 14.22 (Friedm. 31b); 16.13 (Fr. 49a bis)' 20, 23 (Fr. 73a). Siphra Nedaba Par. 4.5 (Weiss 32d). Meṣora' Nega'im Par. 1.13 (W. 70c). Chap. 2.7 (W. 71c). Ḳedoshim 4.9 (W. 8gb). Emor. 13.4 (W. 101b). 16.5 (W. 102d). Behar Par. 3.5 (W. 107c). Siphre Num. 5.15 (Friedm. § 8); 10.8 (§ 75); 18.7 (§ 116); 18.15, 18 (§ 124); 28.26 (§ 148); Deut. 1.1 (Fr. § 1); 6.5 (§ 32); 11.13 (§ 41); 24.1 (§ 269).—Frankel, 100–105; Brüll, 100–103; Derenb., 376–383; Hamb. II, 1196 f.; Bacher, *Tannaiten*, I, 348–358; *JE*, XII, 56 f.; Wolf, *B. H.*, II, 836–838; Schürer, 4th ed., II, 444.

[47] Brüll, 138; Bacher, *Tannaiten*, I, 101, 103 f.

[48] Schürer, 4th ed., III, 435–439; Burkitt a. L. Ginzberg, *JE*, II, 34–38.

[49] Bacher, *Tannaiten*, II, 557 f.; *JE*, VII, 214.

[50] Bacher, *Tannaiten*, I, 289, 324–327; *JE*, IX, 512.

[51] *JE*, VII, 213.

[52] Frankel, 125–127; Brüll, 125–130; Ch. Oppenheim, *Beth Talmud*, V, 138–145, 172–176; Hamb. II, 499–502; Bacher, *Tannaiten*, I, 358–372, 311–313; *JE*, VII, 240 f.

53 Aboth 3.18 a number of Mss. read חַסְמָא. It is unlikely that the name should be sounded חִסְמָא, for nowhere do we find the spelling חיסמא. On the name see Lev. R. 23: R. El. was delivered (אתחסם) from his previous ignorance of the Law. According to Krauss, *Arch.*, II, 657: maker of steel utensils (comp. חִסּוּם Kelim 13.4). Horowitz, *MGWJ*, 1883, 309 f., would derive the name from the halakic utterance of this El. handed down B. M. 92a and its connection with Deut. 25.4 לא תחסום.

54 Aboth 4.4b; Frankel, 131; Brüll, 137 f.; Bacher, *Tannaiten*, I, 448 f. *JE*, VII, 210.

55 Frankel, 129; Brüll, 132 f.; *JE*, XI, 356.

56 Bacher, *Tannaiten*, I, 393–397.

57 Not Ḥanina.

58 Aboth 3.2b; Frankel, 133; Brüll, 140; Hamb. II, 132; Bacher, *Tannaiten*, I, 397–400; *JE*, VI, 209; Büchler, *Der gal. 'Am ha'areṣ*, 282–286.

59 Aboth 6.9b; Bacher, *Tannaiten*, I, 401–403.

60 Comp. פריטא in Palest. Syriac 'money changer'; others think of πρῶτος.—Frankel, 133; Brüll, 140; Bacher, *Tannaiten*, I, 403–406; *JE*, V, 103; Büchler, ibid., 288–290.

61 Pal. Meg. 4.75d.

62 Frankel, 129 f.; Brüll, 133 f.; Hamb. II, 450 f.; Bacher, *Tannaiten*, I, 406–409; *JE*, VII, 340.

63 עַזַּי is abbreviated from Azariah.—Aboth 4.2 f.; Frankel, 135 f.; Brüll, 143–147; Hamb. II, 1119–1121; Bacher, *Tannaiten*, I, 409–424.

64 Pal. Ḥag. 2.77b; Bab. Ḥag. 14b, 15b.

65 Frankel, 136; Brüll, 143 f.; Bacher, *Tannaiten*, I, 425–432; Hamb., *Suppl.*, I, 38–40.

66 Aboth 4.20a.—Raph. Lévy, *Un Tanah*, 128–154; Brüll, 213–215; Hamb. II, 168–171; Bacher, *Tannaiten*, I, 432–436; L. Ginzberg in *JE*, V, 138 f.; E. Rosenthal, *Elisa ben Abuja*, Breslau, 1895 (13). The publication תולדות אלישע בן אבויה by M. D. Hoffmann (not accessible to me) contains, according to Bacher, 'conjectures which are quite ingenious but for the most art uncritical and untenable.' Of no importance is Sam. Back, *Elischa ben Abuja-Acher quellenmässig dargestellt*, Frankf. o. M. 1891 (37). See also Büchler, ibid., 290–292.

67 Hanina? The Mss. waver.

68 Frankel, 130; Brüll, 134–136; Hamb. II, 131 f.; Bacher, *Tannaiten*, I, 438–441; *JE*, VI, 216; Büchler, l. c., 318–328.

[69] Siphra Ṣaw Par. 2.3 (Weiss 30c); Shemini chap. 2.12 (W. 47d); Bacher, *Tannaiten*, I, 441.

[70] Frankel, 137; Bacher, *Tannaiten*, I, 447 f.

[71] Birtotha? see Strack on Aboth 3.7.

[72] Frankel, 134; Brüll, 142; Bacher, *Tannaiten*, I, 442–445; *JE*, V, 100.

[73] Frankel, 137; Brüll, 149; Bacher, *Tannaiten*, I, 445 f.

[74] Aboth 3.4. Frankel, 136 f.; Brüll I, 148; Bacher, *Tannaiten*, I, 436 f.; *JE*, VI, 208.

[75] Frankel, 137; Bacher, *Tannaiten*, I, 446 f.; *JE*, XI, 358 f.

[76] Frankel, 137; Bacher, *Tannaiten*, I, 447.

[77] חָרֵשׁ proper name I Chr. 9.15. Others: Ḥarash.

[78] Aboth 4.15b; Yoma 8.6. Frankel, 130f.; Brüll, I, 136f.; Bacher, *Tannaiten*, I, 385–389; *JE*, VIII, 380.

[79] Others: Bethera.

[80] Frankel, 94–97; Brüll, 29–32; Bacher, *Tannaiten*, I, 379–385; *JE*, II, 598 f.; Halevy, I e, 681 to 688. The Tannaim belonging to the family B. are often difficult to distinguish (comp. also H. Grätz, *MGWJ*, I (1852), 112–120).

[81] Frankel, 137; Bacher, *Tannaiten*, I, 389–393; *JE*, VI, 207; Halevy, I e, 689–697.

NOTES TO CHAPTER XIII, § 5, P. 114

[1] Comp. Frankel, 143–149; Brüll, 151–156; Bacher, *Tannaiten*, II, 335–350; D. Hoffmann, *Magazin*, 1884, 17–30, a.: *Einl. in die halach. Midraschim*, Berlin, 1887, esp. 18–20.

[2] Frankel, 146–149; Bacher, *Tannaiten*, II, 351–364; *JE*, VII, 296, 233 f.

[3] The passages are listed by Hoffmann, *Einl.*, p. 85 f. Jonathan occurs in the Mishna only Aboth 4.9; in the Tosephta only Nidda 2.2 (ed. Zuckerm., p. 642) a. with mutilated name: Nathan bar Joseph Terumoth 8.8 (p. 39) and Kelim II, 3.8 (p. 581). Josiah only in the Tosephta Shebu. 1.7 (p. 447).

[4] Frankel, 137; Bacher, *Tannaiten*, I, 131, 149; II, 354; *JE*, VI, 204.

[5] For a characterization see Frankel 149–153.

[6] מיישא see *Diḳd.* Er. 13b, p. 38.

[7] Er. 13b.

[8] Sanh. 38b.

[9] See p. 22.

[10] His name is absent only in 4 tractates; R. H., Ḥag., Tamid, Zabim.

[11] On Meir comp. M. Joel, *MGWJ*, 1855, 88 ff., 125 ff.; Frankel, 154–158; Brüll, 160–169; Ros., *Entstehung*, II, § 17–27; Hamb. II, 705–715; Grätz, 4th ed., IV, 171–178 a. n. 19; Bacher, *Tannaiten*, II, 1 to 69; Is. Broydè, *JE*, VIII, 432–435; Halevy, I e, 788–796 (R. Meir and his associates 796 ff.); Raph. Lévy, *Un Tanah. Etude sur la vie et l'enseignement d'un docteur Juif du IIe siecle*, Paris, 1873 (167; with especial reference to Meir); A.Blumenthal, *Rabbi Meir*, Frankf. o. M., 1888 (143); A. H. Rewson, תולדות ר' מאיר, Warsaw, 1889 (27).

[12] יוחאי abbreviated from Johanan.

[13] Moshe Kuniz, ספר בן יוחאי, Vienna 1815 fol. (154; much that is superficial); M. Pinner, *Compendium des Hierosolymitan. u. Babyl. Thalmud*, I, Berlin, 1832, 4to; M. Joel, *MGWJ*, 1856, 365 ff., 401 ff.; Frankel, 168–173; Brüll, 185–195; Ros., *Entstehung*, II, 41–51; Hamb. II, 1124 to 1133; Grätz, 4th ed., IV, 178–182 a. n. 20; Bacher, *Tannaiten*, II, 70–149; M. Seligsohn, *JE*, XI, 359 to 363; Halevy, I e, 785–791; L. Lewin, *R. Simon ben Jochai*, Frankf. o. M., 1893 (94). For a long time Simeon ben Johai was held to have been the author of the Zohar; in reality, however, this standard work of the Cabala was composed in the second half of the 13th cent. by Moses ben Shem Tob de Leon in Spain. Jacob Emden, *Mitpaḥath Sepharim*, Altona, 1768 already asserted that in its present form the Zohar was not by S. ben J.; nevertheless he likewise considered it as sacred.

[14] M. Joel, *MGWJ*, 1857, 83–91; Frankel, 164–168; Brüll, 178–185; Ros., *Entstehung*, II, 38–51; Hamb. II, 493–498; Bacher, *Tannaiten*, II, 150–190; a. (on the polemical utterance Derek Ereṣ Rabba 11) in *MGWJ*, 1898, 505–507; M. Seligsohn, *JE*, VII, 241 f.; Halevy. I e, 781–788. On R. Jose as author of the tractate Kelim see above p. 22.

[15] Abbreviated from Eleazar or, as Dalman, *Gramm. des. jüd.-paläst. Aram.*, 2d ed., 179, would have it, from אֶלְיוֹעֵינַי I chr. 3.23 etc.

[16] M. Joel, *MGWJ*, 1857, 125–134; Frankel, 158–164; Brüll, 169–178; Ros., *Entstehung*, II, 28–40a; Hamb. II, 452–460; Bacher, *Tannaiten*, II, 191–224, comp. 225–228 a. 237–274; Lauterbach, *JE*, VII, 343 f. To him goes back the groundwork of the halakic Midrash Siphra on Levit. Comp. also p. 71 (Simanim) and Bacher, *Rabbanan*, Budapest, 1914, p. 23–30 (on the controversies of Judah a. Nehemiah with anonymous scholars).

[17] Frankel, 176; Brüll, 198–200; Bacher, *Tannaiten*, II, 255–274. On the Tosephta see chap. VIII.

[18] Aboth 4.12.—Frankel, 173 f.; Brüll, 195–197; Hamb. II, 159; Bacher, *Tannaiten*, II, 275–282; *JE*, V, 94 f.; Halevy, I e, 806–809.

19 Not: Eleazar.

20 See above p. 110.

21 Aboth 4.11a.—Frankel, 176; Brüll, 198; Bacher, *Tannaiten*, II, 283–291; *JE*, V, 116. S. Horovitz is inclined to look upon Siphre Zuṭa as having proceeded from his school (Hor., *Siphre*, p. xviii).

22 Aboth 4.11b.—Frankel, 175 f.; Brüll, 198; Bacher, *Tannaiten*, II, 365 f.; *JE*, VII, 213 f.

23 This reading is better attested than: Eleazar.

24 Frankel, 186; Brüll, 212; Hamb. II, 158 f.; Bacher, *Tannaiten*, II, 292–307; *JE*, VII, 717. On the 32 hermeneutic rules see chap. XI, § 4.

25 Others: Ḳorḥa.

26 Frankel, 178; Brüll, 202; Bacher, *Tannaiten*, II, 308–321; *JE*, VII, 293.

27 See above p. 112.—*JE*, V, 120.

28 Yeb. 98b.

29 Mek. on Ex. 19.10 (Friedm. 63b).—Comp. Bacher, *MGWJ*, 1901, 300 f.; 1902, 83 f.

30 B. M. 84b f.—Aboth 1. 17 f.—Frankel, 178–185; Ph. Bloch, *MGWJ*, 1864, 81 ff., 121 ff.; Brüll, 203–209; Ros., *Entstehung*, III, 52–60; Hamb. II, 1121–1124; Grätz, 4th ed., IV, 171, 185–188; Bacher, *Tannaiten*, II, 322–334; Lauterbach, *JE*, XI, 347 f.; Halevy, I e, 764–775. Ad. Büchler, 'La conspiration de R. Nathan er de R. Meir contre le Patriarche Simon ben Gamaliel,' *REJ*, XXVIII, 60–74.

31 Aboth 4.5a.—Frankel, 185 f.; Brüll, 209 f.; Bacher, *Tannaiten*, II, 369 f.; *JE*, VI, 650.

32 Aboth 2.8c.—Frankel, 176 f.; Brüll, 200–202; Bacher, *Tannaiten*, II, 366–369; *JE*, XI, 78. Lewy, *Über einige Fragmente aus der Mischna des Abba Saul*, Berlin, 1876, 4to (36); comp. D. Hoffmann, *Magazin*, 1877, 114–120 a. J. Egers, *MGWJ*, 1878, 187–192, 227–235.

33 Or: Akiba.

34 Above p. 109.

35 Shab. 83b.—Frankel, 186; Brüll, 211 f.; Bacher, *Tannaiten*, II, 370; *JE*, VI, 208.

36 Frankel, 187; Brüll, 212; Bacher, *Tannaiten*, II, 376; *JE*, VI, 208.

37 Also: Jose.

38 Bacher, *Tannaiten*, II, 371–373. Not identical with the one immediately following, against D. Hoffmann, *Einl.*, p. 38 f.

39 Abbreviated from Jose, Joseph.

40 Frankel, 174 f.

[41] Aboth 4.20b.—Brüll, 245 f.; Bacher, *Tannaiten*, II, 373–376. On his מגלת סתרים see above p. 16.

[42] Aboth 4.14 (comp. Shab. 147b).—Bacher, *Tannaiten*, II, 377 to 383.

[43] *Zunz-Festschr.* 197.

[44] *Tannaiten*, II, 230.

[45] א' is according to Grätz a. S. Krauss Στρόβιλος; according to Bacher a. Klein, Aristobulus.—Bacher, *Tannaiten*, II, 383 f.; *JE*, X, 388. S. Klein, 'Eine Tannaimfamilie in Rom,' *Jeschurun*, ed. by J. Wohlgemuth, III, 424–445, Berlin, 1916, thinks that R. lived in Rome at the time of R. Simon ben Johai.

[46] Bacher, *Tannaiten*, II, 388 f.

NOTES TO CHAPTER XIII, § 6, P. 116

[1] Bacher, *Tannaiten*, II, 385–387; *JE*, IV, 642 f.

[2] On this place name, which is also written כפר עכום a. כ' עכן, see H. Hildesheimer, *Beiträge zur Georgr. Palästinas*, Berlin, 1886, p. 12, 81.—Franel, 199; Brüll, 232 f.; Bacher, *Tannaiten*, II, 392; *JE*, XI, 352.

[3] Bacher, *Tannaiten*, II, 393 f.; *JE*, I, 382 f.

[4] So according to Ḳid. 39b.—Aboth 4.16.—Frankel, 202; Brüll, 242 f.; Bacher, *Tannaiten*, II, 395–397; *JE*, VII, 26.

[5] Frankel, 198; Brüll, 230 f.; Bacher, *Tannaiten*, II, 397.

[6] Frankel, 203; Brüll, 245; Bacher, *Tannaiten*, II, 397–399.

[7] Shebiith 2.18 כיפור.—Bab. Ber. 63a.—Bacher, *Tannaiten*, I, 390δ; II, 276.

[8] Bacher, *Tannaiten*, II, 389 f.

[9] Bacher, *Tannaiten*, II, 390–392; *JE*, IV, 643.

[10] Frankel, 199 f.; Brüll, 235 f.; Hamb. II, 159–161; Bacher, *Tannaiten*, II, 400–407; *JE*, V, 104 f.; S. Krauss, 'R. El'azar ben Sim'on als römischer Befehlshaber,' *MGWJ*, 1894, 151–156.

[11] Brüll, 240 f.; Bacher, *Tannaiten*, II, 495–499; Is. Broydè, *JE*, X, 20 f.

[12] Aboth 4.7 f.—Brüll, 247; Bacher, *Tannaiten*, II, 407–411; *JE*, VI, 650; B. Koenigsberger, *R. Ismael ben R. Jose*, Pleschen, 1902 (28).

[13] Brüll, 246 f.; Bacher, *Tannaiten*, II, 412 to 415; *JE*, V, 99 f.

[14] Frankel, 199; Brüll, 233 f.; Bacher, *Tannaiten*, II, 415 f.

[14a] Bacher, *Tannaiten*, II, 416; on the name (אוורדימס?) *Bab. Amoräer*, 64δ.

[15] Aboth 4.20b.—Frankel, 198 f.; Brüll, 231 f.; Ros., *Entstehung*, III, 64; Bacher, *Tannaiten*, II, 417 to 421; *JE*, VII, 243.

[16] Brüll, 249; Bacher, *Tannaiten*, II, 494 f.; *JE*, VII, 345 f.

[17] Frankel, 199; Brüll, 233. Bacher, *Tannaiten*, II, 417δ, holds him to be identical with the teacher of the same name from Bartotha (above p. 114).

[18] Frankel, 200 f.; Brüll, 236–238; Bacher, *Tannaiten*, II, 422–436; *JE*, XI, 349.

[19] Frankel, 201; Brüll, 238 f.; Bacher, *Tannaiten*, II, 489.

[20] Frankel, 188–189; Brüll, 218–223; Hamb. II, 846–850; Bacher, *Tannaiten*, II, 437–453; *JE*, IX, 176 f.; Halevy, I e, 819–830.

[21] This form is better attested than: Eliezer.

[22] Comp. Syriac *ḳuphra* = כַּפָּר?; Levy, IV. 357 'dealer in rubber.' Others of Ḳappar.

[23] Aboth 4.21 f.—Frankel, 202 f.; Brüll, 243 f.; Bacher, *Tannaiten*, II, 500–502; *JE*, V, 101 f.

[24] G. = Gamaliel?; comp. also *Diḳd.* on Men. 54b.—Frankel, 203; Brüll, 244.

[25] Bacher, *Tannaiten*, II, 488 f.; *JE*, XI, 351.

[26] Aboth 6.8 f.—Frankel, 202; Brüll, 239 f.; Bacher, *Tannaiten*, II, 489–494; *JE*, XI, 355 f.

[27] Abbreviated from Menahem, as also is מני.

[28] Palest. Shebiith 37aα; Palest. Ber. 4bα.

[29] Bacher, *Paläst. Amoräer*, III, 443.

[30] Aboth 5.20.—Frankel, 202; Brüll, 242; Bacher, *Tannaiten*, II, 556 f.

[31] Yeb. 45a.

[32] Pes. 37a; Shab. 156a.

[33] See e. g. Shab. 118b.

[34] Soṭa 49b; B. Ḳ. 82b f.

[35] Palest. Shab. 10.12c.—On this teacher see Klein in *Israelit. Monatsschrift* (Supplement to *Jüdische Presse* X), 1910, No. 3.

[36] S. Klein, *JQR*, N. S., II, 544–556.

[37] *Mar Samuel*, Leipzig, 1873.

[38] Vol. II.

[39] *Magazin*, 1892, 50, 252–254 and, which is particularly noteworthy, in *ZHBg*, 1901, 101, 105 (review of Halevy's work).

[40] Comp. Moses Kuniz, מעשה חכמים, Part I, Vienna 1805 (79 leaves; see Cat. Ros. No. 1203); Abr. Krochmal, החלוץ, II (1853), 63–93; III (1854), 118–146; A. Bodek, *Marc. Aurel. Antoninus als Zeitgenosse des Rabbi Jehuda ha-Nasi*, Leipzig, 1868 (158; p. 11–64 on time and year of death); H. W. Schneeberger, *The Life and Works of Rabbi Jehuda ha-nasi* (*Rabbi*), Berlin

1870 (65); S. Gelbhaus, *Rabbi Jehuda Hanassi u. die Redaktion der Mischna*, Vienna, 1876 (98) [as a matter of fact it appeared in 1880. To be used only with caution, see *Theol. Litztg.*, 1881, No. 3]; A. Büchler, 'Der Patriarch R. Jehuda u. die griechischrömischen Städte Palästinas,' *JQR*, 1901, 683–740; A. Büchler, 'Die Maultiere u. die Wagen des Patriarchen Jehuda I.,' *MGWJ*, 1904, 193–208. In addition; Frankel, 191–197; Brüll, 223 to 230; Hamb. II, 440–450; Grätz, 4th ed., IV, 192–205, 208 f.; Bacher, *Tannaiten*, II, 454–486, a. *JE*, VII, 333–337; Halevy, I e, 809 ff. J. Fürst, 'Antoninus u. Rabbi,' *Magazin*, 1889, 41–45; D. Hoffmann, 'Die Ant.-Agadot,' *Magazin*, 1892, 33–55, 245–255; S. Krauss, *Ant. u. Rabbi*, Vienna, 1910 (148) [Ant. identified with Avidius Cassius!] ; R. Leszynsky, *Die Lösung des Ant.-Rätsels*, Berlin, 1910 (64). S. Krauss, 'La Légende de la naissance de Rabbi,' *REJ*, LVIII, 65–74 (according to Bereshith Rabbathi etc.).

NOTES TO CHAPTER XIII, § 7, P. 118

1 Keth. 103b beginning. Three sayings by him Aboth 2.2–4. Comp. in addition Weiss, III, 42–44; Bacher, *Tannaiten*, II, 554; Halevy, II, 19–23; *JE*, V, 562.

2 The name is probably abbreviated from אֲחִיָּה, comp. חִירָם a. אֲחִירָם in a bilingual inscription Ειας, see *Ephemeris f. semit. Epigraphik*, I, 189, 350.

3 See p. 13, 16, 17.

4 Chap. VIII (Mishnayoth of H., see Halevy, II, 114–119, 121–123).

5 Ḥul. 141a bottom.—Hamb. II, 137–140; Bacher, *Tannaiten*, I, 520–530; B. Baer in *Magazin*, 1890, 28–49; 119–135; Is. Broydé, *JE*, VI, 430 f.

6 So ordinarily in the Talmud.

7 See above p. 117.

8 Since ברבי (son of Rabbi . . ., *JE*, III, 52) is repeatedly wanting, it becomes doubtful whether the father or the son is meant by ר"א הקפר. Comp. also D. Hoffmann, *Einl. in die halach. Midraschim*, 1887, p. 83.

9 Concerning his Mishnayoth see Halevy, II, 114 ff., 123–126. See in addition Hamb., *Suppl.* I, 36–39; Grätz, 4th ed., IV, 196 f., 209. Bacher, *Tannaiten*, II, 503–520; L. Ginzberg, *JE*, II, 503–505.

10 Bacher, *Tannaiten*, II, 530–536; Lauterbach, *JE*, XI, 349 f.

11 E. g. Yoma 24a.

12 Not to be confounded with the Amora, the Haggadist R. Levi, see p. 124. Bacher, *Tannaiten*, II, 536–539; Halevy II, 119–121; *JE*, VIII, 36;

B. Ratner, 'Die Mischna des L. b. S.,' *Harkavy-Festschrift*, 117–122; A. M. Padua in חוט המשולש (see above p. 308, n. 40), p. 61–104.

[13] Bacher, *Tannaiten*, II, 543–546; Halevy II, 52–56.

[14] So Babyl. Talmud, Mek., Siphre.

[15] Others: Benaiah.

[16] See p. 121.—Bacher, *Tannaiten*, I, 539–543; L. Ginzberg, *JE*, II, 494 f.

[17] B. B. 8a; Ḥag. 20a; A. Z. 26b.

[18] Bacher, *Paläst. Amoräer*, III, 598 f.

[19] Tos. Ahiloth 4.8 (Zuck. p. 601); B. Ḳ. 81a; Midr. Ḳoh. 1.8; 7.26.

[20] Palest. Kil. 9.32b. S. Funk, I, 32 a. n. 4; *JE*, V, 289.—On the Babylonian Tannaim see Halevy II, 181–193. Tannaim whose time cannot be determined with certainty are named by Bacher, *Tannaiten*, II, 547–561.

NOTES TO CHAPTER XIII, § 8, P. 119

[1] Palest. Nidda 2.49d; Bacher, *Paläst. Amoräer*, I, 89 f.; *JE*, VI, 186 f.

[2] Comp. ἀπφῦς?

[3] Bacher, *Paläst. Amoräer*, I, 2, 91, 341; *JE*, V, 50 f.

[4] At times: Ḥanina bar Ḥama.

[5] Bacher, *Paläst. Amoräer*, I, 1–34; Grätz, 4th ed., IV, 232–234; Halevy II, 258 ff.; *JE*, VI, 216 f.

[6] Hamb. II, 430 f.; Bacher, *Paläst. Amoräer*, I, 35–47; Halevy II, 273–282.

[7] Bacher, *Paläst. Amoräer*, I, 48–57; Halevy, II, 282 to 293.

[8] Bacher, *Paläst. Amoräer*, I, 58–88; Halevy II, 297 f.; *JE*, VII, 234 f.

[9] Frankel, Introd., 70b; comp. Bacher, *Paläst. Amoräer*, I, 124 f.; *JE*, VII, 355 f.

[10] In the Palest. Talmud usually אושעיא.

[11] Bacher, *Paläst. Amoräer*, I, 89–108; Halevy II, 253–258; *JE*, VI, 475 f. W. Bacher, 'The Church father Origen and Hoshaya,' *JQR*, III, 357–360.

[12] In the Palest. Talmud. רבי יהודה נשיאה or רבי יודן נשייא.

[13] Hamb. II, 898–901; Grätz, 4th ed., IV, 220–228; Bacher, *Paläst. Amoräer*, III, 581 a. *JE*, VII, 337 f.; Halevy II, 23–52. A. Marmorstein, 'L'opposition contre le patriarche R. Juda II.,' *REJ*, LXIV, 59–66.

[14] Bacher, *Paläst. Amoräer*, I, 109–118.

[15] Bacher, *Paläst. Amoräer*, I, 119–123; *JE*, XI, 351.

[16] Aboth 6.2b; Hamb. II, 520–526; Bacher, *Paläst. Amoräer*, I, 124–194;

Grätz, 4th ed., IV, 240 f.; Halevy II, 293–296; *JE*, VII, 293 f.; J. Rachlin, בר ליואי, תולדות ר' יהושע בן לוי הלוי, New York, 1906 (92).

[17] Bacher, *Paläst. Amoräer*, III, 640–642 a. *Proöm.* 44 f.; *JE*, XII, 626.

[18] Bacher, *Paläst. Amoräer*, II, 85; III, 559 f.; *JE*, VI, 432.

[19] Bacher, *Babyl. Amoräer*, 35; Halevy II, 223–225.

[20] Fürst, *Kultur-u. Lit. geschichte*, I, 92; Bacher, *Babyl. Amoräer*, 34 a. *JE*, I, 29; Halevy, II, 225–228.

[21] Shab. 156a Ḥanina, not Ḥiyya, is the correct reading.

[22] Bacher, *Paläst. Amoräer*, III, 644; *JE*, XII, 652b.

[23] Sanh. 17b according to the correct reading (see I. Pick's marginal gloss).

[24] Sanh. 30b; B. Ḳ. 47b. 4aγ. Bacher, *Babyl. Amoräer*, 34 f.; הַקֶּדֶם, II (1908), 148–150.

[25] D. Hoffmann, *Mar Samuel*, 74 ff.; Bacher, *Babyl. Amoräer*, 34; Felix Lazarus in Brüll's *Jahrbücher*, X, 74–84; S. Funk, I, 44, 63 a. n. 4; *JE*, V, 289. On the other hand Grätz, 4th ed., IV, note 27; Halevy, II, 246–252.

[26] Babyl. Pes. 4a.

[27] Nidda 24b.

[28] Comp. Bekor. 24a.

[29] Er. 50b; B. B. 42a; Sanh. 83b top (comp. R. Ḥiyya B. M. 5a).—M. J. Mühlfelder, *Rabh. Ein Lebensbild zur Geschichte des Talmud*, Leipzig, 1871 (83); Bacher, *Babyl. Amoräer*, 1–33 a. *JE*, I, 29 f.; Grätz, 4th ed., IV, 256–261; Hamb. II, 956–966; Halevy II, 210 to 223, 400–410; Funk, I, 42–56; Umanski in Gräber's אוצר ספרות, V (Cracow 1896), 159–212; Albek, משפחות סופרים, I (Warsaw 1903), 28–73; J. S. Zuri (Schesak), *Rab, sein Leben u. seine Anschauungen*, Zurich, 1918 (151); J. E. Melamed, רבן של כל בני הגולה, *Leben u. Tätigkett des Tannaiten Rab*, Wilna, 1914 (242).

[30] Sanh. 5a. In the printed editions frequently Rabbah bar bar Ḥana (see p. 128), e. g. Ḥul. 8b, 44b, 100a. *JE*, X, 290.

[31] Sanh. 29b, 36b; B. Ḳ. 80a. Halevy II, 228; *JE*, II, 230 f.

[32] B. M. 85b.

[33] B. Ḳ. 113a.

[34] D. Hoffmann, *Mar Samuel, Rector der jüdischen Akademie zu Nehardea in Babylonien*, Leipzig, 1873 (79); Sigm. Fessler, *Mar Samuel, der bedeutendste Amora*, Breslau, 1879 (68); F. Kanter, *Beiträge zur Kenntniss des Rechtssystems u. der Ethik Mar Samuels*, Bern, 1895 (47); D. Schapiro, 'Les connaissances médicales de Mar Samuel,' *REJ*, XLII, 14–26; Hamb. II, 1072–1079; Bacher, *Babyl. Amoräer*, 37–45; Grätz, 4th ed., IV, 261–265; Sokolow in האסיף, II (1885), 262–274; Funk I, 56–65; Halevy II, 400–410; Lauterbach, *JE*, XI, 29–31.

NOTES TO CHAPTER XIII, § 9, P. 121

[1] See Pes 118a.

[2] Comp. Bondi, p. 236–241.—Hamb. II, 473–489; Bacher, *Paläst. Amoräer*, I, 205–339 a. *Proöm.* 39 f.; Grätz, 4th ed., IV, 234–238 a. Note 26; Halevy II, 298–332; J. Bondi, *JbJLG*, I, 233–268 [follows Halevy]; S. Mendelsohn, *JE*, VII, 211–213; Löwenmayer, *MGWJ*, IV, (1855), 285–294, 321–328; Horowitz, in *Literaturblatt* of the *Jüdische Presse*, Berlin, 1871–1873 (an unfinished biography); Witkind, חוט המשולש, Wilna, 1877, p. 105 to 142; S. A. Jordan, *Rabbi Jochanan bar Nappacha*, I, Budapest, 1895 (96); S. J. Zuri, *R. Jochanan*, Berlin, 1918 (176).—As to Johanan's connections with the compilation of the Palestinian Talmud see above p. 65.

[3] Bacher, *Paläst. Amoräer*, I, 340–418; Grätz, 4th ed., IV, 238 to 240; Halevy II, 317–327 (followed by Bondi, 1. c., 248–253); *JE*, XI, 354 f.

[4] In the Babyl. Talmud אילפא.

[5] Taan. 21a. Bacher, *Paläst. Amoräer*, I, 209f.

[6] Yoma 78a (read Isaac for Zadok).

[7] M. Ḳ. 25b.—Frankel, *Introd.*, 107a.

[8] Properly to be sounded Alexandrai.

[9] Bacher. *Paläst. Amoräer*, I, 195–204; *JE*, I, 361. Ibid., p. 360f., on a somewhat older Amora of the same name.

[10] Edited by S. Buber, Lyck 1868.

[11] Bacher, *Paläst. Amoräer*, III, 607–609.

[12] See Halevy II, 228ff.

[13] Bacher, *Paläst. Amoräer*, III, 560.

[14] Not to be confounded with the Tanna of the same name.

[15] Bacher, *Paläst. Amoräer*, I, 419–446 a. *Proöm.* 41 f.

[16] Bacher, *Paläst. Amoräer*, I, 447–476 a. *Proöm.* 42 f.; *JE*, VI, 187.

[17] Bacher, *Paläst. Amoräer*, III, 614–616; *JE*, VIII, 397.

[18] Thus Rab speaks of him as Lyddian לודאה.

[19] Bacher, *Paläst. Amoräer*, II, 552–566 (controversy with spokesmen of Christian dogma p. 555–557); Frankel, *Introd.*, 127a; Grätz, 4th ed., IV, 241–246.

[20] Bacher, *Paläst. Amoräer*, III, 557 f. a. *Proöm.* 46.

[21] Bacher, *Paläst. Amoräer*, III, 592–594; *JE*, VII, 234.

[22] Bacher, *Paläst. Amoräer*, III, 444, 612, 751 a. *Yerushalaim*, IX (1911), 392–395.

[23] P. 119.

[24] P. 126.

[25] P. 131.—Bacher, *Paläst. Amoräer*, III, 79–86.

[26] Frankel, *Introd.*, 66b f., Bacher, *Paläst. Amoräer*, III, 533–535.

[27] In the Palest. Talmud for the most part corrupted into עילאי.

[28] Bacher, *Paläst. Amoräer*, III, 627–636 a. *Proöm.* 45 f.; *JE*, XII, 42 f.

[29] Bacher, *Babyl. Amoräer*, 52–60; Grätz, 4th ed., IV, 289–292; Halevy II, 411ff., 417ff.; *JE*, VI, 492 f.; S. Funk, I, 111–116; A. Lapidot in Rabbinowitz's כנסת ישראל, III, 297–303.

[30] Ḳidd. 72a.

[31] Ḳidd. 33b.

[32] Nidda 24b.—Hamb. II, 491 f.; Bacher, *Babyl. Amoräer*, 47–52; Grätz, 4th ed., IV, 292–297; Halevy II, 421 ff.; Lauterbach, *JE*, VII, 342 f.; Funk, I, 133–142.

[33] L. Bank, *REJ*, XXXIX, 191–198.

[34] Funk, I, 107 to 109 a. Note 4; *JE*, V, 289.

[35] Bacher, *Babyl. Amoräer*, III, 564 f.; Hyman, *Toldoth*, 202 f.

[36] Bacher, *Babyl. Amoräer*, 71–73.

[37] Gen. R. on 23.1.

[38] Palest. Taan. 3.67a = Babyl. Taan. 20b. Bacher, *Babyl. Amoräer*, 74 f.; *JE*, I, 185 f.

[39] Bacher, 46, 81; Funk, I, 110; *JE*, X, 289 f.

[40] Bacher, *Babyl. Amoräer*, 83–85 a. *Proöm.* 87.

[41] In the Palest. Talmud R. Jeremiah bar Wa ווה or simply R. J.

[42] Frankel, *Introd.*, 108a; Bacher, *Babyl. Amoräer*, 7, 51 a. *Paläst. Amoräer*, III, 582f.; *JE*, VII, 109.

NOTES TO CHAPTER XIII, § 10, P. 124

[1] In the Babyl. Talmud, sometimes also in the Palest.: bar Naḥmani.

[2] Bacher, *Paläst. Amoräer*, I, 477–551; *JE*, XI, 25 f.

[3] Bacher, *Babyl. Amoräer*, 79 f., 86 a. *Paläst. Amoräer*, II, 205–295 a. *Proöm.*, 49–55; *JE*, XII, 615 f.

[4] Bacher, *Paläst. Amoräer*, II, 296–436 a. *Proöm.* 55–60; *JE*, VIII, 21f.

[5] Not to be confounded with the Tannaite Eleazar ben Shammua. In the Palest. Talmud (except in Ber.) לעזר.

[6] Frankel, *Introd.*, 111b–113a; Bacher, *Paläst. Amoräer*, II, 1–87; Halevy II, 327–332 (followed by Bondi, *JbJLG*, I, 253–256); *JE*, V, 95 f.

[7] Frequently mispronounced as Abuhu.

[8] Hamb. II, 4–8; Perlitz in *MGWJ*, 1887 (Febr. to April, June, July); Grätz, 4th ed., IV, 282–287; Bacher, *Paläst. Amoräer*, II, 88–142; K. Kohler, *JE*, I, 36 f.

[9] In the Palest. Talmud also אימי, i. e. Emmi or Immi.

[10] Hamb. II, 56 f.; *JE*, I, 522 f. On Ammi a. Asi see Bacher.

[11] So the Babyl. Talmud; in the Palest. usually יוסי, but also איסי, אסי, אסא, comp. Frankel, *Introd.*, 100a, b. The name is prob. shortened from יוסף.

[12] Hamb. II, 76 f.; Halevy II, 232; *JE*, II, 231.

[13] In the Palest. Talmud ר' יהודה נשיאה or ר' יודן נשייא.

[14] Grätz, 4th ed., IV, 276 f.; Halevy II, 333 ff.; Bacher, *JE*, VII, 338 f.

[15] Bacher, *Babyl. Amoräer*, 86 f. a. *Paläst. Amoräer*, II, 174–201; Grätz, 4th ed., IV, 280 f.

[16] In the Palest. Talm. ordinarily minus a title. In the Babyl. Talm. Sanh. 14a רב שמן!

[17] Bacher, *Paläst. Amoräer*, II, 201–204; Grätz, 4th ed., IV, 280 f.; *JE*, XI, 348.

[18] So in Palestine with Grecized name.

[19] Bacher, *Paläst. Amoräer*, II, 437–474 a. *Proöm.* 63–65; *JE*, XI, 356 f.

[20] Z. I. is not to be confounded with the later Palestinian Z., who was a pupil of Jeremiah.

[21] Palest. Maas. 3.51a.—Bacher, *Paläst. Amoräer*, III, 1–34; Grätz, 4th ed., IV, 300–302; *JE*, XII, 651 f.; Halevy II, 242 ff. a. esp. L. Bank, *REJ*, XXXVIII, 47–63, who distinguishes three bearers of this name, to wit, two Babylonians (Rab Judah's pupil a. a contemporary of Abaye and Rabba) a. the Palestinian. See also S. Berman, לוח א"י X, 145–154.

[22] Bacher, *Paläst. Amoräer*, III, 517–525 a. *JE*, I, 29.

[23] Bacher, *Paläst. Amoräer*, III, 34–54.

[24] אילעא, אילא; Frankel, *Introd.*, 75b records other mutilated forms of this name.

[25] Palest. Yoma 3.40c; Palest. Giṭ. 7.48 γ.

[26] Bacher, *Paläst. Amoräer*, III, 699 to 702; *JE*, V, 88.

[27] In the Palest. Talm. also Zeriḳan.

[28] Bacher, *Paläst. Amoräer*, III, 754 f.; *JE*, XII, 662.

[29] Bacher, *Paläst. Amoräer*, III, 550–552, 565.

[30] Bacher, *Paläst. Amoräer*, III, 572 f.

[31] Bacher, *Paläst. Amoräer*, III, 603 f.

[32] Bacher, *Paläst. Amoräer*, III, 599–603 a. *Proöm.* 67.

33 In the Palest. Talm.: R. Ba.

34 Bacher, *Paläst. Amoräer*, III, 530–532.

35 Bacher, *Paläst. Amoräer*, III, 571 f.

36 Bacher, *Paläst. Amoräer*, I, 131; III, 440.

37 Comp. Ezr. 2. 11.

38 Bacher, *Paläst. Amoräer*, III, 667–669; *JE*, II, 619.

39 Bacher, *Paläst. Amoräer*, II, 475–512 a. *Proöm.* 60–63. See above p. 122.

40 So the Babyl. Talm. פפי a. פפא Aramaized Πάππος. In the Palest. Talm. for the most part חיננא, in the Midrashim mostly חנינא b. Pappa.

41 Bacher, *Paläst. Amoräer*, II, 513–532 a. *Proöm.* 65 f.; *JE*, VI, 218 f.

42 See p. 129.

43 Bacher, *Paläst. Amoräer*, III, 661–666 a. *Proöm.* 83 f.; *JE*, III, 31.

44 Bacher, *Paläst. Amoräer*, III, 540–546 a. *Proöm.* 66.

45 Above p. 125.

46 Bacher, *Paläst. Amoräer*, III, 636–639 a. *Proöm.* 48 f.; *JE*, XII, 43.

47 Bacher, *Paläst. Amoräer*, III, 526.

48 Funk, I, 142 f.

49 Er. 67a.—Bacher, *Babyl. Amoräer*, 61–71; Grätz, 4th ed., IV, 297; Halevy, II, 421 f.; *JE*, VI, 422 f.; Funk, I, 116–123.

50 Bacher, *Babyl. Amoräer*, 73 f.; *JE*, VI, 201.

51 Bacher, *Babyl. Amoräer*, 62 f.

52 Bacher, *Babyl. Amoräer*, 64 f. a. *Proöm.* 87. On the name אבדימי see below § 11, n. 22.

53 Hisda is the one just mentioned. Bacher, *Babyl. Amoräer*, 75 f.

54 Er. 67a; Shebu. 41b.—Bacher, *Babyl. Amoräer*, 76–79; Grätz, 4th ed., IV, 289; *JE*, XI, 285 f.

55 Beṣa 25b.

56 Ned. 32a; Meg. 15b.

57 B. M. 16b.

58 Hamb. II, 819f.; Bacher, *Babyl. Amoräer*, 79–83; Grätz, 4th ed., IV, 298–300; Halevy II, 412ff., 419ff.; Funk, I, 123–132; *JE*, IX, 143f.

59 See Mann, *JQR*, N. S., VIII, 352f.

60 Palest. Talm.: Abba.

61 The father's name was Abba bar Ḥana, hence בר twice.

62 Comp. L. Stern, *Über den Talmud*, Würzburg, 1875, 18 ff.; K. Fischer, *Gutmeinung über den T. der Hebräer*, Vienna, 1883, 75 ff.—Bacher, *Babyl. Amoräer*, 87–93; Lauterbach, *JE*, X, 290 f.

[63] In the Babyl. Talm. עולא with the father unnamed; in the Palest. Talm. likewise minus a title.

[64] Bacher, *Babyl. Amoräer*, 93–97; *JE*, XII, 340.

[65] Bacher, *Babyl. Amoräer*, 97–101; Grätz, 4th ed., IV, 320–325; Halevy II, 435–440; Lauterbach, *JE*, X, 292 f.; Funk, II, 25–33.

[66] Pes. 13b, 52b.

[67] Bacher, *Babyl. Amoräer*, 101–107; Grätz, 4th ed., IV, 325 f.; Halevy II, 440 ff.; Funk, II, 25–34.

NOTES TO CHAPTER XIII, § 11, P. 128

[1] Bacher, *Paläst. Amoräer*, III, 95–106; Halevy II, 356–366; *JE*, VII, 108 f.

[2] Bacher, *Paläst. Amoräer*, III, 670–673.

[3] Bacher, *Paläst. Amoräer*, III, 54–63.

[4] Bacher, *Paläst. Amoräer*, III, 106–160 a. *Proöm.* 69–71; *JE*, I, 276 f.

[5] In the Palest. Talm. also Abun a. Bun.

[6] So for the most part in the Babyl. Talm.

[7] Bacher, *Paläst. Amoräer*, III, 397–432.

[8] Bacher, *Paläst. Amoräer*, III, 744–748.

[9] Bacher, *Paläst. Amoräer*, III, 681–685; *JE*, VI, 218.

[10] Bacher, *Paläst. Amoräer*, III, 679 f. a. *Proöm.* 84.

[11] Bacher, *Paläst. Amoräer*, III, 674–676 a. *Proöm.* 84.

[12] Bacher, *Paläst. Amoräer*, III, 37–72 a. *Proöm.* 73 f.

[13] Also חונא, חוניא, נחוניא.

[14] Bacher, *Paläst. Amoräer*, III, 272–302 a. *Proöm.* 74; *JE*, VI, 493.

[15] Frankel, *Introd.*, 90.

[16] In the Palest. Talm. also for short: J. b. P.; frequently also simply R. Judah.

[17] Bacher, *Paläst. Amoräer*, III, 160–220 a. *Proöm.* 71–73.

[18] Bacher, *Paläst. Amoräer*, III, 63 to 79 a. *Proöm.* 68 f.

[19] Bacher, *Paläst. Amoräer*, III, 303–309.

[20] Once for short: Ḥanina of Caesarea.—Bacher, *Paläst. Amoräer*, 13.

[21] Bacher, *Paläst. Amoräer*, III, 656–659 a. *Proöm.* 83; *JE*, I, 281.

[22] A bilingual inscription reads Αβουδεμμος i. e. אבוה דְאֶמִּיה, *Ephemeris für semit. Epigraphik*, I, 189, 350.

[23] Bacher, *Paläst. Amoräer*, III, 691–693; *JE*, IV, 603.

[24] Palest. Ber. 1.5aγ; Ter. 1.41a.

[25] Grätz, 4th ed., IV, 316–318; *JE*, VI, 400.—Sanh. 99a probably another Hillel is meant, see Bacher, *Paläst. Amoräer*, III, 703 f.

[26] Hamb. II, 1–4; Grätz, 4th ed., IV, 327–329; Bacher, *Babyl. Amoräer*, 107–113 a. *JE*, I, 27 f.; Halevy II, 473–480; Funk II, 34–40.

[27] Sukka 28a.

[28] Er. 15a; Sanh. 27a.—Bacher, *Babyl. Amoräer*, 108 f., 150 a. *Proöm.* 88; Grätz, 4th ed., IV, 329–335; A. J. Joffe. *Magazin*, 1885, 217 to 224; Halevy, II, 473–480, 494–496; S. Funk, II, 66–77 a. in *JbJLG*, IV, 204–213 [follows Halevy]; *JE*, X, 288 f.; Antokolski in האסיף (by Straschun), I, 2d divis., 194–201 (supplemented by A. Lapidot, כנסת ישראל, III, 333–340).

[29] B. B. 22a; Taan. 8a; Funk, II, 89.

[30] Hamb. II, 820 f.; Bacher, *Babyl. Amoräer*, 133–137 a. *Proöm.* 88; Funk, II, 86–88; Halevy, II, 499–502; *JE*, IX, 143.

[31] *JE*, X, 314. Hyman, *Toldoth*, 1101 f.

[32] *JE*, VI, 555; Hyman, 140 f.

[33] Hyman, 751 f.

[34] Bacher, *Babyl. Amoräer*, 124–127; *JE*, X, 291 f.

[35] פפוניא belonging to the district of Pum Beditha; prob. Epiphaneia. Bacher, *Babyl. Amoräer*, 137–139; *JE*, I, 278.

[36] Bacher, *Babyl. Amoräer*, 139 f.; *JE*, X, 288.

[37] Bacher, *Babyl. Amoräer*, 140 f.

NOTES TO CHAPTER XIII, § 12, P. 130

[1] Bacher, *Paläst. Amoräer*, III, 220–231; Halevy, II, 366 ff.; on Jonah see also *JE*, VII, 230 f.

[2] Bacher, *Paläst. Amoräer*, III, 231–237.

[3] Bacher, *Paläst. Amoräer*, III, 310–344 a. *Proöm.* 74 f.; *JE*, X, 20.

[4] Bacher, *Paläst. Amoräer*, III, 690 f.

[5] Bacher, *Paläst. Amoräer*, III, 344–396 a. *Proöm.* 74–79; *JE*, III, 52 f.

[6] Bacher, *Paläst. Amoräer*, III, 449,724–729; *JE*, VII, 240.

[7] Bacher, *Paläst. Amoräer*, III, 749; *JE*, XI, 20.

[8] See above p. 128.

[9] Bacher, *Paläst. Amoräer*, III, 397 f., 404, 407 a. *Proöm.* 79–81.

[10] Abbreviated from Menahem.

[11] Bacher, *Paläst. Amoräer*, III, 397, 443–457.

[12] Also Ḥanina.

[13] Bacher, *Paläst. Amoräer*, III, 673 f., 446 f.

[14] Bacher, *Paläst. Amoräer*, III, 432–443.

[15] Bacher, *Paläst. Amoräer*. III, 723.

[16] Palest. Ber. 12c.—Bacher, *Paläst. Amoräer*, III, 465–511; *Proöm.* 89–102; Lauterbach, *JE*, XII, 44. As to his supposed native place Nave נוה, נוי, ננוה Shab. 30a, see Bacher, 508 f.; Schürer, 4th ed., II, 17 f.; Klein, *JQR*, N. S. VI, 550–554; *Corpus Inscriptionum*, 84 f.; *Jeschurun*, IX, 164 ff.

[17] To be kept apart from the elder N., son of Samuel bar N., a. from the Babylonian Rab N. bar Jacob. Bacher, *Paläst. Amoräer*, III, 739–743.

[18] Bacher, *Paläst. Amoräer*, III, 458–465 a. *Proöm.* 82 f.

[19] Halevy, II, 571–573.

[20] Bacher, *Paläst. Amoräer*, III, 17, 99, 106, 225, 449.

[21] Bacher, *Babyl. Amoräer*, 141–143; Grätz, 4th ed., IV, 336 f.; Halevy, II, 505 to 517; *JE*, IX, 510; Pijoska in אוצר הספרות (by Gräber), V, 213–218; Funk II, 89–93.

[22] Bacher, *Babyl. Amoräer*, 141; Halevy, II, 505 ff.; *JE*, VI, 493.

[23] Ḥag. 4b; Ber. 6a; *JE*, II, 620.

[24] Sanh. 17b.

[25] Grätz, 4th ed., IV, 336 f.; *JE*, VI, 186; Funk, II, 88 f.

[26] Hyman, 1031 f.

[27] *JE*, IV, 604.

[28] Shab. 82a.

[29] Weiss, III, 207; Halevy, III, 85–89; Hyman, 1105.

[30] *JE*, XII, 645.

NOTES TO CHAPTER XIII, § 13, P. 132

[1] Bacher, *Babyl. Amoräer*, 146; *JE*, I, 490 f.; Halevy, II, 515; III, 68–73.

[2] Halevy, II, 515–517.

[3] Halevy, II, 536–550; III, 74–85; comp. *JE*, X, 300.

[4] *JE*, VI, 493 f.; Hyman, 355 f.

[5] Keth. 22a.

[6] Bacher, *Babyl. Amoräer*, 144–147 a. *JE*, II, 187 f.; Grätz, 4th ed., IV, 348–353; Halevy, II, 536–539; Funk, II, 98–110, 140–143. As to Ashi's relation to the exilarch Huna bar Nathan see L. Bank, *REJ*, XXXII, 51–55.

[7] Above p. 130.

[8] Ḥul. 93b; *JE*, I, 278; Hyman, 130–132.

[9] Bacher, *Babyl. Amoräer*, 147. A consolatory prayer on the occasion of a death Ber. 46b. See also Ber. 55b.

[10] Bacher, *Babyl. Amoräer*, 145.

NOTES TO CHAPTER XIII, § 14, P. 133

[1] Halevy, III, 64–68; Funk, II, 112 f.

[2] Hyman, 141.

[3] Grätz, 4th ed., IV, 369–372; Halevy, III, 93 f.; Bacher, *JE*, XI, 665.

[4] The spelling רבא with א seems to be better attested than רבה, see *Diḳd.*, Ber. 50a a. M. Ḳ. 4a. The name T. probably from the native home Thospitis. Halevy, III, 95–98; *JE*, X, 293.

[5] Halevy, III, 7–15, 100–102.

[6] *JE*, V, 578; Funk, II, 102.

[7] Halevy, III, 85–89; Hyman, 1029.

[8] Hyman, 1029.

[9] Hyman, 749 f.; Brüll, *Jahrbücher*, II, 23–25.

NOTES TO CHAPTER XIII, § 15, P. 133

[1] N. Brüll, 'Die Entstehungsgeschichte des B. T. als Schriftwerkes,' *Jahrbücher*, II, 23–49; Halevy, III, 23–63; W. Bacher, *JE*, X, 610–612.

[2] See D. Hoffmann, *Magazin*, 1876, 26 f.; 1877, 159.

[3] Epistle, ed. Neubauer, 34 f.; ed. Lewin, 98 f.

[4] Neub., 25.

[5] *JE*, I, 282.

[6] Ḥul. 59b.

[7] Var.: אמוסא.

[8] Var.: תחינא.

[9] Funk, II, 124 f.

[10] See W. Bacher, *JE*, V, 675.

[11] Comp. Sherira: ואמרין דגאון הוה.

[12] Comp. Halevy, III; A. Epstein a. W. Bacher, *JE*, V, 567 to 572.

[13] See Sam. Poznański, *REJ*, LI, 52–58. Comp. also S. P., *Babylonische*

Geonim in nachgeonäischer Zeit, Berlin, 1914 (144); 'Die Anfänge des palästin. Gaonats', *Schwarz-Festschrift*, 471–488. L. Ginzberg, *Geonica*, 2 volumes, New York, 1909.

NOTES TO CHAPTER XIV, § 5, P. 163

[1] The dealer in asphalt? Abraham ibn Ezra calls him בן קוורא; comp. also Harkavy, *Responsen*, 374.

NOTES

PART II

NOTES TO CHAPTER XV, § 1, P. 201

1 Comp. the articles 'Midrash,' 'Midrash-Haggadah,' 'Midrash-Halakah' by J. Theodor, J. Z. Lauterbach, S. Horovitz in *JE*, VIII, 548–580. Abraham ben Elijah of Wilna, ספר רב פעלים, edited by Sh. Ḥones, Warsaw 1894 (160) [Alphabetical list of Midrashim with statements as to which ancient authors mention them.] Corrections and additions in: S. Buber a. S. Chones, מחברת יריעות שלמה, Warsaw 1896 (52). See in addition D. Kaufmann, *MGWJ*, XXXIX, 136–139.

2 2.10 ff.

3 Levit. 6.20; Num. 19.22.

4 See chap. II, § 1 (in the same place also on the 'oral Torah'). As to the word Midrash see chap. I, § 6.

5 See chap. I, § 7.

6 See chap. II, § 3.

7 See chap. VIII.

8 See chap. I, § 3.

9 See chap. XVI.

10 See the passages adduced by me in *PRE.*, 3d ed., IX, 767, l. 35 ff.

11 Comp. Aboth 5.22 הפוך בה והפוך בה דכולא בה.

12 See chap. I, § 8.

13 Zunz, *Gottesdienstl. Vorträge*, 349 f.

14 See Zunz. l. c., esp. chap. 20; Hamb. II, 921–934 (article: 'Predigt, religiöse Rede'). As to the Rules governing the exposition of Scripture see chap. XI.

NOTES TO CHAPTER XV, § 2, P. 203

1 E. g. Palest. Maas. 1.48d; Palest. Yeb. 4.5cγ; Weiss, III, 121.

2 Babyl. Sanh. 57b.

3 See above p. 13γ.

4 Ber. 10a; Erub. 21b; Yoma 38b a. elsewhere; Weiss, III, 141; Bacher, *Terminologie*, II, 133.

5 Chap. II, § 2.

6 We possess the oldest written specimen of a Midrash in IV Esdras 7,

132–139; that is a Midrash on Exod. 34.6 f., with regard to the naming of the 13 Middoth or divine attributes. See D. Simonsen, *Lewy-Festschrift*, 270–278.

[7] Berlin 1832.

[8] Genesis R. by J. Theodor, 1903 ff. a. Siphre by S. Horovitz, 1917.

[19] Comp. Num. Rabba.

NOTES TO CHAPTER XV, § 3, P. 204

[1] On these Sedarim comp. Ad. Büchler, *JQR*, V (1893), 420–468; VI, 1–73; Jos. Jacobs, *JE*, XII, 254–257; Ism. Elbogen, *Der jüdische Gottesdienst in seiner geschichtlichen Entwicklung*, Berlin 1913, § 25, 4 and esp. J. Theodor, 'Die Midrashim zum Pent. u. der dreijährige paläst. Zyklus,' *MWGJ*, 1885–1887; esp. 1885, p. 356. (The exceptions taken by A. Berliner, *Über den Einfluss des ersten hebr. Buchdruckes . . .*, Frankf. o. M. 1896, 36 f., 49, are untenable.)

[2] Comp. Theodor, *MGWJ*, 1879, 169; M. Lerner, *Magazin*, 1880, 202.

[3] Theodor, 170; Lerner, 204.

[4] Lerner, 169.

[5] For more detailed studies on the proems in the Pesiḳtha Kahana see Theodor, 108, 110–113, 164–175, 271–278; on those in Gen. R., Lerner, 168–174, 197–207. As to the proems, see in adition Ph. Bloch, 'Studien zur Aggada,' *MGWJ*, 1885, 1886; S. Maybaum, *Die ältesten Phasen in der Entwickelung der jüd. Predigt*, Berlin 1901, I, 14–27; W. Bacher, *Die Proömien der alten jüd. Homilie*, Leipzig 1913 (126). The publications by D. Künstlinger (*Altjüd. Bibeldeutung*, Berlin 1911; *Die Petiḥot der Pesikta de Rab Kahana*, Cracow 1912; *Die P. des Midr. Rabba zu Levit.*, 1913; *zur Gen.*, 1914) are, according to Bacher, whose criticism is probably too severe, 'altogether undemonstrated and unclear'; see *MGWJ*, 1911, 503–509.

[6] Sanh. 38b.

[7] Bacher, *Paläst. Amoräer*, III, 508.

[8] Shab. 30a.

[9] Zunz, *GV.*, 354; Grätz, *MGWJ*, 1881, 329.

[10] Comp. Num. R. sect. 15–17 a. 20–23; Deut. R., Yelammedenu a. Pesiḳtha Rabbathi (Zunz, 258; 252; 227,231; 242 f.). The halakic introduction opens in the two works mentioned first with 'Halakah,' in the two others with the formula יְלַמְּדֵנוּ רַבֵּנוּ.

[11] Comp. Theodor, *MGWJ*, 1879, 166 against Zunz, 195, 227, 355.

[12] See Theodor, *MGWJ*, 1879, 108 f.

NOTES TO CHAPTER XVI, P. 206

[1] Frankel 307–311; Weiss, II, 225–239; D. Hoffmann, *Zur Einleitung in die halachischen Midraschim*, Berlin 1887.

[2] Isr. Lewy, *Über die 'Mechilta des R. Simon,'* p. 2, explains prob. correctly: 'Academy of Rab.' Even then one is materially justified in thinking of the school of Akiba.

[3] See above p. 112 f., 95 f.

[4] Comp. Hoffmann, 43 ff.; Bacher, *Terminologie*, I.

[5] See above p. 94; Bacher, *Terminologie*, I, 14 f., 44 f., 149 α.

[6] See above p. 96.

[7] Comp. in addition S. Horovitz, *Siphre*, p. vi–ix.

NOTES TO CHAPTER XVI, § 1, P. 206

[1] So in particular: 8.1–10.7 (dedication of the tabernacle, ed. Weiss 40c–46b); 18.1–5; a number of verses at the beginning of Ḳedoshim, 19.1–3, 15–18; furthermore 22.32 ff. and on the Benedictions and Curses 26.3–46.

[2] According to Asi of the third generation of Palestinian Amoraim (see above p. 125), an old established custom, Levit. R. 7. Yoma 27a, a piece is preserved of the instruction which Abaye imparted to his son.

[3] Sanh. 86a: סתם ספרא ר׳ יהודה.

[4] See above p. 119.

[5] See Hoffmann, 27 f.

[6] Wayyiḳra Nedaba; Wayyiḳra Ḥoba (commences Levit. 4.1); Saw 6.1; Mekiltha Milluim 8.1; Shemini 9.1; Tazri'a 12.1; Tazri'a Nega'im 13.1; Meṣora' Nega'im 14.1; Meṣora' Zabim 14.1; Aḥare Moth 16.1; Ḳedoshim 19.1; Emor 21.1; Behar 25.1; Beḥuḳḳothai 26.1.

[7] See, however, p. 208 a. n. 8 on Midrash Tannaim.

[8] D. Hoffmann, *Mechilta de-Rabbi Simon ben Jochai, ein halachischer u. haggadischer Midrasch zu Ex . . . reconstruirt u. mit Anmerkungen*, Frankf. o. M. 1905 (180); comp. the same author's paper, 'Zur Einl. in . . .,' *JbJLG*, III, 191–205 a. Isr. Lewy, *Ein Wort über die Mechilta des R. Simon*, Breslau 1889 (40).

[9] 'Der Anteil R. Simons an der ihm zugeschriebenen M.,' *Lewy-Festschrift*, 403–436.

[10] *Zur Erklärung u. Textkritik der Mechilta des R. Simon*, Breslau 1919 (33. Programme, important also for textual criticism). Comp. also L. Blau,

'Zur Erklärung der M.,' *Lewy-Festschrift*, 54 to 65.—Main source: Midrash ha-gadol.

¹¹ See § 2b. Excerpts are found in Yalḳuṭ Shimeoni, in Num. R. 4.21–7 a. in Midrash ha-gadol; add the fragment Num. 31.23 ff. published by S. Schechter, *JQR*, VI (1894), 657–663, from the Genizah.

NOTES TO CHAPTER XVI, § 2, P. 207

¹ According to Güdemann, *MGWJ*, 1870, 273, properly: compendium, from כּוֹל.

² בֹּא almost one-half, בְּשַׁלַּח almost entirely, also the greater part of יִתְרוֹ.

³ Bo or פָּסְחָא Passover, begins at Exod. 12.1; Beshallaḥ 13.17; Ha-shira 15.1; Wayyassa' 15.22, Manna; Amaleḳ 17.8 (18.1 ff. usually cited as 'Jethro'); Baḥodesh 19.1, revelation on Sinai; Neziḳin 21.1, Book of the Covenant Dekaspa, after the initial words Im keseph 22.34; Shabbatta.

⁴ So 6.22 to 27 (the Priestly Blessing); 7.1–18 a. 84–89 (gifts and offerings by the princes of the tribes); 10.9 f., 29–36 (Hobab a. the battle cries); ch. 11, 12 etc. Strangely enough such elucidations are wanting 13, 14 (the spies) 16, 17 (Korah's uprising and the consequences), 20–24 (brazen serpent), Sihon a. Og, Balaam etc.

⁵ 1.1–30; 3.23–29; 6.4–9; 11.10–32.

⁶ Haggadic matter at the end: 30.14; ch. 32–34.

⁷ See Hoffmann, *Einl.*, 18–20, 73–77.

⁸ *Midrash Tannaim zum Deut.*, Berlin 1908, 1909 (264).

⁹ See on this point Hoffmann, 'Zur Einl. . . .,' *JbJLG*, VI, 304–323. His 'Likkute Mechilta' in the *Hildesheimer-Festschrift* a. *Neue Collectaneen aus einer M. zu Deut.*, Berlin 1897, have been superseded by the publication named in n. 8.

NOTES TO CHAPTER XVII, § 1, P. 210

¹ *GV.*, ch. 11.

² *Ha-shaḥar*, III (1872), 43–66.

³ Buber counts 32; but he omits No. 31; 22 a. 30 are duplicated; דְּרָשׁוּ, with Buber No. 24, is not original. More about the question of the genuineness of certain discourses in Theodor, *MGWJ*, 1879, 104 f.

[4] 3 discourses with messages of evil, Nos. 13–15, before the ninth of Ab; 7 of consolations after the ninth of Ab and 1 or 2 penitential haphtaras towards New Year.

[5] מסקיד, מסאסא.

[6] דברי ירמיהו. Jer. 1.1.

[7] Buber, introd., No. 2; Bacher, *Paläst. Amöraer*, II, 504.

[8] See *MGWJ*, 1879, 109, 166.

[9] Buber, p. XLIX.

[10] See Zunz, *GV.*, 240 f.

[11] 195.

[12] Introd., No. 9.

[13] *MGWJ*, 1879, 102–104.

[14] See Theodor, p. 105, n. 2.

[15] Zunz, 192; see also Buber, introd., No. 1.—Editions: S. Buber, פסיקתא, Lyck 1868 (50 pp. a. 207 leaves). See Abr. Geiger, *Jüd. Zeitschrift*, VII (1869), 187–195. Introductory points are discussed by: Weiss, III, 277–283; Theodor, *MGWJ*, 1879, 97 ff., 164 ff., 271 ff., 337 ff., 455 ff. (particularly on the proems) a. *JE*, VIII, 559 f.; Bloch, *MGWJ*, 1885, 166 ff., 210 ff., 257 ff., 385 ff. a. 1886, 165 ff., 389 ff.—The Pisḳoth for the three mourning Sabbaths have been translated by Bloch in *Steinschneider-Festschrift*, p. 41–71.

NOTES TO CHAPTER XVII, § 2, P. 211

[1] Nos. 2, 5 a. 21 each to the second verse, after in Nos. 1, 4 a. 20 each time the first verse is subject of the homily.

[2] Comp. Nos. 20, 27–30 with Pesiḳtha Kahana Nos. 27, 9, 8, 23, 28; but par. 21 is wrongly printed by Buber against the evidence of the manuscripts as continuation of Pesiḳtha Kahana 20 (174b ff.).

[3] *GV.*, 181–186.

[4] III, 261.

[5] *JE*, XII, 478 f.

[6] Manuscripts: British Museum Add. 27,169 (also Gen. R.); Oxford, Bodleian Library 147 a. 2,335 (Neubauer's Catalogue); Paris, Public Library 149. In the first named Ms. the three first sections are without the additions which appear in the prints and are derived from Tanna d'be Eliyyahu (in the first edition as well as the Venice print they are placed at the end of the Midrash as 'other text'); in par. 26 'R. Levi in the name of R. Ḥama bar Ḥanina' to the end is omitted and on the margin there is a reference to Midrash

Samuel 24; in par. 28 right at the beginning there is a reference to Pesiḳtha Kahana 8 (communication by J. Theodor). For the printed editions see p. 340, n. 13 on Gen. R. See also Theodor, *MGWJ*, 1886, 307–313, 406–415; 1885, 353, 405 a. (esp. on the point of proverbs) 1881, 500–510; *JE*, VIII, 560; XII, 478 f.

NOTES TO CHAPTER XVII, § 3, P. 212

[1] So Bacher, *Paläst. Amoräer*, III, 502 f.

[2] See above p. 131.

[3] Editions: a. Tanḥuma: Constantinople 1520-22; Venice 1545; Mantua 1563 (on the additions in this print which have passed over also into the later editions see Buber, introd., 163–180); Verona 1595 a. elsewhere; with the commentaries עץ יוסף a. ענף יוסף, Wilna-Grodno 1831; Vienna 1863; Stettin 1864; Cat. Bodl. Nos. 3795–3801. b. L. Grünhut undertook to collect the citations from Yelammedenu, esp. on Num., scattered in any number of places, in ס' הליקוטים IV–VI, Jerusalem 1900–1903. c. S. Buber, מדרש תנחומא Wilna 1885 (5 parts in 3 volumes). According to Mss. in Oxford (5) Rome, Parma, Munich. In the judgment of Theodor, Buber should have based his text on cod. Vatic. Ebr. 34 rather than on Oxford Opp. 20 = Neubauer Cat. 154; moreover, the arrangement of the Midrash by homilies should have been signalized. The text published by Buber diverges in Gen. and Exod. markedly from that of the other editions, whereas in Levit., Num. a. Deut. there is essential agreement. See also Zunz, *GV.*, 226–238; Weiss, III, 268–273; A. Epstein, קדמות התנחומא, Pressburg 1886 (reprint from Bet Talmud V); Theodor, *MGWJ*, 1885, 354 ff., 405 ff., 424 ff. a. volumes 1886, 1887 (concerning the connection with the Sedarim of the Pentateuch) a. *JE*, VIII, 560; M. Lerner, 'Jel. Rabbenu,' *JbJLG*, I (1903), 203–212; Ad. Neubauer, 'Le Midrash Tanhuma et extraits du Yelamdenu,' *REJ*, XIII (1886), 224–238; XIV, 92–107, 111–114; L. Grünhut, *Sepher ha-liḳḳutim*, I (1898) a. A. Epstein, ibid., II (1899); Lauterbach, *JE*, XII, 45 f. On fragments of a Tanḥuma closely related to the text of Buber see J. Bassfreund, *MGWJ*, 1894, 167–176, 214–219.

NOTES TO CHAPTER XVII, § 4, P. 213

[1] Comp. also No. 38 a. 45.

[2] *GV.*, 239–251.

[3] Friedmann's edition 1b.

[4] *REJ*, XXXII, 278 to 282; XXXV, 224–229.

[5] XXXIII, 40–46.

[6] Friedm. 135b.

[7] De Rossi erroneously took it for the Lekaḥ Ṭob of Tobiah ben Eliezer, see his Catalogue, III, 117 ff.

[8] Editions: first Prague about 1656, 4to (sine 1. et a.); Sklow 1806; Breslau 1831 with commentary by Zeeb Wolf; Lemberg 1833 with two commentaries; M. Friedmann, Vienna 1880 (26 pp. a. 205 leaves). See also *JE*, VIII, 561 f.

NOTES TO CHAPTER XVII, § 5, P. 214

[1] The editions Constantinople 1512 a. Venice 1545 have only 10, since נצבים Deut. 29.10 a. וילך 31.1 are joined.

[2] See p. 226.

[3] This name also in cod. Munich Hebr. 229.

[4] See also Zunz, *GV.*, 251–253; Weiss, III, 268; Theodor, *MGWJ*, 1886, 559–564; 1887, 35–48, 322; *JE*, IV, 487 f.; VIII, 562.—The manuscript tradition is not unanimous. The manuscripts of the Bodleian 147 a. 2335 contain the Midrash Rabba on the entire Pentateuch. Codex Epstein has on Deut. 1.1–7.11 דברים a. ואתחנן wholly different homilies; 7.12–30.20 עקב to נצבים squares with our Deut. R. (nevertheless נצבים with additions); the two last pericopes האזינו a. וזאת הברכה coincide with the Tanḥuma prints. Likewise cod. Munich Hebr. 229; but ואתחנן (3.23 ff.), האזינו a. וזאת הב' are wanting. S. Buber has published from this codex the pericope דברים (1.1–3.22) a. the additions in נצבים in לקוטים ממדרש אלה הדברים זוטא, Vienna 1885, 10–32 (see above p. 209).

[5] So in the first print Constantinople 1512.

[6] Zunz.

[7] Of the passages adduced by Zunz, 259, the one concerning the interpretation of the numerical value of צִיצִת, which he discusses himself, is alone of a certainly older date.

[8] Theodor, *MGWJ*, 1879, 276.

[9] In the preface to אות אמת, Saloniki 1565.

[10] See in addition Zunz, *GV.*, 258–262; Weiss, III, 266 f.; Theodor, *MGWJ*, 1886, 443–459, 558, as well as 1885, 405 f., 427–430 a. *JE*, II, 669–671; VIII,

562.—Manuscripts: Oxford Bodleian 147. 2335 (Catal. Neubauer); Paris Ms. Hebr. 149 has section 1–5.

[11] See the text edited by Buber.

[12] Comp. e. g. section 20 a. 29 with this Pes. 6 a. 12 a. the sources and parallels signalized in Wünsche's translation, 349–358.

[13] Section 15 to Pes. K. 5 a. section 39 to Tanḥuma.

[14] 256–258.

[15] See also Weiss, III, 260, 265 f.; Theodor, *MGWJ*, 1886, 212–218, 252–265 a. 1885, 405; *JE*, VIII, 562.—Manuscripts: Oxford Bodl. 147 a. 2335 of Neubauer's Catalogue.

NOTES TO CHAPTER XVII, § 6, P. 215

[1] Gen. 6.5 a. 18.25 were likewise, according to a division differing from the one most familiar, beginnings of Sedarim.

[2] Comp. Zunz, *GV.*, 256; Theodor, *JE*, VIII, 562.—Editions: First Venice 1618 at the end of שתי ידות by Menahem di Lonsano; Jellinek's Beth ha-midrash, IV; Warsaw 1876; Benj. Epstein, מדרש אגדת בראשית with commentary נחלת בנימין, Zhitomir 1899 (132); S. Buber, 'אגדת ב, Cracow 1903 (48 a. 165).

[3] *Sepher Ha-liḳḳuṭim*, I, 2a–20a.

[4] Haggadic pieces I. 4a, 19a, 25a, 33a, 76b, 115a, 121b, 128b; II. 34b, 128a, 138a. See in addition Zunz, *GV.*, 281, *Schriften*, III, 251–259; Geiger, *Jüd. Zeitschrift*, XI, 94–103; Abr. Wilna, *Rab Pe 'alim*, 48–51; Theodor, *JE*, VIII, 563.—J. M. Freimann, ספר והזהיר, I (Exod.), Leipzig 1873; II (Levit., Num.), Warsaw 1880.

[5] Published by Jellinek in *Beth ha-midrash*, I, 137 ff. (Hanukkah); VI, 36–70 (Passover, Weeks, Tabernacles, Purim, New Year, Day of Atonement).

[6] Translated in *Israels Lehrhallen*, 5b.

[7] Collected by L. Grünhut, *Sepher ha-liḳḳuṭim*, II, 16a–19b.

[8] Comp. Zunz, *GV.*, 281, *Schriften*, III, 252; Abr. Wilna, *Rab Pe'alim*, 52 f.; Theodor, *JE*, VIII, 579.

[9] Attested by Eleazar of Worms, about 1200; see Brüll, *Jahrbücher*, I, 146; *Rab Pe'alim*, 1, note.

[10] Comp. the excerpts in Yalḳuṭ § 132, 234, 235 (Jannes a. Jambres), 241, 243.

[11] The excerpts in Yalḳuṭ have been collected by S. Buber in *Ha-shaḥar*, XI (Vienna 1883) as well as in *Rab Pe'alim*, 133–147. See also Zunz, *GV.*, 282 f.; VIII, 572 f.

NOTES TO CHAPTER XVIII, § 1, P. 217

[1] So רבא, with א at the end, is the best attested spelling.

[2] Lerner, *Magazin*, 1880, 157; Theodor, *MGWJ*, 1894, 518 a. *JE*, III, 64.

[3] The appellation Rabba was later on transferred to that haggadic Midrash on the other books of the Torah (ויקרא רבה in Aruk, אלה הדברים רבה in Yalkuṭ) and then also on the five Megilloth (Song of Songs, Ruth, Lamentations, Ḳoheleth, Esther) which in each case was the most widely known; the latter, however, for the first time it seems in the edition Venice 1545, part 1 מדרש רבות על חמשה חומשי תורה, part 2 מדרש חמש מגלות רבתא. Only With two of the Midrashim on the five 'Scrolls' does the title read there מדרש איכה רבתי, שיר השירים רבה; with the other three simply: M. Ruth, M. Ḳoh. a. Megillath Esther. The edition Amsterdam 1641 is the first to say מ' רות רבה, the Wilna edition the first to add רבה also to Midrash Esther. (The first print of these Midrashim on the Pentateuch, 1512, opens with בשם אל רבה אתחיל בראשית רבה; the title of the first print of the Midrash on the Megilloth, 1519, reads מדרש חמש מגלות). The appellation Rabba has nothing to do with the epithet רבה 'the Elder' or 'the Great' by which Oshaia was known (see Theodor on parasha 1.1).

[4] See Bacher, *Terminologie*, II, 236 f.

[5] See 2.24; 4.4; 8.17; 9.6, 24; 12.3.

[6] From parasha 75 (Sabbath pericope וישלח Gen. 32.4 ff.) on extensive portions take on the character of the more recent haggada (esp. par. 75.8–13; 91.5, 6; 93.7, 8, which are wanting in cod. Vat. Hebr. 30).

[7] In par. 93, 94, ויגש 44.18–46.27 the exposition does not proceed any onger verse by verse, but passes over many verses; the parashas 95 a. 96 are Tanḥuma homilies on Gen. 46.28 a. 47.28 f.; in par. 97 exposition sets in once more beginning with 48.15 (hence 48.1–14 remains ignored!). Theodor has discovered in cod. Vat. Hebr. 30 three parashas, numbered 95–97, hitherto unknown, but proved genuine by the evidence of Midrash ha-gadol, by which the gap between 94 a. 97 of the prints and the other Mss. is filled up (in par. 97 exposition of Gen. 48.1–14), see *Guttmann-Festschrift*, 148–171. Accordingly, since after par. 94 two parashas are to be excised and three to be inserted, we shall in the future designate the last four not as 97–100, but as 98–101.

[8] On this שִׁטָּה חֲדָשָׁה see Theodor, 153 f.

[9] *Die ältesten Phasen in der Entwicklung der jüd. Predigt*, I (Berlin 1901), 43.

[10] Buber 33a.

[11] Comp. *MGWJ*, 1895, 488 ff.

[12] See above p. 217 γ.

[13] a. Rabboth. Editions. On the Pentateuch: Constantinople 1512; on the Megilloth: (Pesaro?) 1519, Constantinople 1520. Editions comprising both the Pentateuch and the Megilloth: Venice 1545 (comp. *MGWJ*, 1893, 452). With commentary by Issachar Baer ben Naphtali Cohen מתנות כהונה (completed in 1550), Cracow 1587–88; by Samuel Japheh Ashkenazi יפה תואר, Venice 1597 ff. (Gen.). 1657 (Exod.), Constantinople 1648 (Levit.); by David Luria a. Samuel Straschun e. g. Wilna 1843–45; by Wolf Einhorn e. g. Wilna 1855 ff. The latest and best edition is that of Wilna 1878, in which the long chapters are divided into paragraphs thus facilitating citation. Important textual corrections for these Midrashim as well as for the tannaitic Midrashim, Tanḥuma, Yalḳuṭ etc. in Meir Benveniste's אות אמת, Saloniki 1565, Prague 1624.—Comp. also Cat. Bodl. No. 3753–3784, Cat. Ros. p. 808–813 (this full and exact Catalogue should be consulted also with the other Midrashim). As to translations see chap. XXIV, § 2.

b. Gen. R. alone. Manuscripts, see *MGWJ*, 1893, 169 ff. Editions: Venice 1567 with the commentary falsely attributed to Rashi in the book named אור השכל, which, edited by Abraham ben Gedaliah ibn Asher, contains also his own commentary entitled מעדני מלך [Gen. 49.20], see A. Epstein, *Magazin*, 1887, 1–17; Theodor, *MGWJ*, 1893, 171 a. in *Lewy-Festschrift*, Hebr. part, 132–154. Of J. Theodor's 'Bereschit Rabba mit krit. Apparate u. Kommentare' Bojanowo 1903 ff. there have appeared up to date 720 pages; see Bacher's review in *Deutsche Literaturzeitung*, 1912, No. 9, col. 517–521. Introductional points: Zunz, *GV.*, 174–179, 254–256 (see Theodor, *MGWJ*, 1894, 517–524); Weiss, III, 252–260; M. Lerner, *Anlage des Bereschith Rabba u. seine Quellen*, Berlin 1882 (148. Previously printed in *Magazin*, 1880, 1881). Theodor, 'Die Midrašim zum Pentat. u. der dreijährige palästinensische Zyklus,' *MGWJ*, 1885; 'Der Midr. B. R.,' ibid., 1893 (on the manuscripts), 1894 f. (as to the London Ms. Brit. Mus. Add. 27, 169 agreeing with the citations in Aruk. The Genizah fragment, 3 leaves, 2 containing the beginning, which was described by E. Levine, *JQR*, 1908, 777–783, comes likewise quite close to the London Ms.); *JE*, III, 62–65 a. VIII, 557–559. Bamberger, *Die Schöpfungsgeschichte nach Darstellung des Midr. B. R.*, Mayence 1903 (48. Transl. of par. 1–4): N. Netter, *Die Geschichte Noahs u. der Sündflut*, Midr. R. Gen., Strassburg 1891 (132); S. Auscher, *Die Geschichte Josefs . . . B.R.*, Berlin 1897 (47); M. Margel, *Der Segen Jakobs, Midr. B. R.*, Frankf. o. M. 1901 (82).

NOTES TO CHAPTER XVIII, § 2, P. 218

[1] Comp. what is related Pal. Shab. 15c of Judah ha-nasi, Ishmael ben Jose and Ḥiyya.

[2] See e. g. 1.2 and the passage Pal. Taan. 4.59d–60c which occupies three columns; however, the marked textual divergences point rather to a common source. But when we compare that which is said on 1. 2 in connection with Ps. 77.7 f. with the proem to Pesiḳtha K. No. 17 (ותאמר ציון for the second Sabbath of consolation after the ninth of Ab) we should judge that it was borrowed from this Pesiḳtha.

[3] On 1.15, ed. Buber 39a.

[4] Editions see on Gen. R.; S. Buber, מדרש איכה רבה, *herausgegeben* [after a Ms. in Rome and one in the British Museum], *commentirt u. mit einer Einl.*, Wilna 1899 (76 a. 160). According to Alex. Marx this text represents an Italo-Palestinian recension, while that of the earlier editions is Spanish-Babylonian. Otherwise comp. Zunz, *GV.*, 179–181; Weiss, III, 262 f.; Jos. Abrahams, *The Sources of the Midrash Echah rabbah*, Dessau 1881 (60); A. Winkler, *Beiträge zur Kritik des Midrasch Threni*, Kaschau 1894 (69); J. Theodor, *JE*, V, 85–87; VIII, 559.

NOTES TO CHAPTER XIX, § 1, P. 220

[1] See chap. XVIII, § 2.

[2] See on 2.4.

[3] See Zunz, *GV.*, 263 f.; Weiss, III, 264 f.; S. Salfeld, *Magazin*, 1878, 120–125, a. esp. Theodor, *MGWJ*, 1879, 337 ff., 408 ff., 455 ff.; 1880, 19 ff.; the same writer, 1879, 271–275 a, *JE*, VIII, 564; Lauterbach, *JE*, XI, 291 f. —The Library of the Jewish Theological Seminary of America possesses a very good Ms. of Aggadath Shir Hashirim (and Midrash zuṭa on Ḳoheleth, it also includes Midrash Proverbs in an abridged form).

[4] Derived from Gen. R. or Levit. R.; it is found also elsew ere.

[5] This one from Palest. Sanh. 2.

[6] So on 3.13 Meir a. his teacher Elisha (see Palest. Ḥag 2.77).

[7] Comp. Zunz, *GV.*, 265; Weiss, III, 273; Theodor, *JE*, VIII, 565; M. Seligsohn, *JE*, X, 577 f.; P. D. Hartmann, *Das Buch Ruth in der Midrash-Litteratur*, Frankf. o. M. 1901 (100).

[8] 5. 5 (א' באבות) comp. 7.11.

[9] See above chap. VII, § 2.

[10] 5.9.

[11] Comp. Zunz, *GV.*, 265 f.; Weiss, III, 274; Theodor, *MGWJ*, 1880, 185 ff. a. *JE*, VII, 529–532; L. Grünhut, *Kritische Untersuchung des Midrash Kohelet Rabba, Quellen u. Redactionszeit*, Frankf. o. M. 1892 (57).

[12] See Babyl. Meg. 10b ff.

[13] Comp. Zunz, *GV.*, 264 f.; Weiss, III, 274; IV, 209; Theodor, *JE*, V, 241; VIII, 565 f.— Mordecai's Dream was edited in a more correct text by Merx, *Chrestomathia Targumica*, 157–164.

NOTES TO CHAPTER XX, P. 223

[1] On Bereshith R. major, Leḳaḥ Ṭob, Sekel Ṭob see chap. XXII.

[2] Section 2.10, Erub. 64a.

[3] Prints: Constantinople 1517, Venice 1546, Stettin 1860; S. Buber, *Midrasch Samuel . . . kritisch bearbeitet, commentirt u. mit einer Einl.*, Cracow 1893 (142), whereon see *MGWJ*, 1895, 331 to 336, 368–370. See in addition Zunz, *GV.*, 269 f.; W. Bacher, *REJ*, XXVI, 304–309 (Bacher regards this Midrash as older than the one on the Psalter); *JE*, XI, 13. Translation in *Israels Lehrhallen*, Va.

[4] II, 550 f.

[5] Printed in Jellinek's *Beth Ha-midrash*, I.

[6] See Zunz, *GV.*, 270 f.; Theodor, *JE*, VIII, 566.—Prints: Prague 1595 a. Altona (s. a., about 1770), both times in the back of the Travel of R. Pethahiah; three recensions in the collection of Horovitz. Translated in *Israels Lehrhallen*, II.

[7] *GV.*, 266–268.

[8] See Yalḳuṭ.

[9] See as early as Pal. Kil. 9.32b.

[10] Comp. M. on the Song and M. Koh.

[11] See above p. 97 f.

[12] Editions: together with M. Samuel a. M. Prov. Venice 1546, Prague 1613, Amsterdam 1730; by itself as M. Shoḥer Ṭob Constantinople 1512 (the second part was prob. printed in Fez), Lemberg 1851; Warsaw 1873; S. Buber, מדרש תהלים [according to cod. Parma de Rossi 1332 collated with 7 other Mss.] . . . *commentirt u. mit einer ausführlichen Einl.*, Wilna 1892 (128 a 542). See also Cat. Bodl. No. 3788 to 4792; Jellinek, *Beth Ha-midrash*, V, introd., p. 29–32 a. Hebr. text 70–86; Lauterbach, *JE*, X, 248–250. Translated by Wünsche.

[13] Comp., however, 1.1 the four riddles put forth to Solomon by the queen of Sheba; 9.2 the death of Akiba.

[14] So chap. 3 entire, chap. 7 a. 18 almost entire.

[15] Printed editions: Constantinople (about 1512–17), Venice 1546, Stettin 1861: S. Buber, *Midrash Mischle* [according to codex Paris 152] . . . *commentirt u. mit einer ausführl. Einl.*, Wilna 1893 (112). See also Zunz, *GV.*, 268 f.; Weiss, III, 276; Lauterbach, *JE*, X, 231.

[16] *Leḳeṭ midrashim*, Jerusalem 1903. More fully Jerusalem 1921. See also Zunz, *GV.*, 270; Brüll, *Jahrbücher*, V–VI, 99; *JE*, VIII, 567 (Ma'yan Gannim see chap. XXII i).

NOTES TO CHAPTER XXI, § 1, P. 225

[1] See above chap. II, § 2, p. 15.

[2] Zunz, *GV.*, 85; M. Seligsohn, *JE*, XI, 147–149.—B. Ratner, מבוא להסדר עולם רבה, Wilna 1894; *Seder Olam Rabba. Die grosse Weltchronik. Nach Handschriften u. Druckwerken mit krit. Noten u. Erklärungen* [in Hebrew], Wilna 1897 (151 p.). A new critical edition is in course of preparation by Al. Marx; as an earnest his Königsberg dissertation: *Seder Olam* (*Kap.* 1–10) . . . *herausgegeben, übersetzt u. erklärt* (35 a. 21).

[3] E. g. in Aruk and in Rashi.

[4] See above p. 111.

[5] See S. Friedmann, *Jüd. Literaturblatt*, Magdeburg 1879, p. 30 f., 34 f.

[6] See Zunz, *Schriften*, III, 242; A. Epstein, *Beiträge zur jüd. Altertumskunde*, I, 21 ff.

[7] Editions: Constantinople 1514; Venice 1544. 1608; Wilna 1838 with comment. by A. A. Broda; Wilna 1838 with comment. by W. Einhorn; Warsaw 1852 fol. with comment, by D. Luria. Latin translation a. notes were published by Guil. Henr. Vorstius, *Capitula R. Elieser*, Leiden 1644 (without the Hebrew text). Ger. Friedlander, *Pirke de-Rabbi Eliezer* [according to codex A. Epstein, with translation, introduction a. notes], London 1916 (60 a. 490), see hereon *JQR*, N. S., VIII, 477–488. Comp. also Zunz, *GV.*, 271–278; Weiss, III, 290–294; Theodor, *JE*, VIII, 567; A. Ochser, *JE*, X, 58–60.

[8] See Vogelstein a. Rieger, *Geschichte der Juden in Rom*, I (Berlin 1896), 185–200.

[9] Printed for the first time in Mantua 1476–79; then Constantinople 1510, Venice 1544 a. often. J. F. Breithaupt, יוסיפון בן גוריון *sive Josephus Habraicus*.

Latine versus . . . atque notis illustratus, Gotha 1707. See also Zunz, *GV.*, 146–154; Cat. Bodl. No. 6033; M. Schloessinger, *JE.*, VII, 259–261; Trieber in, *Nachrichten der Göttinger Gesellschaft der Wiss.*, 1895, 381 ff.

[10] Comp. Josh. 10.13.

[11] Printed Naples 1552, Venice 1625 a. frequently; English translation: M. M. Noah, *The Book of Yashar*, New York 1840. See also Zunz, *GV.*, 154–156; Cat. Bodl. No. 3581–3586; Cat. Ros. 188 f.; *JE.*, XII, 588 f.

[12] The Passover Haggada does not belong here. See S. Wiener, *Bibliographie der Oster-Haggada* 1500–1900, St. Petersburg 1902 (66 pp. 4to); Cat. Bodl. No. 2671–2751; L. Landshuth, *Maggid mereshith*, Berlin 1856; D. Cassel, *Die Pesach-Haggada*, [text, translation a. short notes], 11th ed., Berlin, 1910.

[13] The text preserved in Yalḳuṭ Gen. 133 was printed a second time in *Beth Ha-midrash*, III; Rab Pe'alim, 153–156; and by R. H. Charles, *Book of Jubilees*, Oxford 1895, Appendix II: see the same author, *The Greek Versions of the Testaments of the Twelve Patriarchs*, 1908, Appendix I. See also Zunz, *GV.*, 145; *JE.*, VIII, 579.

[14] Printed Constantinople 1516, Venice 1544. Comp. Zunz, *GV.*, 145; Rab Pe'alim, 45; *JE.*, VIII, 573 f.; translated in *Israel's Lehrhallen*, I.

[15] Printed Constantinople 1516, Venice 1544, *Beth Ha-midrash*, I, 91–95. See also Zunz, *GV.*, 146; *JE.*, VIII, 575; translated as in preceding note.

[16] The first was printed Constantinople 1516, Venice 1544, *Beth Ha-midrash*, I, 115–129; transl. as in n. 14. A long piece was received into the Yalḳuṭ (Deut. 940), also into Deut. R. The second starts from Prov. 31.29 and was printed *Beth Ha-midrash*, VI, 71–78. A third was edited together with the first in Hebrew a. Latin by G. Gaulmun, *De vita et morte Mosis libri tres*, Paris 1629. See also Zunz, *GV.*, 146; Theodor, *JE.*, VIII, 575 f.; Schürer, 4th ed., III, 301 f.

[17] Constantinople 1519. See Zunz, *GV.*, 140; Cat. Bodl. No. 1400 f. Transl. as in n. 14. A critical edition has been published by Isr. Lévi, *REJ*, LXVIII, 129–160, comp. LXIX, 108–121; LXXI, 51–65, 222.—On other eschatological writings of which the Book of Zerubbabel is a specimen see Buttenwieser, *Outline of Neo-Hebraic Apocalyptic Luterature*, Cincinnati 1901, and OLZ, V, 68–72.

[18] The Aramaic text was published by H. Filipowski at the end of *Mibḥar ha-peninim, The Choice of Pearls* [by Ibn Gebirol], London 1851; subsequently by Jellinek in *Beth Ha-midrash*, VI (1877) a. M. Gaster in *Transactions of the Oriental Congress*, London 1891, II (comp. Ad. Neubauer, *JQR*, 1894, 570–

576). Frequently printed in Hebrew translation, Cat. Bodl. 1382–1388; *Beth Ha-midrash,* I, 142–146; transl. in *Israels Lehrhallen,* II. See in addition Zunz, *GV.,* 134; Dalman, *Grammatik des jüdischpaläst. Aram.,* 2d ed., § 3, 2; L. Ginzberg, *JE,* I, 637 f.; Isr. Lévi, *REJ,* XLV, 172 to 175 (maintains against Ginzberg that it was written in Syria; the name Bagras he takes to be a corruption of Bacchides).

[19] Four recensions are known: the first was printed in *Beth Ha-midrash* II, a. in *Rab Pe'alim,* 157–160 (comp. S. Möbius, *Midrasch der zehn Märtyrer übersetzt,* Leipzig 1854 [32 pp.]), a second a. third in *Beth Ha-midrash,* VI, a fourth in בֵּית אָב (work of Spanish liturgy), Leghorn 1777.—See in addition Zunz, *GV.,* 142; *JE,* VIII, 574.

[20] Text in *Beth Ha-midrash,* IV; reedited by Grünhut, *Sepher ha-likkutim,* III (see *ZHBg,* , 98–100); translated as in n. 18. Comp. *JE.,* VIII, 574.

[21] See p. 226 g.

[22] Printed Constantinople 1519, *Beth Ha-midrash,* I. See also Zunz, *GV.,* 282; Cat. Bodl. 3734 to 3739: Schürer, 4th ed., II, 621 (on Armilus); *JE.,* VIII, 579. Transl. as in n. 14.

[23] Text in *Beth Ha-midrash,* I; a fuller version in חיבור המעשיות, Venice 1551, reprinted e. g. in מעשיות Calcutta 1840 a. Bagdad 1869. See in addition Zunz, *GV.,* 142–144; Cat. Bodl. 3751, 4986[3]; *JE.,* VIII, 573. Translated in *Israels Lehrhallen,* IV.

[24] Collected by Buber in כנסת ישראל, I (Warsaw 1887), 309 ff., also in *Rab Pe'alim,* 147–153. See also Zunz, *GV.,* 279 f.; *JE,* VIII, 574 f.

[25] Text in *Beth Ha-midrash,* VI a. in L. Grünhut, *Sepher ha-likkutim,* I. See also *JE,* VIII, 573.

[26] See Cat. Bodl. 3869–3942; Cat. Ros. 81–83; esp. Steinschneider, *Serapeum,* 1866, 1–12.

NOTES TO CHAPTER XXI, § 2, P. 227

[1] See above p. 74.

[2] Babyl. Keth. 106a.

[3] S. El. R. 10, ed. Friedm., chap. 9, p. 48.

[4] According to the Aruk (סדר), which, however, adduces no citation, the first part has 30, the second 12 chapters; in the edition Venice 1598 (according to a Ms. of the year 1186) the first part has 31, the second 25. Zunz did not fail to recognize that in the latter part the chapters 15–25 constitute a later

addition. Friedmann, who was enabled to base his text upon a Vatican Ms. of the year 1073, replaced the hardly convenient division of the first part by one more to the point into 29 chapters; the second part ends with him at chapter 15 of the Venice edition; the last chapter, however, is not genuine. In the edition by H. M. Horowitz, *Bibliotheca Hagg.*, II, 3–19, S. El. Z. has only 12 chapters. The manuscripts, the prints and the excerpts in Yalḳuṭ differ in regard to S. El. Z. among themselves and one is led to assume divergent recensions. As to the 'new text' of the edition by Sh. Heida, Prague 1677, one should be on his guard. Best edition: M. Friedmann, Vienna 1902. 1900 (150 pp. of introd., 200 pp. of text). Whereon Theodor, *MGWJ*, 1900, 380–384, 550–561; 1903, 70–79. See in addition Zunz, *GV.*, 112–117; Weiss, III, 288–294; Bacher, *Tannaiten*, 2d ed., I, 489 f.; *JE*, VIII, 568.— M. Friedmann, נספחים לסדר אליהו זוטא, *Pseudo-Seder Elijahu zuta* [according to Venice 1598 a. codex de Rossi 1240], Vienna 1904 (56), endeavors to show that of the sections 16–25 of the book printed as Seder Eliyyahu Zuṭa 16–18 represent an old Derek-Ereṣ-Book and 19–25 a Pirḳe-R.-Eliezer-Book. The conclusion of the book is made up of chapters 39–41 of Pirḳe R. Eliezer according to codex de Rossi 1240.

[5] Printed Constantinople 1519, Venice 1544; *Beth Ha-midrash*, II; another recension in Sh. Schönblum, שלשה ספרים נפתחים, Lemberg 1877 (Pirḳa deRabbenu ha-ḳadosh) a. in Grünhut, *Sepher ha-likkutim*, III. See also *Ḥuppath Eliyyahu*, edited by H. M. Horowitz in כבוד חופה, Frankf. o. M. 1888. Zunz, *GV.*, 284 f.; *JE*, VIII, 575. Translated in *Israels Lehrhallen*, IV.

[6] Printed for the first time Saloniki 1514, then Constantinople 1519, Venice 1544; M. Steinschneider, *Alphabetum Syracidis*, Berlin 1854, according to the Venice edition, at the same time with the aid of a Leiden Ms. See Zunz, *GV.*, 105; Cat. Bodl. 1363 ff.; L. Ginzberg, *JE*, II, 678–681 and *ZHBg.*, 1907, 125 f.

[7] Printed for the first time as appendix to Azulai, שם הגדולים, Leghorn 1786, then in *Beth Ha-midrash*, I. See also Zunz, *GV.*, 118; Cat. Bodl. 3793; *Rab Pe'alim*, 123 f.; *JE*, VIII, 578 f.

NOTES TO CHAPTER XXI, § 3, P. 228

[1] See Aug. Wünsche, 'Kabbala', *PRE*, 3d ed., IX, 670–689.

[2] Of other editions we may mention: J. S. Rittangel, Amsterdam 1642, with Latin translation; J. F. v. Meyer, Leipzig 1830, with German translation;

Isidor Kalisch, New York 1877, with English translation; Warsaw 1884 with many commentaries; L. Goldschmidt, *Das Buch der Schöpfung, Text nebst Übersetz., . . . Erklärungen u. . . . Einl.*, Frankf. o. M. 1894 (on the defects of this publication see *REJ*, XXIX, 310–316). See also Zunz, *GV.*, 165 f.; Cat. Bodl. 3562–3574; David Castelli, ספר חכמוני *Il commento di Sabbathai Donnolo sul libro della creazione* [text, notes, introd.], Florence 1880; A. Epstein, *REJ*, XXVIII (1894), 95–108; XXIX, 61–78, a. partic. L. Ginzberg, *JE*, XII, 602–606; in addition Ph. Mordell, 'The Origin of Letters and Numerals according to the Sefer Yesira,' *JQR*, N. S., II (1912), 557–583; III (1913), 517–544.

3 Text in *Beth Ha-midrash*, III, a. in A. Epstein, *Beiträge zur jüd. Alterthumskunde*, Vienna 1887. See also Zunz, *GV.*, 280; Theodor, *JE*, VIII, 578. Translated in *Israels Lehrhallen*, V b.

4 Editions: Venice 1546; Amsterdam 1708; *Beth Ha-midrash*, III; S. A, Wertheimer, מדרש אותיות רבי עקיבא השלם, *in zwei Rezensionen nach alten Handschriften u. Druckwerken, nebst einem* מ' אלפא ביתות, Jerusalem 1914 (16 a. 128). Cat. Bodl. 3395–3401. See Zunz, *GV.*, 168; *Beth Ha-midrash*, VI, introd., p. 40 ff.; *JE*, I, 310 f.; translated in *Israels Lehrhallen*, IV.

5 Edited according to two Mss. by S. A. Wertheimer, Jerusalem 1899 (56). See *JE*, VIII, 576, 578.

6 Printed: Cat. Bodl. 3547–3549; *Beth Ha-midrash*, II, III; edited from a Ms. by Wertheimer, Jerusalem 1890. See Zunz, *GV.*, 166 f.; Ph. Bloch in *Guttmann-Festschrift*, 113–124; *JE*, VI, 332 f. Translated in *Israels Lehrhallen*, III.

7 Prints: Cat. Bodl. 3743–3745; *Beth Ha-midrash*, II; See Zunz, *GV.*, 169. Translated in *Israels Lehrhallen*, III.

8 First print: Amsterdam 1701; see Zunz, *GV.*, 167; Cat. Bodl. 4042; *JE*, X, 335 f.—On the book *Shiur Ḳoma*, The Dimensions of God, produced under gnostic influences, see M. Gaster, *MGWJ*, 1893, 179–185, 213–230; *JE*, XI, 298.

NOTES TO CHAPTER XXII, P. 230

1 E. g. for the Palest. Talm., see above p. 80, No. 7.

2 B. B. 14b.

3 *Kerem Hemed*, VII, 4 ff.

4 *Die Exegese bei den franz. Israeliten*, Leipzig 1873, p. xxii.

5 *Lehrbuch der jüd. Gesch. u. Lit.*, Leipzig 1879.

6 נטעי נעמנים, Breslau 1847, 10 a. *Jüd. Zeitschrift*, XI, 115.

[7] *Literaturblatt des Orients*, V, 253.

[8] ר' שמעון קרא והילקוט שמעוני, Cracow 1891.

[9] See A. Epstein, *REJ*, XXVI, 75–82, against M. Gaster who had argued XXV, 44 ff. in favor of a higher date for Makir.—Editions: Saloniki 1526–27 (part I) a. 1521 (part II): Venice 1566 (with many alterations, see *MGWJ*, 1895, 484), Cracow 1595–96, Leghorn 1650 (important for its textual readings as well as for the commentary), Frankf. o. M. 1687, Warsaw 1876. See also Zunz, *GV.*, 295–305; *JE*, VIII, 569; XII, 585 f. and on the prints: A. Epstein in האשכול, VI (Cracow 1909), 183–210, as well as *REJ*, LXI, 131.

[10] W. Bacher, *Göttingische gelehrte Anzeigen*, 1902, No. 10, p. 808.—Prints: J. Spira, *The Yalkut on Isaiah of Machir ben Abba Mari* [according to codex Leiden in which 20. 4–40. 20 a. 63. 2 to the end are missing], Berlin 1894 (30 a. 278). S. Buber, ילקוט המכירי. . . . *zu den* 150 *Psalmen*, Berdyczew 1899 (354 a. 294). L. Grünhut, ס' ילקוט המכירי על משלי *mit Anmerkungen, Quellennachweis u. Einl.*, Frkf. o. M. 1902 (20 pp. a. 104 leaves); supplements thereto in *Sepher ha-likkutim*, VI. A. W. Greenup edited in London from codex Harley 5704, incomplete at the beginning and at the end (the gap may be supplied from cod. Vatic. 291, discovered by S. Schechter): *The Yalkut of R. Machir bar Abba Mari*: Hosea 1909; Zechariah 1909; Amos, Obadiah, Jonah, Micah, Nahum, Habakkuk 1909, 1910; Joel, Zephaniah, Haggai, Malachi 1913 (comp. *ZHBg*, XIII, 131 ff.; XIV, 131; XVI, 2 ff.). See in addition *JE*, VIII, 246, 569.

[11] See above p. 207, 208.—Manuscripts in Berlin (Ms. Or. Fol. 1204–1208), Oxford (Bodl. 2338), Cambridge (3404–3407), British Museum, New York (Jewish Theological Seminary of America), San Francisco. S. Schechter, *Midrash ha-gadol forming a Collection of Ancient Rabbinic Homilies to the Pentateuch . . . Genesis*, Cambridge 1902 (825) fol. D. Hoffmann, *Midrasch ha-gadol zum Buche Exodus*, first fascicle, Berlin 1913 (80).

[12] *Journal of Philology*, XVI (1887), 131–152.

[13] *GV.*, 287–293.

[14] *Beth Ha-midrash*, VI, introd. xiv–xvi.

[15] In the introd. to *The Fifty-third Chapter of Isaiah according to the Jewish Interpreters*, II (Oxford 1877).

[16] *The Book of Tobit*, Oxford 1878, vii–ix, xx–xxiv, a. in *The Academy*, 1887, Sept. 17 a. 24.

[17] *Magazin*, 1888, 65–99, where there is also more accurate information about the Ms. Bereshith Rabbathi of the Jewish community in Prague, mentioned by Zunz.

[18] Buber, introd., 18, 20–26.

[19] Zunz, *GV.*, 293–295. Comp. Cat. Bodl. 7304.—Prints: Venice 1546 (Levit., Num., Deut.) as: פסיקתא רבתא או זוטרתא, from which with the correct title and a commentary by A. M. Padua (פאדווא) Wilna 1880. S. Buber, *Lekach tob (Pesikta sutarta), ein agadischer Comm. zum ersten u. zweiten Buche Mosis von R. Tobia ben Elieser*, Wilna 1880; see hereon *HBg*, XXI, 29–32. J. Nacht, *Tobia ben Elieser's Comm. zu Threni* [according to Ms. Munich], *mit einer Einl. u. Anmerkungen*, Berlin 1895 (67). S. Bamberger, *Lekach Tob, ein agad. Komm. zur Megillath Ruth*, Aschaffenburg (Frkf. o. M.) 1887 (106). G. Feinberg, *Tobia ben Elieser's Comm. zu Koheleth*, Dissertation Zurich 1904 (110). A. W. Greenup, *The Commentary of R. Tobia ben Elieser on Canticles*, London 1909 (108). L. T. on Esther see in S. Buber, ספרי דאגדתא, Wilna 1886, 85–112.

[20] See *ZHBg*, 1901, 98.

[21] S. Buber, מ' שכל טוב *Midrasch Sechel Tob zum ersten u. zweiten Buch Mose von Rabbi Menachem ben Salomo verfasst im J. 1139* [Gen. 11-Exod. 15; according to two Mss. of the Bodleian], *herausgegeben, . . . commentiert u. mit . . . Einl.*, Berlin 1900–1901 (60 a. 336; 344).

NOTES TO CHAPTER XXIII, § 1, P. 233

[1] See above p. 223.

[2] See above p. 346, n. 5.

NOTES TO CHAPTER XXIII, § 2, P. 233

[1] See above for specific items.

[2] See *PRE*, 3d ed., XX, 196 f.

[3] Above, p. 217 ff., in dealing with the Midrashim there enumerated, I have indicated in each case the volume of this publication in which a translation is available.

INDEXES

I. HEBREW AND ARAMAIC WORDS EXPLAINED

II. TITLES OF BOOKS

O. = Order (see p. 26f), Tr. = Tractate, Md. = Midrash.
Of other Hebrew titles only a selection appears here.

III. PROPER NAMES

A = Amora. B A = Babylon. Amora. The figures (1–7) which follow immediately after A or T indicate the generation to which the teacher referred to belongs. S = one of the Saboraim. G = Gaon. E = Exponent, with reference to authors of Introduction, Commentaries, etc. (Only a selective list.). P = Name of place.

APPENDICES

APPENDIX I

TABULAR SURVEY OF THE TRACTATES IN MISHNA, TALMUD AND TOSEPHTA

"G" indicates that the tractates have Gemara in the Babylonian or Palestinian Talmud (the letter is placed in the respective columns).—The order which we follow here and which rests on that of Maimonides has been maintained by Surenhusius, Rabe and Jost; except that with them (in accordance with the prescription Soṭa 2a) Soṭa is placed immediately after Nazir, hence before Giṭṭin. After 1606, the sequence wavers only in the order Ṭoharoth.

Volume	Babylonian Talmud 1697 ff.	Mishna since 1606	Order	Maimonides	Name, Number of Chapter	Munich Codex 95	Mishna Codices C	Mishna Codices K	Palestinian Talmud	Tosephta Vien. Codex	Tosephta Erfurt Codex	Mishna ed. 1559
I	1G	1	I. Zera'im	1	Berakoth 9	[1]	1	1	1G	1	1	1
	2—	2		2	Pe'a 8	2	2	2	2G	2	2	2
	3—	3		3	Demai 7	3	3	3	3G	3	5	3
	4—	4		4	Kil'aim 9	4	4	4	4G	6	7	4
	5—	5		5	Shebi'ith 10	5	5	5	5G	5	6	5
	6—	6		6	Terumoth 11	6	6	6	6G	4	3	6
	7—	7		7	Ma'asroth 5	7	8	7[2]	7G	7	8	7
	8—	8		8—	Ma'aser Sheni 5	8	7	8	8G	8	9	8
	9—	9		9	Ḥalla 4	9	9	9	9G	10	10	9
	10—	10		10	'Orla 3	10	10	10	10G	9	4	10
	11—	11		11	Bikkurim 3	11	11	11	11G	11	11	11
II	1G	1	II. Mo'ed	1	Shabbath 24	1	1		1G[3]	1		1
	2G	2		2	'Erubin 10	2	2		2G	2		2
III	3G	3		3	Pesaḥim 10	3	3		3G	3		3
IV	11—	11		4	Sheḳalim 8	9[4]	5		5G	4		12
	9G	8		5	Yoma 8	7	4		4G	5		4
	10G	9		6	Sukka 5	6	6		6G	6		5
III	4G	5		7	Beṣa (Yom Ṭob) 5	8	7		8G	7		6
IV	7G	7		8	Rosh Hashana 4	5	8		7G	8		7
	8G	10		9	Ta'anith 4	11	9		9G	9		8
	12G	12		10	Megilla 4	10	10		10G	10		9
III	6G	6		11	Mo'ed Kaṭan 3	12	12		12G	11		11
	5G	4		12	Hagiga 3	4	11		11G	12		10
V	1G	1	III. Nashim	1	Yebamoth 16	1	1	1	1G	1		1
	2G	2		2	Kethubboth 13	2	2	2	3G	2		2
VI	5G	6		3	Nedarim 11	5	3	3	4G	3		5
	6G	7		4	Nazir 9	6	4	5	6G	4		6
	4G	4		5	Giṭṭin 9[5]	4	5	4	5G	6		3
	7G	5		6	Soṭa 9	7[6]	7	6	2G	5		7
V	3G	3		7	Ḳiddushin 4	3	6	7	7G	7		4

Volume	Babylonian Talmud 1697 ff.	Mishna since 1606	Order	Maimonides	Name, Number of Chapter	Münich Codex 95	Mishna Codices C K	Palestinian Talmud	Tosephta	Mishna ed. 1559
VII	1G	1		1	Baba Ḳamma 10	1	1	1G	1	1
	2G	2		2	Baba Meṣi'a 10	2	2	2G	2	2
VIII	3G	3		3	Baba Bathra 10	3	3	3G	3	3
IX	5G	4		4	Sanhedrin 11	4	4	4G	4	4
	6G	5	IV. Neziḳin	5	Makkoth 3	5	5	5G[7]	5	5
	7G	6		6	Shebu'oth 8	6	6	6G	6	6
	9—	7		7	'Eduyyoth 8	9	7	—	7	10
VIII	4G	8		8	'Aboda Zara 5	8	8	7G	8	7
IX	10—	9		9	Aboth 5	[8]	9	—	—	9
	8G	10		10	Horayoth 3[9]	7	10	8G	9	8
X	1G	1		1	Zebaḥim 14	1	1	—	1[10]	1
	2G	2		2	Menaḥoth 13	2	2	—	3	2
XI	4G	3		3	Ḥullin 12	3	3		2	[11]
X	3G	4		4	Bekoroth 9	4	4		4	[11]
XI	5G	5		5	'Arakin 9	5	5		5	3
	6G	6	V. Ḳodashim	6	Temura 7	6	6	not extant	6	4
	7G	7		7	Kerithoth 6	8	7[12]		8	5
	8G	8		8	Me'ila 6	7	8		7	6
	10G[13]	9		9	Tamid 7[14]	9	10		—	7
	11—	10		10	Middoth 5[15]	10	9		—	9
	9—	11		11	Ḳinnim 3	11	11		—	8
XII	2	9		1	Kelim 30	1	1		1	14
	3	4		2	Ohaloth 18	2	2		2	6
	4	5		3	Nega'im 14	3	3		3	7
	5	2		4	Para 12	4	4		4	8
	6	8		5	Ṭoharoth 10	5	5		7	9
	7	1	VI. Ṭoharoth	6	Mikwa'oth 10	6	6	not extant	6	1
	1G	7		7	Nidda 10	7[16]	7	1G[17]	5	2
	8	11		8	Makshirin 6	8	8		8	10
	9	6		9	Zabim 5	9	9		9	11
	10	10		10	Tebûl Yom 4	10	10		11	12
	11	3		11	Yadaim 4	11	11		10	3[11]
	12	12		12	'Ukṣin 3	12	12		12	13

1 In Codex Munich 95, Ber is found between Mo'ed and Nashim; the Mishnayoth for Zera'im (Ber. excepted) and Ṭoharoth (Nidda excepted) follow Ḳodashim in the order given by Maimonides.

2 The scribe of the Kaufm. Codex began M. Sh. after Terumah, apparently following his copy. Then he struck out the written lines and wrote Ma'aser Rishon (Ma'as). At the end of the Order he lists M. Sh. before Ma'as.

3 The Pal. Gemara for chapters 21–24 is no longer extant.

4 With the Pal. Gemara, which for this Tractate also appears in the prints of the Babyl. Talmud.

5 Lippmann Heller and Levi son of Gershon (Introd. to the Pentateuch Comm.) place (according to Soṭa 2a: Nazir, Soṭa) Giṭṭin after Soṭa.

6 Then Nidda, then the Order of Neziḳin. Comp. p. 253, n. 9.

7 Mak. 3 in the Pal. Tal, without Gemara.

8 After the Order Ṭoharoth at the beginning of the so-called small Tractates.

9 Mishna Naples 1492: Horayoth, Aboth.

10 The Erfurt (now Berlin) MS. contains only the Orders I-IV, and Zeb. Chaps. 1–3.

11 Ḥul. and Bek. are placed 4th and 5th respectively in the Order Ṭoharoth.

12 The Kaufm. Codex gives it in the list of the tractates (not in the text) as follows: Me'ila, Kerithoth.

13 In Tamid only chapters 1, 2, 4 have Gem.

14 Chaps. 6 and 7 are combined into one chapter in Codices Cambr. and Kaufm.

15 Mishna Naples 1492: Middoth, Tamid.

16 Midda follows Nashim (see above p. 253, n. 9). The scribe however calls attention to this change at the end of Miḳwaoth: מסכת נדה כתבתי אחר סדר נשים.

17 Mishna chaps. 1–4; of the Gem. only chaps. 1–3 and the three first lines of chap. 4 are extant.

APPENDIX II

ALPHABETICAL LIST OF TRACTATES IN THE MISHNA

Figures in heavy type denote the Order, those in light, the place, within the Order

א Aboth **4**.9
Ohaloth (Ahiloth) **6**.2

ב Baba Bathra **4**.3
Baba Meṣi'a **4**.2
Baba Ḳamma **4**.1
Beṣa **2**.7
Bekoroth **5**.4
Bikkurim **1**.11
Berakoth **1**.1

ג Giṭṭin **3**.5

ד Demai **1**.3

ה Horayoth **4**.10

ז Zebaḥim **5**.1
Zabim **6**.9

ח Ḥagiga **2**.12
Ḥalla **1**.9
Ḥullin **5**.3

ט Ṭebul Yom **6**.10
Ṭoharoth **6**.5

י Yebamoth **3**.1
Yadaim **6**.11
Yoma **2**.5
Yom Ṭob **2**.7

כ Kil'aim **1**.4
Kelim **6**.1
Kippurim **2**.5
Kerithoth **5**.7
Kethubboth **3**.2

מ Megilla **2**.10
Middoth **5**.10
Mo'ed Ḳaṭan **2**.11
Makkoth **4**.5
Makshirin **6**.8
Menaḥoth **5**.2
Me'ila **5**.8
Ma'asroth **1**.7
Ma'aser Sheni **1**.8
Miḳwa'oth **6**.6
Mashkin **2**, 11 (**6**.8)

נ Nega'im **6**.3
Nidda **6**.7
Nedarim **3**.3
Neziḳin **4**.1–3
Nazir **3**.4
(Nashim **3**.1)

ס Soṭa **3**.6
Sukka **2**.6
Sanhedrin **4**.4

ע 'Aboda Zara **4**.8
'Eduyyoth **4**.7
'Uḳṣin **6**.12
'Erubin **2**.2
'Arakin **5**.5
'Orla **1**.10

פ Pe'a **1**.2
Pesaḥim **2**.3
Para **6**.4
Pirḳe Aboth **4**.9

ק Ḳiddushin **3**.7
Ḳinnim **5**.11

ר Rosh Hashana **2**.8

ש Shebu'oth **4**.6
Shebi'ith **1**.5
Shabbath **2**.1
(Sheḥitath Ḥullin **5**.3)
Sheḳalim **2**.4

ת Temura **5**.6
Tamid **5**.9
Ta'anith **2**.9
Terumoth **1**.6

APPENDIX III

The Opening Words of those Chapters in the Babylonian Talmud which have Gemara, in Alphabetical Order.

Considering that before the discovery of printing it was customary to cite the Babylonian Talmud as a rule after the opening words of the Chapter in question and since Jews are still in the habit of this mode of citation, it becomes necessary to know where each chapter may be located (in which Tractate and in which place in the Tractate). For this reason I give here the opening words of those chapters which are provided with Babylonian Gemara. Those chapters which have nothing but Mishna are usually cited by the name of the Tractate and the number of the Chapter. Even of these chapters the opening words are listed in many editions of the Babylonian Talmud in the Appendix to Berakoth (thus e. g. in Pinner, *Berachoth*, fol. (פ"ז); furthermore in: Joh. Buxtorf's *Operis Talmudici brevis recensio*. in Joh. Christ. Wolf's *Bibliotheca Hebraea*, II, 724–741 and in W. H. Lowe, *The Fragment of Talmud Babli Pesachim . . . in the University-Library*, Cambridge, 1879, 50–59.

אור לארבעה עשר Pes. 1
אותו ואת בנו Ḥul. 5
אחד דיני ממונות Sanh. 4
איזהו מקומן Zeb. 5
איזהו נשך B.M. 5
אין בין המוּדָּר Ned. 4
אין בערָכין ʻArak. 2
אין דורשין Ḥag. 2
אין מעמידין A. Z. 2
אין מקדישין Arak. 7
אין עומדין Ber. 5
אין צדין Beṣa 3
אלו דברים בפסח Pes. 6
אלו דברים שֶׁבֵּין Ber. 8
אלו הן הַגּוֹלִין Mak. 2
אלו הן הַלּוֹקִין Mak. 3
אלו הן הממונין Sheḳ. 5
אלו הן הַנֶּחֱנָקִין Sanh. 10
אלו טרֵיפות Ḥul. 3
אלו מְנָחוֹת נִקְמָצוֹת Men. 7
אלו מְצִיאוֹת שֶׁלּוֹ B.B. 2
אלו נֶאֱמָרִין Soṭa 7
אלו נְעָרוֹת Keth. 3
אלו עוברין Pes. 3
אלו קדשים Tem. 3

אלו קְשָׁרִים Shabb. 15
אלמנה לְכֹהֵן גדול Yeb. 7
אלמנה נִיזּוֹנֶת Keth. 11
אם אינן מַכִּירִין R.H. 2
אמר להם הַמְּמוּנֶּה צְאוּ Yoma 3
אמר ר׳ עקיבא Shabb. 9
אמרו לו אָכַלְתָּ Ker. 3
אַף עַל פִּי שֶׁאָמְרוּ Keth. 5
ארבע מיתות Sanh. 7
ארבעה אבות נזיקין B.K. 1
ארבעה אחים Yeb. 3
א׳ מחוסרי כפורים Ker. 3
א׳ נדרים Ned. 3
א׳ ראשי שנים R.H. 1
א׳ שומרין Sheb. 8
ארוסה ושומרת Soṭa 4

באחד באדר Sheḳ. 1
בא לו כֹּהֵן גדול Yoma 7
בא סימן התחתון Nid. 6
בהמה המקשה Ḥul. 4
ביצה שנולדה Beṣa 1
בית כור B.B. 7
בש״א אין מְמָאֲנִין Yeb. 13
בש״א הֶקְדֵּשׁ Nazir 5

בש״א כל־הַנִּתָּנִין Zeb. 4
בְּכֹל מְעָרְבִין Erub. 3
בְּמָה אשה יוצאה Shabb. 6
בְּמָה בְהֵמָה Shabb. 5
במה טומנין Shabb. 4
במה מדליקין Shabb. 2
בנות כותים Nid. 4
בן סורר ומורה Sanh. 8
בני העיר Meg. 4
בראשונה כל מי Yoma 2
בשלשה מקומות הכהנים Tamid 1
בש׳ פרקים בשנה כהנים Ta'an. 4
בש׳ פ׳ ב׳ תורמין Sheḳ. 3
בתולה נשאת Keth. 1

גט פשוט B.B. 10
גיד הנשה Ḥul. 7

דיני ממונות בשלשה, גזלות Sanh. 1
ד׳ מ׳ ב׳ זה בורר Sanh. 3
דַּם הַנִּדָּה Nid. 7
דם חטאת Zeb. 11
דם שחיטה Ker. 5

האומר התקבל Giṭ. 6
האומר לחבירו צא Ḳid. 3
ה׳ ל׳ בית כּוֹר B.B. 7
ה׳ מִשְׁקְלֵי עָלַי Arak. 5
האוֹרֵג Shabb. 13
האיש מְקַדֵּשׁ בּוֹ Ḳid. 2
האשה בִזְמַן Pes. 8
האשה [בתרא] Yeb. 16
האשה נקנֵית Ḳid. 1
האשה [רבה] Yeb. 10
ה׳ שהיא עושָׂה Nid. 9
ה׳ שהלך בעלהּ וצָרָתָהּ Yeb. 16
ה׳ שהלכה היא Yeb. 15
ה׳ . . . שלום Yeb. 15
ה׳ שנָּפְלוּ Keth. 8

ה׳ שֶׁנִּתְאַרְמְלָה Keth. 2
הַבָּא על יְבִמְתּוֹ Yeb. 6
הבונה Shabb. 12
הַבַּיִת וְהָעֲלִיָּה B.B. 10
הגוזל [בתרא] B.K. 10
הגוזל ומאכיל B.K. 10
הגוזל עצים B.K. 9
הגוים אין להם נזק Naz. 9
הדר עם הנכרי Erub. 6
הוציאוּ לו Yoma 5
הורה כהן Hor. 2
הורו בית דין Hor. 1
הזהב קונה B.M. 4
הזורק גט Giṭ. 8
הזורק מרשות Shabb. 11
הַזְּרוֹעַ וְהַלְּחָיַיִם Ḥul. 10
החובל B.K. 8
החולץ ליבמתו Yeb. 4
הֶחָלִיל Suk. 5
היה מֵבִיא Soṭa 2
היה נוטל Soṭa 3
היה קורא Ber. 2
היו בודקין Sanh. 5
הישן תחת המטה Suk. 2
הכונס B.Ḳ. 6
הכותב לאשתו Keth. 9
הכל חייבין Ḥag. 1
הכל ממירין Tem. 1
הכל מעריכין Arak. 1
הכל שוחטין Ḥul. 1
הלוקח בהמה Bekor. 3
ה׳ עוֹבֵר חמורו Bekor. 1
ה׳ עובר פרתו Bekor. 2
המביא אשם תלוי Ker. 6
המביא גט Giṭ. 1
ה׳ גט [תניינא] Giṭ. 2
ה׳ כַּדֵּי יין Beṣa 4
הַמְגָרֵשׁ Giṭ. 9

הַמַּדִּיר את־אשתו Keth. 7
המוכר את־הבית B.B. 4
ה' את הספינה B.B. 5
ה' את שדהו Arak. 9
ה' פירות B.B. 6
הַמּוֹצֵא תפילין Erub. 10
המוציא יין Shabb. 8
הַמִּזְבֵּחַ מְקַדֵּשׁ Zeb. 9
המנחות והנסכים Men. 12
הַמַּנִּיחַ את־הכד B.B. 3
הַמַּפֶּלֶת Nid. 3
הַמַּפְקִיד B.M. 3
המצניע Shabb. 10
המקַבֵּל שדה מחבירו B.M. 9
הַמַּקְדִּישׁ את שדהו Arak. 8
המקנא Soṭa 1
הַנֶּהֱנֶה שָׁוֶה פ' Me'ila 5
הַנּוֹדֵר מן הירק Ned. 7
ה' מן המבושל Ned. 6
הנושא את האשה Keth. 12
הַנִּיזָּקִין Giṭ. 5
הַנִּשְׂרָפִין Sanh. 9
הָעוֹר וְהָרוֹטֶב Ḥul. 9
הֶעָרֵל Yeb. 8
הקומץ את־המנחה לאכול שיריה Men. 2
הקומץ [רבה] את־ה' ל' דבר Men. 3
הקורא . . . למפרַע Meg. 2
הקורא . . . עומד Meg. 3
הָרוֹאָה כֶתֶם Nid. 8
הָרוֹאֶה מקום Ber. 9
הֲרֵינִי נזיר Naz. 2
הרי עָלַי עשרון Men. 13
הַשַּׂג יד Arak. 4
הַשּׂוֹכֵר את האוּמָנִין B.M. 6
ה' את־הפועל A.Z. 5
ה את־הפועלים B.M. 7

השואל את־הפרה B.M. 8
השוחט אחד בעוף Ḥul. 2
השוחט והמעלה Zeb. 13
השולח גט Giṭ. 4
הַשּׁוּתָּפִין שֶׁנָּדְרוּ Ned. 5
ה' שֶׁרָצוּ B.B. 1
הַשָּׁלִיחַ שעשה Me'ila 6
הַתּוֹדָה היתה באה Men. 8
התכלת Men. 4
(האומר) התקבל Giṭ. 6
התרומה מה Sheḳ. 4

(ואלו הן) הנשרפין Sanh. 9
ואלו מגַלְּחִין M.Ḳ. 3
ואלו מוּתָּרִין Ned. 2
ואלו נדרים Ned. 11
(ו)אלו קשרים Shabb. 15
ולד חטאת Tem. 4
ולד חטאת Me'ila 3

זה בורר Sanh. 3

חבית שנשברה Shabb. 22
חומר בַּקּודש Ḥag. 3
חזקת הַבָּתִּים B.B. 3
חַטַּאת העוף שֶׁעֲשָׂאָהּ Zeb. 7
חַלּון (שבין) Erub. 7
חלק Sanh. 11
חמש עשרה נשים Yeb. 1
חרש שנשא Yeb. 14

טבול יום Zeb. 12
טרף בַּקַּלְפֵּי Yoma 4

ידיעות הטומאה Sheb. 2
יום הכִּפּורים Yoma 8
יום טוב שֶׁחָל Beṣa 2
י' ט' של ראש השנה R.H. 4

Pes. 4	מקום שֶׁנָּהֲגוּ
B.K. 7	מְרוּבָּה מִדַּת ת׳
Soṭa 8	מְשׁוּחַ מלחמה
Beṣa 5	מַשִּׁילִין פירות
M.Ḳ. 1	מַשְׁקִין בית הַשְּׁלָחִין
Sanh. 6	נִגְמַר הַדִּין
Shabb. 21	נוֹטֵל אדם
Yeb. 11	נושאין על האנוסה
Ned. 10	נערה המאורסה
Keth. 4	נ׳ שֶׁנִּתְפַּתְּתָה
Ta'an. 3	סדר תעניות אלו
Ta'an. 2	ס׳ ת׳ כיצד
Suk. 1	סוכה שהיא גבוהה
Ker. 4	סָפֵק אָכַל חֵלֶב
Soṭa 9	עֶגְלָה ערופה
Bekor. 4	עד כַּמָּה ישראל
Erub. 2	עושין פַּסִּין
Bekor. 6	על אלו מומין
Pes. 10	עַרְבֵי פסחים
Ḳid. 4	עשרה יוּחֲסִין
Zeb. 14	פָּרַת חַטָּאת שֶׁשְּׂרָפָהּ
Me'ila 4	קָדְשֵׁי המזבח
Zeb. 6	ק׳ קדשים שֶׁשְּׁחָטָן בראש
Me'ila 1	ק׳ ק׳ ש׳ בדרום
Ned. 8	קוֹנָם יַיִן
Tamid 2	רָאוּהוּ אֶחָיו
R.H. 3	ראוהו בית דין
Ḥul. 11	ראשית הַגֵּז
Shabb. 19	ר׳ אליעזר (אומר אם לא הביא כְלִי) [דמילה]
Shabb. 13	ר׳ אל׳ א׳ האורג
Ned. 9	ר׳ אל׳ א׳ פותחין
Shabb. 20	ר׳ אל׳ א׳ תולין
Men. 10	ר׳ ישמעאל אומר עוֹמֶר
A.Z. 4	ר׳ יש׳ א׳ שלש אבנים
Yeb. 5	רבן גמליאל
Shebu. 1	שבועות שְׁתַּיִם .. ידיעות
Shebu. 3	ש׳ שת׳ . . . שבועה
Shebu. 6	שבועת הדיינין
Shebu. 4	ש׳ העדות
Shebu. 5	ש׳ הַפִּקָּדוֹן
Yoma 1	שִׁבְעַת יָמִים קודם
Shabb. 23	שׁוֹאֵל אָדָם
Arak. 6	שום הַיְתוֹמִים
B.Ḳ. 4	שור שֶׁנָּגַח ארבעה
B.Ḳ. 5	שור ש׳ את הפרה
Ḥul. 12	שִׁילּוּחַ הַקַּן
Naz. 6	שלשה מינין
Sheḳ. 6	שלשה עשר שוֹפָרוֹת
Ber. 7	ש׳ שאכלו
Nid. 1	שמאי אומר כל־הַנָּשִׁים
Shabb. 14	שמנה שְׁרָצִים
Keth. 13	שְׁנֵי דַיָּנֵי גז׳
Naz. 8	שני נזירים
Yoma 6	שני שְׂעִירֵי
B.M. 1	שְׁנַיִם אוחזין
Men. 11	שתי הַלֶּחֶם
Men. 10	שתי מִדּוֹת
Shabb. 20	תּוֹלִין
Nid. 10	תִּינוֹקֶת
Pes. 5	תמיד נִשְׁחַט
Ber. 4	תְּפִלַּת השחר

The German Protestant theologian and Orientalist HERMANN L. STRACK was born in 1848 and died in 1924. From 1877 he was professor of Old Testament exegesis and Semitic languages at the University of Berlin. He was the foremost Christian authority of his day on Talmudic and rabbinic literature, having studied rabbinics under Moritz Steinschneider. Although Professor Strack was active in the conversionary Institutum Judaicum, he was vigorous in his defense of Jews and Judaism against resurgent German anti-Semitism. Among his numerous works are the *Einleitung in das Alte Testament* and *Kurzgefasster Kommentar zu den Schriften des Alten und Neuen Testaments.* Professor Strack was also a member of the foreign advisory board of the famous *Jewish Encyclopedia.*

Atheneum Paperbacks

TEMPLE BOOKS—*The Jewish Publication Society*

T1 JEWISH LIFE IN THE MIDDLE AGES *by Israel Abrahams*
T2 FOR THE SAKE OF HEAVEN *by Martin Buber*
T3 A HISTORY OF THE CONTEMPORARY JEWS *by Solomon Grayzel*
T4 THE ZIONIST IDEA *edited by Arthur Hertzberg*
T5 A HISTORY OF MEDIAEVAL JEWISH PHILOSOPHY *by Isaac Husik*
T6 THREE JEWISH PHILOSOPHERS *edited by Hans Lewy, Alexander Altmann and Isaak Heinemann*
T7 THE JEW IN THE MEDIEVAL WORLD *by Jacob R. Marcus*
T8 A HISTORY OF THE JEWISH PEOPLE *by Max L. Margolis and Alexander Marx*
T9 THE CONFLICT OF THE CHURCH AND THE SYNAGOGUE *by James Parkes*
T10 INTRODUCTION TO THE TALMUD AND MIDRASH *by Hermann L. Strack*
T11 AKIBA: SCHOLAR, SAINT AND MARTYR *by Louis Finkelstein*
T12 OF JEWISH LAW AND LORE *by Louis Ginzberg*
T13 JUDAISM AND MODERN MAN *by William Herberg*
T14 STUDIES IN JUDAISM *by Solomon Schechter*
T15 JEWISH MAGIC AND SUPERSTITION *by Joshua Trachtenberg*
T16 THE WILD GOATS OF EIN GEDI *by Herbert Weiner*
T17 JUDAISM AND CHRISTIANITY *by Leo Baeck*
T18 THEODORE HERZL *by Alex Bein*
T19 AMERICAN JEWRY AND THE CIVIL WAR *by Bertram W. Korn*
T20 SELECTED ESSAYS OF AHAD HA-'AM *by Leon Simon*
T21 NATIONALISM AND HISTORY *by Simon Dubnow*
T22 HELLENISTIC CIVILIZATION AND THE JEWS *by Victor Tcherikover*
T23 ANTHOLOGY OF HOLOCAUST LITERATURE *edited by Glatstein, Knox and Margoshes*
T24 FROM RESISTANCE TO DIPLOMACY *by Yehuda Bauer*
T25 JOSEPHUS *by Lion Feuchtwanger*
T26 BETWEEN EAST AND WEST *by André N. Choraqui*
T27 THE BUNKER *by Charles Goldstein*

PHILOSOPHY AND RELIGION

6 ROGER WILLIAMS *by Perry Miller*
9 MATTER, MIND AND MAN *by Edmund W. Sinnott*
19 BUDDHISM IN TRANSLATIONS *by Henry Clarke Warren*
31 PHILOSOPHY OF MATHEMATICS AND NATURAL SCIENCE *by Hermann Weyl*
38 TOWARD REUNION IN PHILOSOPHY *by Morton White*
52 RELIGION IN TWENTIETH CENTURY AMERICA *by Herbert W. Schneider*
60 HERACLITUS *by Philip Wheelwright*
69 ON THE USE OF PHILOSOPHY *by Jacques Maritain*
75 RELIGIOUS PHILOSOPHY *by Harry Austryn Wolfson*
97 THE EIGHTEENTH CENTURY CONFRONTS THE GODS *by Frank E. Manuel*
183 GENERALIZATION IN ETHICS *by Marcus Singer*
185 KARL MARX IN HIS EARLIER WRITINGS *by H. P. Adams*

Atheneum Paperbacks

HISTORY–AMERICAN–BEFORE 1900

6 ROGER WILLIAMS *by Perry Miller*
17 MYTHS AND REALITIES *by Carl Bridenbaugh*
32 STRANGERS IN THE LAND *by John Higham*
40 THE UNITED STATES AND MEXICO *by Howard F. Cline*
51 TURMOIL AND TRADITION *by Elting E. Morison*
84 THE DIMENSIONS OF LIBERTY *by Oscar and Mary Handlin*
86 THE CORPORATION IN MODERN SOCIETY *edited by Edward S. Mason*
110 DRED SCOTT'S CASE *by Vincent C. Hopkins, S.J.*
111 THE DECLINE OF AMERICAN LIBERALISM *by Arthur A. Ekirch, Jr.*
113 HARVARD GUIDE TO AMERICAN HISTORY *edited by Oscar Handlin, Arthur Meier Schlesinger, Samuel Eliot Morison, Frederick Merk, Arthur Meier Schlesinger, Jr., Paul Herman Buck*
115 THE ROOTS OF AMERICAN LOYALTY *by Merle Curti*
116 THE POLITICS OF PREJUDICE *by Roger Daniels*
117 CENTURY OF STRUGGLE *by Eleanor Flexner*
118 BOSTON'S IMMIGRANTS *by Oscar Handlin*
123 THE AMERICAN APPROACH TO FOREIGN POLICY *by Dexter Perkins*
125 THE EIGHTEENTH-CENTURY COMMONWEALTHMAN *by Caroline Robbins*
126 THE AMERICAN AS REFORMER *by Arthur M. Schlesinger*
132 ASA GRAY *by A. Hunter Dupree*
134 THE COLONIAL MERCHANTS AND THE AMERICAN REVOLUTION—1763–1776 *by Arthur M. Schlesinger*
136 THE ROAD TO APPOMATTOX *by Bell Irvin Wiley*
137 FREE SPEECH IN THE UNITED STATES *by Zechariah Chafee, Jr.*
139 CONSERVATION AND THE GOSPEL OF EFFICIENCY *by Samuel P. Hays*
142 THE PROFESSIONAL ALTRUIST *by Roy Lubove*
144 POVERTY AND PROGRESS *by Stephan Thernstrom*
145 STREETCAR SUBURBS *by Sam B. Warner*
150 THE DECLINE OF AGRARIAN DEMOCRACY *by Grant McConnell*
151 POLITICS AND POWER *by David J. Rothman*
161 QUANTIFICATION IN AMERICAN HISTORY *by Robert P. Swierenga*
166 THE CATTLE TOWNS *by Robert R. Dykstra*
169 POLICING THE CITY: BOSTON: 1822-1885 *by Roger Lane*
186 WITCHCRAFT IN OLD AND NEW ENGLAND *by George Lyman Kittredge*

Atheneum Paperbacks

HISTORY–AMERICAN–1900 TO THE PRESENT

2 POWER AND DIPLOMACY *by Dean Acheson*

7 THE REPUBLICAN ROOSEVELT *by John Morton Blum*

40 THE UNITED STATES AND MEXICO *by Howard F. Cline*

43 A&B HOLMES-LASKI LETTERS: THE CORRESPONDENCE OF JUSTICE OLIVER WENDELL HOLMES AND HAROLD J. LASKI *1916–1935 edited by Mark De Wolfe Howe, abridged by Alger Hiss, 2 vols.*

51 TURMOIL AND TRADITION *by Elting E. Morison*

86 THE CORPORATION IN MODERN SOCIETY *edited by Edward S. Mason*

111 THE DECLINE OF AMERICAN LIBERALISM *by Arthur A. Ekirch, Jr.*

113 HARVARD GUIDE TO AMERICAN HISTORY *edited by Oscar Handlin, Arthur Meier Schlesinger, Samuel Eliot Morison, Frederick Merk, Arthur Meier Schlesinger, Jr., Paul Herman Buck*

115 THE ROOTS OF AMERICAN LOYALTY *by Merle Curti*

116 THE POLITICS OF PREJUDICE *by Roger Daniels*

117 CENTURY OF STRUGGLE *by Eleanor Flexner*

123 THE AMERICAN APPROACH TO FOREIGN POLICY *by Dexter Perkins*

126 THE AMERICAN AS REFORMER *by Arthur M. Schlesinger*

129 THE LEGEND OF HENRY FORD *by Keith Sward*

137 FREE SPEECH IN THE UNITED STATES *by Zechariah Chafee, Jr.*

140 MASSACHUSETTS PEOPLE AND POLITICS, 1919–1933 *by J. Joseph Huthmacher*

142 THE PROFESSIONAL ALTRUIST *by Roy Lubove*

149 THE COMMUNIST CONTROVERSY IN WASHINGTON *by Earl Latham*

150 THE DECLINE OF AGRARIAN DEMOCRACY *by Grant McConnell*

151 POLITICS AND POWER *by David J. Rothman*

160 UP AGAINST THE IVY WALL *by Jerry Avorn and members of the staff of the* Columbia Daily Spectator

161 QUANTIFICATION IN AMERICAN HISTORY *by Robert P. Swierenga*

162 PROHIBITION AND THE PROGRESSIVE MOVEMENT *by James H. Timberlake*

163 FARM POLICIES AND POLITICS IN THE TRUMAN YEARS *by Allen J. Matusow*

167 SENATOR ROBERT F. WAGNER AND THE RISE OF URBAN LIBERALISM *by J. Joseph Huthmacher*

173 THE IMAGE *by Daniel J. Boorstin*

175 SECOND CHANCE *by Robert A. Divine*

178 THE END OF THE AMERICAN ERA *by Andrew Hacker*

Atheneum Paperbacks

HISTORY

3 SIX MEDIEVAL MEN AND WOMEN *by H. S. Bennett*
10 TRAVEL AND DISCOVERY IN THE RENAISSANCE *by Boies Penrose*
58 TROTSKY'S DIARY IN EXILE—1935 *translated by Elena Zarudnaya*
63 THE SINO-SOVIET CONFLICT 1956–1961 *by Donald S. Zagoria*
83 KARAMZIN'S MEMOIR ON ANCIENT AND MODERN RUSSIA *by Richard Pipes*
97 THE EIGHTEENTH CENTURY CONFRONTS THE GODS *by Frank E. Manuel*
103 JACOBEAN PAGEANT *by G. P. V. Akrigg*
104 THE MAKING OF VICTORIAN ENGLAND *by G. Kitson Clark*
107 RUSSIA LEAVES THE WAR *by George F. Kennan*
108 THE DECISION TO INTERVENE *by George F. Kennan*
121 DRIVING FORCES IN HISTORY *by Halvdan Koht*
124 THE FORMATION OF THE SOVIET UNION *by Richard Pipes*
127 THE THREE LIVES OF CHARLES DE GAULLE *by David Schoenbrun*
128 AS FRANCE GOES *by David Schoenbrun*
141 SERGEI WITTE AND THE INDUSTRIALIZATION OF RUSSIA *by Theodore Von Laue*
152 A HISTORY OF THE WEIMAR REPUBLIC *by Erich Eyck,*
A&B *2 vols.*
161 QUANTIFICATION IN AMERICAN HISTORY *by Robert P. Swierenga*
181 THE COURT AND THE COUNTRY *by Perez Zagorin*

HISTORY—ASIA

44 CHINA'S RESPONSE TO THE WEST *by Ssu-Yü Teng and John K. Fairbank*
63 THE SINO-SOVIET CONFLICT 1956–1961 *by Donald S. Zagoria*
87 A DOCUMENTARY HISTORY OF CHINESE COMMUNISM *by Conrad Brandt, Benjamin Schwartz and John K. Fairbank*
147 AFTER IMPERIALISM *by Akira Iriye*
153 CHINA'S EARLY INDUSTRIALIZATION *by Albert Feuerwerker*
154 LI TA-CHAO AND THE ORIGINS OF CHINESE MARXISM *by Maurice Meisner*
164 COMMUNISM AND CHINA: IDEOLOGY IN FLUX *by Benjamin I. Schwartz*
168 LITERARY DISSENT IN COMMUNIST CHINA *by Merle Goldman*
176 THE COMMUNISTS AND THE CHINESE PEASANT REBELLIONS *by James P. Harrison*

Atheneum Paperbacks

POLITICAL SCIENCE

2 POWER AND DIPLOMACY *by Dean Acheson*
15 CALL TO GREATNESS *by Adlai E. Stevenson*
20 DOCUMENTS ON FUNDAMENTAL HUMAN RIGHTS *edited by Zechariah*
A&B *Chafee, Jr., 2 vols.*
23 THE CONSTITUTION AND WHAT IT MEANS TODAY *by Edward S. Corwin*
27 COURTS ON TRIAL *by Jerome Frank*
34 THE DIPLOMACY OF ECONOMIC DEVELOPMENT *by Eugene R. Black*
40 THE UNITED STATES AND MEXICO *by Howard F. Cline*
41 THE DIPLOMATS, 1919-1939 *edited by Gordon A. Craig and Felix Gilbert,*
A&B *2 vols.*
44 CHINA'S RESPONSE TO THE WEST *by Ssu-Yü Teng and John K. Fairbank*
46 THE FUTURE OF FEDERALISM *by Nelson A. Rockefeller*
53 THE BILL OF RIGHTS *by Learned Hand*
54 STRATEGIC SURRENDER *by Paul Kecskemeti*
63 THE SINO-SOVIET CONFLICT, 1956-1961 *by Donald S. Zagoria*
72 MR. JUSTICE HOLMES AND THE SUPREME COURT *by Felix Frankfurter*
74 STALIN'S FOREIGN POLICY REAPPRAISED *by Marshall D. Shulman*
105 DILEMMAS OF URBAN AMERICA *by Robert C. Weaver*
107 RUSSIA LEAVES THE WAR *by George F. Kennan*
108 THE DECISION TO INTERVENE *by George F. Kennan*
110 DRED SCOTT'S CASE *by Vincent C. Hopkins, S.J.*
130 THE REVOLUTION OF THE SAINTS *by Michael Walzer*
138 OF LAW AND LIFE AND OTHER THINGS THAT MATTER *by Felix Frankfurter, edited by Philip B. Kurland*
147 AFTER IMPERALISM *by Akira Iriye*
148 POLITICAL CHANGE IN A WEST AFRICAN STATE *by Martin Kilson*
149 THE COMMUNIST CONTROVERSY IN WASHINGTON *by Earl Latham*
150 THE DECLINE OF AGRARIAN DEMOCRACY *by Grant McConnell*
156 VARIETIES OF POLICE BEHAVIOR *by James Q. Wilson*
157 AFRICA: FROM INDEPENDENCE TO TOMORROW *by David Hapgood*
160 UP AGAINST THE IVY WALL *by Jerry Avorn and other members of the staff of the* Columbia Daily Spectator
170 THE POLITICS OF AUTHENTICITY *by Marshall Berman*
175 SECOND CHANCE *by Robert A. Divine*
178 THE END OF THE AMERICAN ERA *by Andrew Hacker*
179 CONGRESS AND THE PUBLIC TRUST *by James C. Kirby, Jr.*
188 POLITICAL OBLIGATION *by Richard Flathman*
189 MACHIAVELLI AND THE NATURE OF POLITICAL THEORY *edited by Martin Fleisher*
195 MAN AND SOCIALISM IN CUBA *edited by Bertram Silverman*
196 THE RADICAL PROBE *by Michael W. Miles*
197 THE CRUEL CHOICE *by Denis Goulet*
198 POLITICS, LANGUAGE AND TIME *by J. G. A. Pocock*

Atheneum Paperbacks

STUDIES IN AMERICAN NEGRO LIFE

NL1 THE NEGRO IN COLONIAL NEW ENGLAND *by Lorenzo Johnston Greene*
NL2 SEPARATE AND UNEQUAL *by Louis R. Harlan*
NL3 AFTER FREEDOM *by Hortense Powdermaker*
NL4 FREDERICK DOUGLASS *by Benjamin Quarles*
NL5 PREFACE TO PEASANTRY *by Arthur F. Raper*
NL6 W.E.B. DU BOIS: PROPAGANDIST OF THE NEGRO PROTEST *by Elliott Rudwick*
NL7 THE BLACK WORKER *by Sterling D. Spero and Abram L. Harris*
NL8 A&B THE MAKING OF BLACK AMERICA *edited by August Meier and Elliott Rudwick, 2 vols.*
NL9 BLACK MANHATTAN *by James Weldon Johnson*
NL10 THE NEW NEGRO *edited by Alain Locke*
NL11 THE NEGRO'S GOD AS REFLECTED IN HIS LITERATURE *by Benjamin Mays*
NL12 NEGRO POETRY AND DRAMA AND THE NEGRO IN AMERICAN FICTION *by Sterling Brown*
NL13 WHEN NEGROES MARCH *by Harbert Garfinkel*
NL14 PHILOSOPHY AND OPINIONS OF MARCUS GARVEY *by Marcus Garvey, edited by Amy Jacques-Garvey*
NL15 FREE NEGRO LABOR AND PROPERTY HOLDING IN VIRGINIA, 1830–1860 *by Luther Porter Jackson*
NL16 SEA ISLAND TO CITY *by Clyde Vernon Kiser*
NL17 NEGRO EDUCATION IN ALABAMA *by Horace Mann Bond*
NL18 POLITICS, PRINCIPLE AND PREJUDICE, 1865–1866 *by LaWanda and John H. Cox*
NL19 NEGRO POLITICAL LEADERSHIP IN THE SOUTH *by Everett Carll Ladd, Jr.*
NL20 BLACK RECONSTRUCTION IN AMERICA, 1860–1880 *by W. E. B. Du Bois*
NL21 NEGROES IN CITIES *by Karl E. and Alma F. Taeuber*
NL22 TWO JAMAICAS *by Philip De Armond Curtin*
NL23 VASSOURASS: A BRAZILIAN COFFEE COUNTY, 1850–1900 *by Stanley J. Stein*
NL24 THE ROYAL AFRICAN COMPANY *by K. G. Davies*
NL25 STRANGE ENTHUSIASM: A LIFE OF THOMAS WENTWORTH HIGGINSON *by Tilden G. Edelstein*
NL26 THE *Guardian* OF BOSTON: WILLIAM MONROE TROTTER *by Stephen R. Fox*
NL27 LEWIS TAPPAN AND THE EVANGELICAL WAR AGAINST SLAVERY *by Bertram Wyatt-Brown*
NL28 THE NEGRO IN BRAZILIAN SOCIETY *by Florestan Fernandes*
NL29 THE NEGRO AND THE COMMUNIST PARTY *by Wilson Record*
NL30 RACE RIOT *by William M. Tuttle, Jr.*
NL31 RACE RIOT AT EAST ST. LOUIS, JULY 2, 1917 *by Elliott Rudwick*
NL32 J. E. SPINGARN AND THE RISE OF THE NAACP *by B. Joyce Ross*

Atheneum Paperbacks

THE WORLDS OF NATURE AND MAN

5 OF MEN AND MOUNTAINS *by William O. Douglas*
18 THE SUDDEN VIEW *by Sybille Bedford*
22 SPRING IN WASHINGTON *by Louis J. Halle*
33 LOST CITY OF THE INCAS *by Hiram Bingham*
45 THE SEA SHORE *by C. M. Yonge*
61 THE NEW YORK TIMES GUIDE TO DINING OUT IN NEW YORK
82 BIRDS AND MEN *by Robert H. Welker*
95 THE FIRMAMENT OF TIME *by Loren Eiseley*
190 HOW TO EAT (AND DRINK) YOUR WAY THROUGH A FRENCH (OR ITALIAN) MENU *by James Beard*
192 THE SENSES OF ANIMALS AND MEN *by Lorus and Margery Milne*

LIFE SCIENCES AND ANTHROPOLOGY

9 MATTER, MIND AND MAN *by Edmund W. Sinnott*
16 THE HORMONES IN HUMAN REPRODUCTION *by George W. Corner*
26 THE OLD STONE AGE *by Miles C. Burkitt*
28 MORPHOGENESIS *by John Tyler Bonner*
33 LOST CITY OF THE INCAS *by Hiram Bingham*
35 GENETICS, PALEONTOLOGY, AND EVOLUTION *edited by Glenn L. Jepsen, Ernst Mayr and George Gaylord Simpson*
45 THE SEA SHORE *by C. M. Yonge*
48 TRISTES TROPIQUES *by Claude Lévi-Strauss*
62 TERRITORY IN BIRD LIFE *by Eliot Howard*
71 HEREDITY AND EVOLUTION IN HUMAN POPULATIONS *by L. C. Dunn*
85 THE INTEGRITY OF THE BODY *by F. M. Burnet, F.R.S.*
88 SPEECH AND BRAIN-MECHANISMS *by Wilder Penfield and Lamar Roberts*
91 CELLS AND SOCIETIES *by John Tyler Bonner*
95 THE FIRMAMENT OF TIME *by Loren Eiseley*
98 IDEAS ON HUMAN EVOLUTION *edited by William Howells*
101 COMMUNICATION AMONG SOCIAL BEES *by Martin Lindauer*
106 ON THE ORIGIN OF SPECIES *by Charles Darwin, a Facsimile of the First Edition, edited by Ernst Mayr*
109 AFRICAN HOMICIDE AND SUICIDE *edited by Paul Bohannon*
155 PEOPLE OF RIMROCK *edited by Evon Z. Vogt and Ethel M. Albert*
192 THE SENSES OF ANIMALS AND MEN *by Lorus and Margery Milne*
193 WATER AND LIFE *by Lorus and Margery Milne*